CASE CLOSED™

VOLUME 56

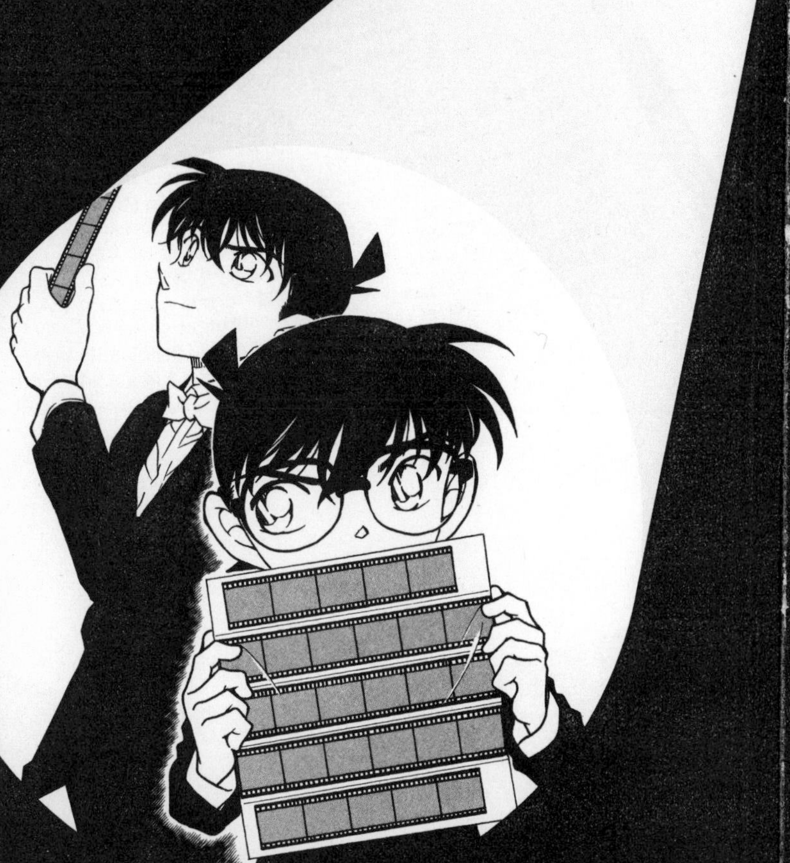

Gosho Aoyama

Case Briefing:

Subject: Jimmy Kudo, a.k.a. Conan Edogawa
Occupation: High School Student/Detective
Special Skills: Analytical thinking and deductive reasoning, Soccer
Equipment: Bow Tie Voice Transmitter, Super Sneakers,
                        Homing Glasses, Stretchy Suspenders

The subject is hot on the trail of a pair of suspicious men in black when he is attacked from behind and administered a strange substance which physically transforms him into a first grader. When the subject confides in the eccentric inventor Dr. Agasa, they decide to keep the subject's true identity a secret for the safety of everyone around him. Assuming the new identity of first grader Conan Edogawa, the subject continues to assist the police force on their most baffling cases. The only problem is that most crime-solving professionals won't take a little kid's advice!

Table of Contents

File 1: Engagement Ring?! (1) 5
File 2: Engagement Ring?! (2) 21
File 3: Engagement Ring?! (3) 37
File 4: The Witch Legend Mystery (1) 53
File 5: The Witch Legend Mystery (2) 69
File 6: The Witch Legend Mystery (3) 85
File 7: Evidence from the West 101
File 8: Location of the Photograph 117
File 9: The Company 133
File 10: Wrong Number 149
File 11: Blood Will Tell 165

CONFIDEN

CASE CLOSED
Volume 56
Shonen Sunday Edition

Story and Art by **GOSHO AOYAMA**

MEITANTEI CONAN Vol. 56
by Gosho AOYAMA
© 1994 Gosho AOYAMA
All rights reserved.
Original Japanese edition published by SHOGAKUKAN.
English translation rights in the United States of America, Canada,
the United Kingdom and Ireland arranged with SHOGAKUKAN.

Translation
Tetsuichiro Miyaki

Touch-up & Lettering
Freeman Wong

Cover & Graphic Design
Andrea Rice

Editor
Shaenon K. Garrity

Printed in the U.S.A.

Published by VIZ Media, LLC
P.O. Box 77010
San Francisco, CA 94107

10 9 8 7 6 5 4 3 2 1
First printing, October 2015

FILE 1: ENGAGEMENT RING?! ①

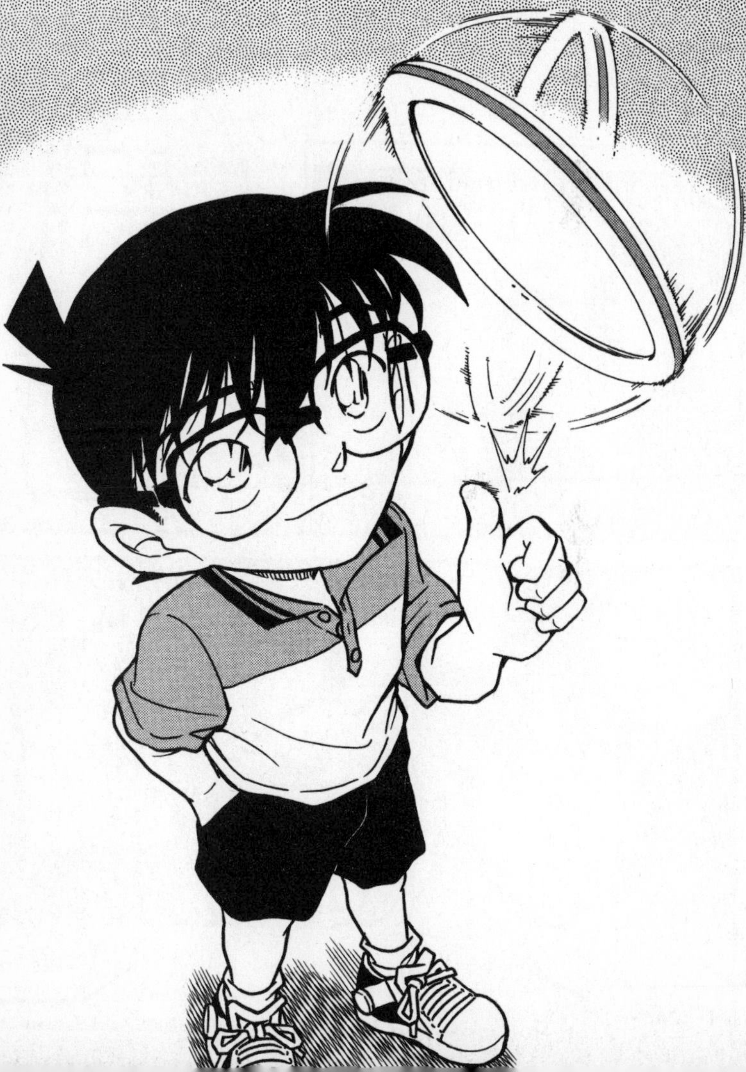

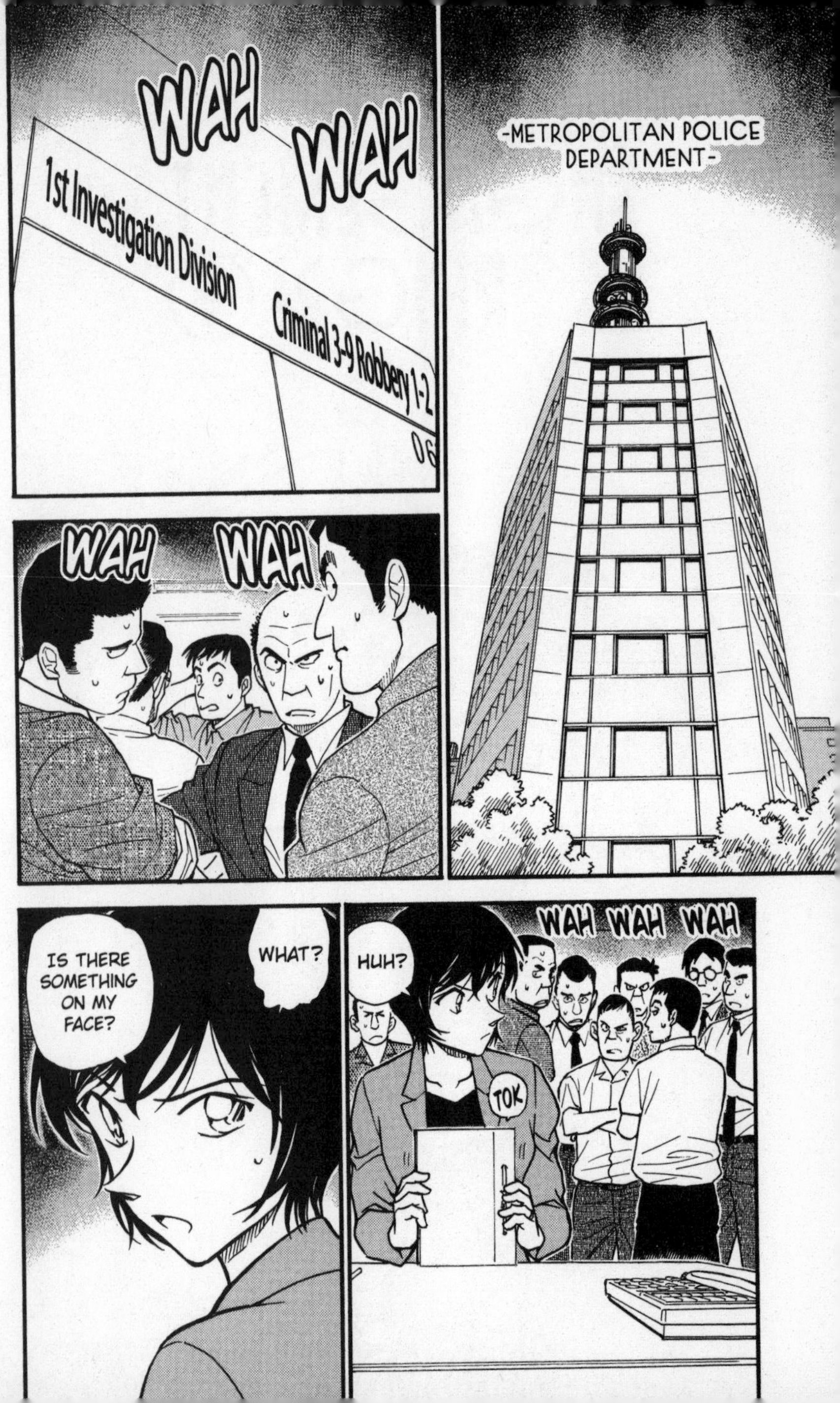
-METROPOLITAN POLICE DEPARTMENT-
WAH
WAH
1st Investigation Division
Criminal 3-9 Robbery 1-2
WAH
WAH
WAH WAH WAH
HUH?
TOK
WHAT?
IS THERE SOMETHING ON MY FACE?

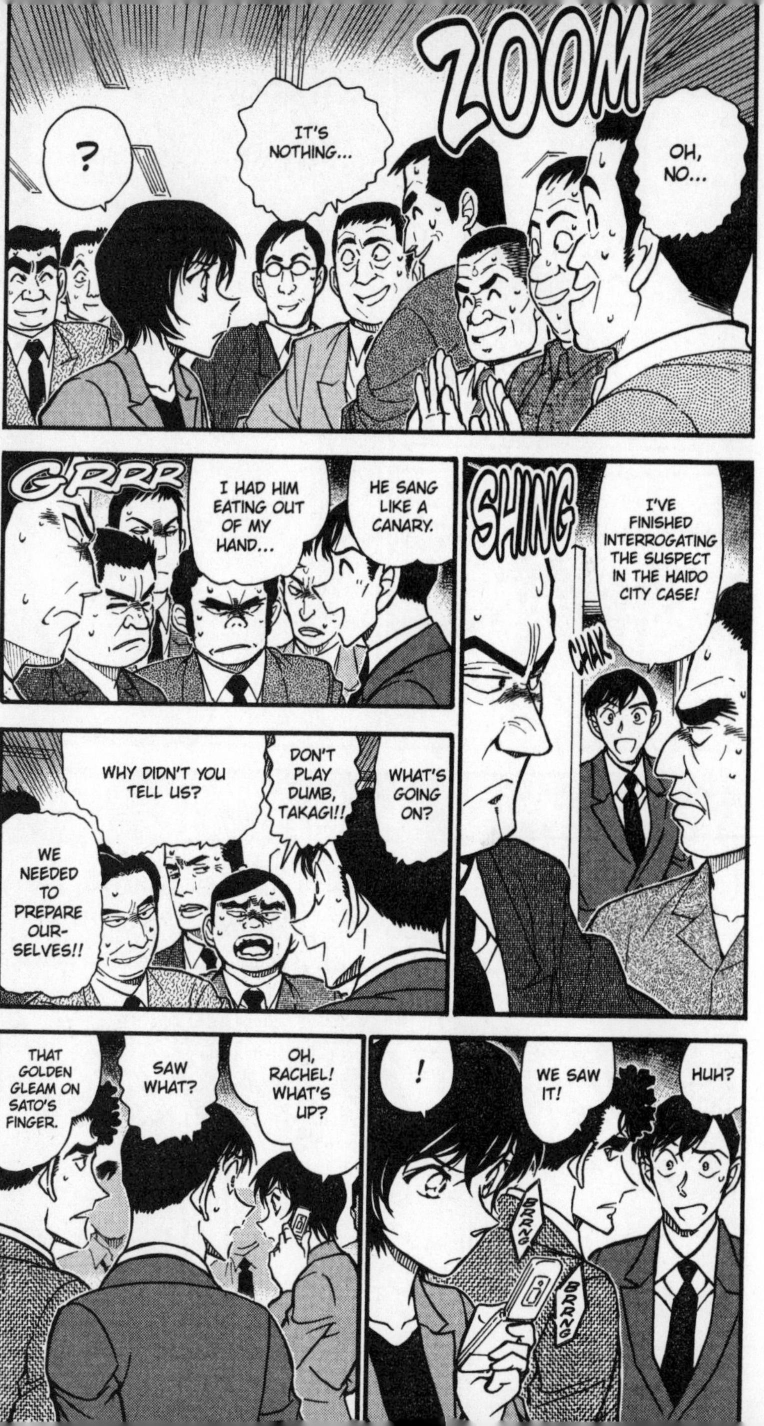
ZOOM
OH, NO...
IT'S NOTHING...
?
SHING
I'VE FINISHED INTERROGATING THE SUSPECT IN THE HAIDO CITY CASE!
CHAK
HE SANG LIKE A CANARY.
I HAD HIM EATING OUT OF MY HAND...
GRRR
WHAT'S GOING ON?
DON'T PLAY DUMB, TAKAGI!!
WHY DIDN'T YOU TELL US?
WE NEEDED TO PREPARE OUR-SELVES!!
HUH?
WE SAW IT!
!
BRRNG
BRRNG
OH, RACHEL! WHAT'S UP?
SAW WHAT?
THAT GOLDEN GLEAM ON SATO'S FINGER.

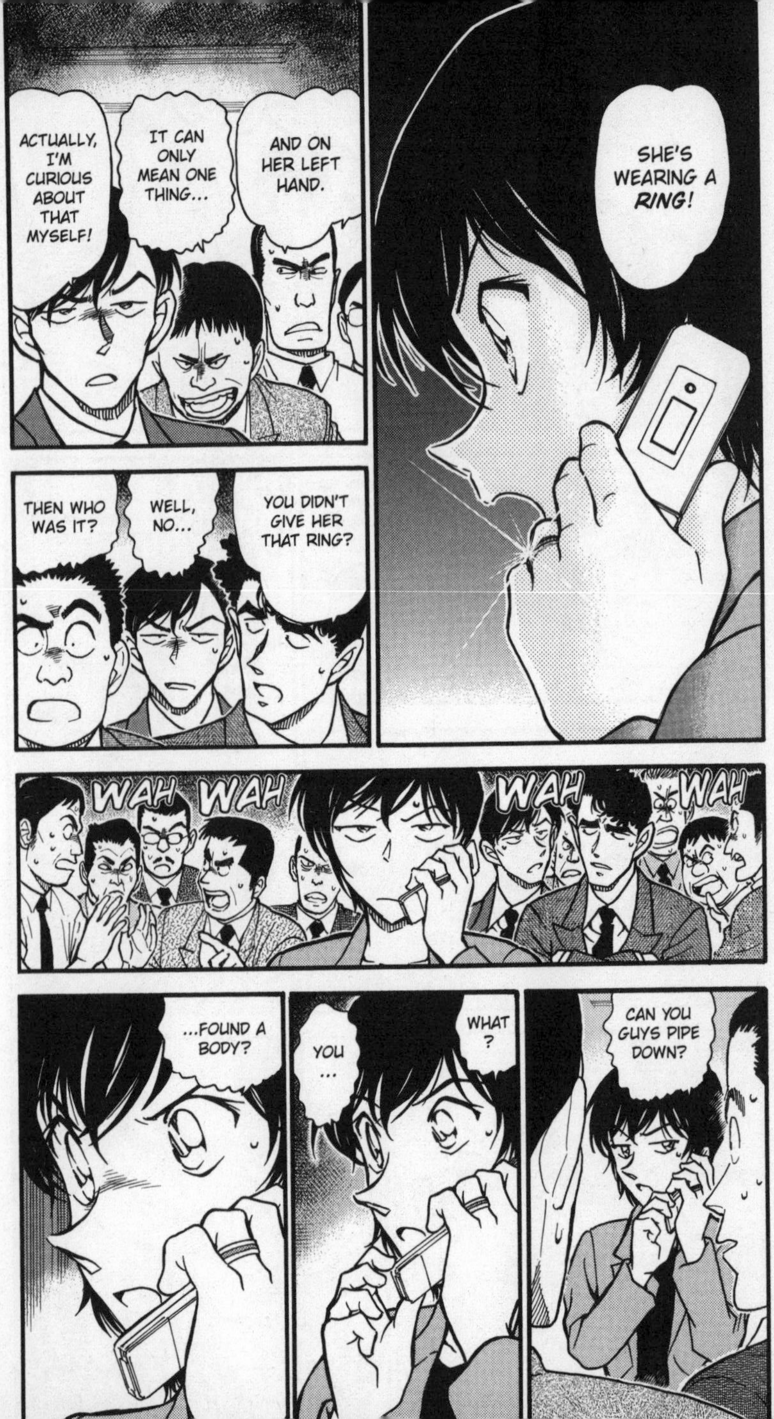
SHE'S WEARING A RING!
AND ON HER LEFT HAND.
IT CAN ONLY MEAN ONE THING...
ACTUALLY, I'M CURIOUS ABOUT THAT MYSELF!
YOU DIDN'T GIVE HER THAT RING?
WELL, NO...
THEN WHO WAS IT?
WAH
WAH
WAH
WAH
CAN YOU GUYS PIPE DOWN?
WHAT?
YOU...
...FOUND A BODY?

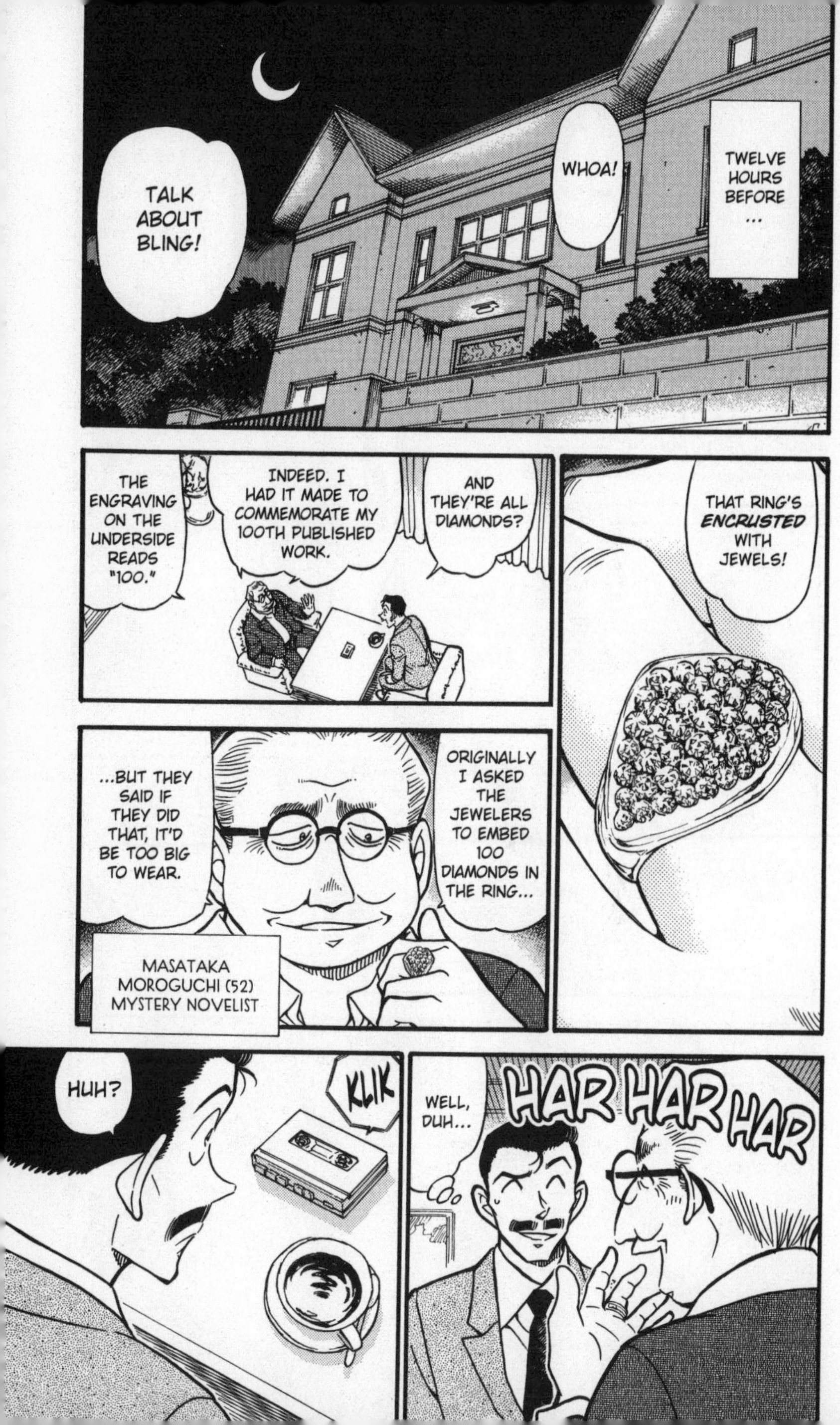
TWELVE HOURS BEFORE ...
WHOA!
TALK ABOUT BLING!
THAT RING'S ENCRUSTED WITH JEWELS!
AND THEY'RE ALL DIAMONDS?
INDEED. I HAD IT MADE TO COMMEMORATE MY 100TH PUBLISHED WORK.
THE ENGRAVING ON THE UNDERSIDE READS "100."
ORIGINALLY I ASKED THE JEWELERS TO EMBED 100 DIAMONDS IN THE RING...
...BUT THEY SAID IF THEY DID THAT, IT'D BE TOO BIG TO WEAR.
MASATAKA MOROGUCHI (52) MYSTERY NOVELIST
HAR HAR HAR
WELL, DUH...
KLIK
HUH?

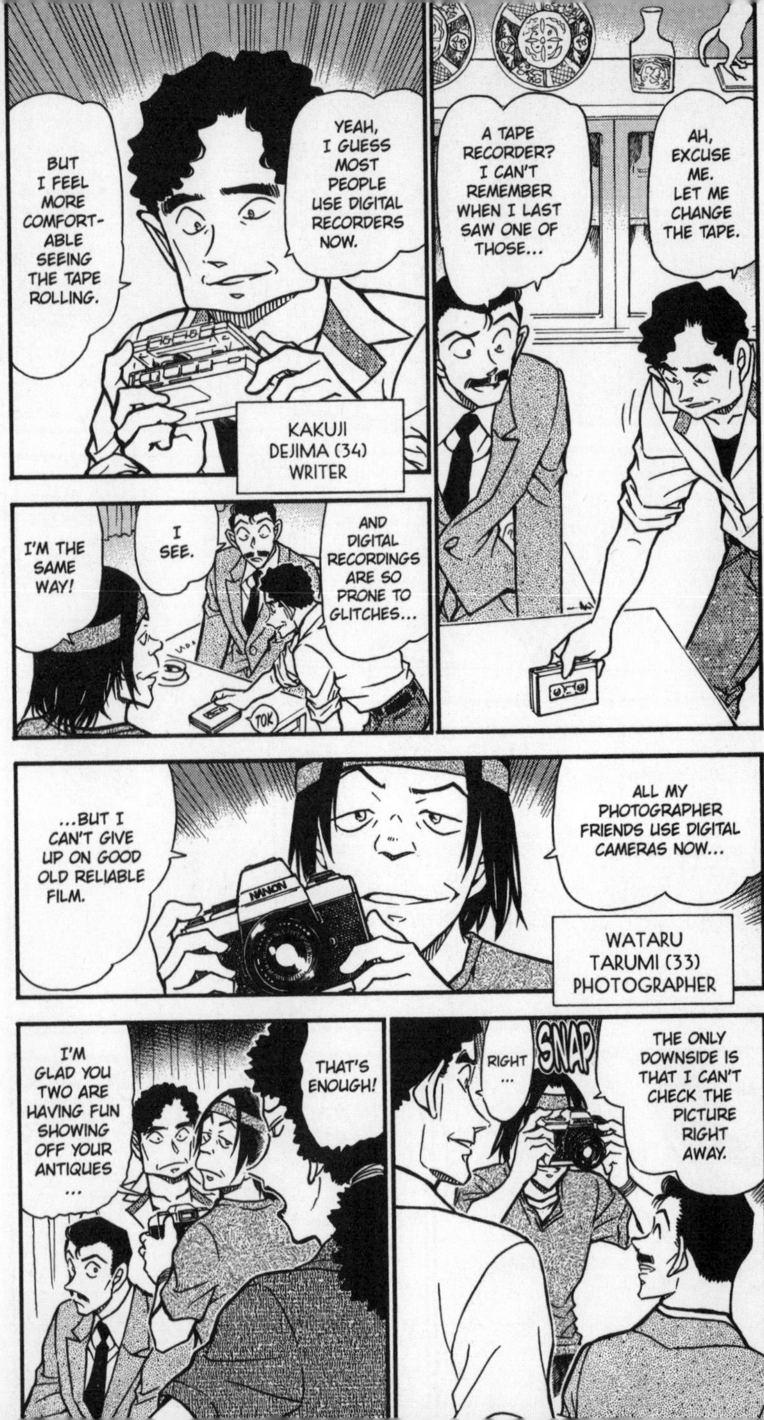
AH, EXCUSE ME. LET ME CHANGE THE TAPE.
A TAPE RECORDER? I CAN'T REMEMBER WHEN I LAST SAW ONE OF THOSE...
YEAH, I GUESS MOST PEOPLE USE DIGITAL RECORDERS NOW.
BUT I FEEL MORE COMFORT-ABLE SEEING THE TAPE ROLLING.
KAKUJI DEJIMA (34) WRITER
AND DIGITAL RECORDINGS ARE SO PRONE TO GLITCHES...
TOK
I SEE.
I'M THE SAME WAY!
ALL MY PHOTOGRAPHER FRIENDS USE DIGITAL CAMERAS NOW...
WATARU TARUMI (33) PHOTOGRAPHER
...BUT I CAN'T GIVE UP ON GOOD OLD RELIABLE FILM.
THE ONLY DOWNSIDE IS THAT I CAN'T CHECK THE PICTURE RIGHT AWAY.
SNAP
RIGHT ...
THAT'S ENOUGH!
I'M GLAD YOU TWO ARE HAVING FUN SHOWING OFF YOUR ANTIQUES ...

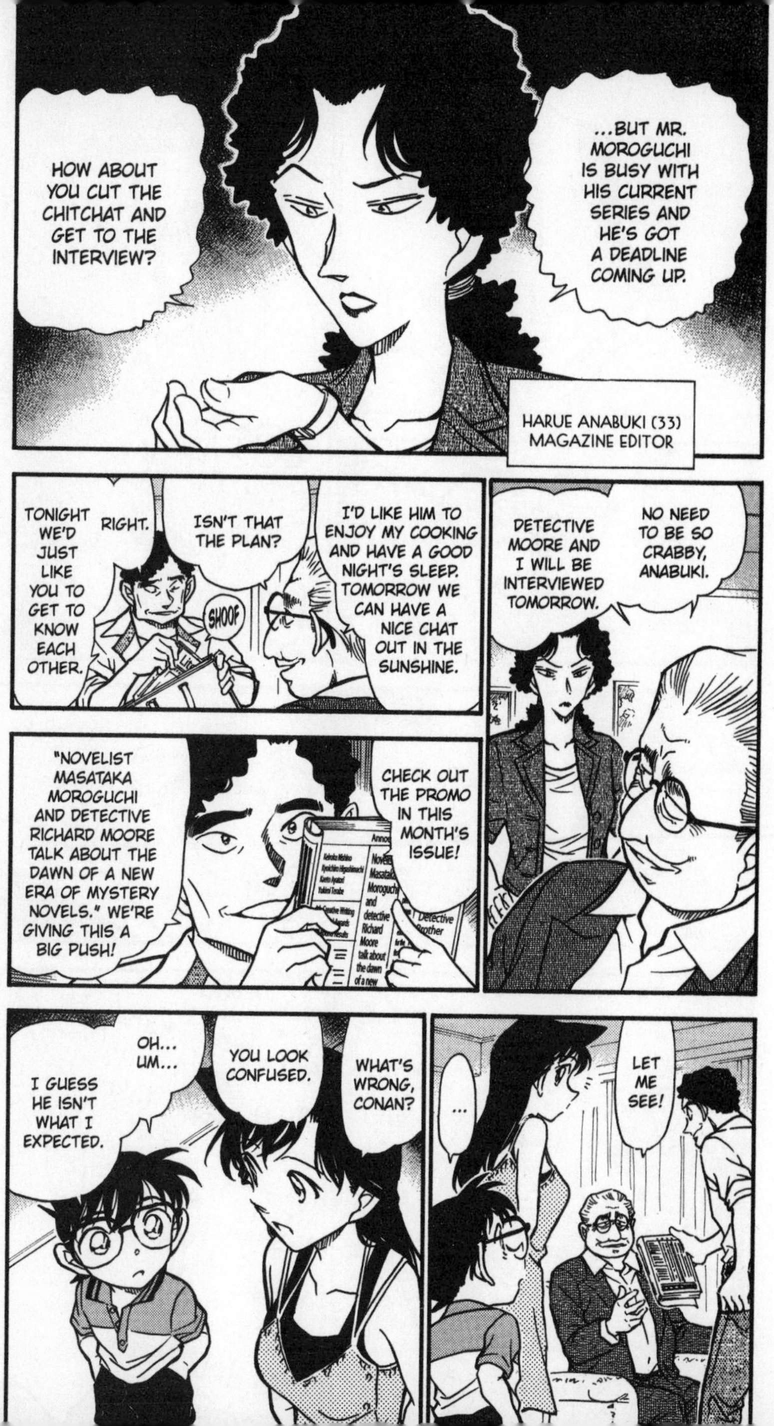
...BUT MR. MOROGUCHI IS BUSY WITH HIS CURRENT SERIES AND HE'S GOT A DEADLINE COMING UP.
HOW ABOUT YOU CUT THE CHITCHAT AND GET TO THE INTERVIEW?
HARUE ANABUKI (33) MAGAZINE EDITOR
NO NEED TO BE SO CRABBY, ANABUKI.
DETECTIVE MOORE AND I WILL BE INTERVIEWED TOMORROW.
I'D LIKE HIM TO ENJOY MY COOKING AND HAVE A GOOD NIGHT'S SLEEP. TOMORROW WE CAN HAVE A NICE CHAT OUT IN THE SUNSHINE.
ISN'T THAT THE PLAN?
SHOOF
RIGHT.
TONIGHT WE'D JUST LIKE YOU TO GET TO KNOW EACH OTHER.
CHECK OUT THE PROMO IN THIS MONTH'S ISSUE!
"NOVELIST MASATAKA MOROGUCHI AND DETECTIVE RICHARD MOORE TALK ABOUT THE DAWN OF A NEW ERA OF MYSTERY NOVELS." WE'RE GIVING THIS A BIG PUSH!
LET ME SEE!
...
WHAT'S WRONG, CONAN?
YOU LOOK CONFUSED.
OH... UM...
I GUESS HE ISN'T WHAT I EXPECTED.

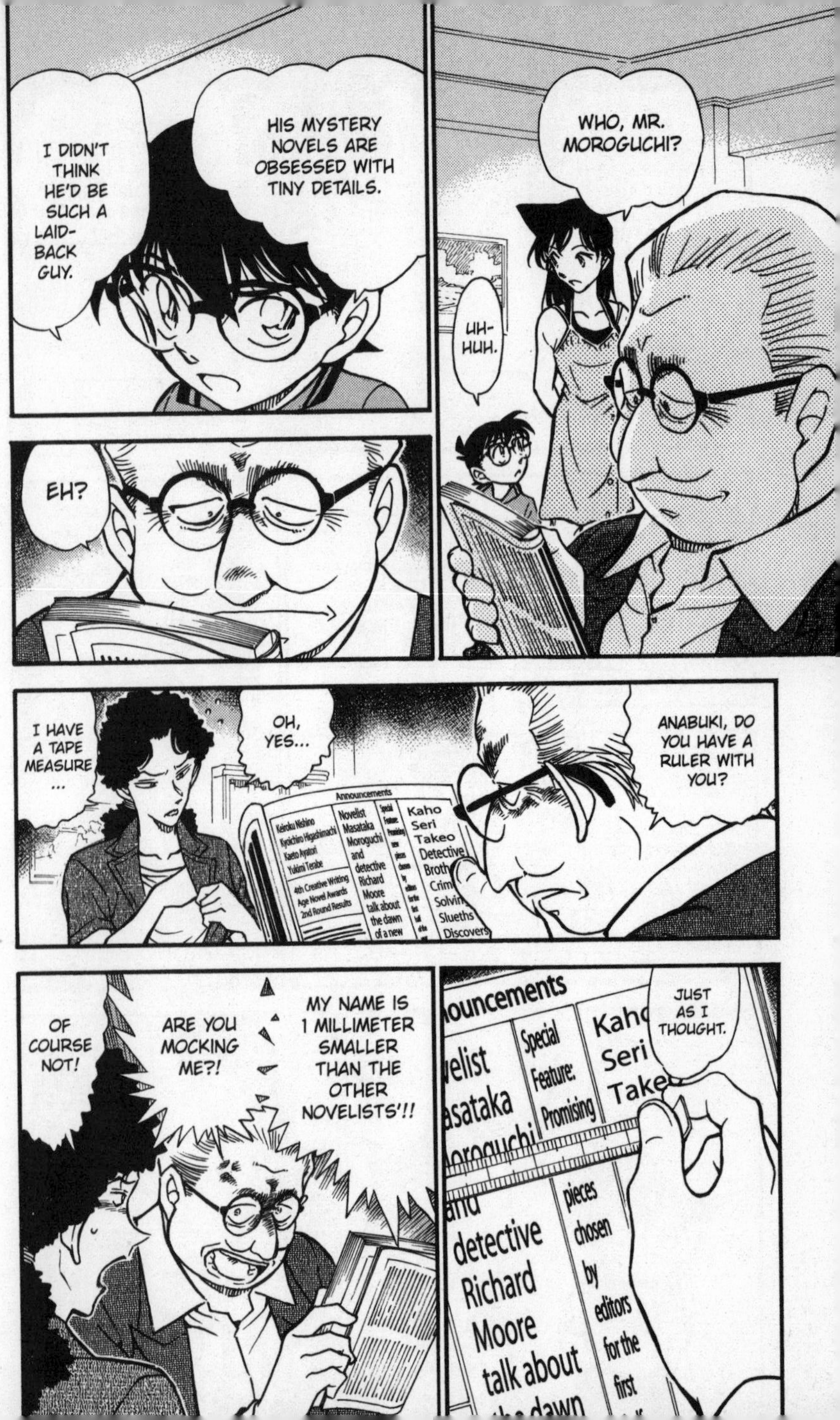
WHO, MR. MOROGUCHI?
UH-HUH.
HIS MYSTERY NOVELS ARE OBSESSED WITH TINY DETAILS.
I DIDN'T THINK HE'D BE SUCH A LAID-BACK GUY.
EH?
ANABUKI, DO YOU HAVE A RULER WITH YOU?
OH, YES...
I HAVE A TAPE MEASURE ...
Announcements
Kaho Seri Takeo Detective Broth Crim Solvin Slueths Discovers
Novelist Masataka Moroguchi and detective Richard Moore talk about the dawn of a new
Keiroku Nishino Kyoichiro Higashimachi Kaeto Ayatori Yukimi Terabe
4th Creative Writing Age Novel Awards 2nd Round Results
JUST AS I THOUGHT.
nouncements
Kaho Seri Take
Special Feature: Promising
velist asataka oroguchi
pieces chosen by editors for the first
and detective Richard Moore talk about
MY NAME IS 1 MILLIMETER SMALLER THAN THE OTHER NOVELISTS'!!
ARE YOU MOCKING ME?!
OF COURSE NOT!

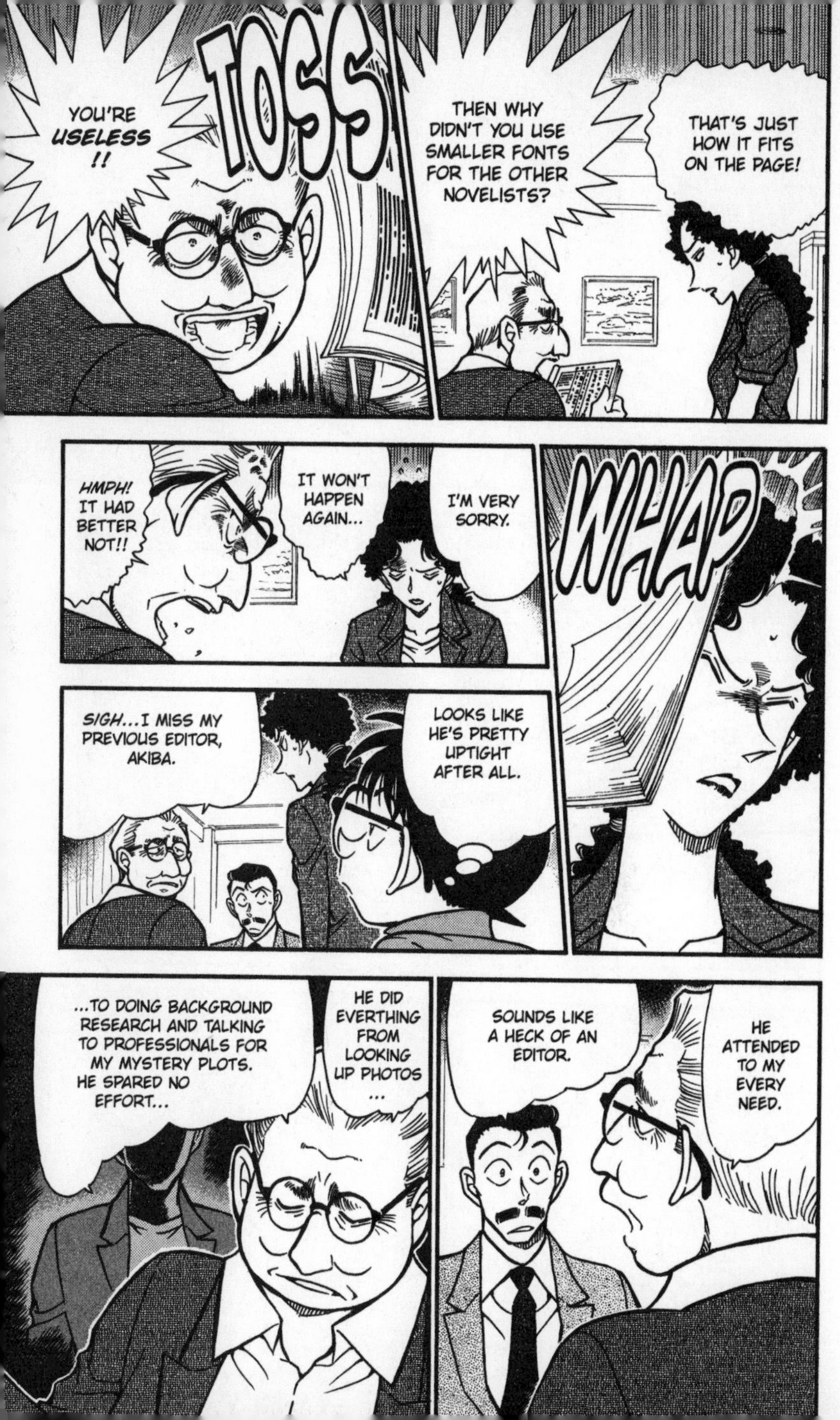
THAT'S JUST HOW IT FITS ON THE PAGE!
THEN WHY DIDN'T YOU USE SMALLER FONTS FOR THE OTHER NOVELISTS?
TOSS
YOU'RE USELESS !!
WHAP
I'M VERY SORRY.
IT WON'T HAPPEN AGAIN...
HMPH! IT HAD BETTER NOT!!
LOOKS LIKE HE'S PRETTY UPTIGHT AFTER ALL.
SIGH...I MISS MY PREVIOUS EDITOR, AKIBA.
HE ATTENDED TO MY EVERY NEED.
SOUNDS LIKE A HECK OF AN EDITOR.
HE DID EVERTHING FROM LOOKING UP PHOTOS ...
...TO DOING BACKGROUND RESEARCH AND TALKING TO PROFESSIONALS FOR MY MYSTERY PLOTS. HE SPARED NO EFFORT...

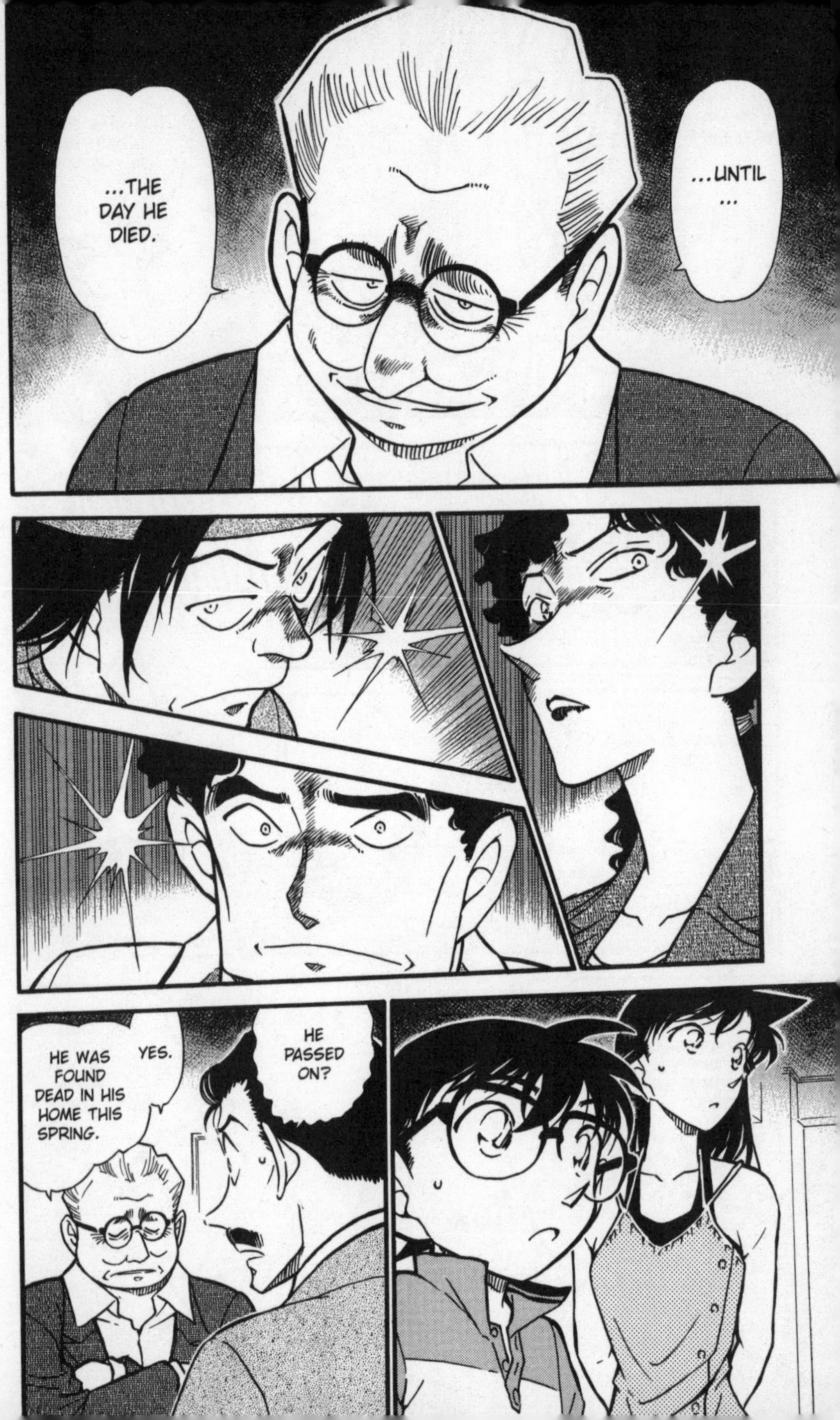
...UNTIL ...
...THE DAY HE DIED.
HE PASSED ON?
YES.
HE WAS FOUND DEAD IN HIS HOME THIS SPRING.

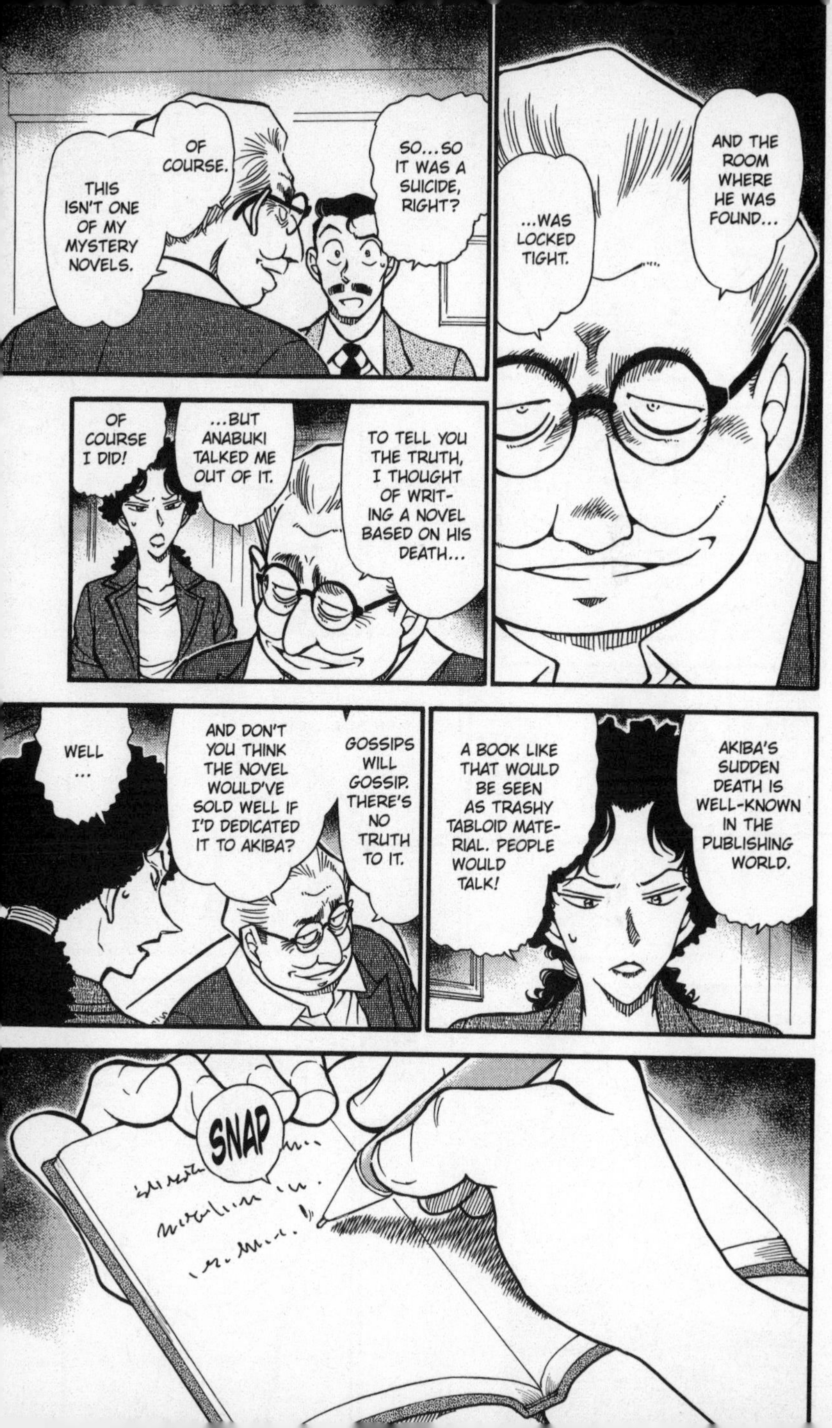
AND THE ROOM WHERE HE WAS FOUND...
...WAS LOCKED TIGHT.
SO...SO IT WAS A SUICIDE, RIGHT?
OF COURSE.
THIS ISN'T ONE OF MY MYSTERY NOVELS.
TO TELL YOU THE TRUTH, I THOUGHT OF WRITING A NOVEL BASED ON HIS DEATH...
...BUT ANABUKI TALKED ME OUT OF IT.
OF COURSE I DID!
AKIBA'S SUDDEN DEATH IS WELL-KNOWN IN THE PUBLISHING WORLD.
A BOOK LIKE THAT WOULD BE SEEN AS TRASHY TABLOID MATERIAL. PEOPLE WOULD TALK!
GOSSIPS WILL GOSSIP. THERE'S NO TRUTH TO IT.
AND DON'T YOU THINK THE NOVEL WOULD'VE SOLD WELL IF I'D DEDICATED IT TO AKIBA?
WELL ...
SNAP

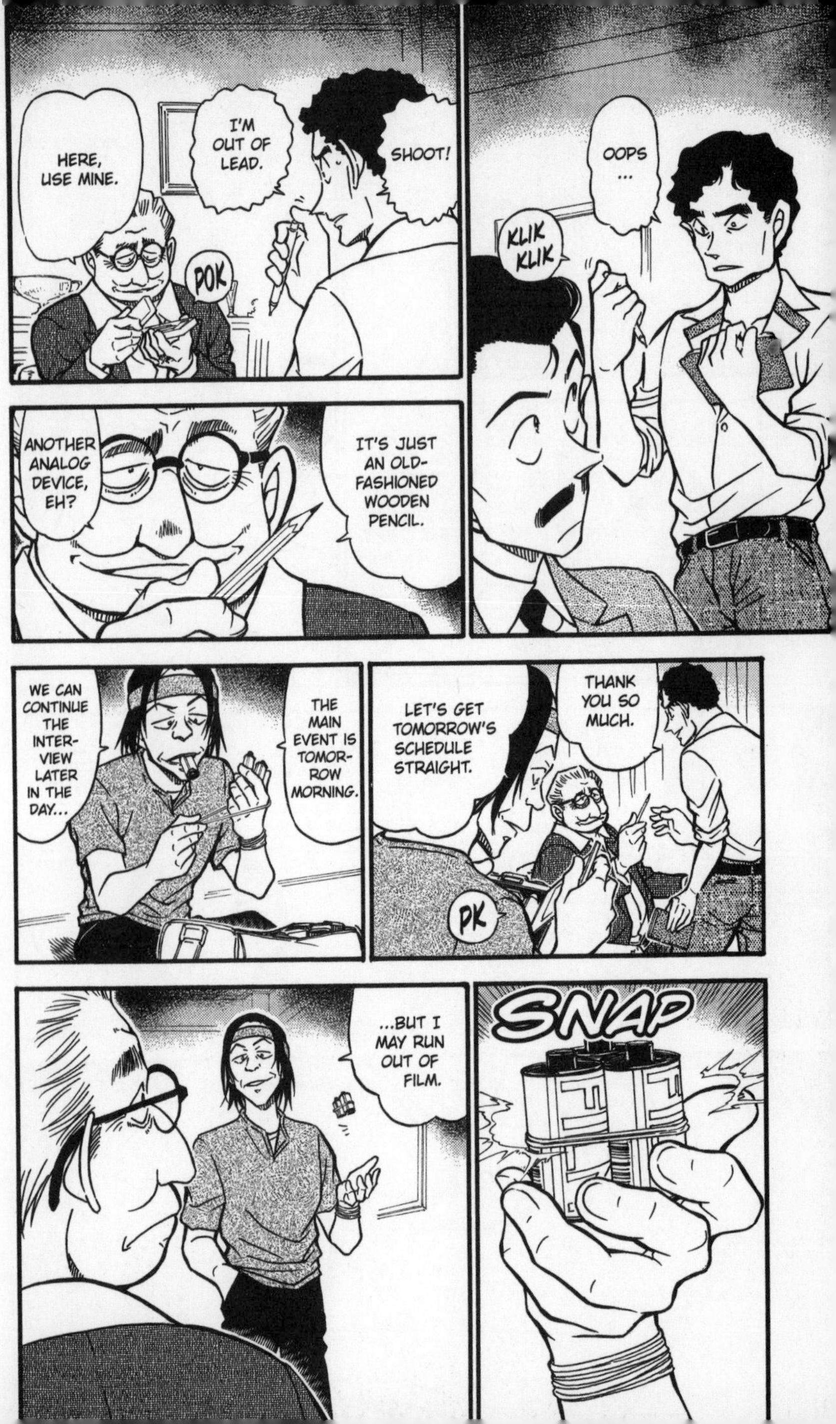
OOPS ...
KLIK KLIK
SHOOT!
I'M OUT OF LEAD.
HERE, USE MINE.
POK
IT'S JUST AN OLD-FASHIONED WOODEN PENCIL.
ANOTHER ANALOG DEVICE, EH?
THANK YOU SO MUCH.
LET'S GET TOMORROW'S SCHEDULE STRAIGHT.
PK
THE MAIN EVENT IS TOMORROW MORNING.
WE CAN CONTINUE THE INTERVIEW LATER IN THE DAY...
SNAP
...BUT I MAY RUN OUT OF FILM.

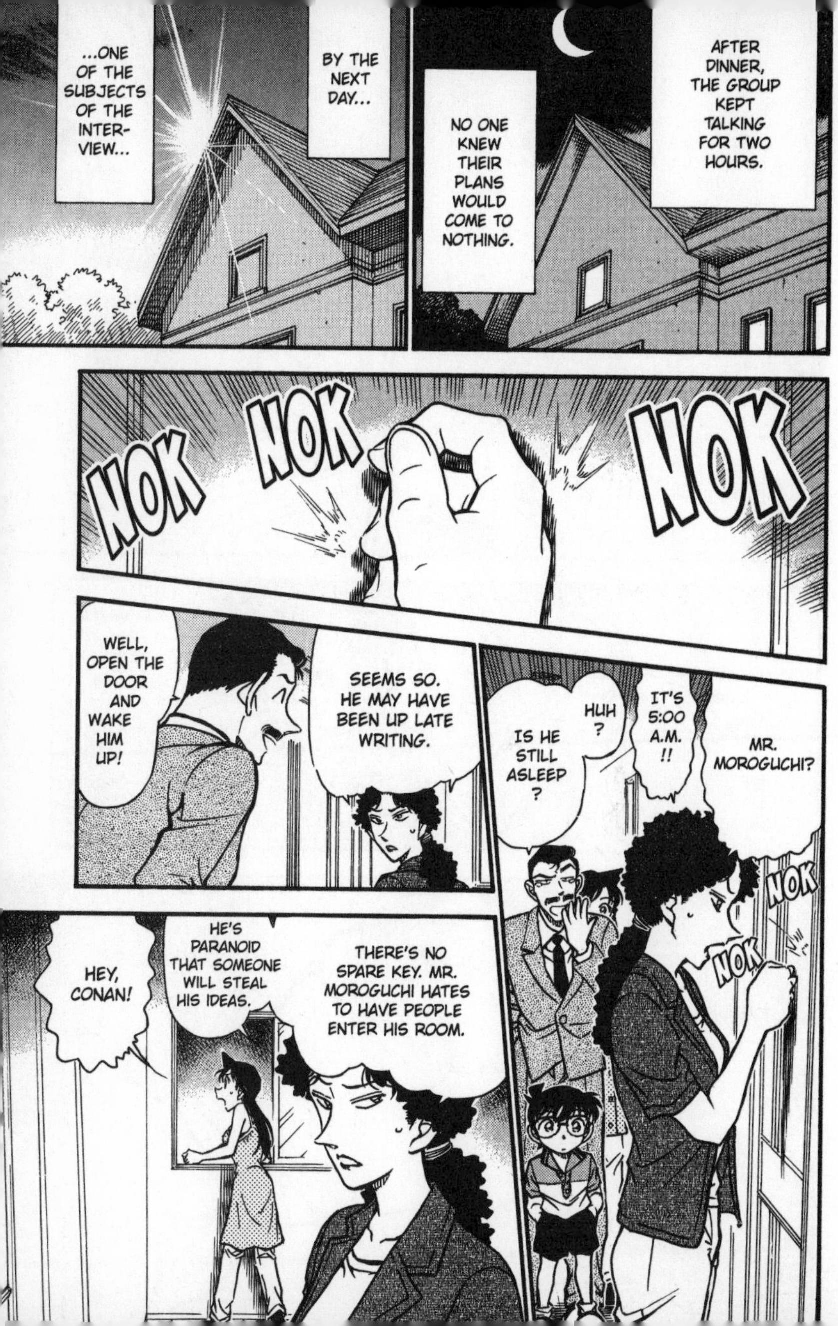
AFTER DINNER, THE GROUP KEPT TALKING FOR TWO HOURS.
NO ONE KNEW THEIR PLANS WOULD COME TO NOTHING.
BY THE NEXT DAY...
...ONE OF THE SUBJECTS OF THE INTER-VIEW...
NOK
NOK
NOK
MR. MOROGUCHI?
IT'S 5:00 A.M. !!
HUH?
IS HE STILL ASLEEP?
NOK
NOK
SEEMS SO. HE MAY HAVE BEEN UP LATE WRITING.
WELL, OPEN THE DOOR AND WAKE HIM UP!
THERE'S NO SPARE KEY. MR. MOROGUCHI HATES TO HAVE PEOPLE ENTER HIS ROOM.
HE'S PARANOID THAT SOMEONE WILL STEAL HIS IDEAS.
HEY, CONAN!

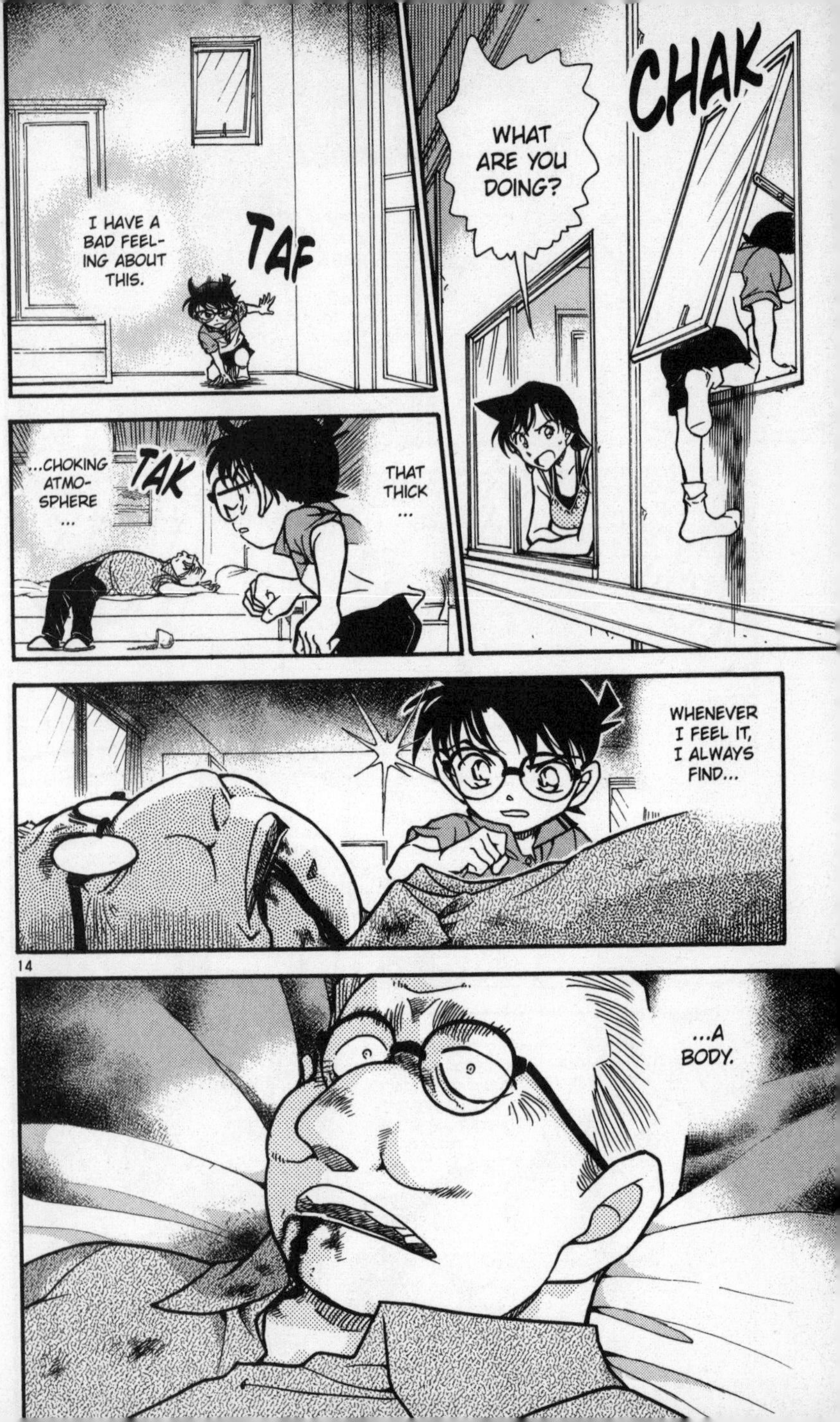
CHAK
WHAT ARE YOU DOING?
I HAVE A BAD FEEL-ING ABOUT THIS.
TAF
THAT THICK ...
...CHOKING ATMO-SPHERE ...
TAK
WHENEVER I FEEL IT, I ALWAYS FIND...
...A BODY.

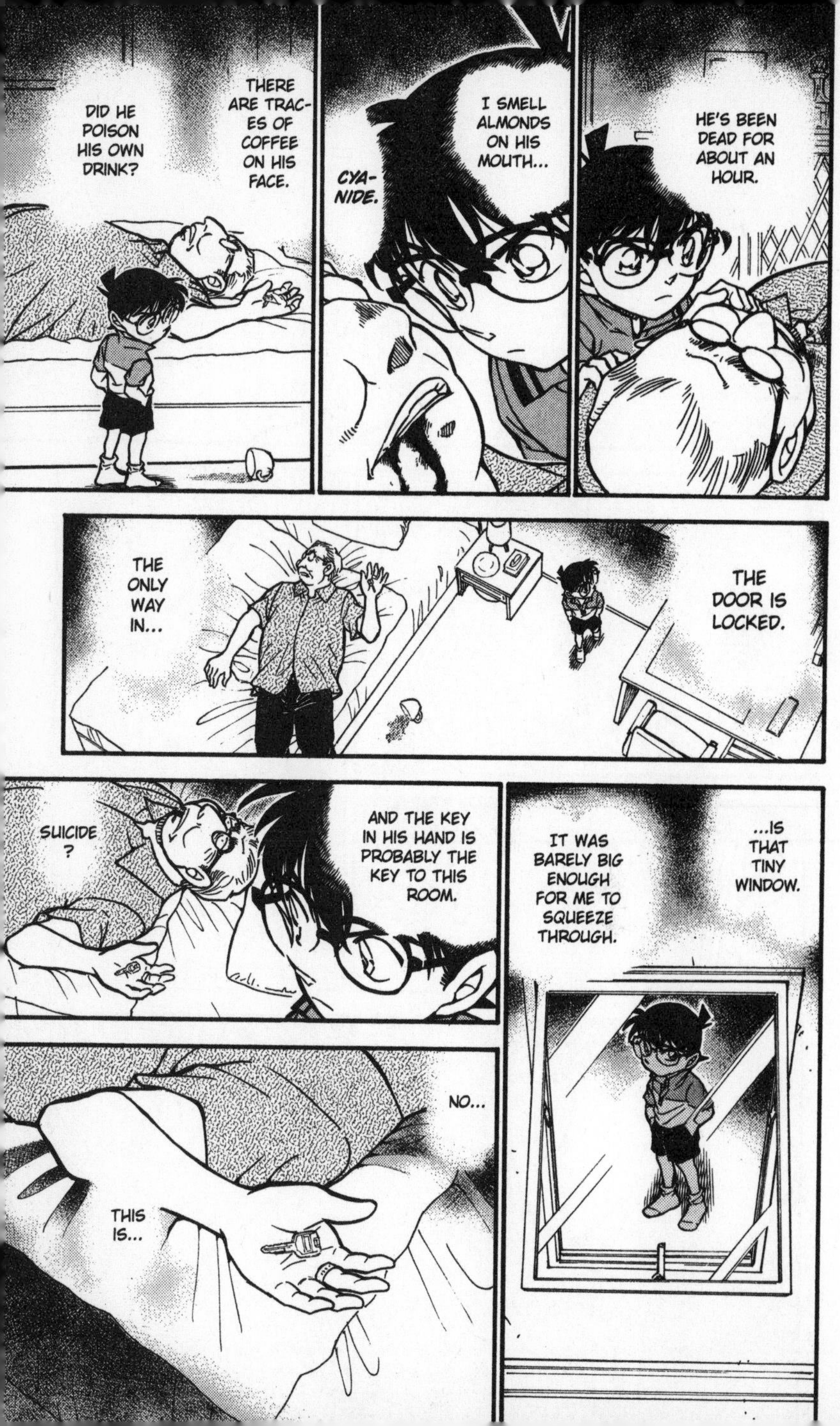
HE'S BEEN DEAD FOR ABOUT AN HOUR.
I SMELL ALMONDS ON HIS MOUTH...
CYA-NIDE.
THERE ARE TRAC-ES OF COFFEE ON HIS FACE.
DID HE POISON HIS OWN DRINK?
THE DOOR IS LOCKED.
THE ONLY WAY IN...
...IS THAT TINY WINDOW.
IT WAS BARELY BIG ENOUGH FOR ME TO SQUEEZE THROUGH.
AND THE KEY IN HIS HAND IS PROBABLY THE KEY TO THIS ROOM.
SUICIDE?
NO...
THIS IS...

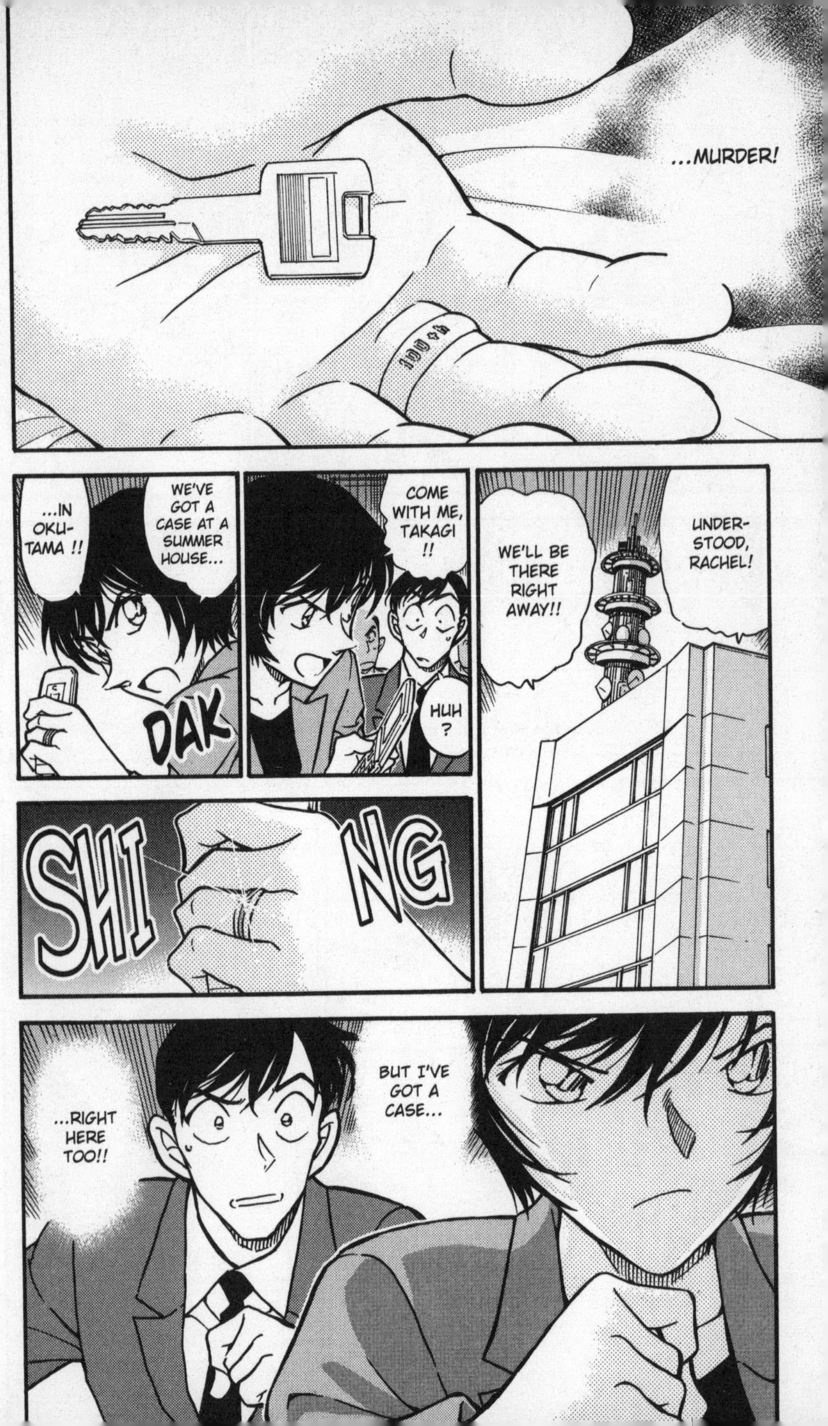
...MURDER!
UNDER-STOOD, RACHEL!
WE'LL BE THERE RIGHT AWAY!!
COME WITH ME, TAKAGI !!
HUH ?
WE'VE GOT A CASE AT A SUMMER HOUSE...
...IN OKU-TAMA !!
DAK
SHING
BUT I'VE GOT A CASE...
...RIGHT HERE TOO!!

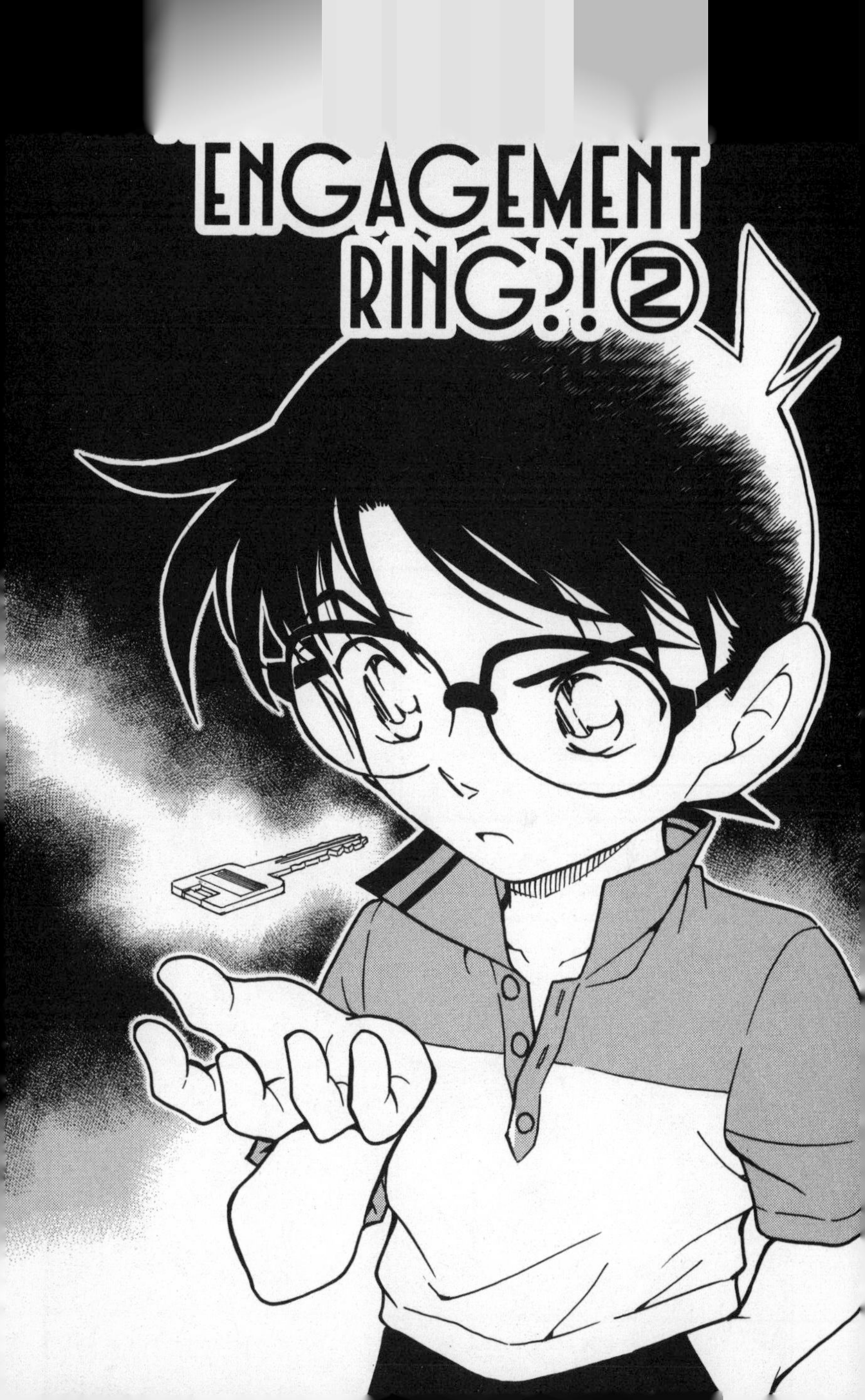
ENGAGEMENT RING?! ②

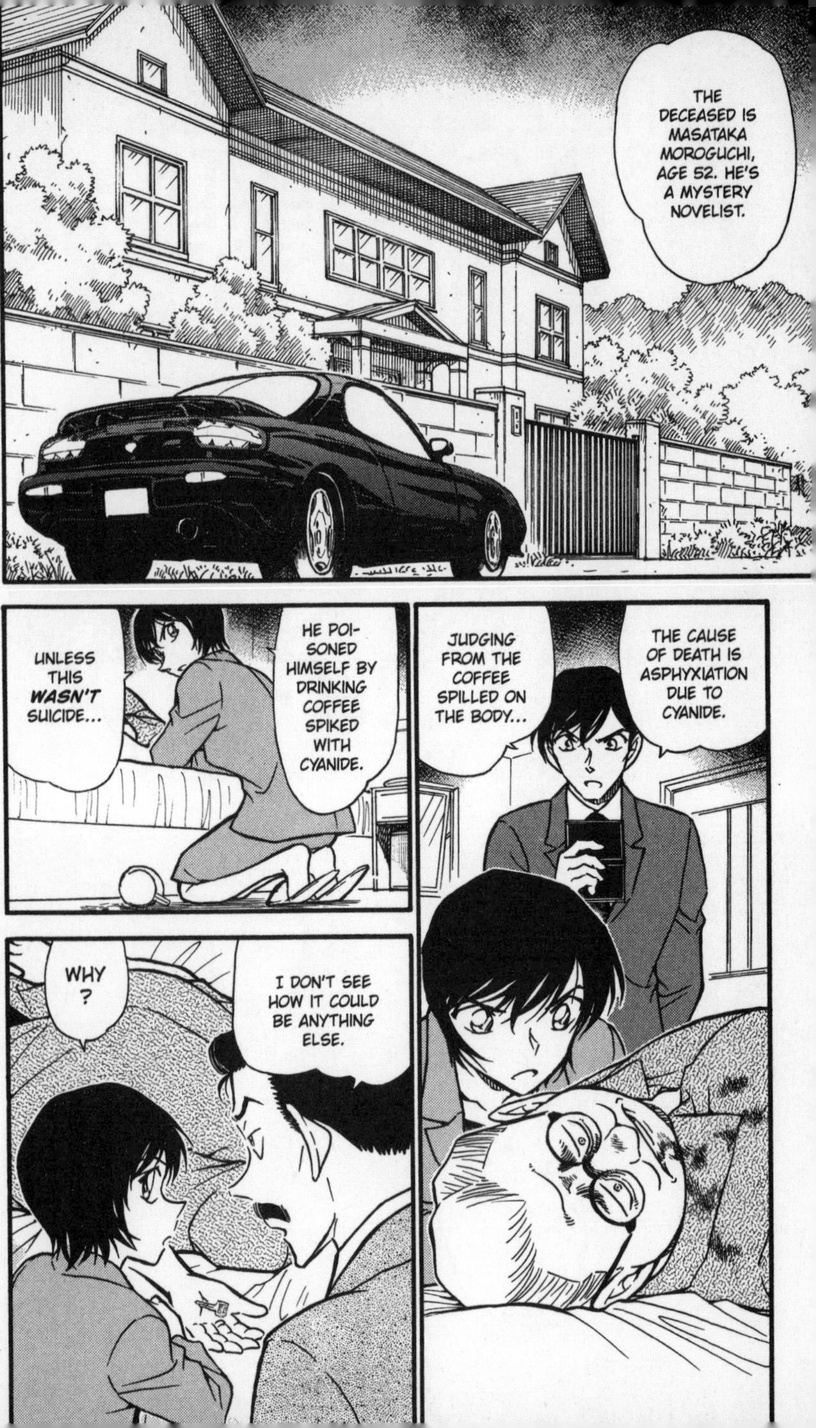
THE DECEASED IS MASATAKA MOROGUCHI, AGE 52. HE'S A MYSTERY NOVELIST.
THE CAUSE OF DEATH IS ASPHYXIATION DUE TO CYANIDE.
JUDGING FROM THE COFFEE SPILLED ON THE BODY...
HE POI-SONED HIMSELF BY DRINKING COFFEE SPIKED WITH CYANIDE.
UNLESS THIS ***WASN'T*** SUICIDE...
I DON'T SEE HOW IT COULD BE ANYTHING ELSE.
WHY?

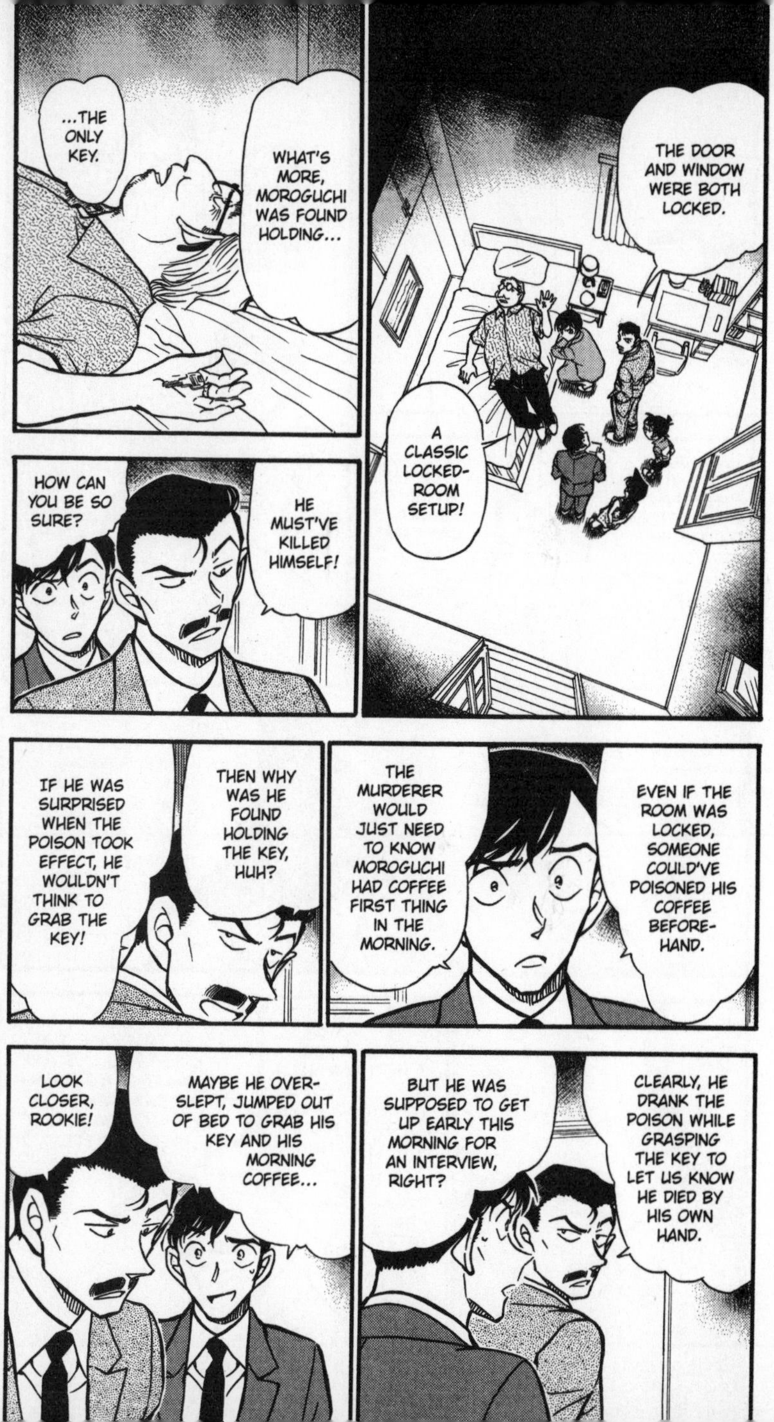
THE DOOR AND WINDOW WERE BOTH LOCKED.
A CLASSIC LOCKED-ROOM SETUP!
WHAT'S MORE, MOROGUCHI WAS FOUND HOLDING...
...THE ONLY KEY.
HE MUST'VE KILLED HIMSELF!
HOW CAN YOU BE SO SURE?
EVEN IF THE ROOM WAS LOCKED, SOMEONE COULD'VE POISONED HIS COFFEE BEFORE-HAND.
THE MURDERER WOULD JUST NEED TO KNOW MOROGUCHI HAD COFFEE FIRST THING IN THE MORNING.
THEN WHY WAS HE FOUND HOLDING THE KEY, HUH?
IF HE WAS SURPRISED WHEN THE POISON TOOK EFFECT, HE WOULDN'T THINK TO GRAB THE KEY!
CLEARLY, HE DRANK THE POISON WHILE GRASPING THE KEY TO LET US KNOW HE DIED BY HIS OWN HAND.
BUT HE WAS SUPPOSED TO GET UP EARLY THIS MORNING FOR AN INTERVIEW, RIGHT?
MAYBE HE OVER-SLEPT, JUMPED OUT OF BED TO GRAB HIS KEY AND HIS MORNING COFFEE...
LOOK CLOSER, ROOKIE!

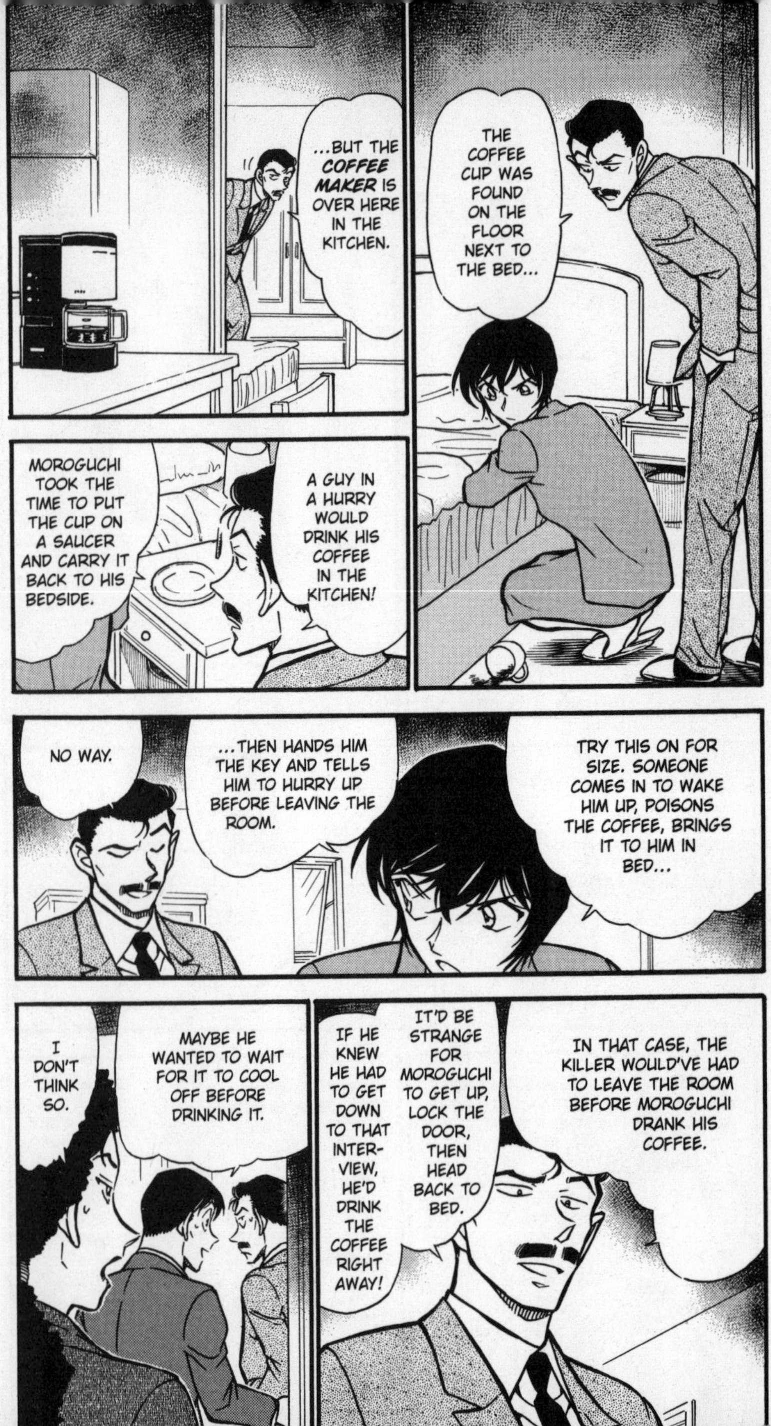
THE COFFEE CUP WAS FOUND ON THE FLOOR NEXT TO THE BED...
...BUT THE **COFFEE MAKER** IS OVER HERE IN THE KITCHEN.
A GUY IN A HURRY WOULD DRINK HIS COFFEE IN THE KITCHEN!
MOROGUCHI TOOK THE TIME TO PUT THE CUP ON A SAUCER AND CARRY IT BACK TO HIS BEDSIDE.
TRY THIS ON FOR SIZE. SOMEONE COMES IN TO WAKE HIM UP, POISONS THE COFFEE, BRINGS IT TO HIM IN BED...
...THEN HANDS HIM THE KEY AND TELLS HIM TO HURRY UP BEFORE LEAVING THE ROOM.
NO WAY.
IN THAT CASE, THE KILLER WOULD'VE HAD TO LEAVE THE ROOM BEFORE MOROGUCHI DRANK HIS COFFEE.
IT'D BE STRANGE FOR MOROGUCHI TO GET UP, LOCK THE DOOR, THEN HEAD BACK TO BED.
IF HE KNEW HE HAD TO GET DOWN TO THAT INTER-VIEW, HE'D DRINK THE COFFEE RIGHT AWAY!
MAYBE HE WANTED TO WAIT FOR IT TO COOL OFF BEFORE DRINKING IT.
I DON'T THINK SO.

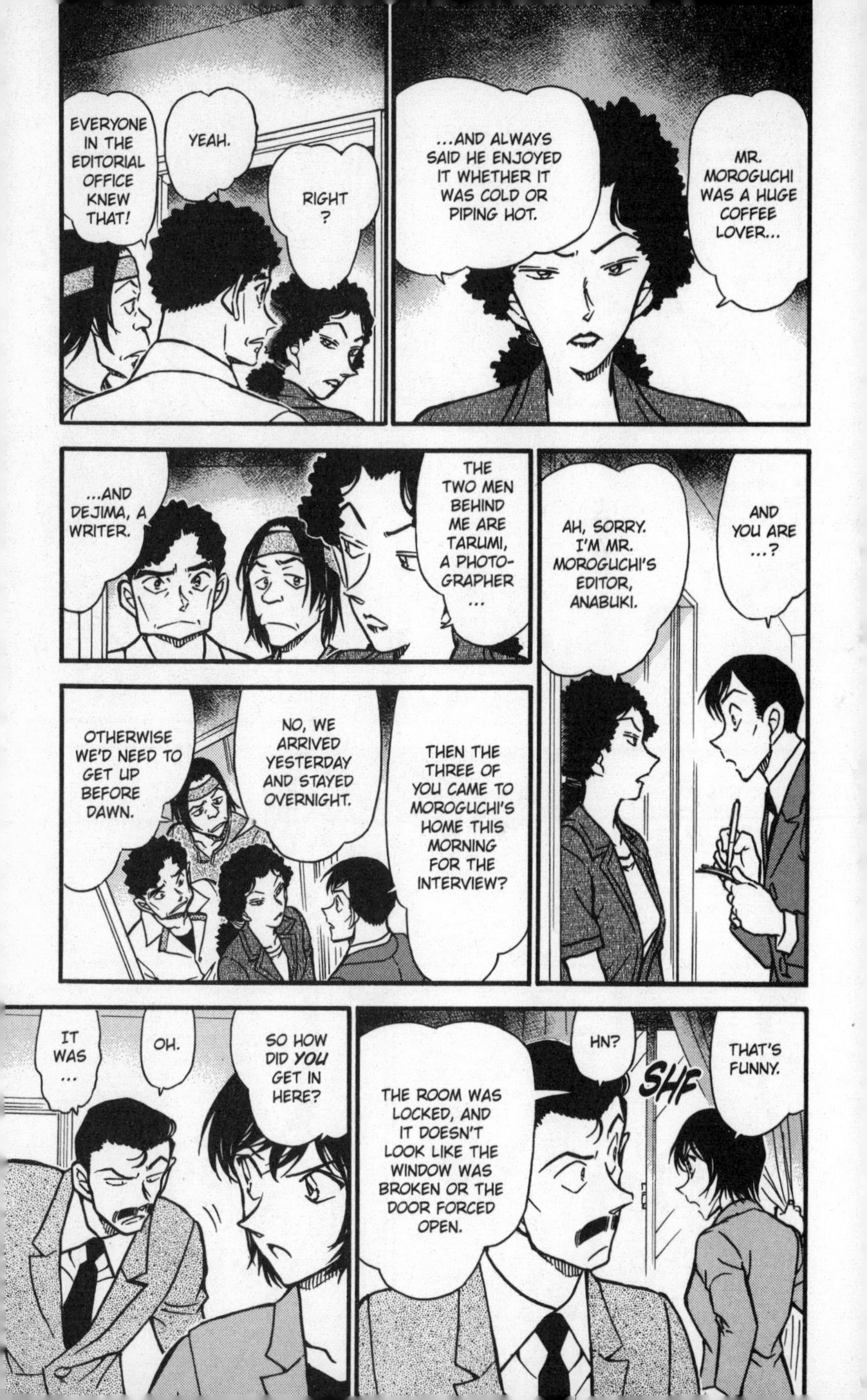
MR. MOROGUCHI WAS A HUGE COFFEE LOVER...
...AND ALWAYS SAID HE ENJOYED IT WHETHER IT WAS COLD OR PIPING HOT.
RIGHT?
YEAH.
EVERYONE IN THE EDITORIAL OFFICE KNEW THAT!
AND YOU ARE ...?
AH, SORRY. I'M MR. MOROGUCHI'S EDITOR, ANABUKI.
THE TWO MEN BEHIND ME ARE TARUMI, A PHOTOGRAPHER ...
...AND DEJIMA, A WRITER.
THEN THE THREE OF YOU CAME TO MOROGUCHI'S HOME THIS MORNING FOR THE INTERVIEW?
NO, WE ARRIVED YESTERDAY AND STAYED OVERNIGHT.
OTHERWISE WE'D NEED TO GET UP BEFORE DAWN.
THAT'S FUNNY.
HN?
SHF
THE ROOM WAS LOCKED, AND IT DOESN'T LOOK LIKE THE WINDOW WAS BROKEN OR THE DOOR FORCED OPEN.
SO HOW DID *YOU* GET IN HERE?
OH.
IT WAS ...

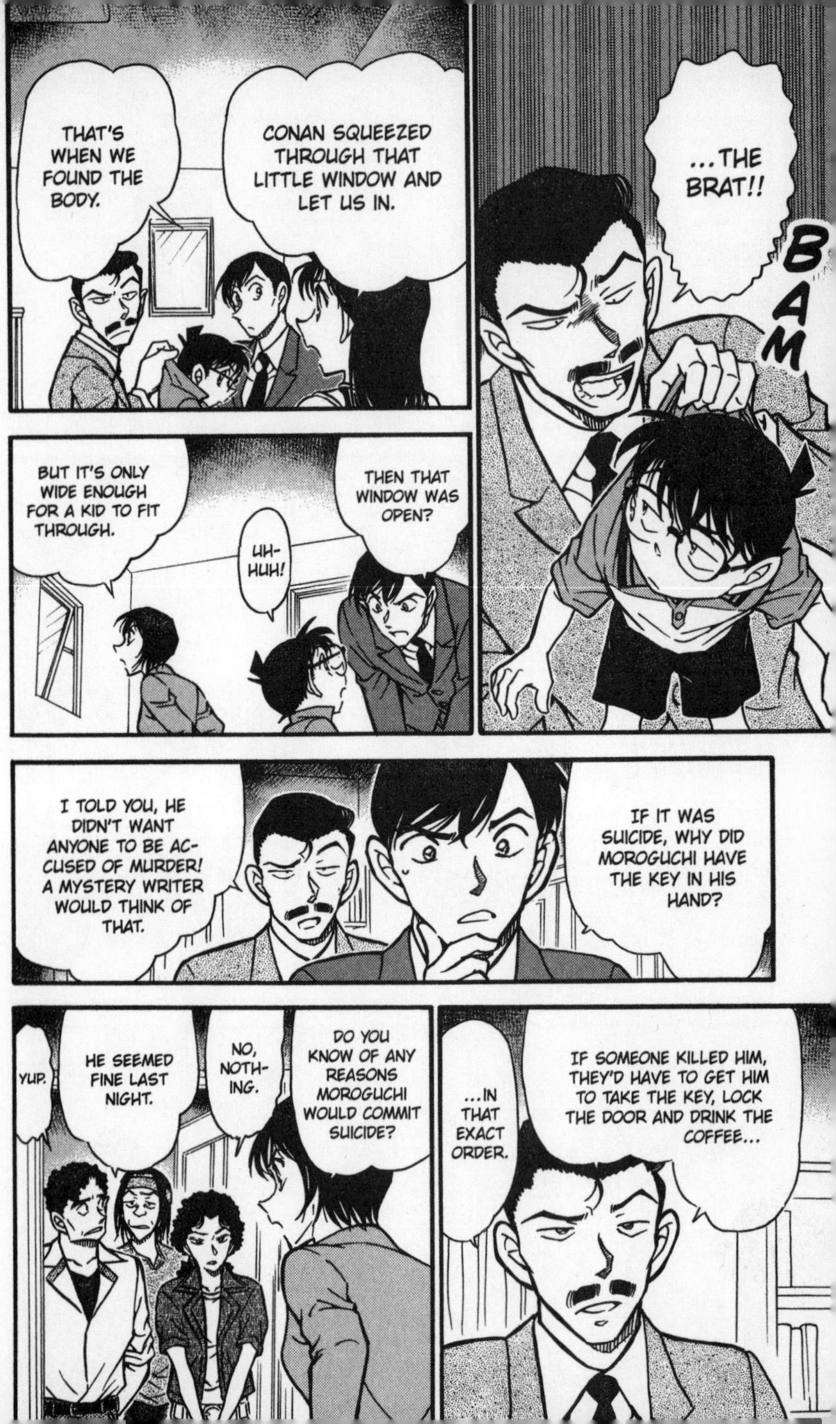
...THE BRAT!!
BAM
CONAN SQUEEZED THROUGH THAT LITTLE WINDOW AND LET US IN.
THAT'S WHEN WE FOUND THE BODY.
THEN THAT WINDOW WAS OPEN?
UH-HUH!
BUT IT'S ONLY WIDE ENOUGH FOR A KID TO FIT THROUGH.
IF IT WAS SUICIDE, WHY DID MOROGUCHI HAVE THE KEY IN HIS HAND?
I TOLD YOU, HE DIDN'T WANT ANYONE TO BE AC-CUSED OF MURDER! A MYSTERY WRITER WOULD THINK OF THAT.
IF SOMEONE KILLED HIM, THEY'D HAVE TO GET HIM TO TAKE THE KEY, LOCK THE DOOR AND DRINK THE COFFEE...
...IN THAT EXACT ORDER.
DO YOU KNOW OF ANY REASONS MOROGUCHI WOULD COMMIT SUICIDE?
NO, NOTH-ING.
HE SEEMED FINE LAST NIGHT.
YUP.

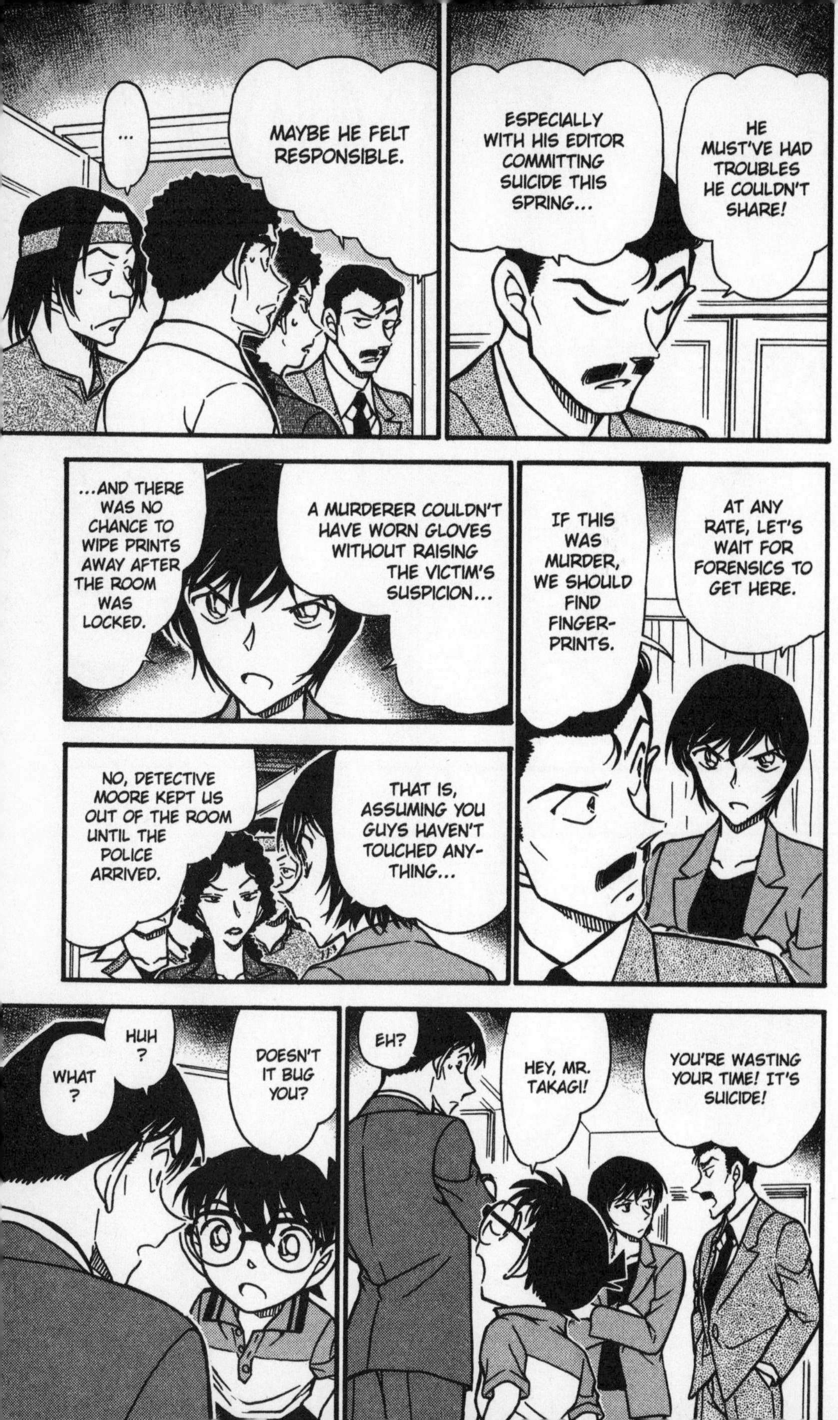
HE MUST'VE HAD TROUBLES HE COULDN'T SHARE!
ESPECIALLY WITH HIS EDITOR COMMITTING SUICIDE THIS SPRING...
MAYBE HE FELT RESPONSIBLE.
...
AT ANY RATE, LET'S WAIT FOR FORENSICS TO GET HERE.
IF THIS WAS MURDER, WE SHOULD FIND FINGER-PRINTS.
A MURDERER COULDN'T HAVE WORN GLOVES WITHOUT RAISING THE VICTIM'S SUSPICION...
...AND THERE WAS NO CHANCE TO WIPE PRINTS AWAY AFTER THE ROOM WAS LOCKED.
THAT IS, ASSUMING YOU GUYS HAVEN'T TOUCHED ANY-THING...
NO, DETECTIVE MOORE KEPT US OUT OF THE ROOM UNTIL THE POLICE ARRIVED.
YOU'RE WASTING YOUR TIME! IT'S SUICIDE!
HEY, MR. TAKAGI!
EH?
DOESN'T IT BUG YOU?
HUH?
WHAT?

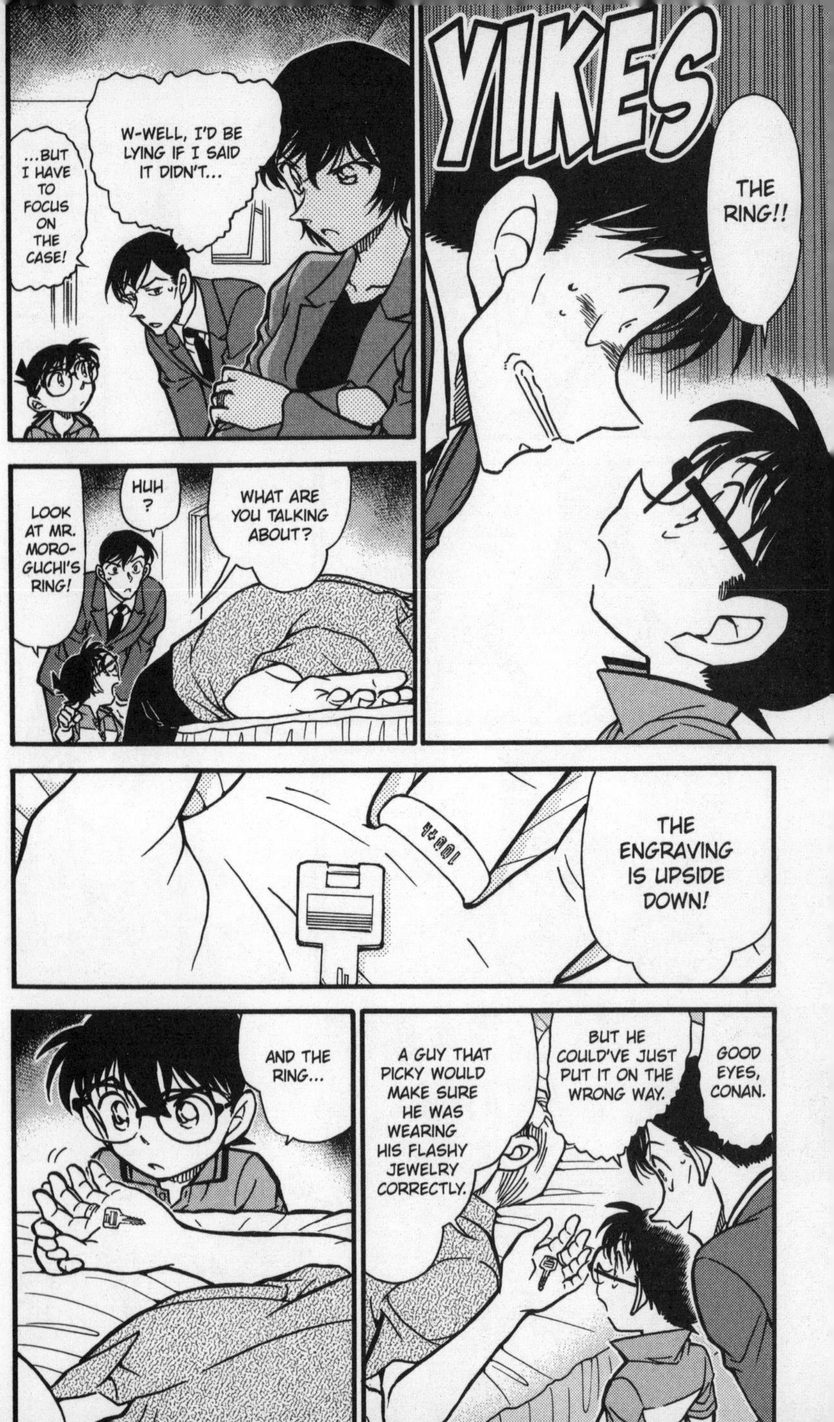
YIKES
THE RING!!
W-WELL, I'D BE LYING IF I SAID IT DIDN'T...
...BUT I HAVE TO FOCUS ON THE CASE!
WHAT ARE YOU TALKING ABOUT?
HUH?
LOOK AT MR. MOROGUCHI'S RING!
THE ENGRAVING IS UPSIDE DOWN!
GOOD EYES, CONAN.
BUT HE COULD'VE JUST PUT IT ON THE WRONG WAY.
A GUY THAT PICKY WOULD MAKE SURE HE WAS WEARING HIS FLASHY JEWELRY CORRECTLY.
AND THE RING...

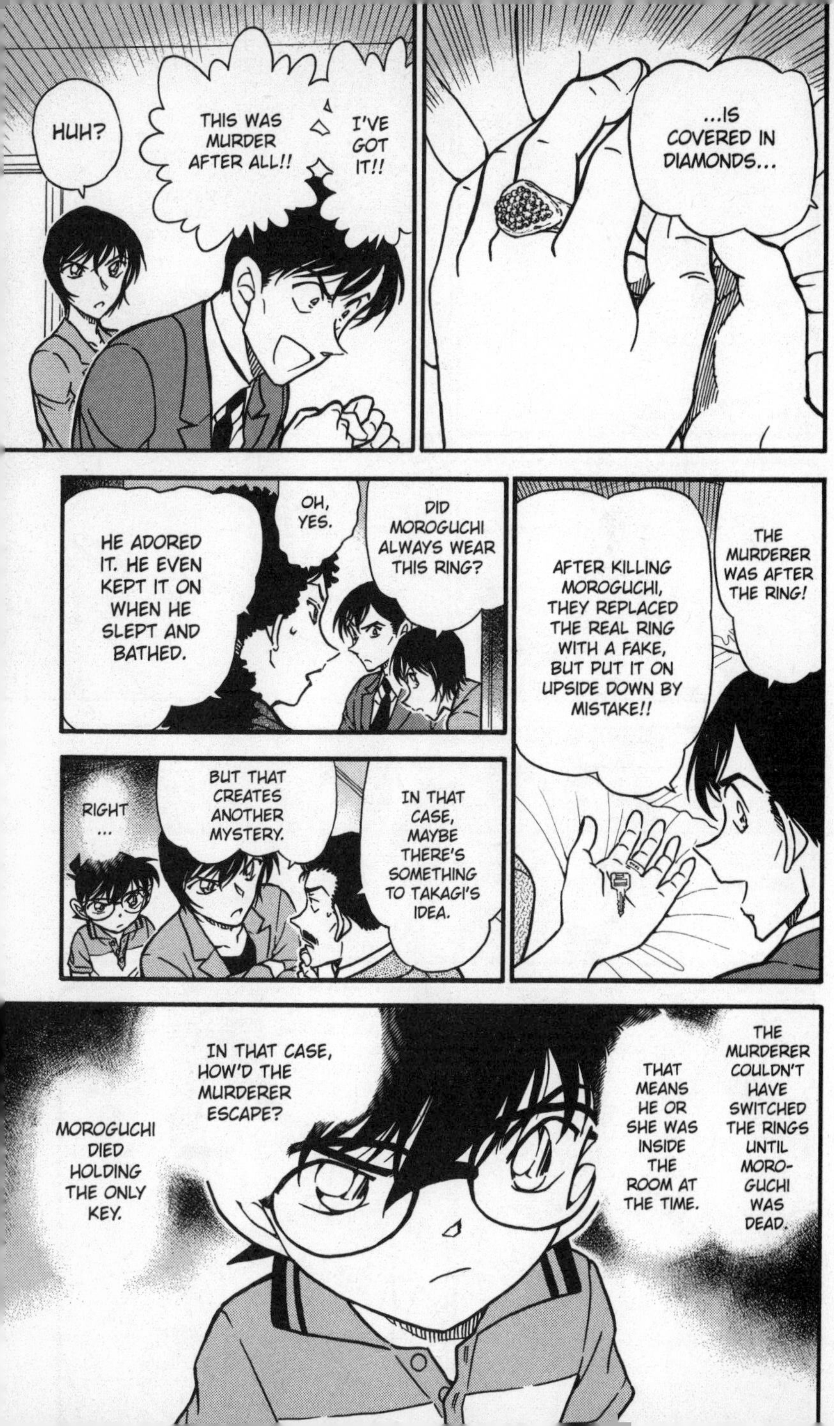
...IS COVERED IN DIAMONDS...
I'VE GOT IT!!
THIS WAS MURDER AFTER ALL!!
HUH?
THE MURDERER WAS AFTER THE RING!
AFTER KILLING MOROGUCHI, THEY REPLACED THE REAL RING WITH A FAKE, BUT PUT IT ON UPSIDE DOWN BY MISTAKE!!
DID MOROGUCHI ALWAYS WEAR THIS RING?
OH, YES.
HE ADORED IT. HE EVEN KEPT IT ON WHEN HE SLEPT AND BATHED.
IN THAT CASE, MAYBE THERE'S SOMETHING TO TAKAGI'S IDEA.
BUT THAT CREATES ANOTHER MYSTERY.
RIGHT ...
THE MURDERER COULDN'T HAVE SWITCHED THE RINGS UNTIL MORO-GUCHI WAS DEAD.
THAT MEANS HE OR SHE WAS INSIDE THE ROOM AT THE TIME.
IN THAT CASE, HOW'D THE MURDERER ESCAPE?
MOROGUCHI DIED HOLDING THE ONLY KEY.

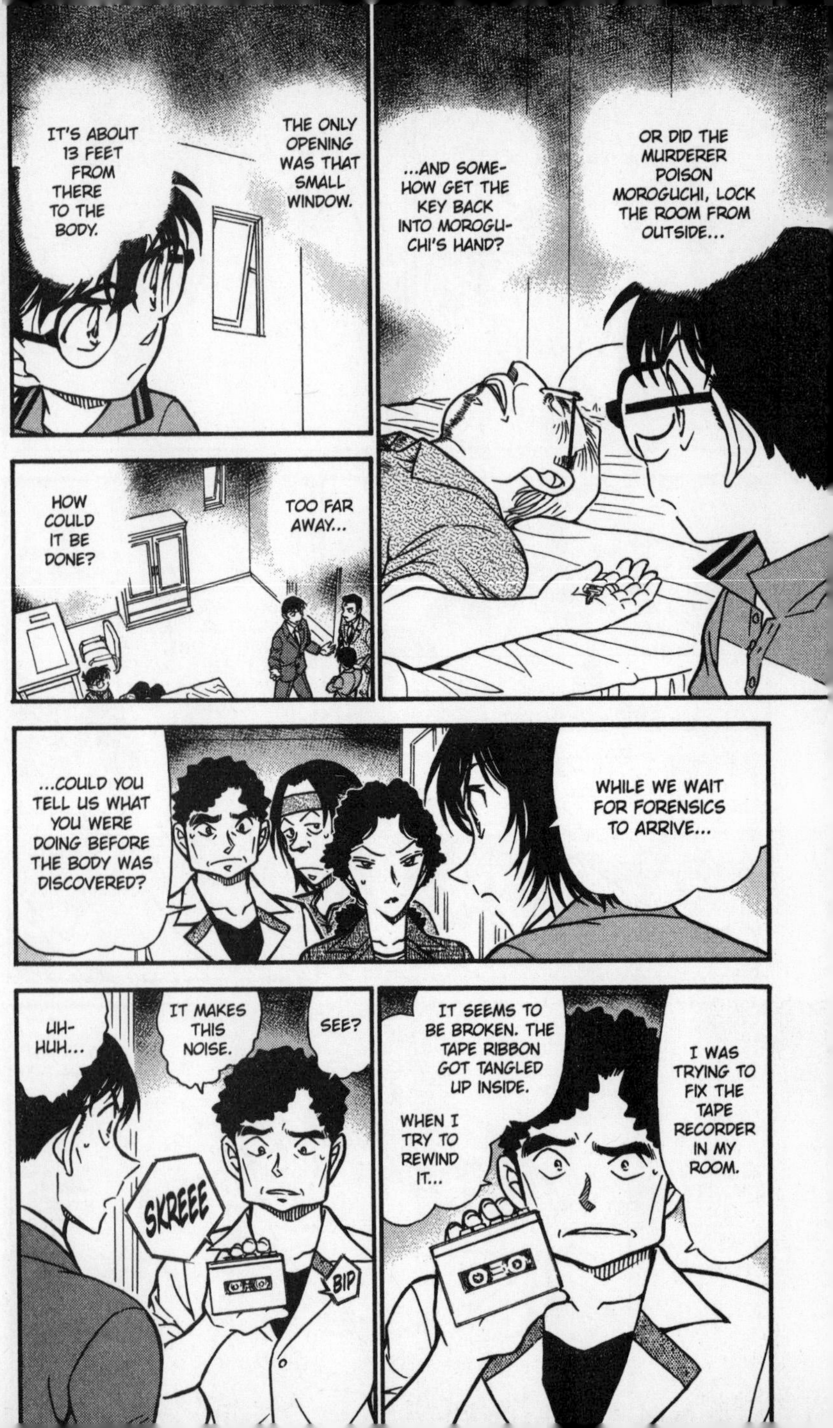
OR DID THE MURDERER POISON MOROGUCHI, LOCK THE ROOM FROM OUTSIDE...
...AND SOME-HOW GET THE KEY BACK INTO MOROGU-CHI'S HAND?
THE ONLY OPENING WAS THAT SMALL WINDOW.
IT'S ABOUT 13 FEET FROM THERE TO THE BODY.
TOO FAR AWAY...
HOW COULD IT BE DONE?
WHILE WE WAIT FOR FORENSICS TO ARRIVE...
...COULD YOU TELL US WHAT YOU WERE DOING BEFORE THE BODY WAS DISCOVERED?
I WAS TRYING TO FIX THE TAPE RECORDER IN MY ROOM.
IT SEEMS TO BE BROKEN. THE TAPE RIBBON GOT TANGLED UP INSIDE.
WHEN I TRY TO REWIND IT...
SEE?
BIP
IT MAKES THIS NOISE.
SKREEE
UH-HUH...

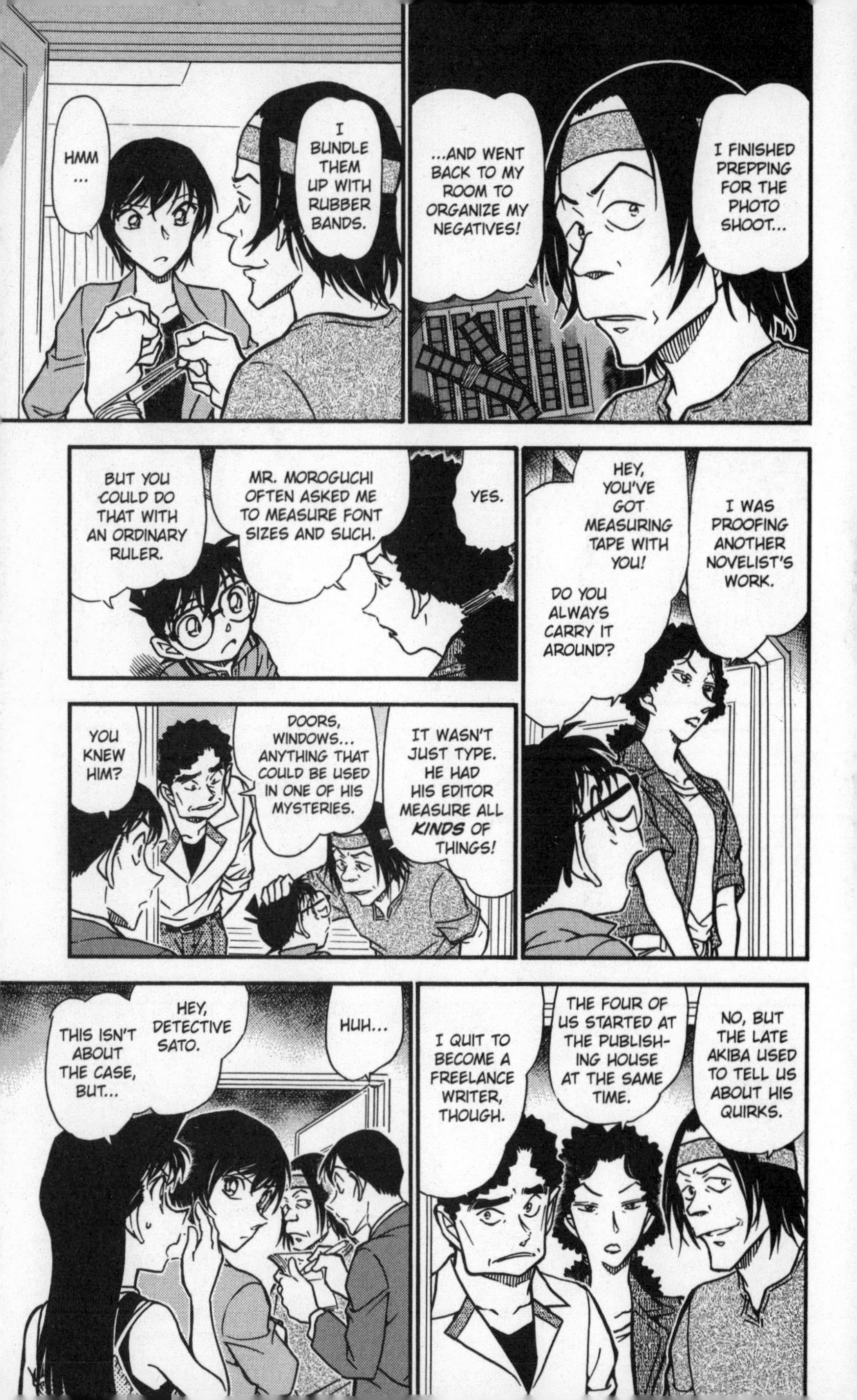
I FINISHED PREPPING FOR THE PHOTO SHOOT...
...AND WENT BACK TO MY ROOM TO ORGANIZE MY NEGATIVES!
I BUNDLE THEM UP WITH RUBBER BANDS.
HMM...
I WAS PROOFING ANOTHER NOVELIST'S WORK.
HEY, YOU'VE GOT MEASURING TAPE WITH YOU!
DO YOU ALWAYS CARRY IT AROUND?
YES.
MR. MOROGUCHI OFTEN ASKED ME TO MEASURE FONT SIZES AND SUCH.
BUT YOU COULD DO THAT WITH AN ORDINARY RULER.
IT WASN'T JUST TYPE. HE HAD HIS EDITOR MEASURE ALL *KINDS* OF THINGS!
DOORS, WINDOWS... ANYTHING THAT COULD BE USED IN ONE OF HIS MYSTERIES.
YOU KNEW HIM?
NO, BUT THE LATE AKIBA USED TO TELL US ABOUT HIS QUIRKS.
THE FOUR OF US STARTED AT THE PUBLISHING HOUSE AT THE SAME TIME.
I QUIT TO BECOME A FREELANCE WRITER, THOUGH.
HUH...
HEY, DETECTIVE SATO.
THIS ISN'T ABOUT THE CASE, BUT...

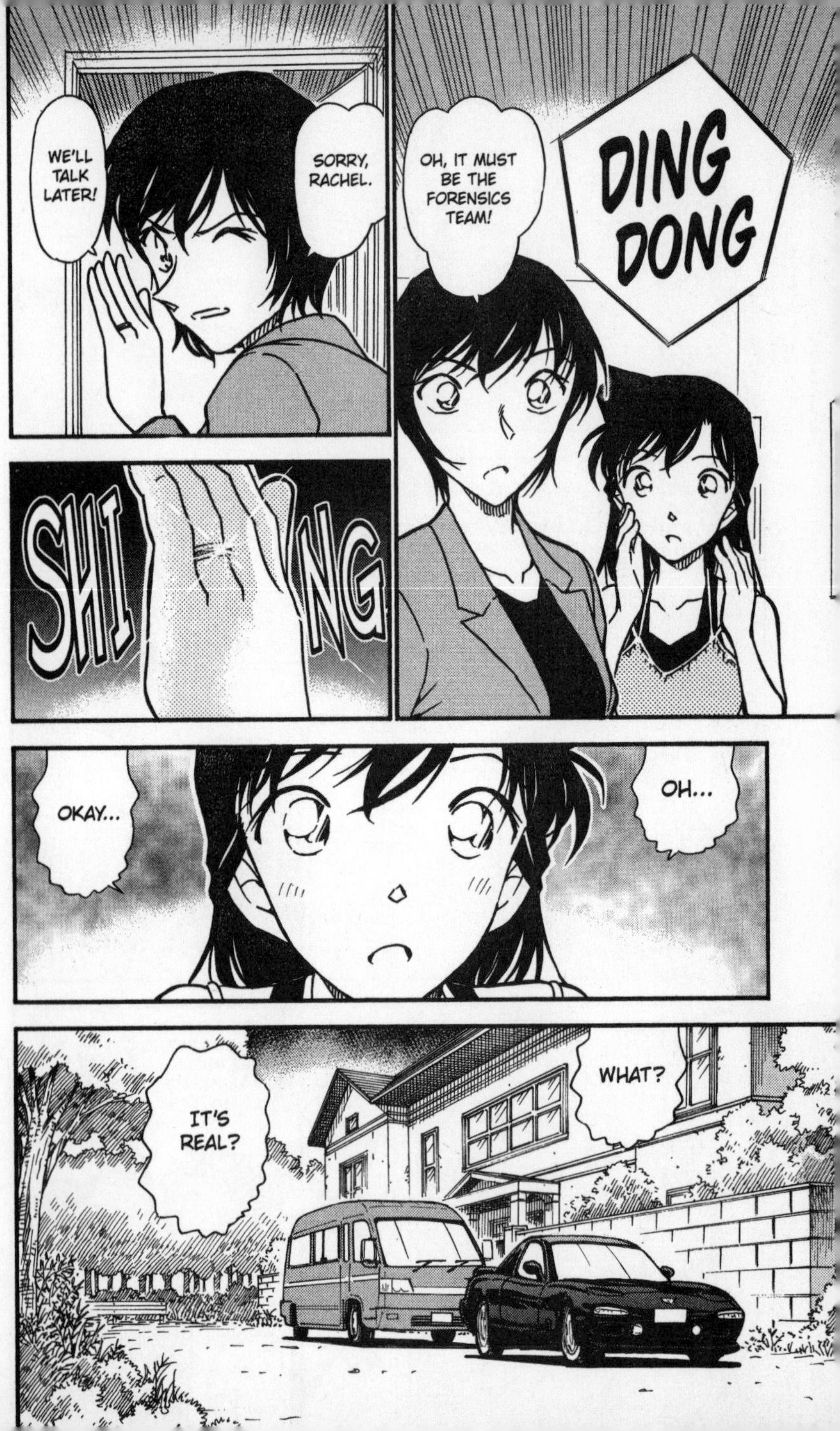
DING DONG
OH, IT MUST BE THE FORENSICS TEAM!
SORRY, RACHEL.
WE'LL TALK LATER!
SHI
NG
OH...
OKAY...
WHAT?
IT'S REAL?

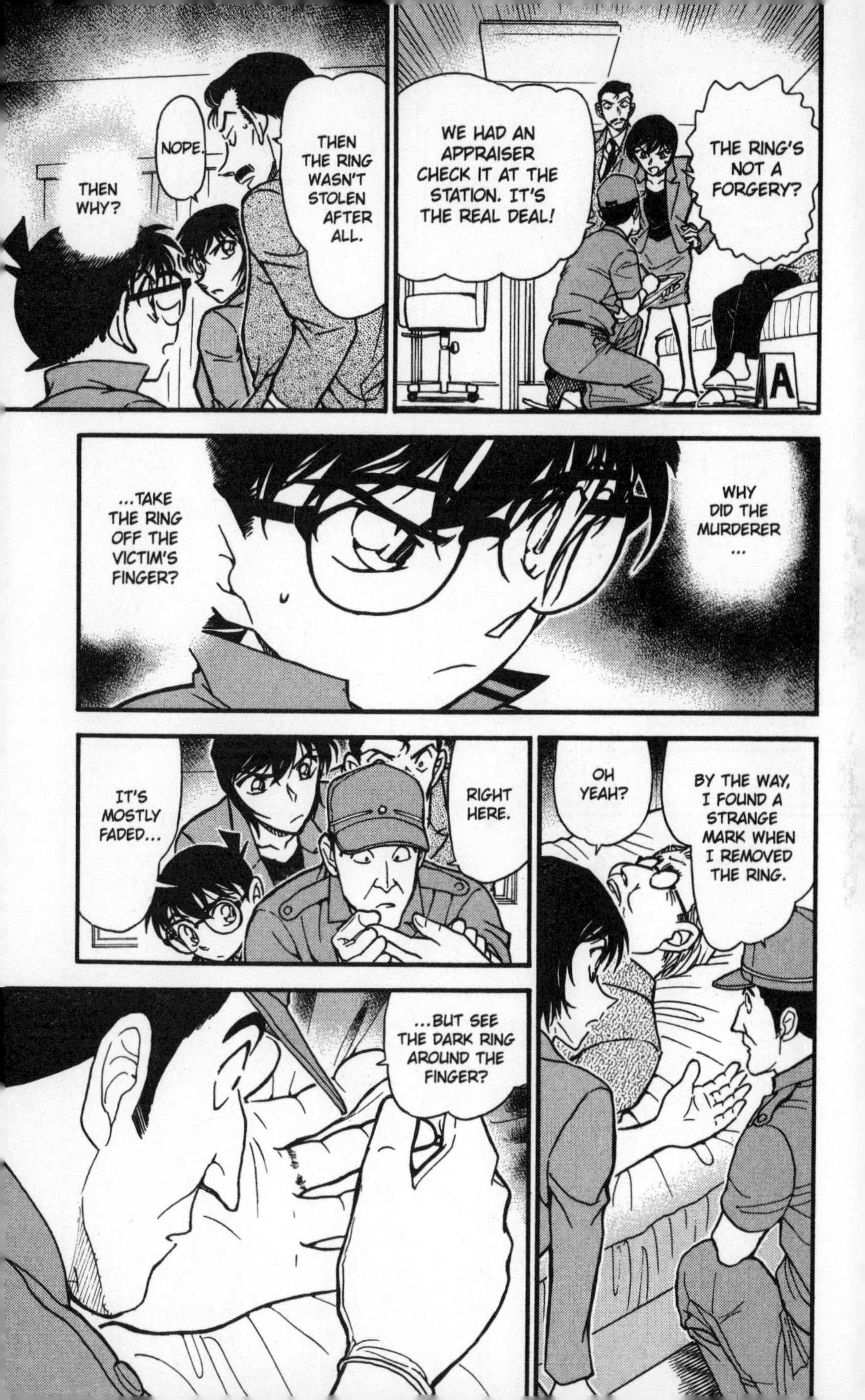
THE RING'S NOT A FORGERY?
WE HAD AN APPRAISER CHECK IT AT THE STATION. IT'S THE REAL DEAL!
A
THEN THE RING WASN'T STOLEN AFTER ALL.
NOPE.
THEN WHY?
WHY DID THE MURDERER ...
...TAKE THE RING OFF THE VICTIM'S FINGER?
BY THE WAY, I FOUND A STRANGE MARK WHEN I REMOVED THE RING.
OH YEAH?
RIGHT HERE.
IT'S MOSTLY FADED...
...BUT SEE THE DARK RING AROUND THE FINGER?

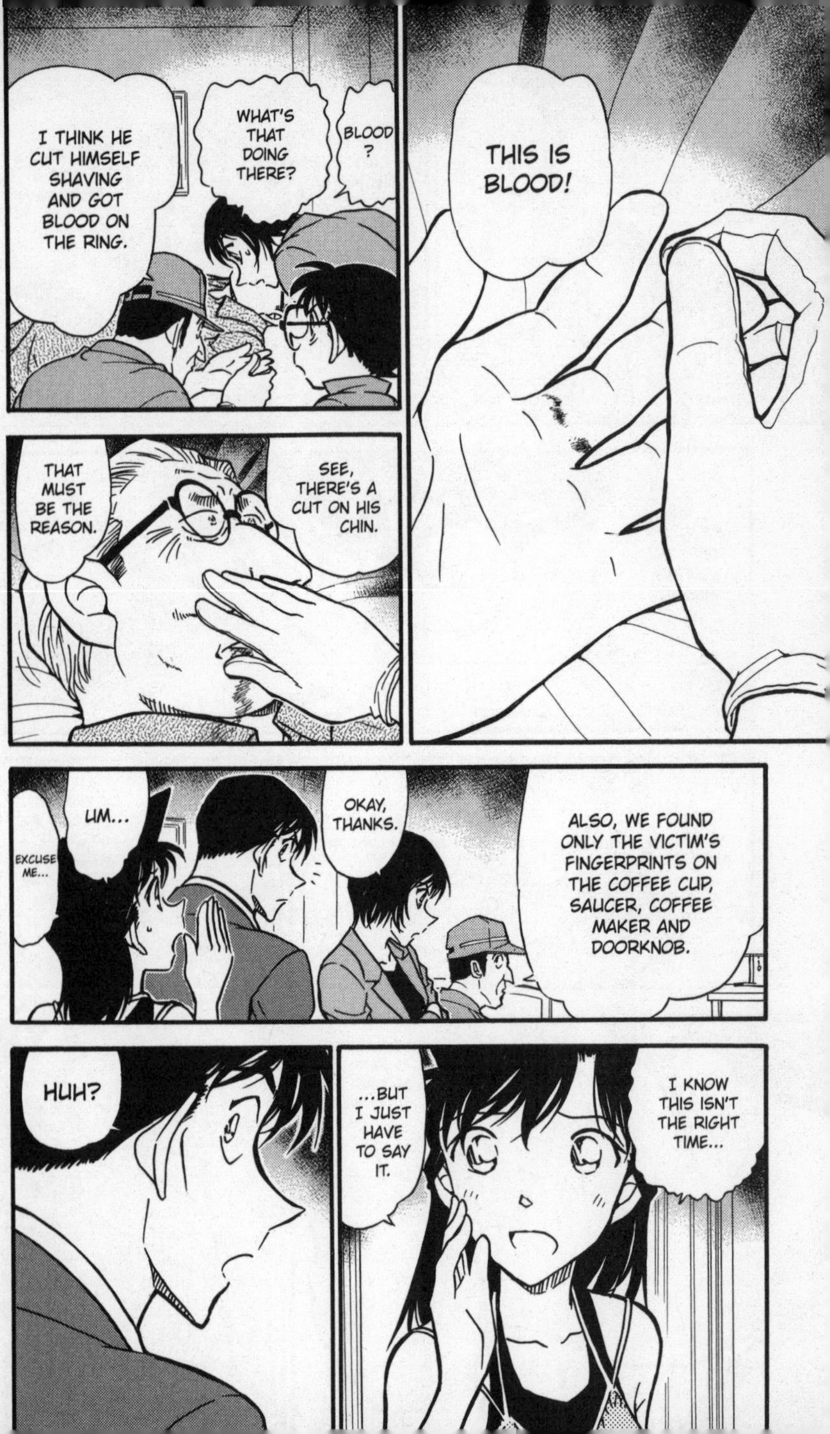
THIS IS BLOOD!
BLOOD?
WHAT'S THAT DOING THERE?
I THINK HE CUT HIMSELF SHAVING AND GOT BLOOD ON THE RING.
SEE, THERE'S A CUT ON HIS CHIN.
THAT MUST BE THE REASON.
ALSO, WE FOUND ONLY THE VICTIM'S FINGERPRINTS ON THE COFFEE CUP, SAUCER, COFFEE MAKER AND DOORKNOB.
OKAY, THANKS.
UM...
EXCUSE ME...
I KNOW THIS ISN'T THE RIGHT TIME...
...BUT I JUST HAVE TO SAY IT.
HUH?

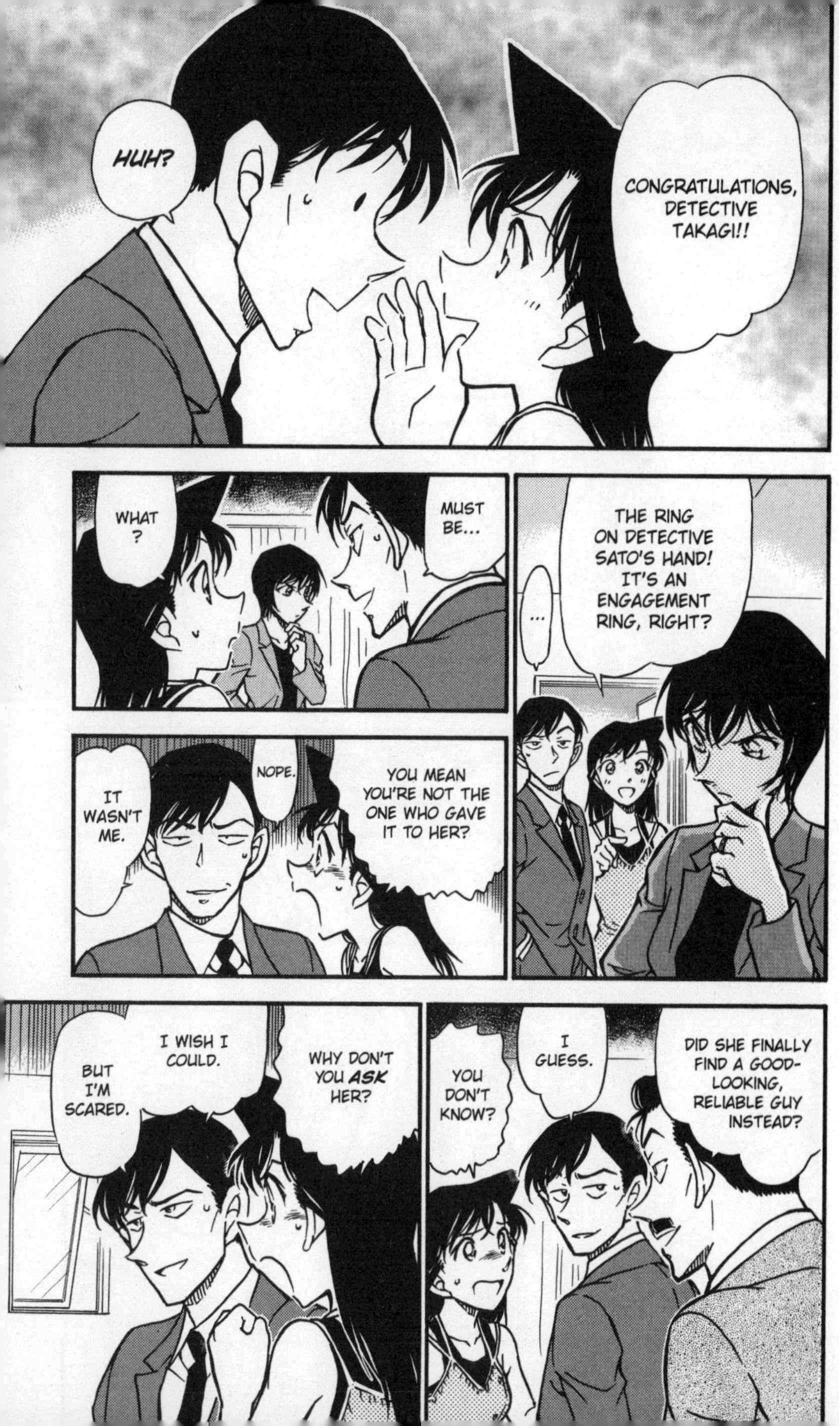
CONGRATULATIONS, DETECTIVE TAKAGI!!
HUH?
THE RING ON DETECTIVE SATO'S HAND! IT'S AN ENGAGEMENT RING, RIGHT?
...
MUST BE...
WHAT?
YOU MEAN YOU'RE NOT THE ONE WHO GAVE IT TO HER?
NOPE.
IT WASN'T ME.
DID SHE FINALLY FIND A GOOD-LOOKING, RELIABLE GUY INSTEAD?
I GUESS.
YOU DON'T KNOW?
WHY DON'T YOU *ASK* HER?
I WISH I COULD.
BUT I'M SCARED.

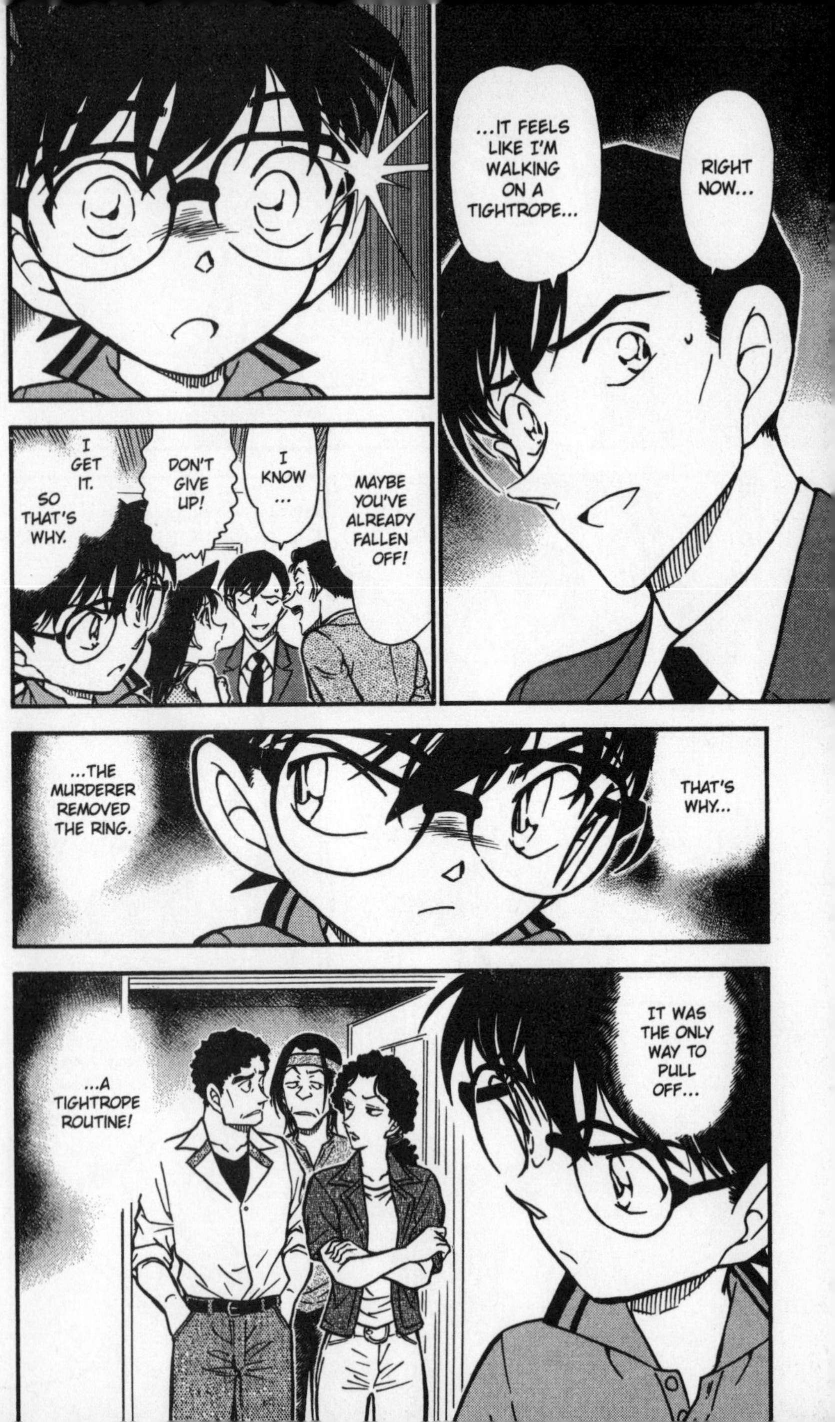
RIGHT NOW...
...IT FEELS LIKE I'M WALKING ON A TIGHTROPE...
MAYBE YOU'VE ALREADY FALLEN OFF!
I KNOW ...
DON'T GIVE UP!
I GET IT.
SO THAT'S WHY.
THAT'S WHY...
...THE MURDERER REMOVED THE RING.
IT WAS THE ONLY WAY TO PULL OFF...
...A TIGHTROPE ROUTINE!

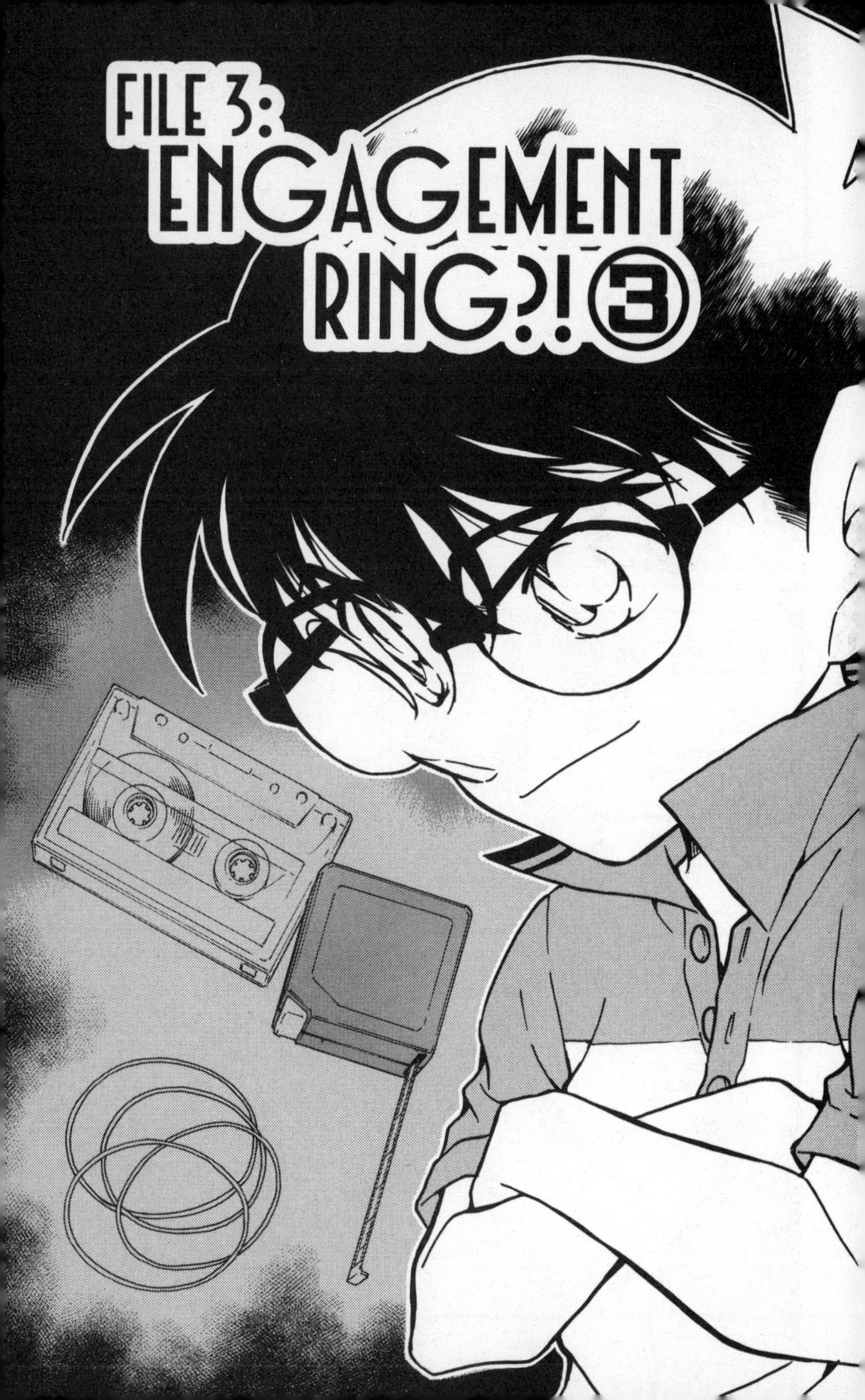
FILE 3:
ENGAGEMENT RING?! ③

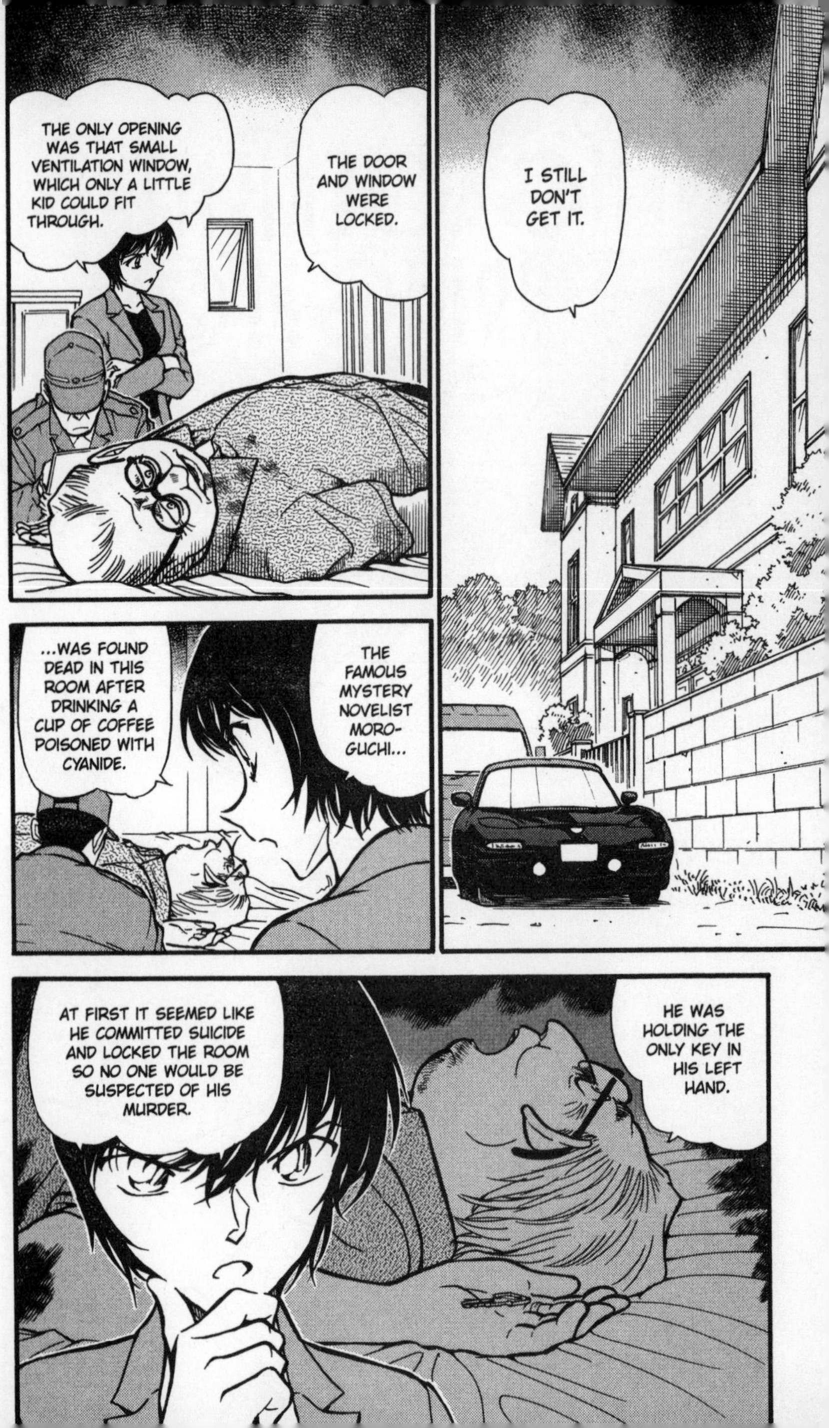
I STILL DON'T GET IT.
THE DOOR AND WINDOW WERE LOCKED.
THE ONLY OPENING WAS THAT SMALL VENTILATION WINDOW, WHICH ONLY A LITTLE KID COULD FIT THROUGH.
THE FAMOUS MYSTERY NOVELIST MORO-GUCHI...
...WAS FOUND DEAD IN THIS ROOM AFTER DRINKING A CUP OF COFFEE POISONED WITH CYANIDE.
HE WAS HOLDING THE ONLY KEY IN HIS LEFT HAND.
AT FIRST IT SEEMED LIKE HE COMMITTED SUICIDE AND LOCKED THE ROOM SO NO ONE WOULD BE SUSPECTED OF HIS MURDER.

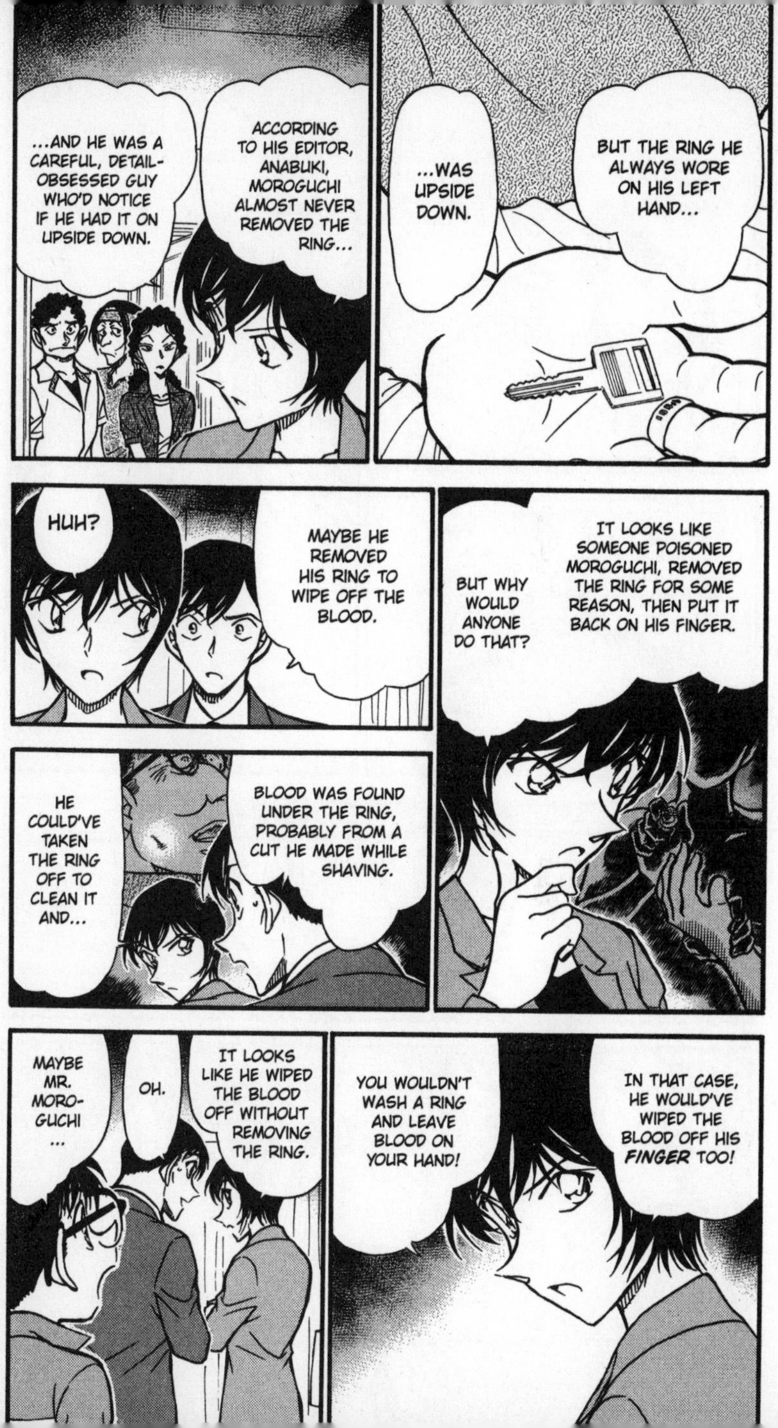
BUT THE RING HE ALWAYS WORE ON HIS LEFT HAND...
...WAS UPSIDE DOWN.
ACCORDING TO HIS EDITOR, ANABUKI, MOROGUCHI ALMOST NEVER REMOVED THE RING...
...AND HE WAS A CAREFUL, DETAIL-OBSESSED GUY WHO'D NOTICE IF HE HAD IT ON UPSIDE DOWN.
IT LOOKS LIKE SOMEONE POISONED MOROGUCHI, REMOVED THE RING FOR SOME REASON, THEN PUT IT BACK ON HIS FINGER.
BUT WHY WOULD ANYONE DO THAT?
MAYBE HE REMOVED HIS RING TO WIPE OFF THE BLOOD.
HUH?
BLOOD WAS FOUND UNDER THE RING, PROBABLY FROM A CUT HE MADE WHILE SHAVING.
HE COULD'VE TAKEN THE RING OFF TO CLEAN IT AND...
IN THAT CASE, HE WOULD'VE WIPED THE BLOOD OFF HIS *FINGER* TOO!
YOU WOULDN'T WASH A RING AND LEAVE BLOOD ON YOUR HAND!
IT LOOKS LIKE HE WIPED THE BLOOD OFF WITHOUT REMOVING THE RING.
OH.
MAYBE MR. MORO-GUCHI...

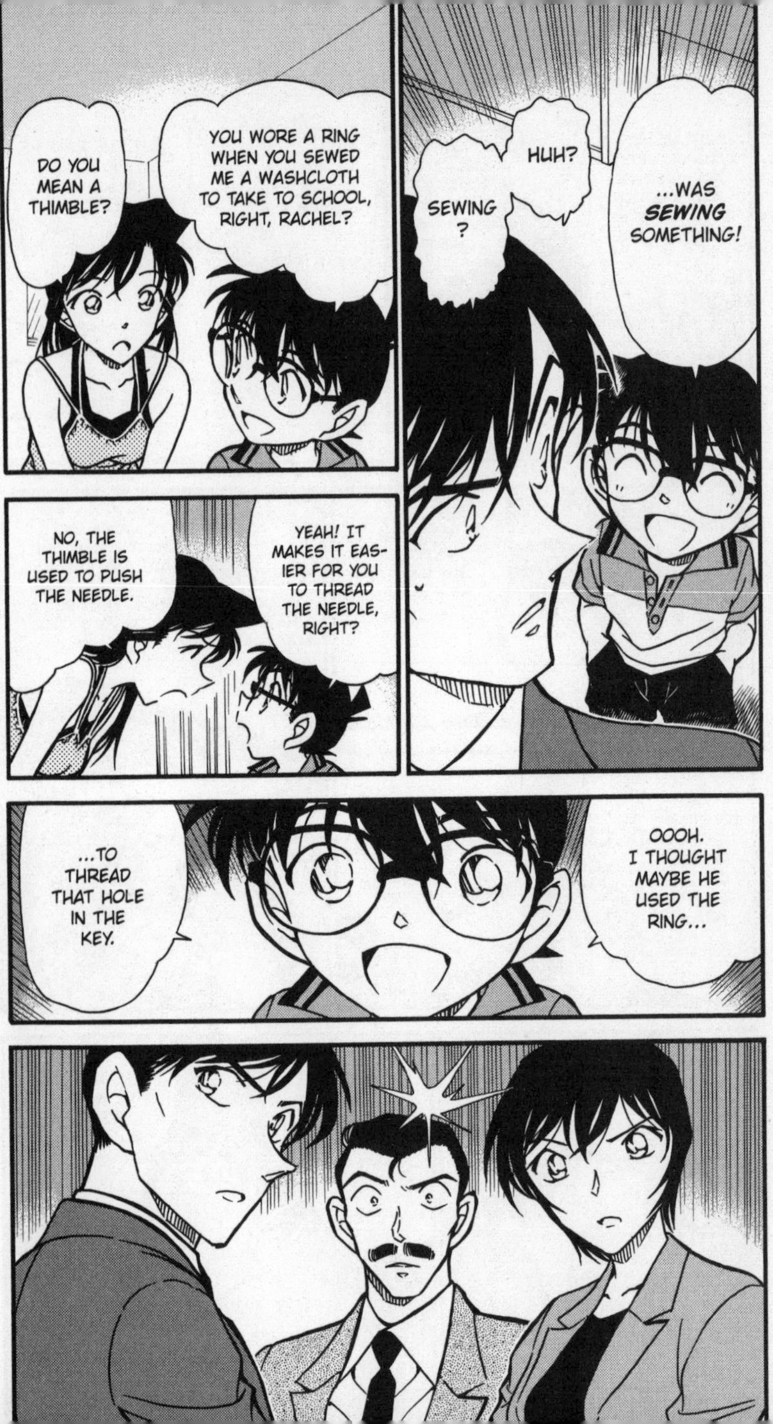
...WAS *SEWING* SOMETHING!
HUH?
SEWING ?
YOU WORE A RING WHEN YOU SEWED ME A WASHCLOTH TO TAKE TO SCHOOL, RIGHT, RACHEL?
DO YOU MEAN A THIMBLE?
YEAH! IT MAKES IT EASIER FOR YOU TO THREAD THE NEEDLE, RIGHT?
NO, THE THIMBLE IS USED TO PUSH THE NEEDLE.
OOOH. I THOUGHT MAYBE HE USED THE RING...
...TO THREAD THAT HOLE IN THE KEY.

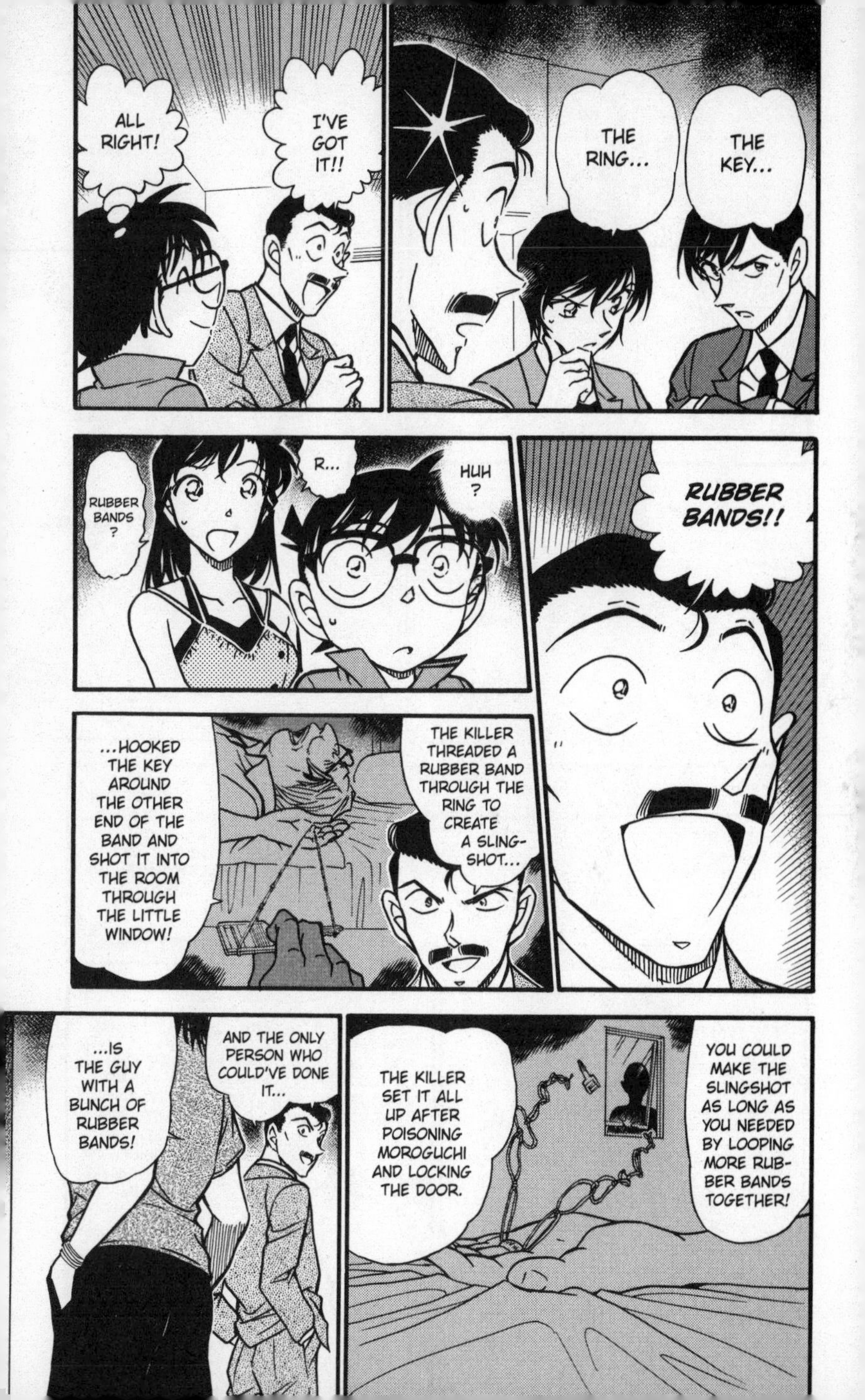
THE KEY...
THE RING...
I'VE GOT IT!!
ALL RIGHT!
RUBBER BANDS!!
HUH ?
R...
RUBBER BANDS ?
THE KILLER THREADED A RUBBER BAND THROUGH THE RING TO CREATE A SLING-SHOT...
...HOOKED THE KEY AROUND THE OTHER END OF THE BAND AND SHOT IT INTO THE ROOM THROUGH THE LITTLE WINDOW!
YOU COULD MAKE THE SLINGSHOT AS LONG AS YOU NEEDED BY LOOPING MORE RUB-BER BANDS TOGETHER!
THE KILLER SET IT ALL UP AFTER POISONING MOROGUCHI AND LOCKING THE DOOR.
AND THE ONLY PERSON WHO COULD'VE DONE IT...
...IS THE GUY WITH A BUNCH OF RUBBER BANDS!

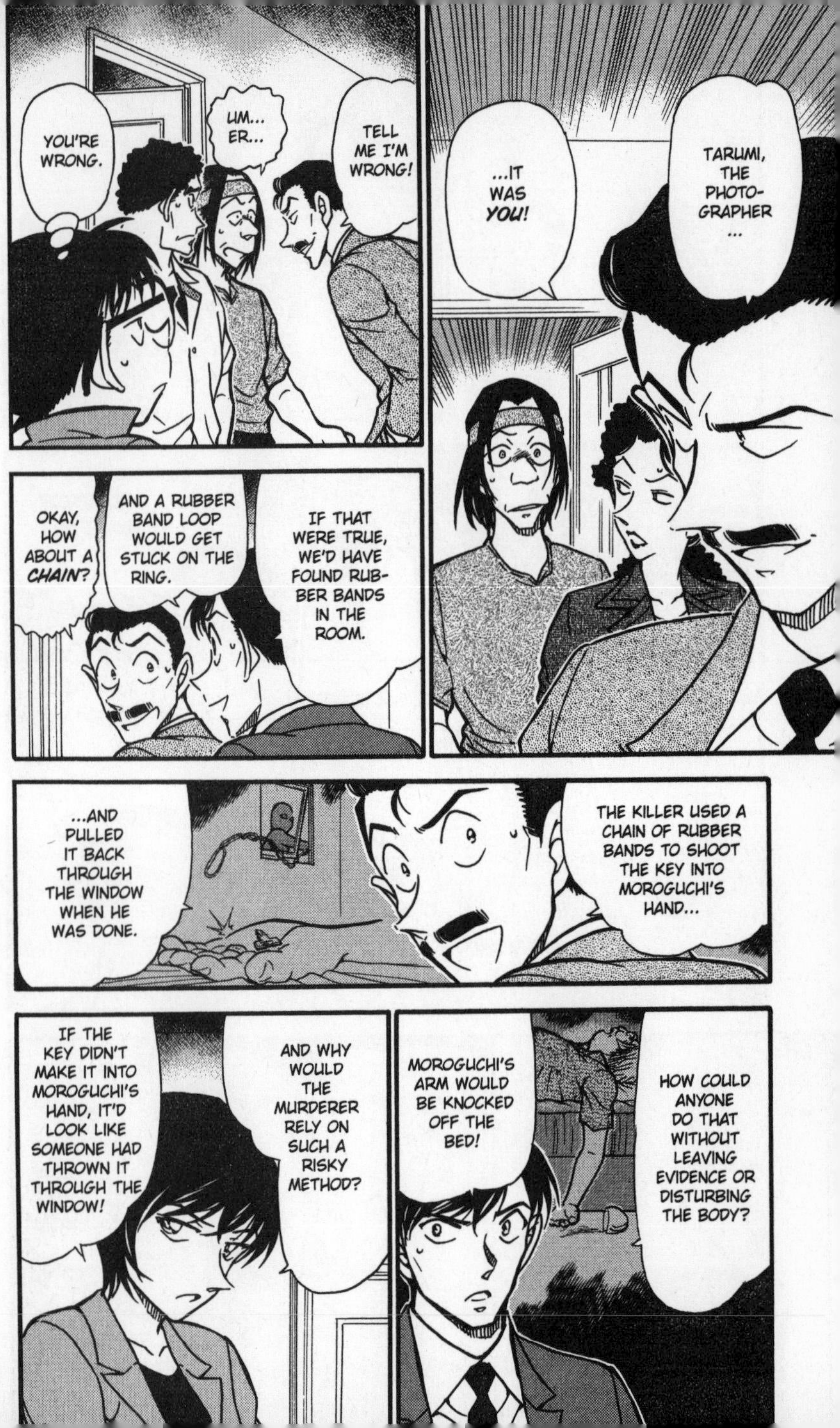
TARUMI, THE PHOTOGRAPHER...
...IT WAS *YOU*!
TELL ME I'M WRONG!
UM... ER...
YOU'RE WRONG.
IF THAT WERE TRUE, WE'D HAVE FOUND RUBBER BANDS IN THE ROOM.
AND A RUBBER BAND LOOP WOULD GET STUCK ON THE RING.
OKAY, HOW ABOUT A *CHAIN*?
THE KILLER USED A CHAIN OF RUBBER BANDS TO SHOOT THE KEY INTO MOROGUCHI'S HAND...
...AND PULLED IT BACK THROUGH THE WINDOW WHEN HE WAS DONE.
HOW COULD ANYONE DO THAT WITHOUT LEAVING EVIDENCE OR DISTURBING THE BODY?
MOROGUCHI'S ARM WOULD BE KNOCKED OFF THE BED!
AND WHY WOULD THE MURDERER RELY ON SUCH A RISKY METHOD?
IF THE KEY DIDN'T MAKE IT INTO MOROGUCHI'S HAND, IT'D LOOK LIKE SOMEONE HAD THROWN IT THROUGH THE WINDOW!

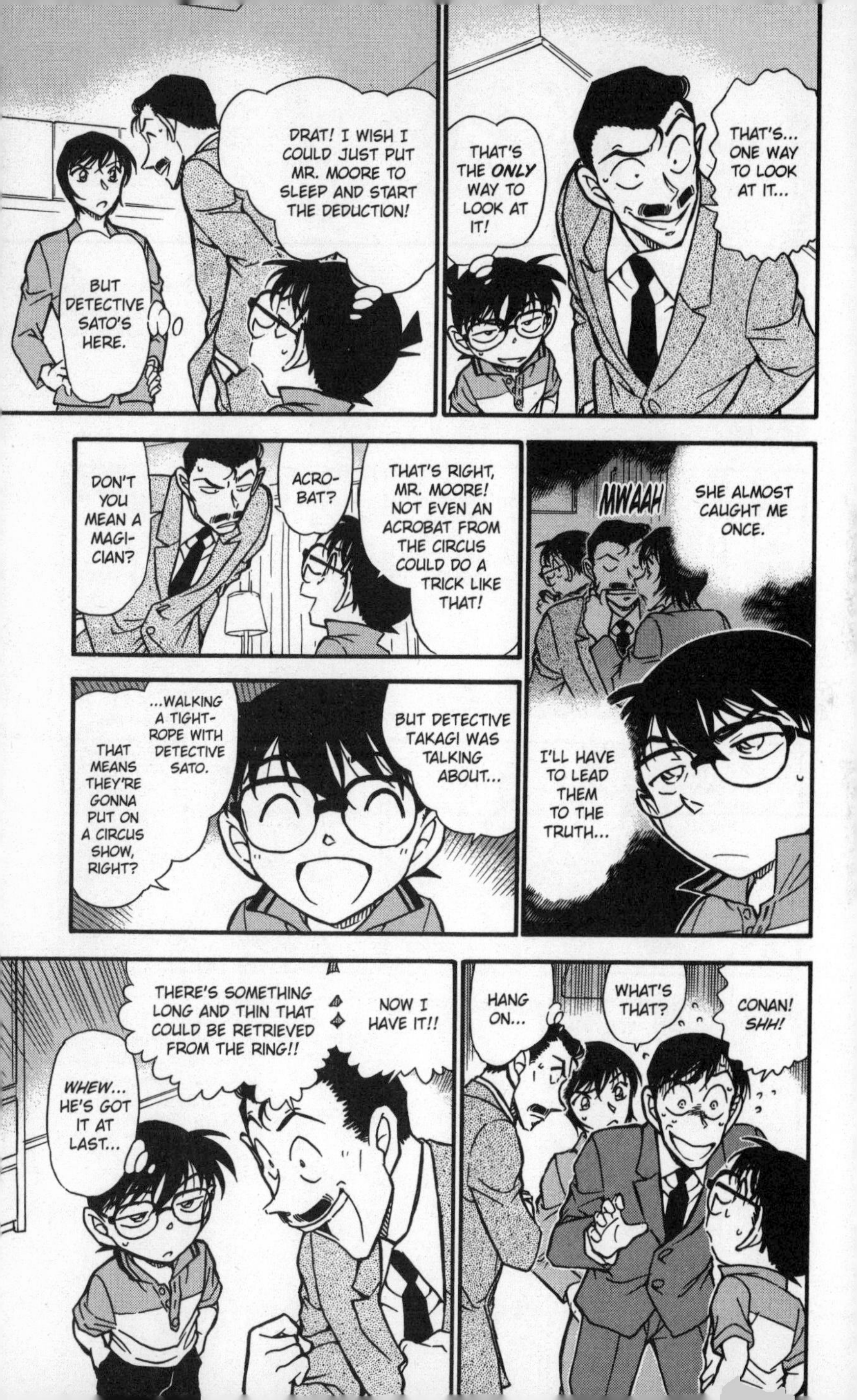
THAT'S... ONE WAY TO LOOK AT IT...
THAT'S THE *ONLY* WAY TO LOOK AT IT!
DRAT! I WISH I COULD JUST PUT MR. MOORE TO SLEEP AND START THE DEDUCTION!
BUT DETECTIVE SATO'S HERE.
MWAAH
SHE ALMOST CAUGHT ME ONCE.
I'LL HAVE TO LEAD THEM TO THE TRUTH...
THAT'S RIGHT, MR. MOORE! NOT EVEN AN ACROBAT FROM THE CIRCUS COULD DO A TRICK LIKE THAT!
ACRO-BAT?
DON'T YOU MEAN A MAGI-CIAN?
BUT DETECTIVE TAKAGI WAS TALKING ABOUT...
...WALKING A TIGHT-ROPE WITH DETECTIVE SATO.
THAT MEANS THEY'RE GONNA PUT ON A CIRCUS SHOW, RIGHT?
CONAN! *SHH!*
WHAT'S THAT?
HANG ON...
NOW I HAVE IT!!
THERE'S SOMETHING LONG AND THIN THAT COULD BE RETRIEVED FROM THE RING!!
WHEW... HE'S GOT IT AT LAST...

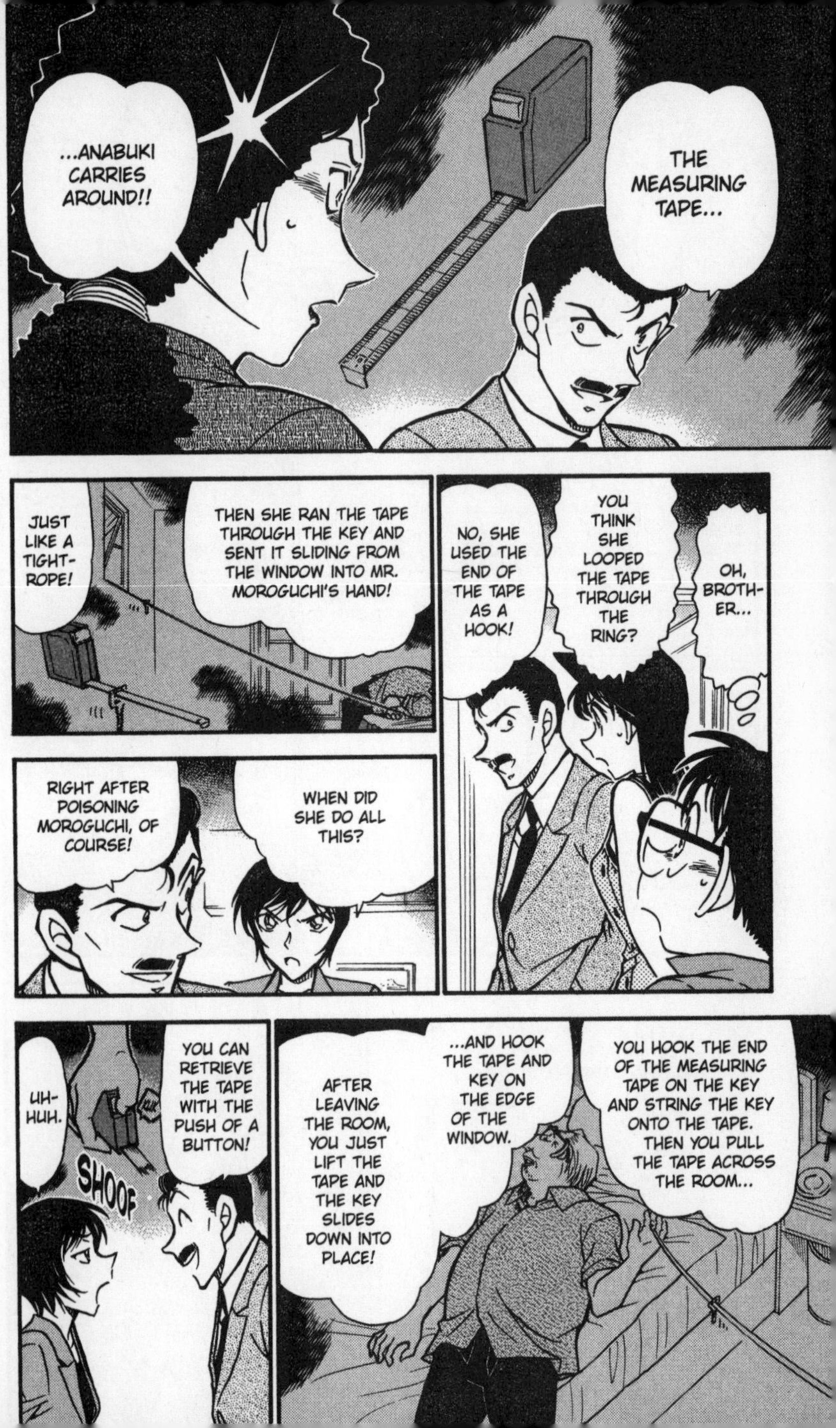
THE MEASURING TAPE...
...ANABUKI CARRIES AROUND!!
OH, BROTHER...
YOU THINK SHE LOOPED THE TAPE THROUGH THE RING?
NO, SHE USED THE END OF THE TAPE AS A HOOK!
THEN SHE RAN THE TAPE THROUGH THE KEY AND SENT IT SLIDING FROM THE WINDOW INTO MR. MOROGUCHI'S HAND!
JUST LIKE A TIGHT-ROPE!
WHEN DID SHE DO ALL THIS?
RIGHT AFTER POISONING MOROGUCHI, OF COURSE!
YOU HOOK THE END OF THE MEASURING TAPE ON THE KEY AND STRING THE KEY ONTO THE TAPE. THEN YOU PULL THE TAPE ACROSS THE ROOM...
...AND HOOK THE TAPE AND KEY ON THE EDGE OF THE WINDOW.
AFTER LEAVING THE ROOM, YOU JUST LIFT THE TAPE AND THE KEY SLIDES DOWN INTO PLACE!
YOU CAN RETRIEVE THE TAPE WITH THE PUSH OF A BUTTON!
SHOOF
UH-HUH.

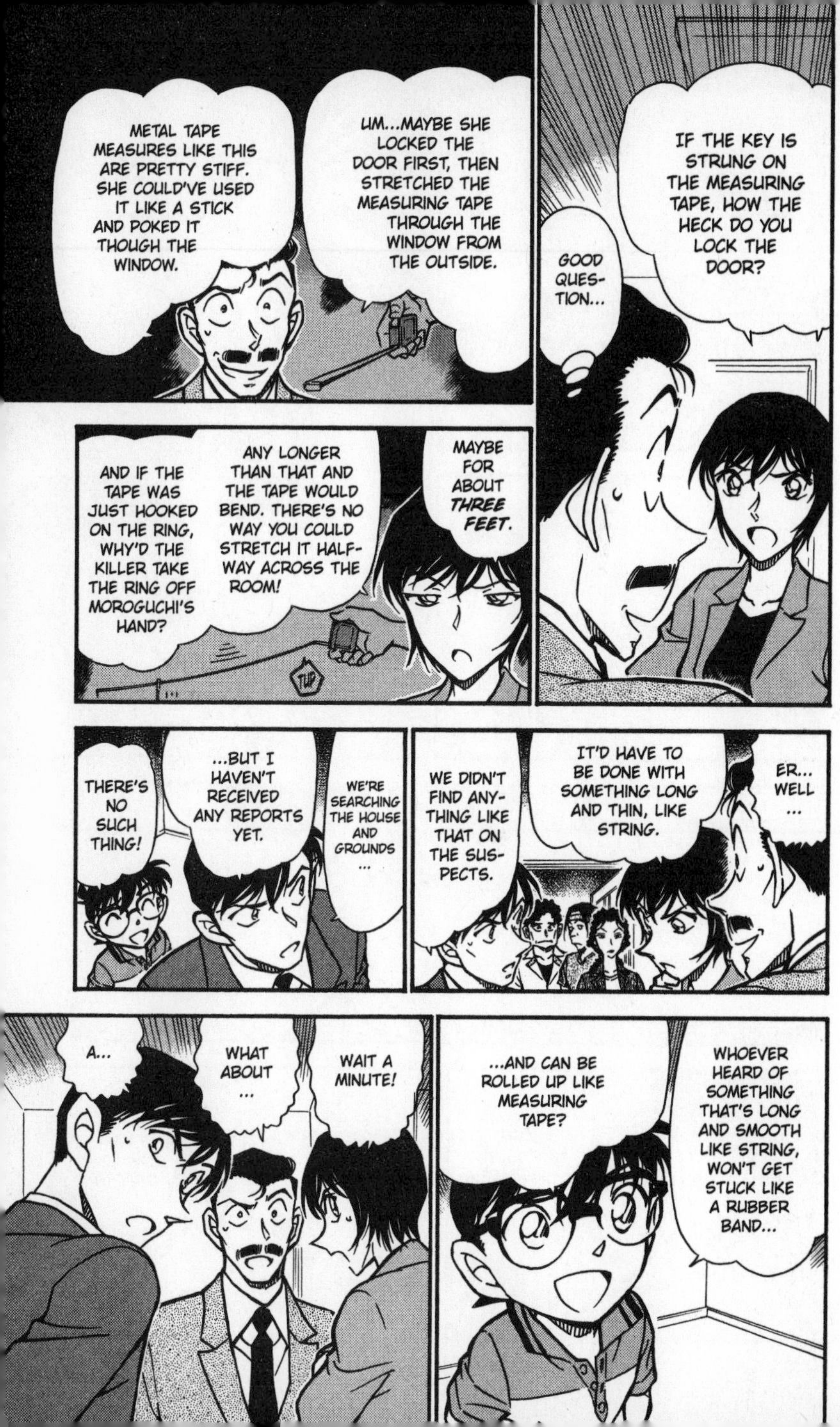
IF THE KEY IS STRUNG ON THE MEASURING TAPE, HOW THE HECK DO YOU LOCK THE DOOR?
GOOD QUES- TION...
UM...MAYBE SHE LOCKED THE DOOR FIRST, THEN STRETCHED THE MEASURING TAPE THROUGH THE WINDOW FROM THE OUTSIDE.
METAL TAPE MEASURES LIKE THIS ARE PRETTY STIFF. SHE COULD'VE USED IT LIKE A STICK AND POKED IT THOUGH THE WINDOW.
MAYBE FOR ABOUT *THREE FEET*.
ANY LONGER THAN THAT AND THE TAPE WOULD BEND. THERE'S NO WAY YOU COULD STRETCH IT HALF-WAY ACROSS THE ROOM!
TUP
AND IF THE TAPE WAS JUST HOOKED ON THE RING, WHY'D THE KILLER TAKE THE RING OFF MOROGUCHI'S HAND?
ER... WELL ...
IT'D HAVE TO BE DONE WITH SOMETHING LONG AND THIN, LIKE STRING.
WE DIDN'T FIND ANY-THING LIKE THAT ON THE SUS-PECTS.
WE'RE SEARCHING THE HOUSE AND GROUNDS ...
...BUT I HAVEN'T RECEIVED ANY REPORTS YET.
THERE'S NO SUCH THING!
WHOEVER HEARD OF SOMETHING THAT'S LONG AND SMOOTH LIKE STRING, WON'T GET STUCK LIKE A RUBBER BAND...
...AND CAN BE ROLLED UP LIKE MEASURING TAPE?
WAIT A MINUTE!
WHAT ABOUT ...
A...

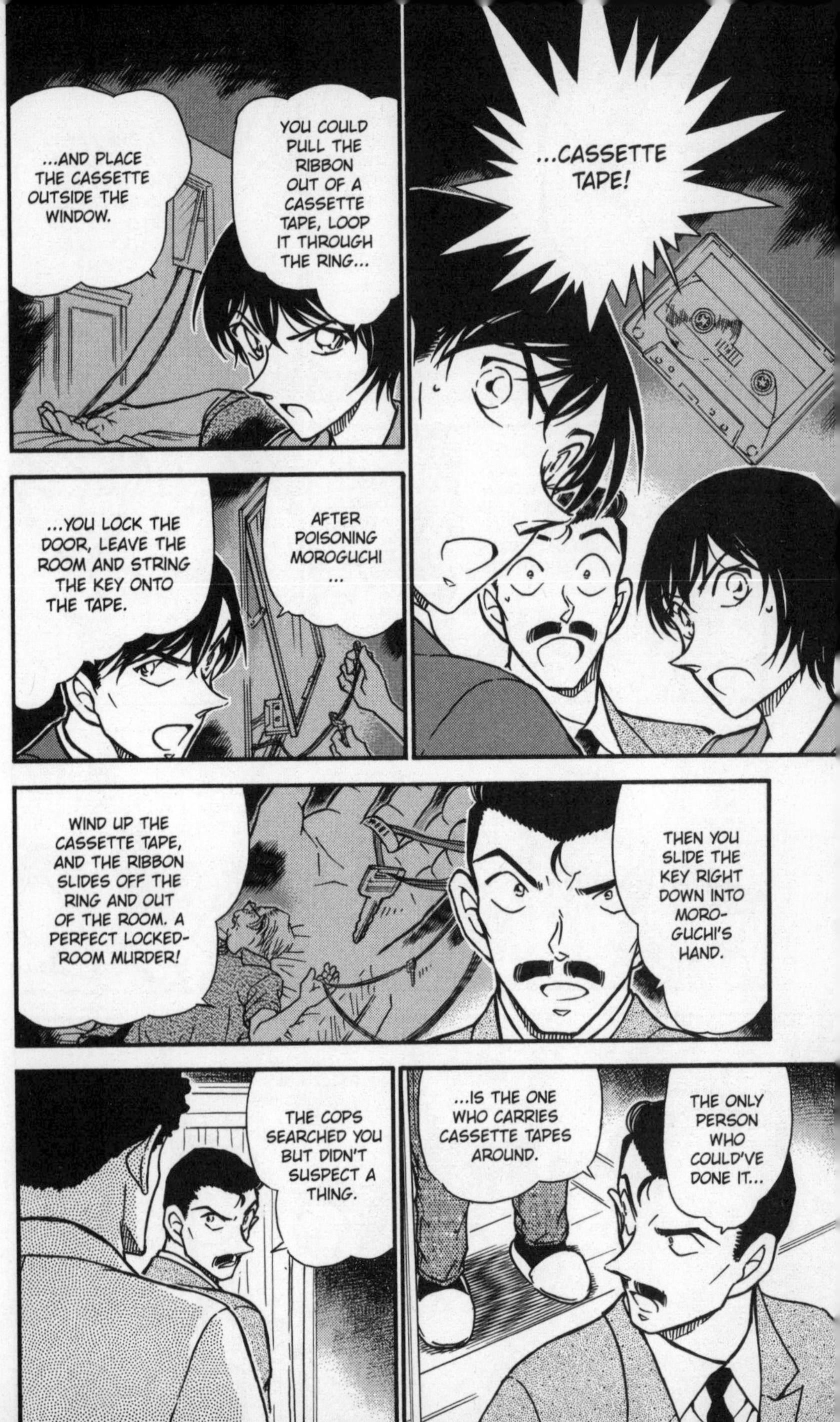

...CASSETTE TAPE!
YOU COULD PULL THE RIBBON OUT OF A CASSETTE TAPE, LOOP IT THROUGH THE RING...
...AND PLACE THE CASSETTE OUTSIDE THE WINDOW.
AFTER POISONING MOROGUCHI ...
...YOU LOCK THE DOOR, LEAVE THE ROOM AND STRING THE KEY ONTO THE TAPE.
THEN YOU SLIDE THE KEY RIGHT DOWN INTO MORO-GUCHI'S HAND.
WIND UP THE CASSETTE TAPE, AND THE RIBBON SLIDES OFF THE RING AND OUT OF THE ROOM. A PERFECT LOCKED-ROOM MURDER!
THE ONLY PERSON WHO COULD'VE DONE IT...
...IS THE ONE WHO CARRIES CASSETTE TAPES AROUND.
THE COPS SEARCHED YOU BUT DIDN'T SUSPECT A THING.

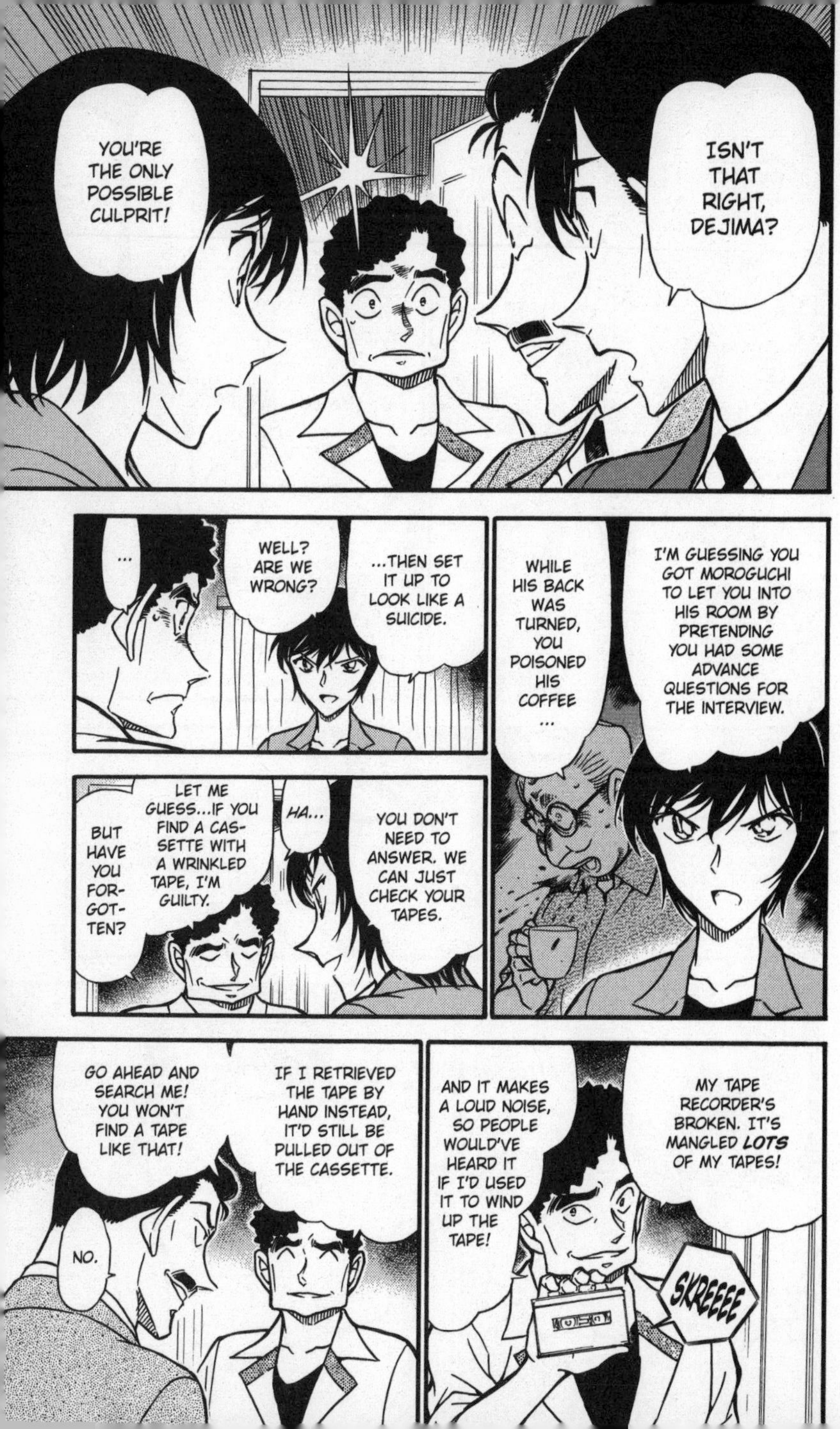
ISN'T THAT RIGHT, DEJIMA?
YOU'RE THE ONLY POSSIBLE CULPRIT!
I'M GUESSING YOU GOT MOROGUCHI TO LET YOU INTO HIS ROOM BY PRETENDING YOU HAD SOME ADVANCE QUESTIONS FOR THE INTERVIEW.
WHILE HIS BACK WAS TURNED, YOU POISONED HIS COFFEE ...
...THEN SET IT UP TO LOOK LIKE A SUICIDE.
WELL? ARE WE WRONG?
...
YOU DON'T NEED TO ANSWER. WE CAN JUST CHECK YOUR TAPES.
HA...
LET ME GUESS...IF YOU FIND A CASSETTE WITH A WRINKLED TAPE, I'M GUILTY.
BUT HAVE YOU FORGOTTEN?
MY TAPE RECORDER'S BROKEN. IT'S MANGLED ***LOTS*** OF MY TAPES!
AND IT MAKES A LOUD NOISE, SO PEOPLE WOULD'VE HEARD IT IF I'D USED IT TO WIND UP THE TAPE!
SKREEEE
IF I RETRIEVED THE TAPE BY HAND INSTEAD, IT'D STILL BE PULLED OUT OF THE CASSETTE.
GO AHEAD AND SEARCH ME! YOU WON'T FIND A TAPE LIKE THAT!
NO.

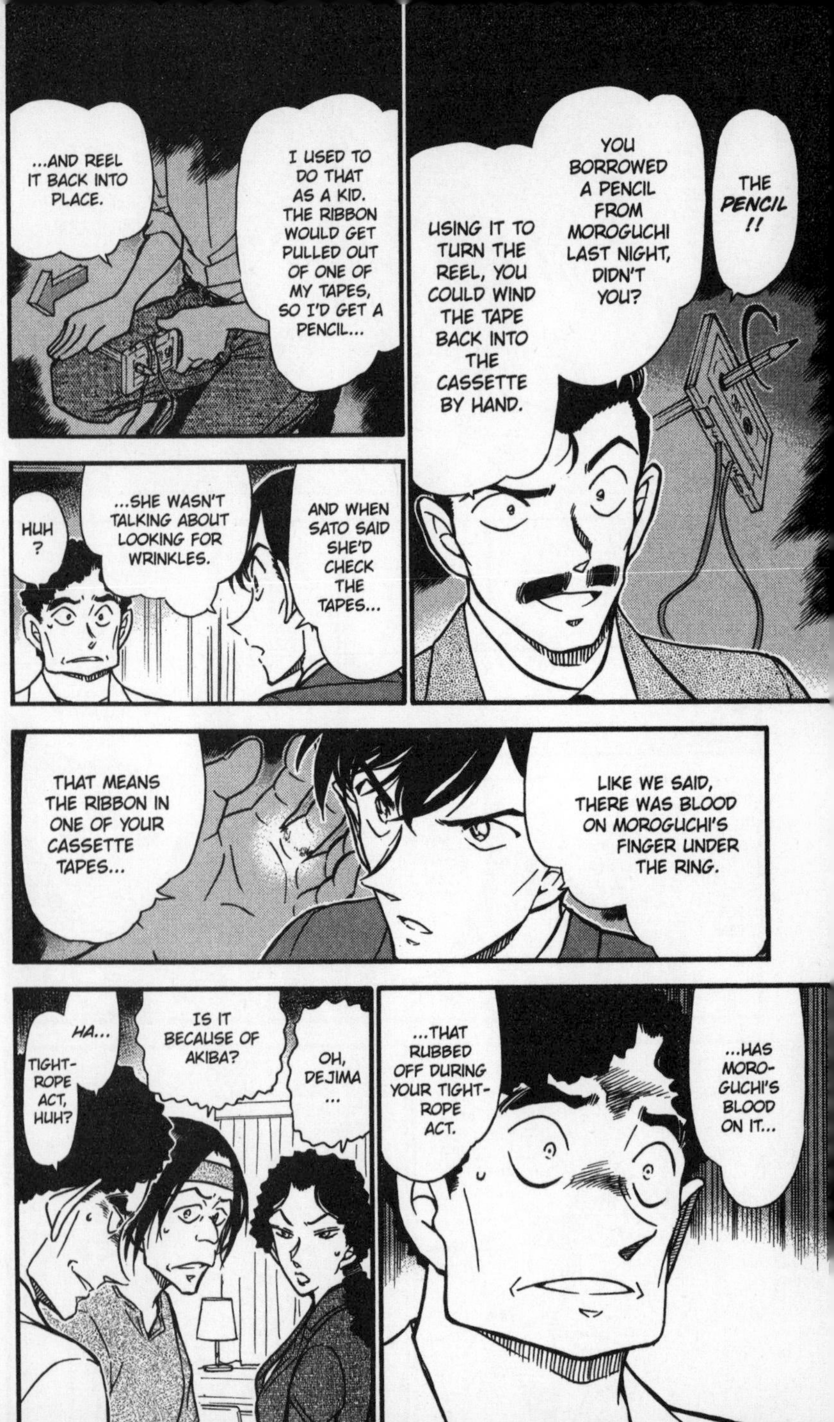
THE PENCIL!!
YOU BORROWED A PENCIL FROM MOROGUCHI LAST NIGHT, DIDN'T YOU?
USING IT TO TURN THE REEL, YOU COULD WIND THE TAPE BACK INTO THE CASSETTE BY HAND.
I USED TO DO THAT AS A KID. THE RIBBON WOULD GET PULLED OUT OF ONE OF MY TAPES, SO I'D GET A PENCIL...
...AND REEL IT BACK INTO PLACE.
AND WHEN SATO SAID SHE'D CHECK THE TAPES...
...SHE WASN'T TALKING ABOUT LOOKING FOR WRINKLES.
HUH?
LIKE WE SAID, THERE WAS BLOOD ON MOROGUCHI'S FINGER UNDER THE RING.
THAT MEANS THE RIBBON IN ONE OF YOUR CASSETTE TAPES...
...HAS MOROGUCHI'S BLOOD ON IT...
...THAT RUBBED OFF DURING YOUR TIGHT-ROPE ACT.
OH, DEJIMA...
IS IT BECAUSE OF AKIBA?
HA... TIGHT-ROPE ACT, HUH?

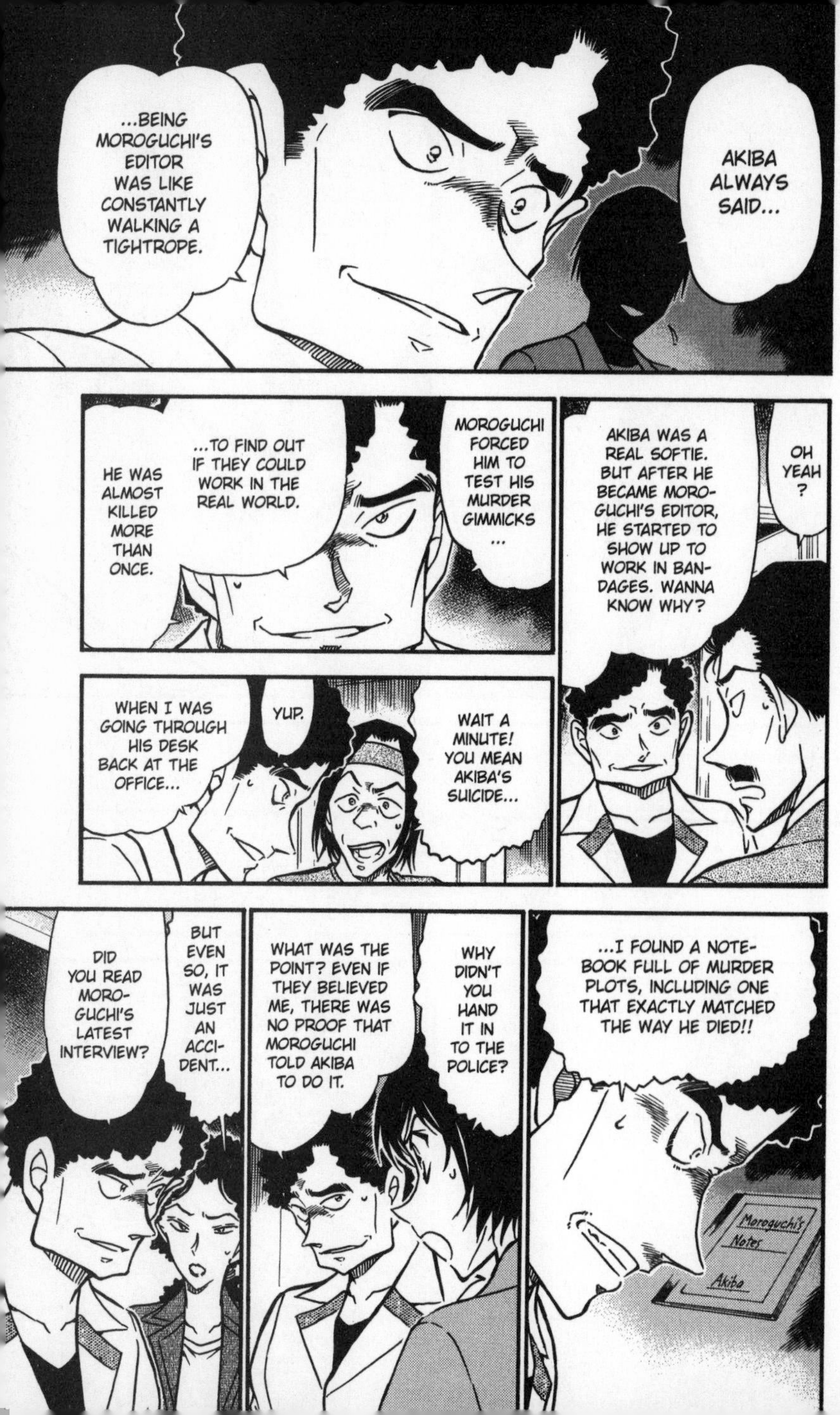
AKIBA ALWAYS SAID...
...BEING MOROGUCHI'S EDITOR WAS LIKE CONSTANTLY WALKING A TIGHTROPE.
OH YEAH?
AKIBA WAS A REAL SOFTIE. BUT AFTER HE BECAME MORO-GUCHI'S EDITOR, HE STARTED TO SHOW UP TO WORK IN BAN-DAGES. WANNA KNOW WHY?
MOROGUCHI FORCED HIM TO TEST HIS MURDER GIMMICKS...
...TO FIND OUT IF THEY COULD WORK IN THE REAL WORLD.
HE WAS ALMOST KILLED MORE THAN ONCE.
WAIT A MINUTE! YOU MEAN AKIBA'S SUICIDE...
YUP.
WHEN I WAS GOING THROUGH HIS DESK BACK AT THE OFFICE...
...I FOUND A NOTE-BOOK FULL OF MURDER PLOTS, INCLUDING ONE THAT EXACTLY MATCHED THE WAY HE DIED!!
Moroguchi's Notes
Akiba
WHY DIDN'T YOU HAND IT IN TO THE POLICE?
WHAT WAS THE POINT? EVEN IF THEY BELIEVED ME, THERE WAS NO PROOF THAT MOROGUCHI TOLD AKIBA TO DO IT.
BUT EVEN SO, IT WAS JUST AN ACCI-DENT...
DID YOU READ MORO-GUCHI'S LATEST INTERVIEW?

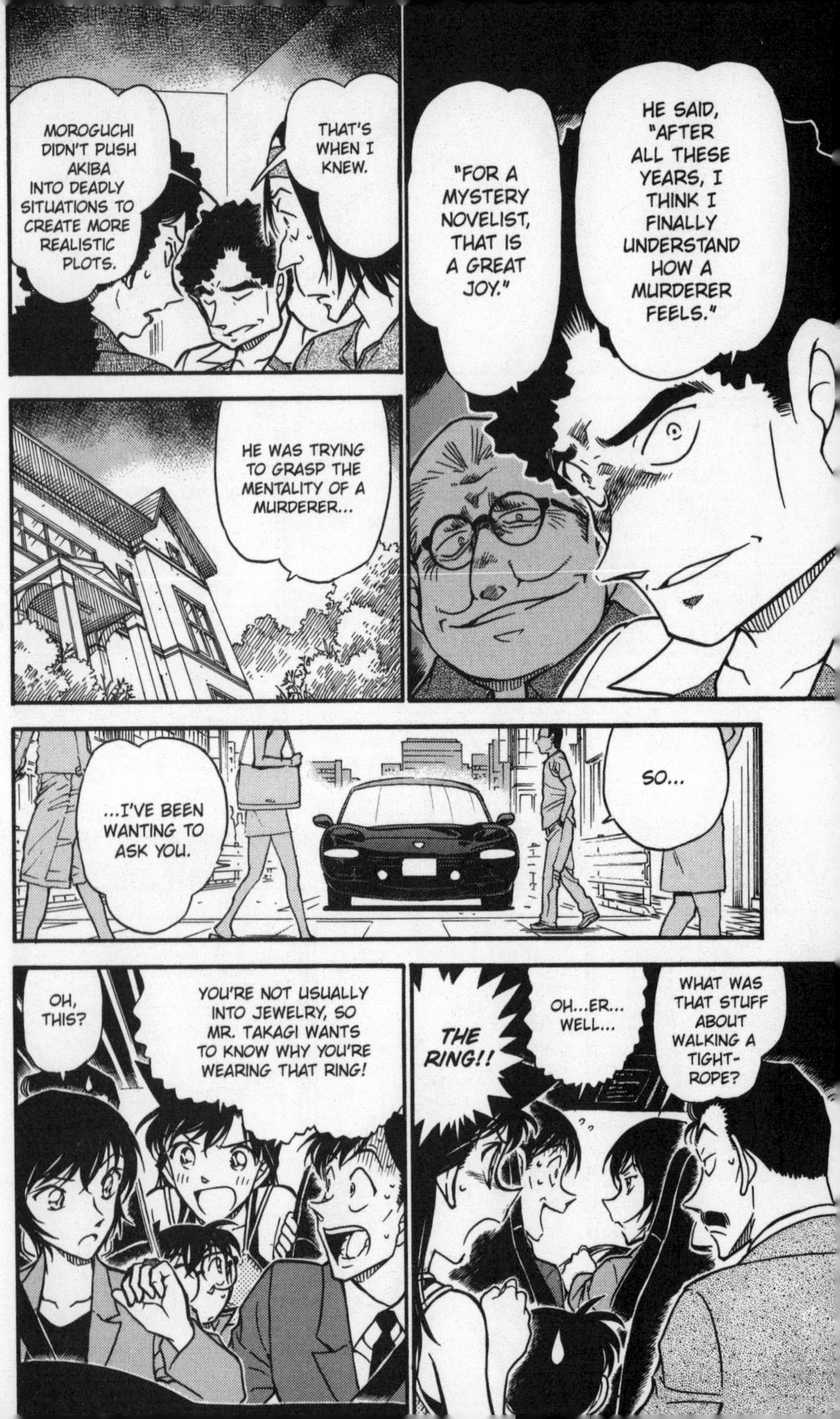
HE SAID, "AFTER ALL THESE YEARS, I THINK I FINALLY UNDERSTAND HOW A MURDERER FEELS."
"FOR A MYSTERY NOVELIST, THAT IS A GREAT JOY."
THAT'S WHEN I KNEW.
MOROGUCHI DIDN'T PUSH AKIBA INTO DEADLY SITUATIONS TO CREATE MORE REALISTIC PLOTS.
HE WAS TRYING TO GRASP THE MENTALITY OF A MURDERER...
SO...
...I'VE BEEN WANTING TO ASK YOU.
WHAT WAS THAT STUFF ABOUT WALKING A TIGHT-ROPE?
OH...ER... WELL...
THE RING!!
YOU'RE NOT USUALLY INTO JEWELRY, SO MR. TAKAGI WANTS TO KNOW WHY YOU'RE WEARING THAT RING!
OH, THIS?

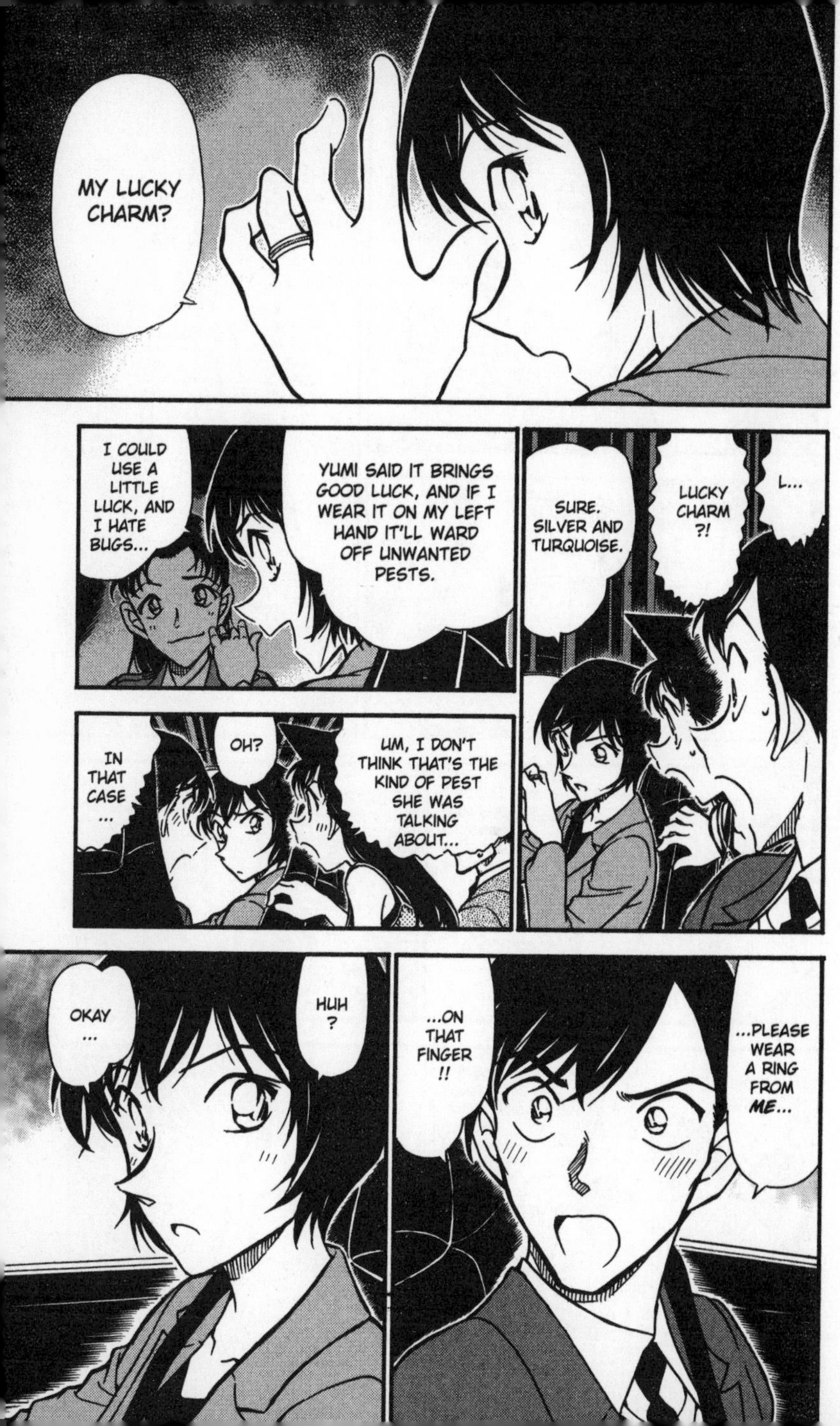
MY LUCKY CHARM?
L...
LUCKY CHARM ?!
SURE. SILVER AND TURQUOISE.
YUMI SAID IT BRINGS GOOD LUCK, AND IF I WEAR IT ON MY LEFT HAND IT'LL WARD OFF UNWANTED PESTS.
I COULD USE A LITTLE LUCK, AND I HATE BUGS...
UM, I DON'T THINK THAT'S THE KIND OF PEST SHE WAS TALKING ABOUT...
OH?
IN THAT CASE ...
...PLEASE WEAR A RING FROM *ME*...
...ON THAT FINGER !!
HUH ?
OKAY ...

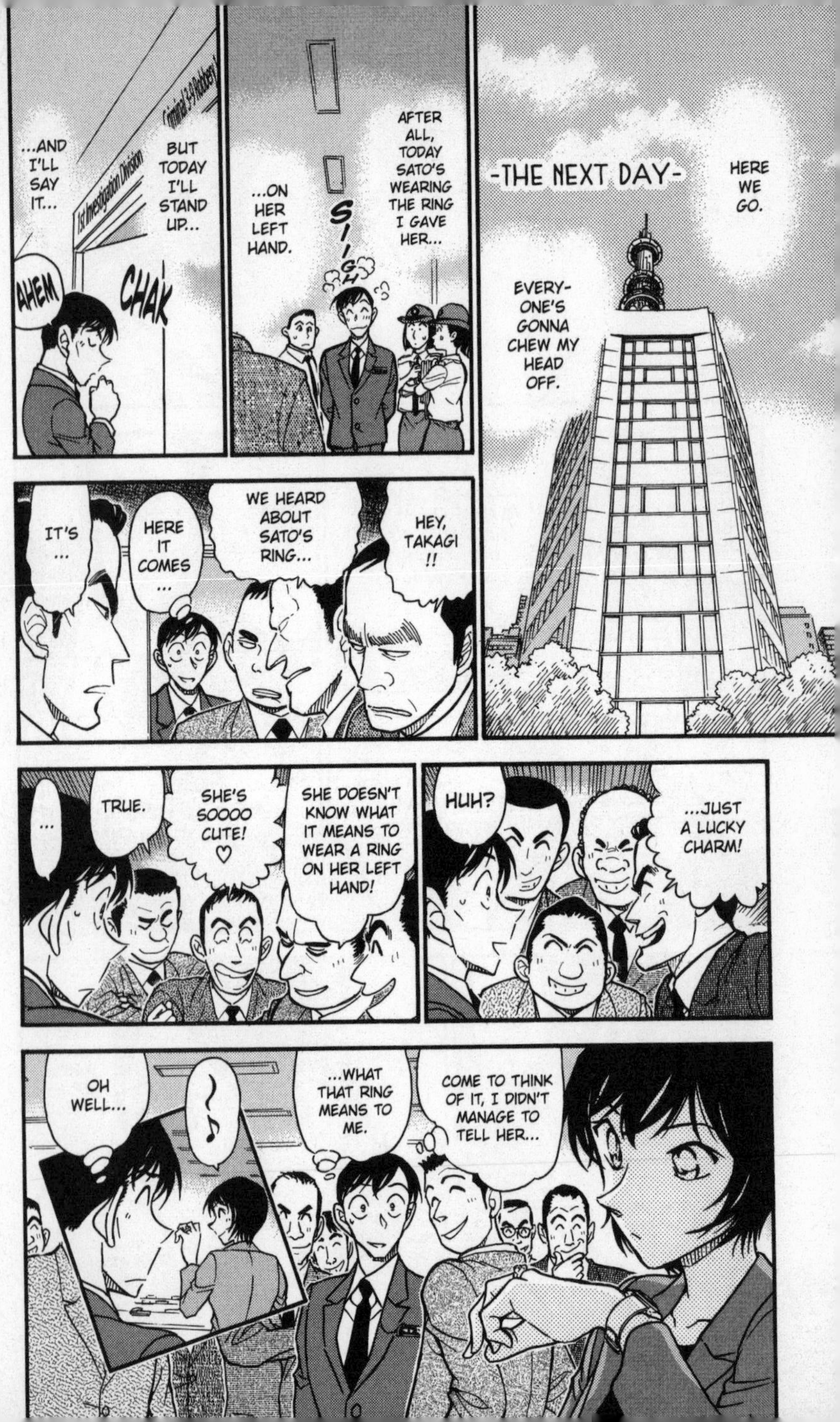
-THE NEXT DAY-
HERE WE GO.
EVERY-ONE'S GONNA CHEW MY HEAD OFF.
AFTER ALL, TODAY SATO'S WEARING THE RING I GAVE HER...
...ON HER LEFT HAND.
SIGH
BUT TODAY I'LL STAND UP...
...AND I'LL SAY IT...
Criminal 3-9 Robbery
1st Investigation Division
AHEM
CHAK
HEY, TAKAGI !!
WE HEARD ABOUT SATO'S RING...
HERE IT COMES ...
IT'S ...
...JUST A LUCKY CHARM!
HUH?
SHE DOESN'T KNOW WHAT IT MEANS TO WEAR A RING ON HER LEFT HAND!
SHE'S SOOOO CUTE! ♡
TRUE.
...
COME TO THINK OF IT, I DIDN'T MANAGE TO TELL HER...
...WHAT THAT RING MEANS TO ME.
?♪
OH WELL...

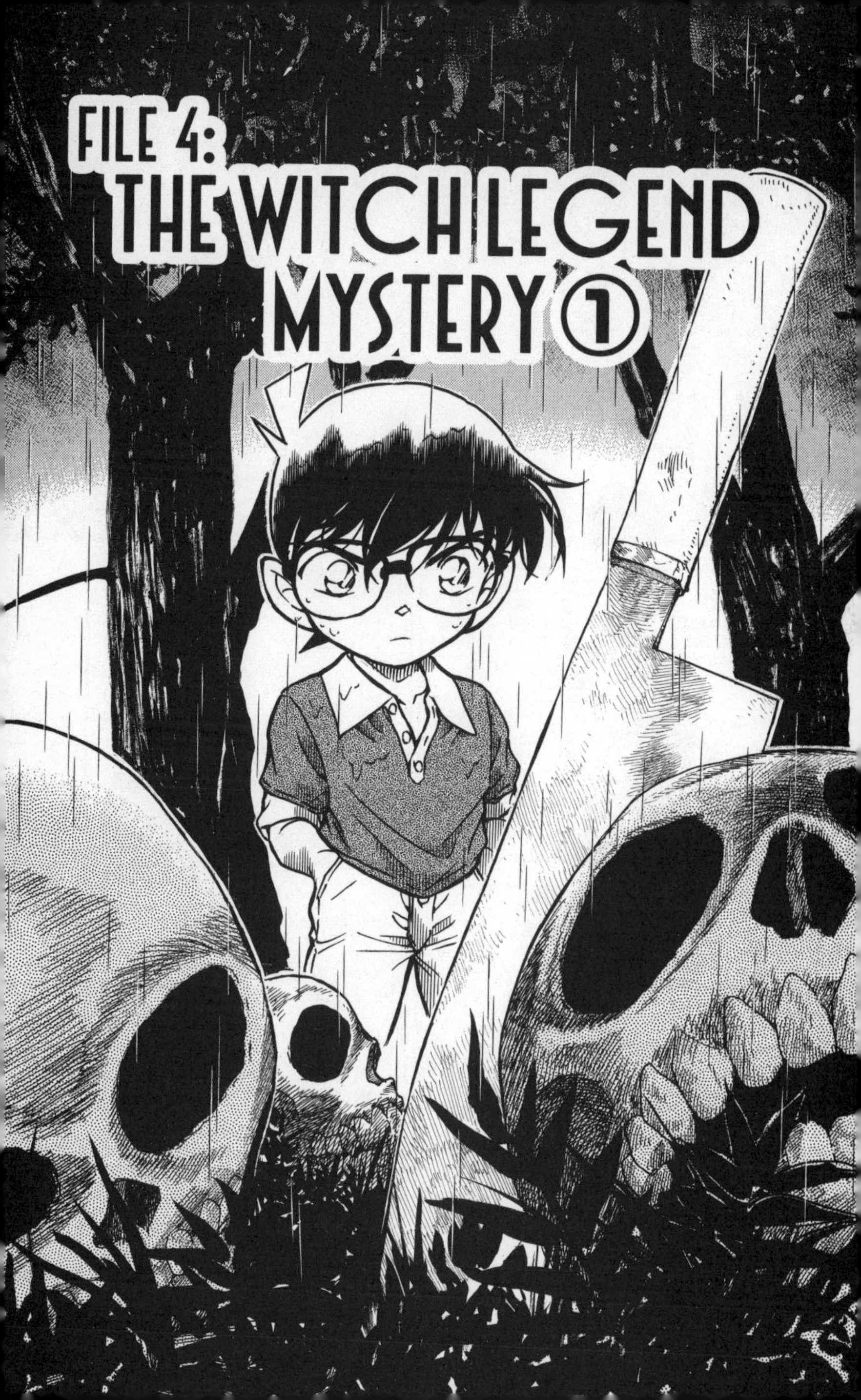
FILE 4:
THE WITCH LEGEND MYSTERY ①

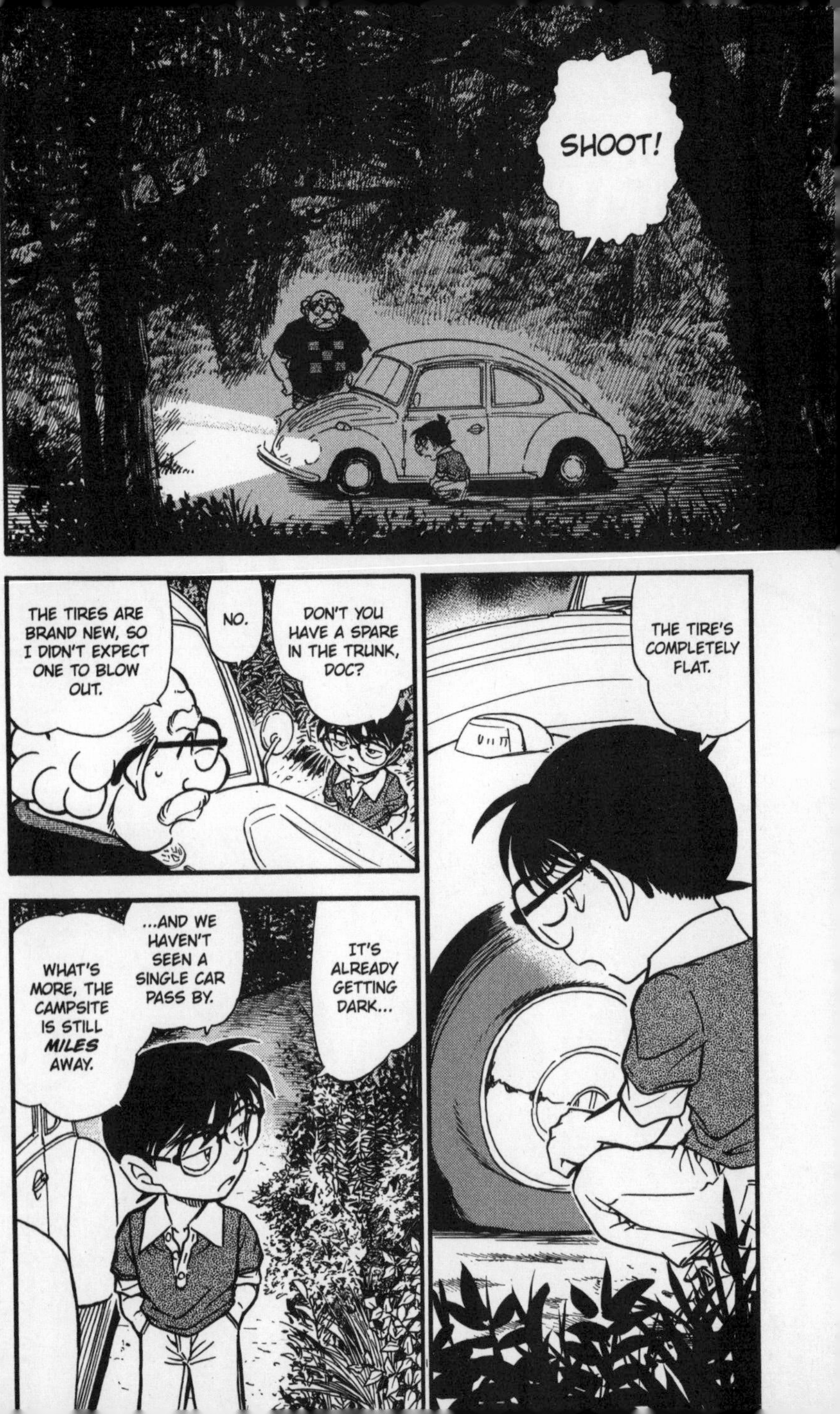
SHOOT!
THE TIRE'S COMPLETELY FLAT.
DON'T YOU HAVE A SPARE IN THE TRUNK, DOC?
NO.
THE TIRES ARE BRAND NEW, SO I DIDN'T EXPECT ONE TO BLOW OUT.
IT'S ALREADY GETTING DARK...
...AND WE HAVEN'T SEEN A SINGLE CAR PASS BY.
WHAT'S MORE, THE CAMPSITE IS STILL *MILES* AWAY.

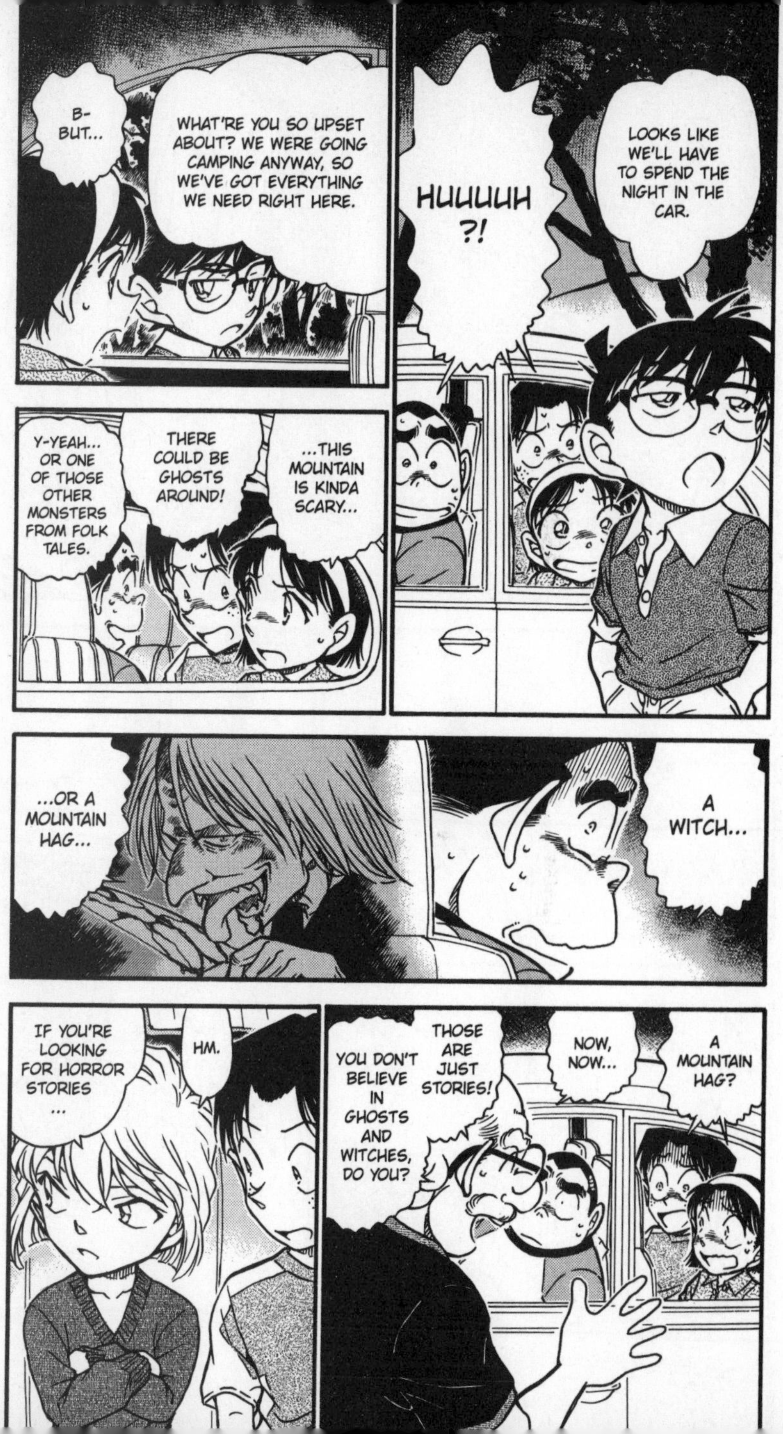
LOOKS LIKE WE'LL HAVE TO SPEND THE NIGHT IN THE CAR.
HUUUUH ?!
WHAT'RE YOU SO UPSET ABOUT? WE WERE GOING CAMPING ANYWAY, SO WE'VE GOT EVERYTHING WE NEED RIGHT HERE.
B- BUT...
...THIS MOUNTAIN IS KINDA SCARY...
THERE COULD BE GHOSTS AROUND!
Y-YEAH... OR ONE OF THOSE OTHER MONSTERS FROM FOLK TALES.
A WITCH...
...OR A MOUNTAIN HAG...
A MOUNTAIN HAG?
NOW, NOW...
THOSE ARE JUST STORIES!
YOU DON'T BELIEVE IN GHOSTS AND WITCHES, DO YOU?
HM.
IF YOU'RE LOOKING FOR HORROR STORIES ...

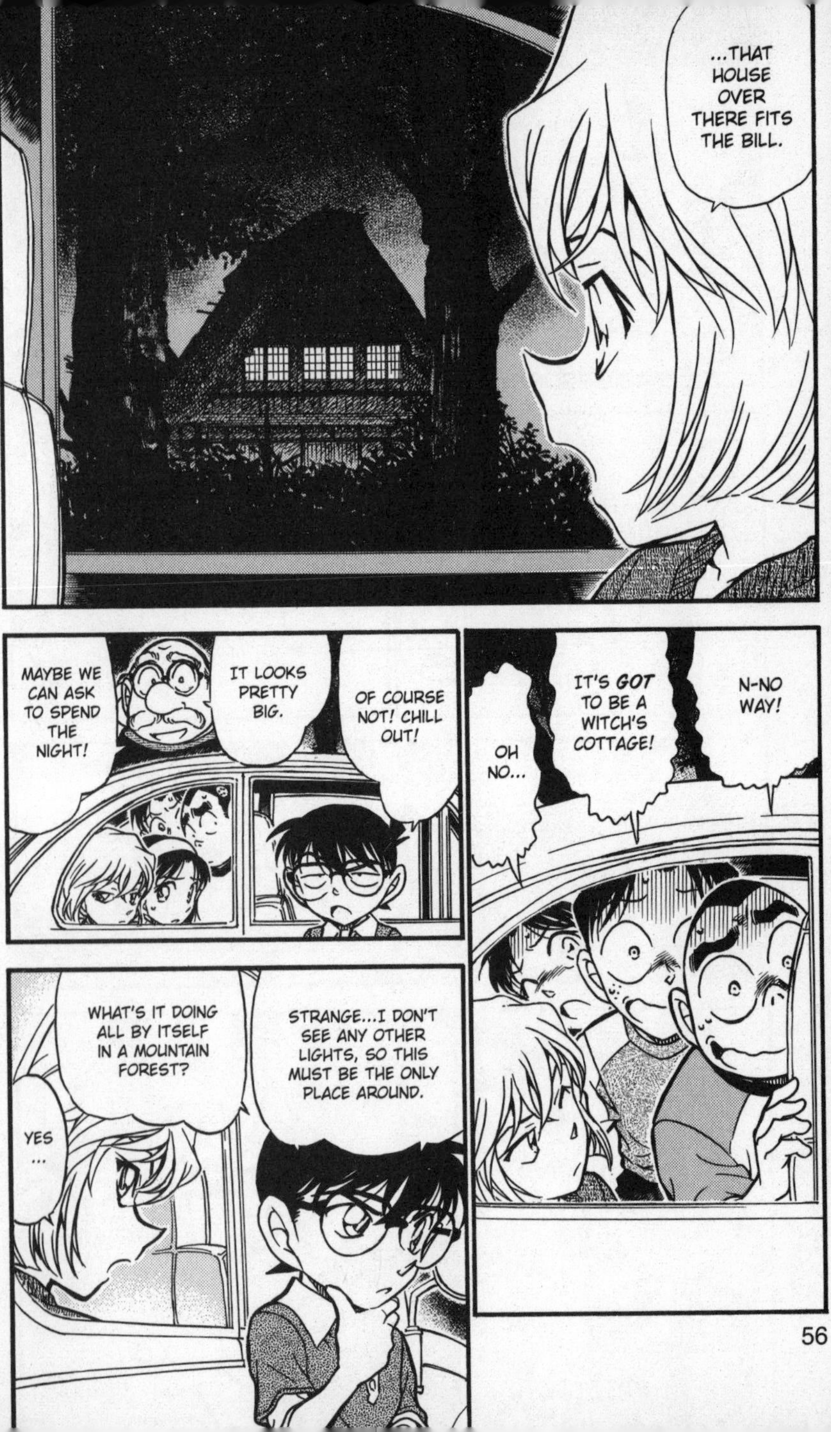
...THAT HOUSE OVER THERE FITS THE BILL.
N-NO WAY!
IT'S **GOT** TO BE A WITCH'S COTTAGE!
OH NO...
OF COURSE NOT! CHILL OUT!
IT LOOKS PRETTY BIG.
MAYBE WE CAN ASK TO SPEND THE NIGHT!
STRANGE...I DON'T SEE ANY OTHER LIGHTS, SO THIS MUST BE THE ONLY PLACE AROUND.
WHAT'S IT DOING ALL BY ITSELF IN A MOUNTAIN FOREST?
YES ...

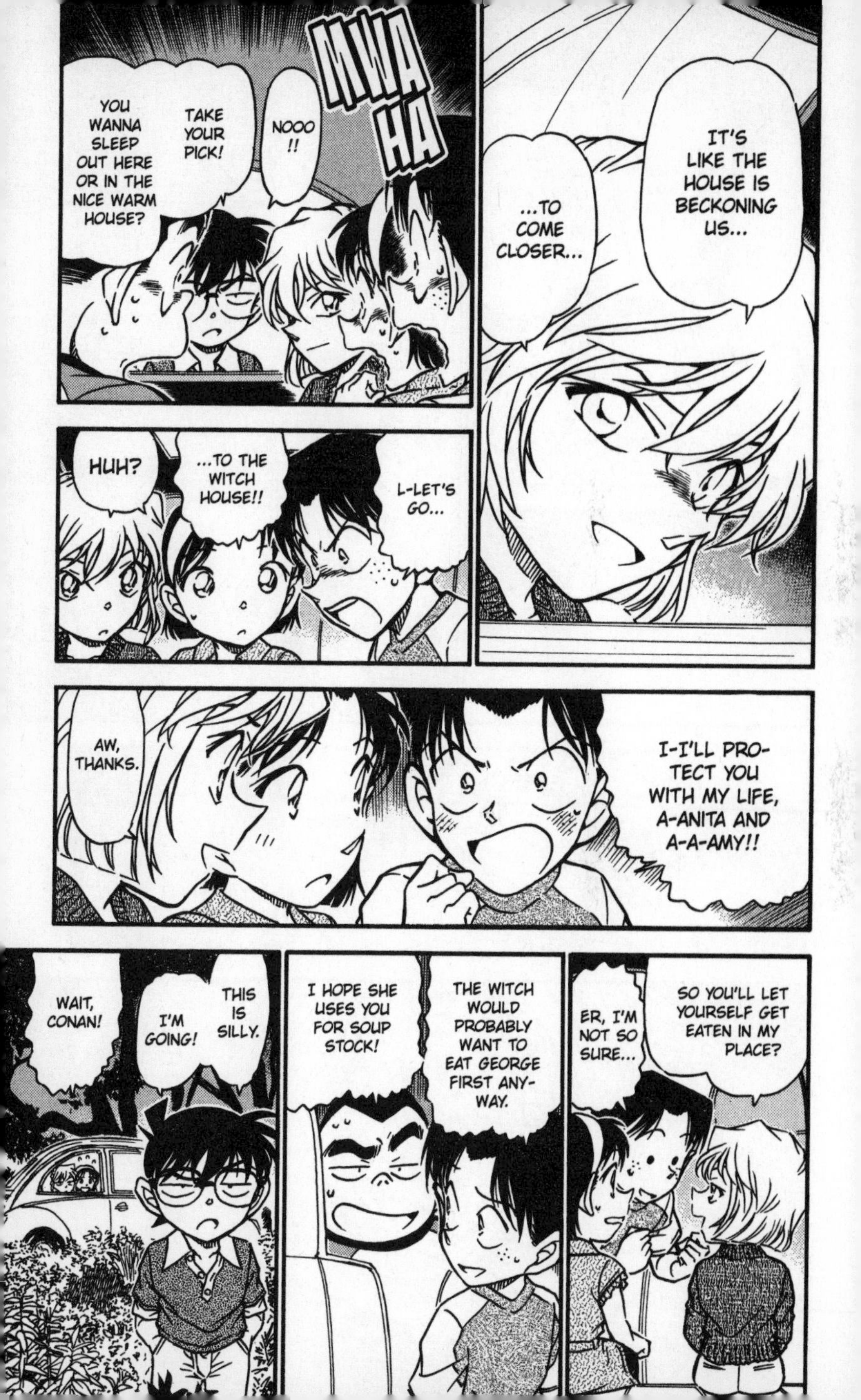
IT'S LIKE THE HOUSE IS BECKONING US...
...TO COME CLOSER...
MWA HA
NOOO!!
TAKE YOUR PICK!
YOU WANNA SLEEP OUT HERE OR IN THE NICE WARM HOUSE?
L-LET'S GO...
...TO THE WITCH HOUSE!!
HUH?
I-I'LL PROTECT YOU WITH MY LIFE, A-ANITA AND A-A-AMY!!
AW, THANKS.
SO YOU'LL LET YOURSELF GET EATEN IN MY PLACE?
ER, I'M NOT SO SURE...
THE WITCH WOULD PROBABLY WANT TO EAT GEORGE FIRST ANYWAY.
I HOPE SHE USES YOU FOR SOUP STOCK!
THIS IS SILLY.
I'M GOING!
WAIT, CONAN!

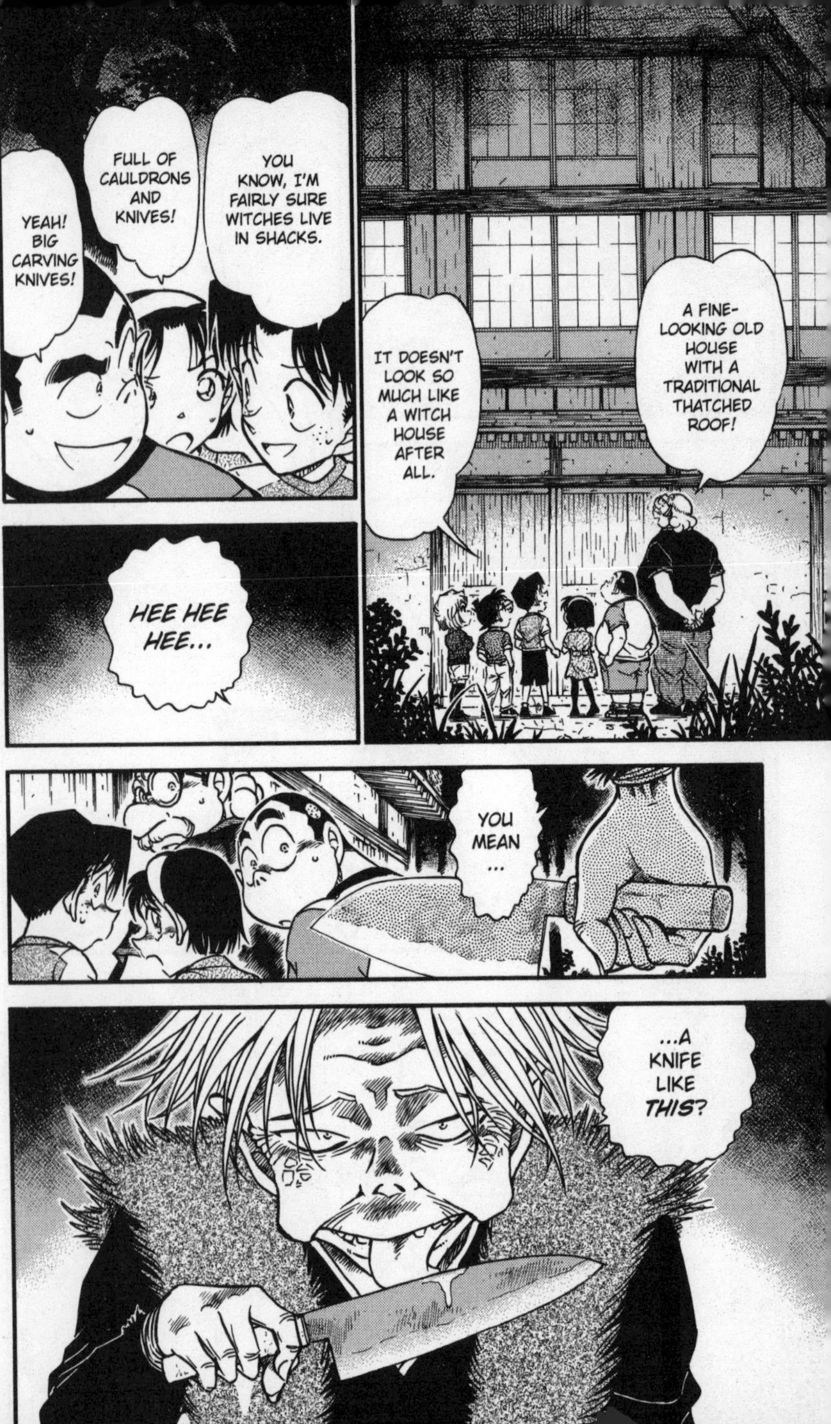
A FINE-LOOKING OLD HOUSE WITH A TRADITIONAL THATCHED ROOF!
IT DOESN'T LOOK SO MUCH LIKE A WITCH HOUSE AFTER ALL.
YOU KNOW, I'M FAIRLY SURE WITCHES LIVE IN SHACKS.
FULL OF CAULDRONS AND KNIVES!
YEAH! BIG CARVING KNIVES!
HEE HEE HEE...
YOU MEAN ...
...A KNIFE LIKE *THIS*?

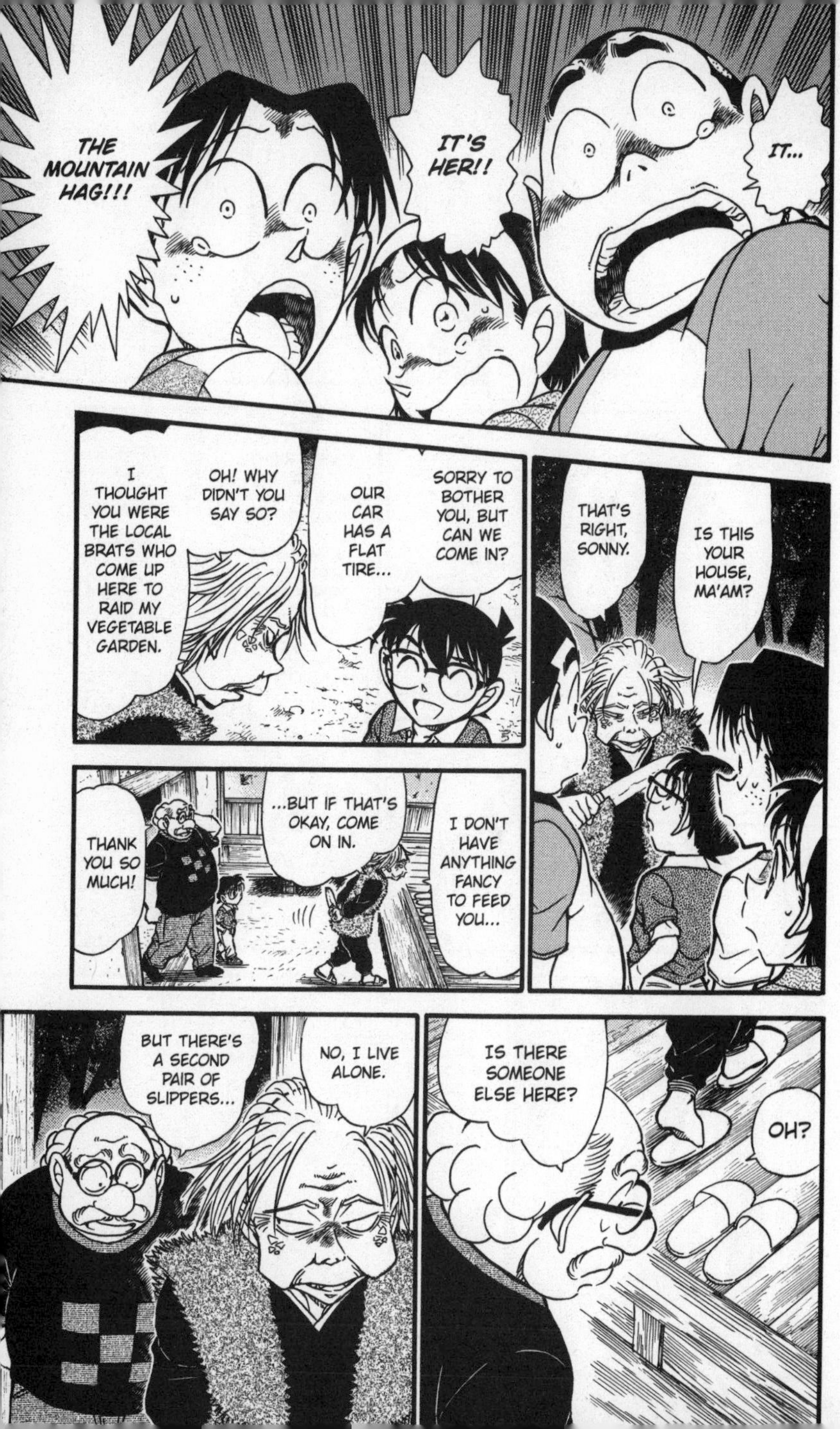
IT...
IT'S HER!!
THE MOUNTAIN HAG!!!
IS THIS YOUR HOUSE, MA'AM?
THAT'S RIGHT, SONNY.
SORRY TO BOTHER YOU, BUT CAN WE COME IN?
OUR CAR HAS A FLAT TIRE...
OH! WHY DIDN'T YOU SAY SO?
I THOUGHT YOU WERE THE LOCAL BRATS WHO COME UP HERE TO RAID MY VEGETABLE GARDEN.
I DON'T HAVE ANYTHING FANCY TO FEED YOU...
...BUT IF THAT'S OKAY, COME ON IN.
THANK YOU SO MUCH!
OH?
IS THERE SOMEONE ELSE HERE?
NO, I LIVE ALONE.
BUT THERE'S A SECOND PAIR OF SLIPPERS...

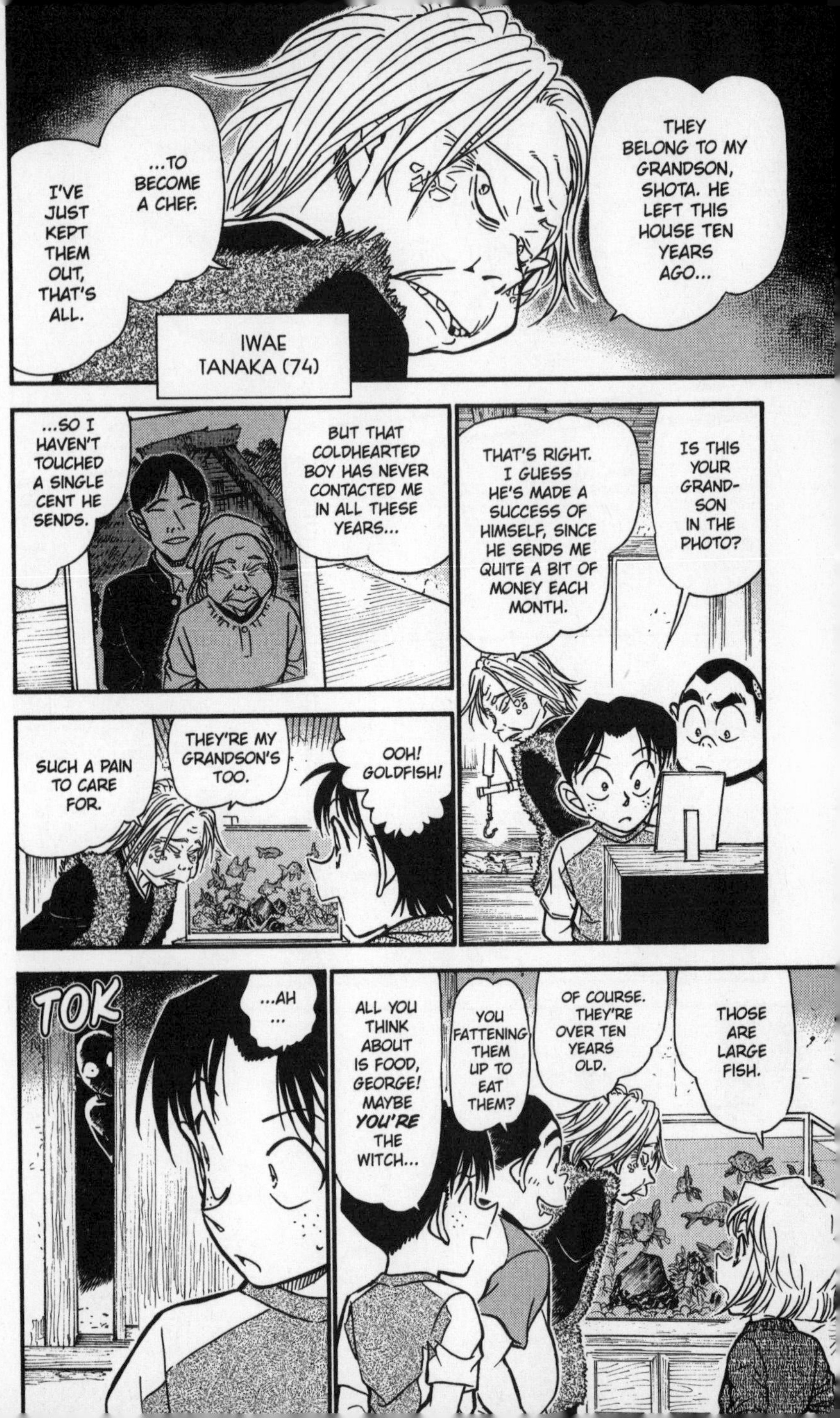
THEY BELONG TO MY GRANDSON, SHOTA. HE LEFT THIS HOUSE TEN YEARS AGO...
...TO BECOME A CHEF.
I'VE JUST KEPT THEM OUT, THAT'S ALL.
IWAE TANAKA (74)
IS THIS YOUR GRAND-SON IN THE PHOTO?
THAT'S RIGHT. I GUESS HE'S MADE A SUCCESS OF HIMSELF, SINCE HE SENDS ME QUITE A BIT OF MONEY EACH MONTH.
BUT THAT COLDHEARTED BOY HAS NEVER CONTACTED ME IN ALL THESE YEARS...
...SO I HAVEN'T TOUCHED A SINGLE CENT HE SENDS.
OOH! GOLDFISH!
THEY'RE MY GRANDSON'S TOO.
SUCH A PAIN TO CARE FOR.
THOSE ARE LARGE FISH.
OF COURSE. THEY'RE OVER TEN YEARS OLD.
YOU FATTENING THEM UP TO EAT THEM?
ALL YOU THINK ABOUT IS FOOD, GEORGE! MAYBE *YOU'RE* THE WITCH...
...AH ...
TOK

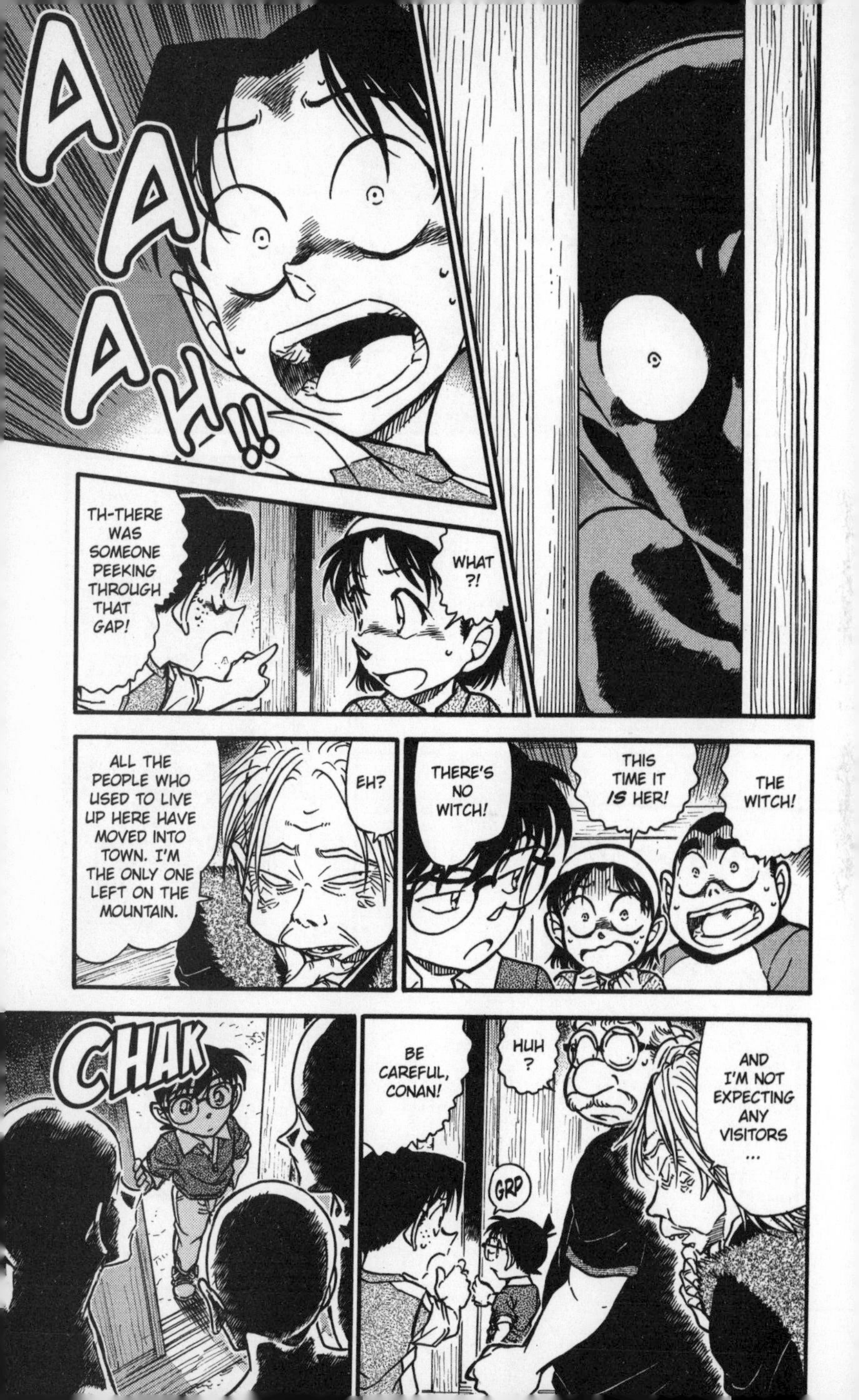
AAAAH!!
TH-THERE WAS SOMEONE PEEKING THROUGH THAT GAP!
WHAT?!
THE WITCH!
THIS TIME IT *IS* HER!
THERE'S NO WITCH!
EH?
ALL THE PEOPLE WHO USED TO LIVE UP HERE HAVE MOVED INTO TOWN. I'M THE ONLY ONE LEFT ON THE MOUNTAIN.
AND I'M NOT EXPECTING ANY VISITORS...
HUH?
BE CAREFUL, CONAN!
GRP
CHAK

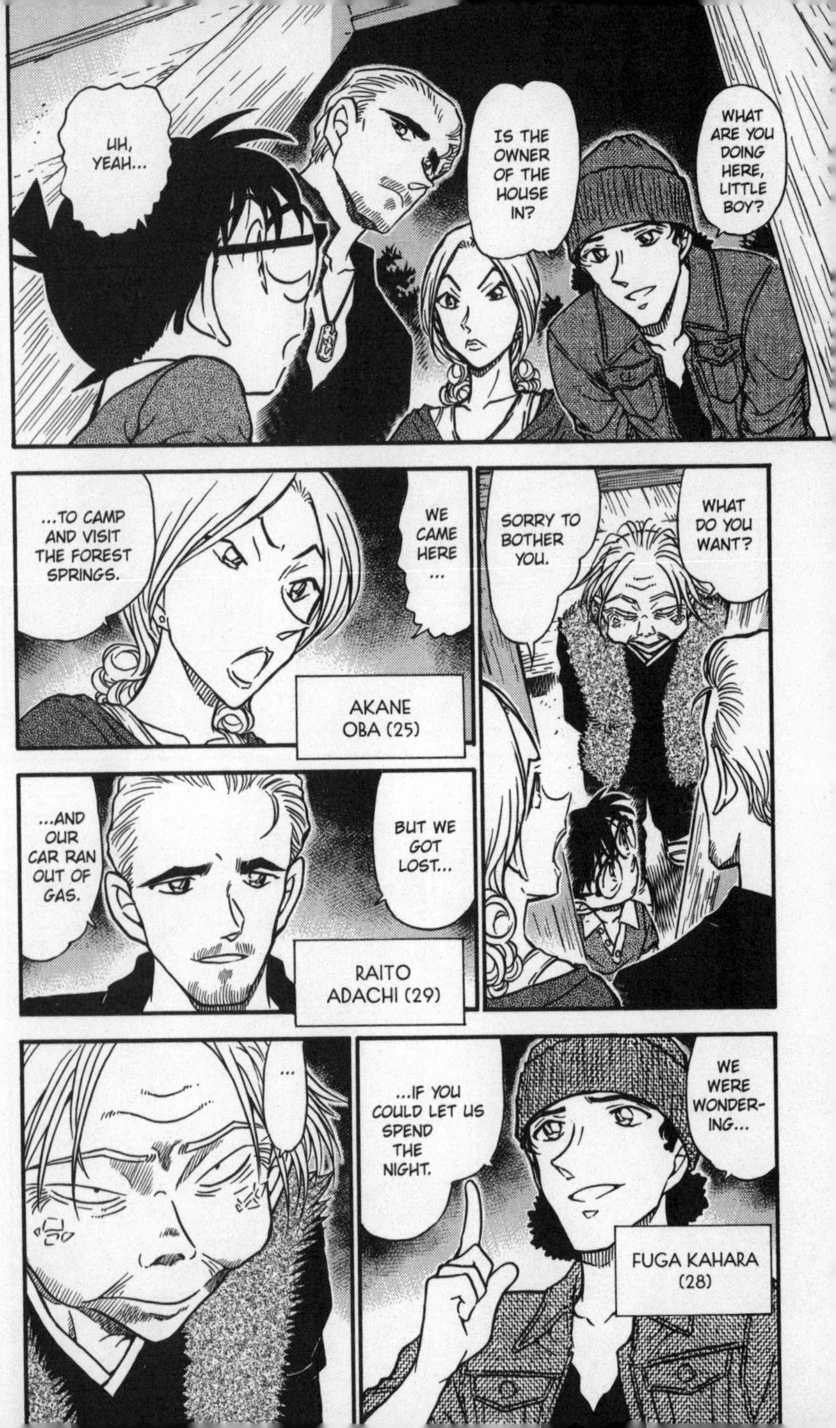
WHAT ARE YOU DOING HERE, LITTLE BOY?
IS THE OWNER OF THE HOUSE IN?
UH, YEAH...
WHAT DO YOU WANT?
SORRY TO BOTHER YOU.
WE CAME HERE ...
...TO CAMP AND VISIT THE FOREST SPRINGS.
AKANE OBA (25)
BUT WE GOT LOST...
...AND OUR CAR RAN OUT OF GAS.
RAITO ADACHI (29)
WE WERE WONDERING...
...IF YOU COULD LET US SPEND THE NIGHT.
FUGA KAHARA (28)
...

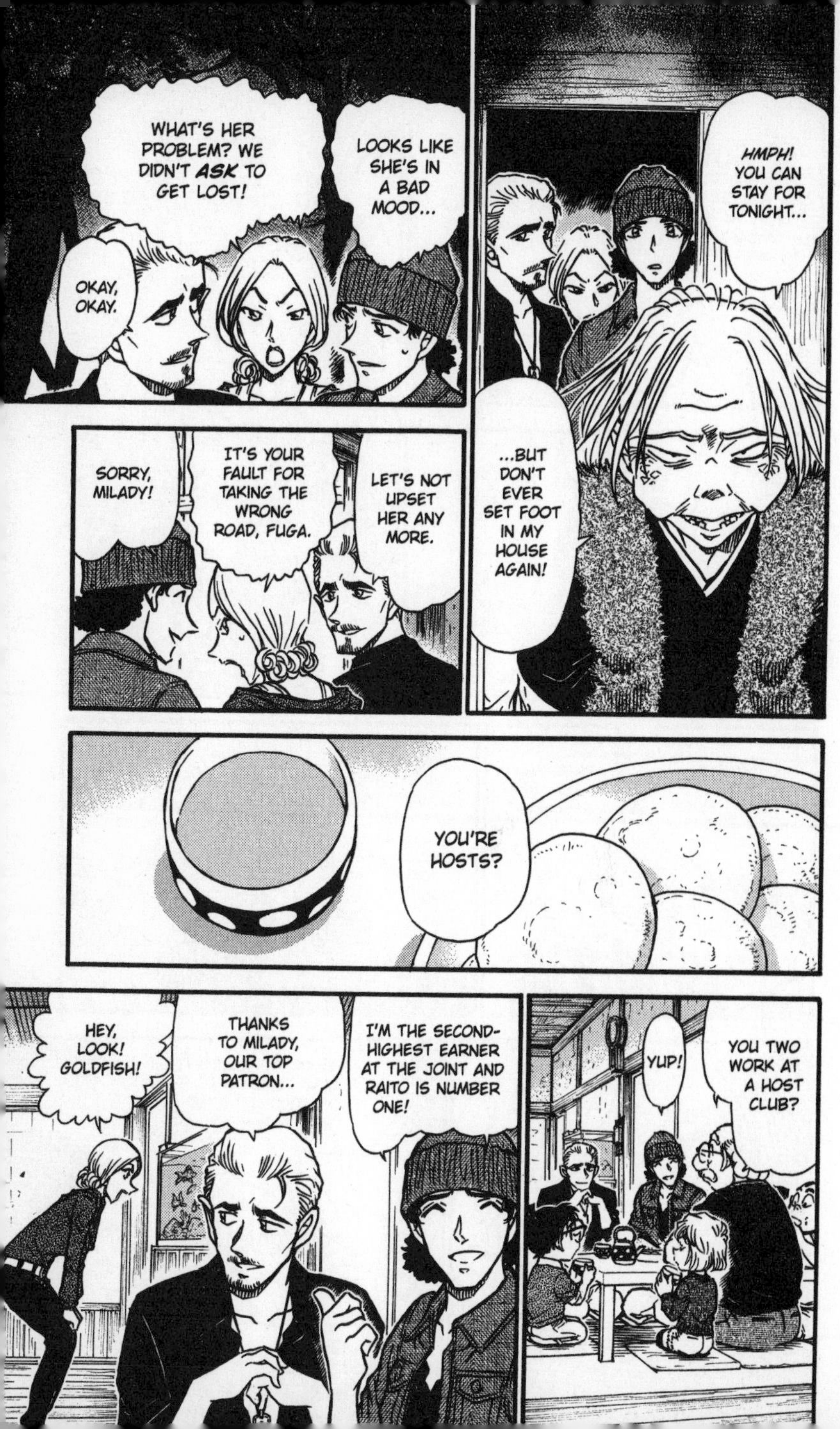
HMPH! YOU CAN STAY FOR TONIGHT...
...BUT DON'T EVER SET FOOT IN MY HOUSE AGAIN!
LOOKS LIKE SHE'S IN A BAD MOOD...
WHAT'S HER PROBLEM? WE DIDN'T ASK TO GET LOST!
OKAY, OKAY.
LET'S NOT UPSET HER ANY MORE.
IT'S YOUR FAULT FOR TAKING THE WRONG ROAD, FUGA.
SORRY, MILADY!
YOU'RE HOSTS?
YOU TWO WORK AT A HOST CLUB?
YUP!
I'M THE SECOND-HIGHEST EARNER AT THE JOINT AND RAITO IS NUMBER ONE!
THANKS TO MILADY, OUR TOP PATRON...
HEY, LOOK! GOLDFISH!

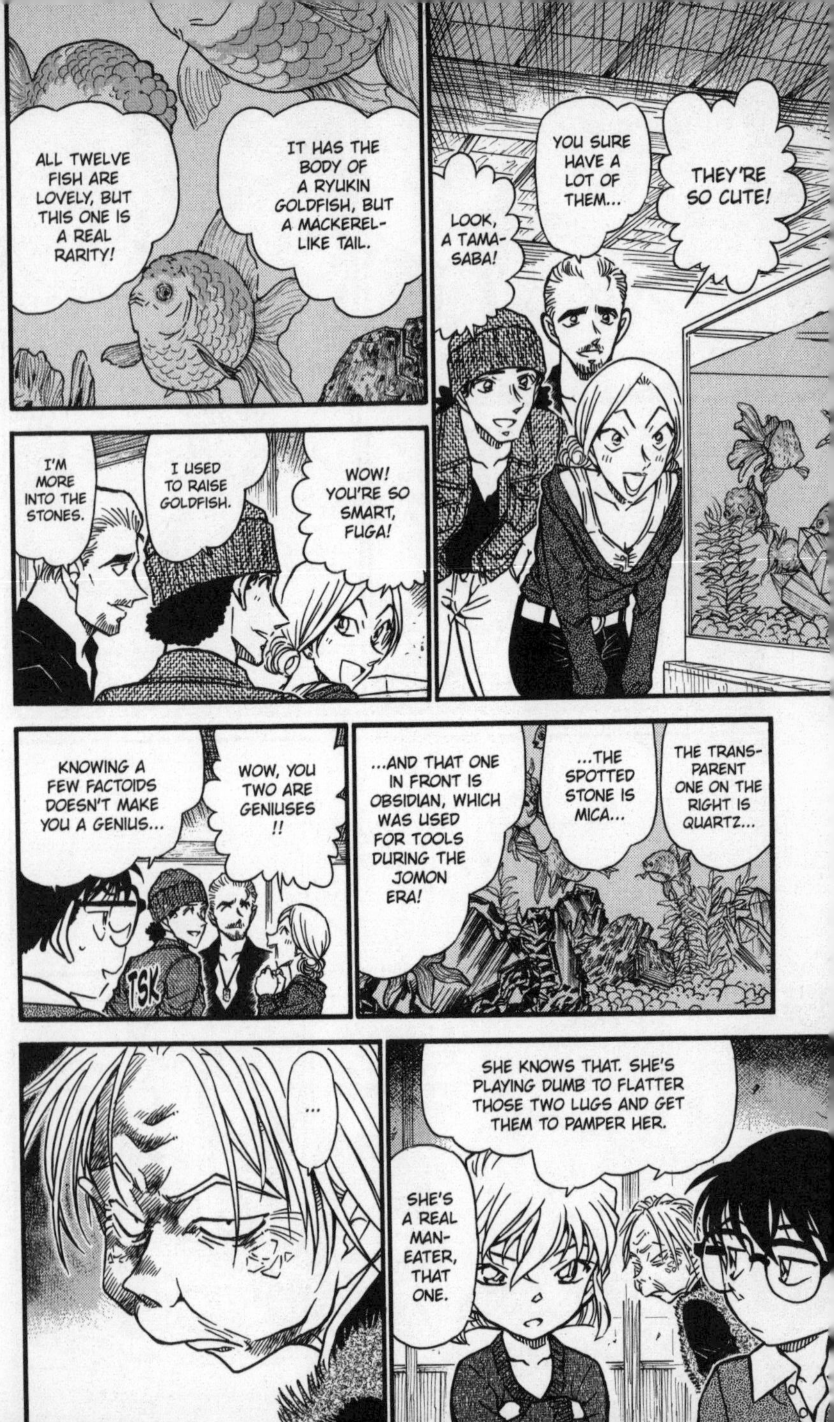
THEY'RE SO CUTE!
YOU SURE HAVE A LOT OF THEM...
LOOK, A TAMA-SABA!
IT HAS THE BODY OF A RYUKIN GOLDFISH, BUT A MACKEREL-LIKE TAIL.
ALL TWELVE FISH ARE LOVELY, BUT THIS ONE IS A REAL RARITY!
WOW! YOU'RE SO SMART, FUGA!
I USED TO RAISE GOLDFISH.
I'M MORE INTO THE STONES.
THE TRANS-PARENT ONE ON THE RIGHT IS QUARTZ...
...THE SPOTTED STONE IS MICA...
...AND THAT ONE IN FRONT IS OBSIDIAN, WHICH WAS USED FOR TOOLS DURING THE JOMON ERA!
WOW, YOU TWO ARE GENIUSES !!
KNOWING A FEW FACTOIDS DOESN'T MAKE YOU A GENIUS...
TSK
SHE KNOWS THAT. SHE'S PLAYING DUMB TO FLATTER THOSE TWO LUGS AND GET THEM TO PAMPER HER.
SHE'S A REAL MAN-EATER, THAT ONE.
...

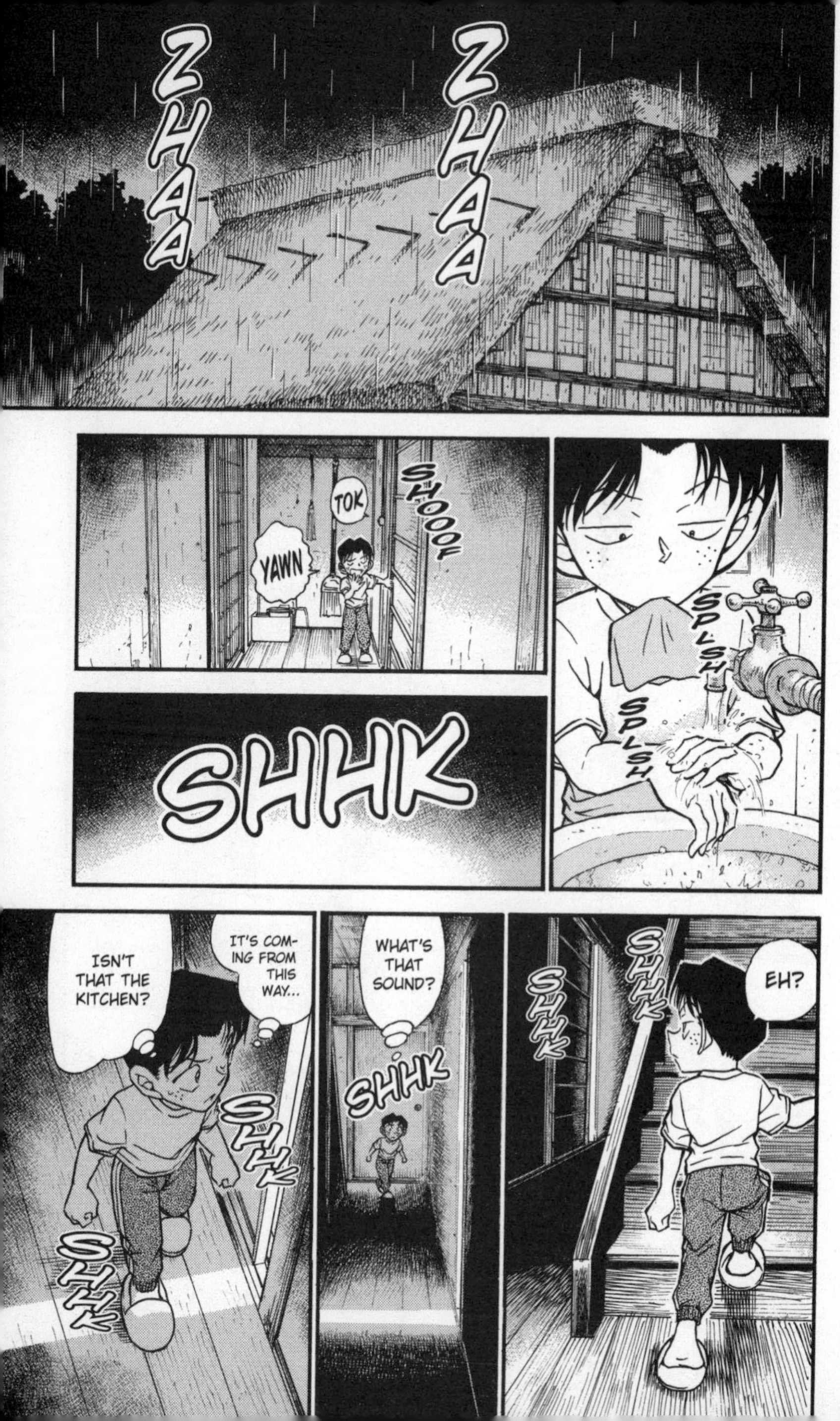
ZHAA
ZHAA
SPLSH
SPLSH
SHOOOOF
TOK
YAWN
SHHK
EH?
SHHK
SHHK
WHAT'S THAT SOUND?
SHHK
IT'S COMING FROM THIS WAY...
ISN'T THAT THE KITCHEN?
SHHK
SHHK

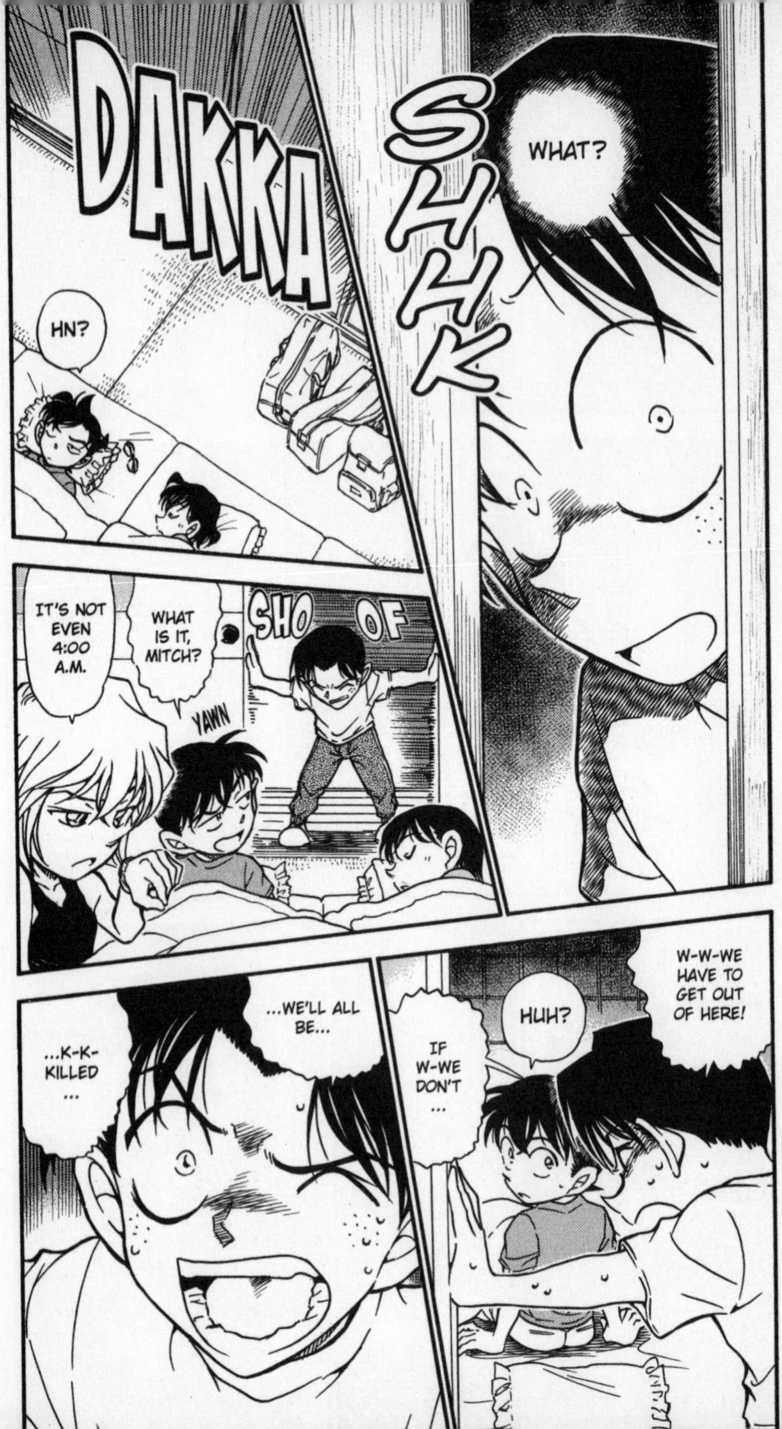
SHHK
WHAT?
DAKKA
HN?
SHO OF
WHAT IS IT, MITCH?
IT'S NOT EVEN 4:00 A.M.
YAWN
W-W-WE HAVE TO GET OUT OF HERE!
HUH?
IF W-WE DON'T ...
...WE'LL ALL BE...
...K-K-KILLED ...

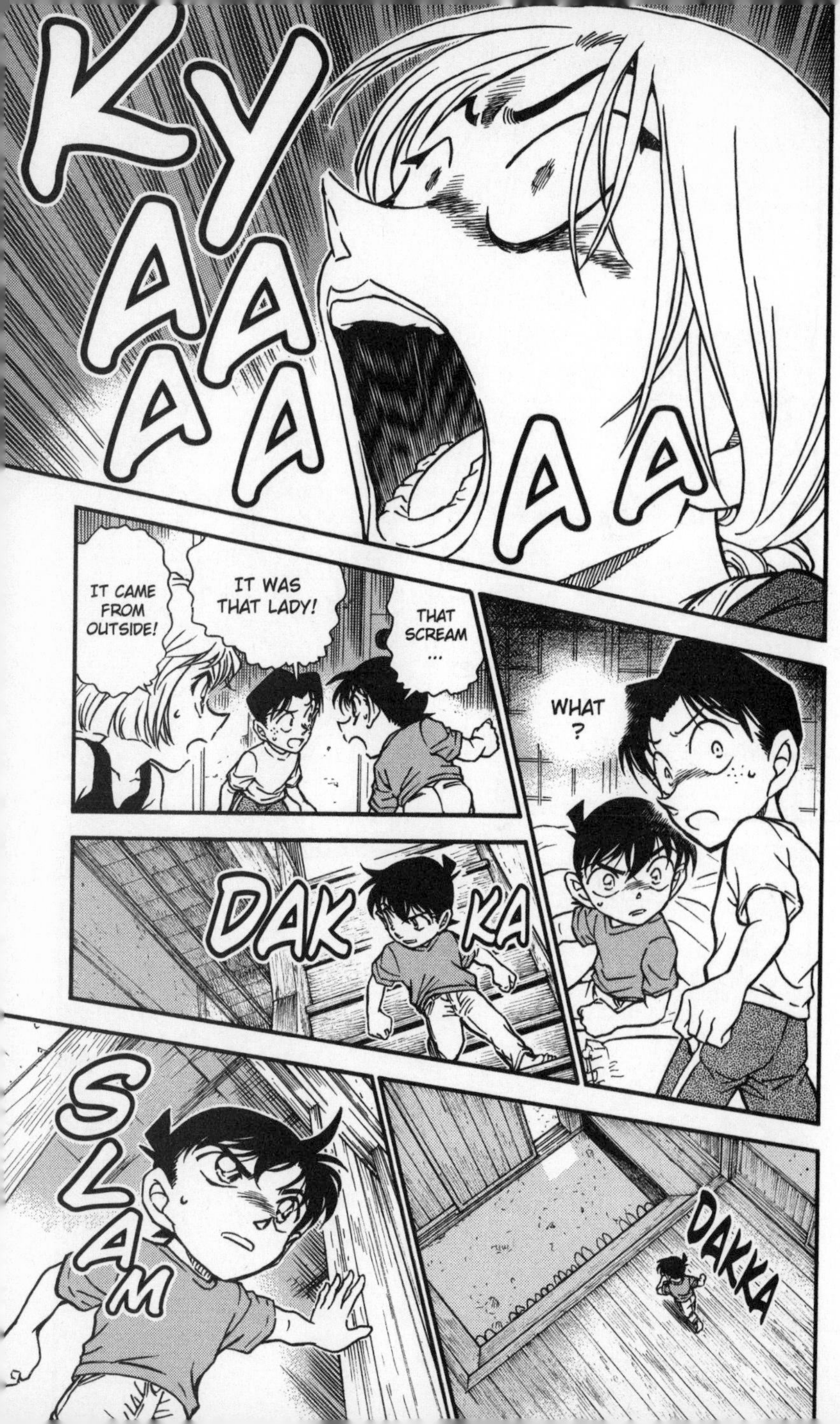
KYAAAAAA
WHAT ?
THAT SCREAM ...
IT WAS THAT LADY!
IT CAME FROM OUTSIDE!
DAK KA
DAKKA
SLAM

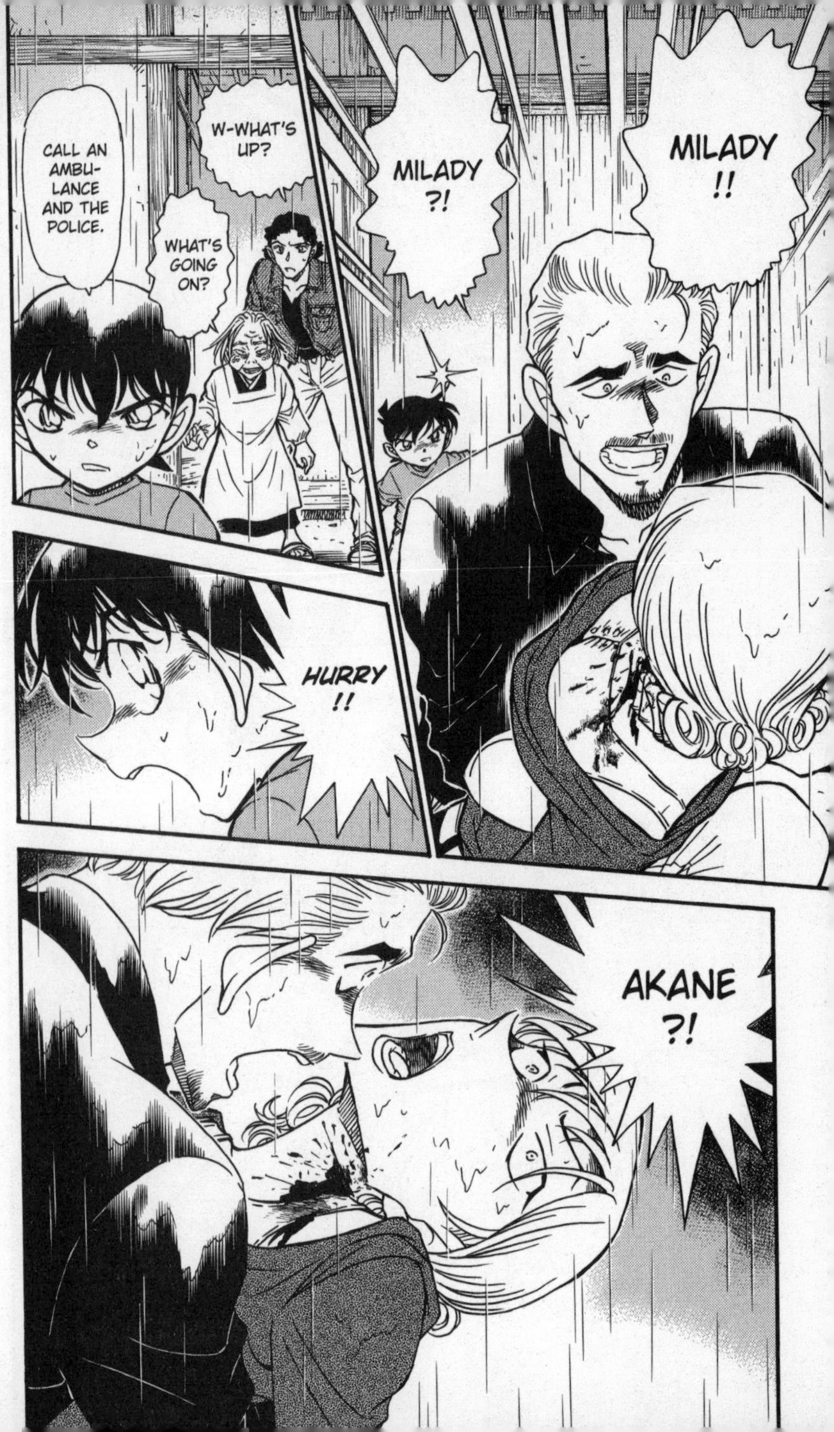
MILADY !!
MILADY ?!
W-WHAT'S UP?
WHAT'S GOING ON?
CALL AN AMBULANCE AND THE POLICE.
HURRY !!
AKANE ?!

THE WITCH LEGEND MYSTERY ②

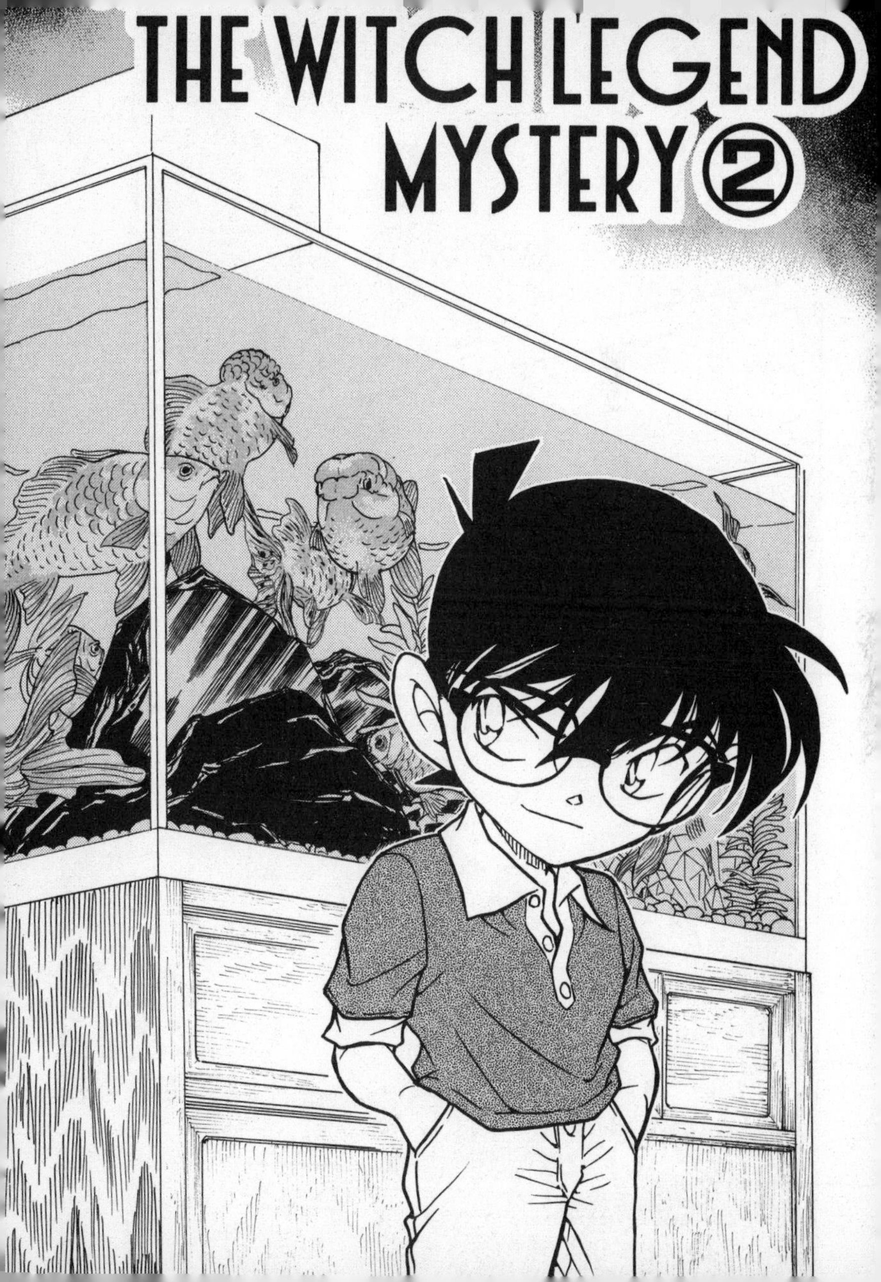

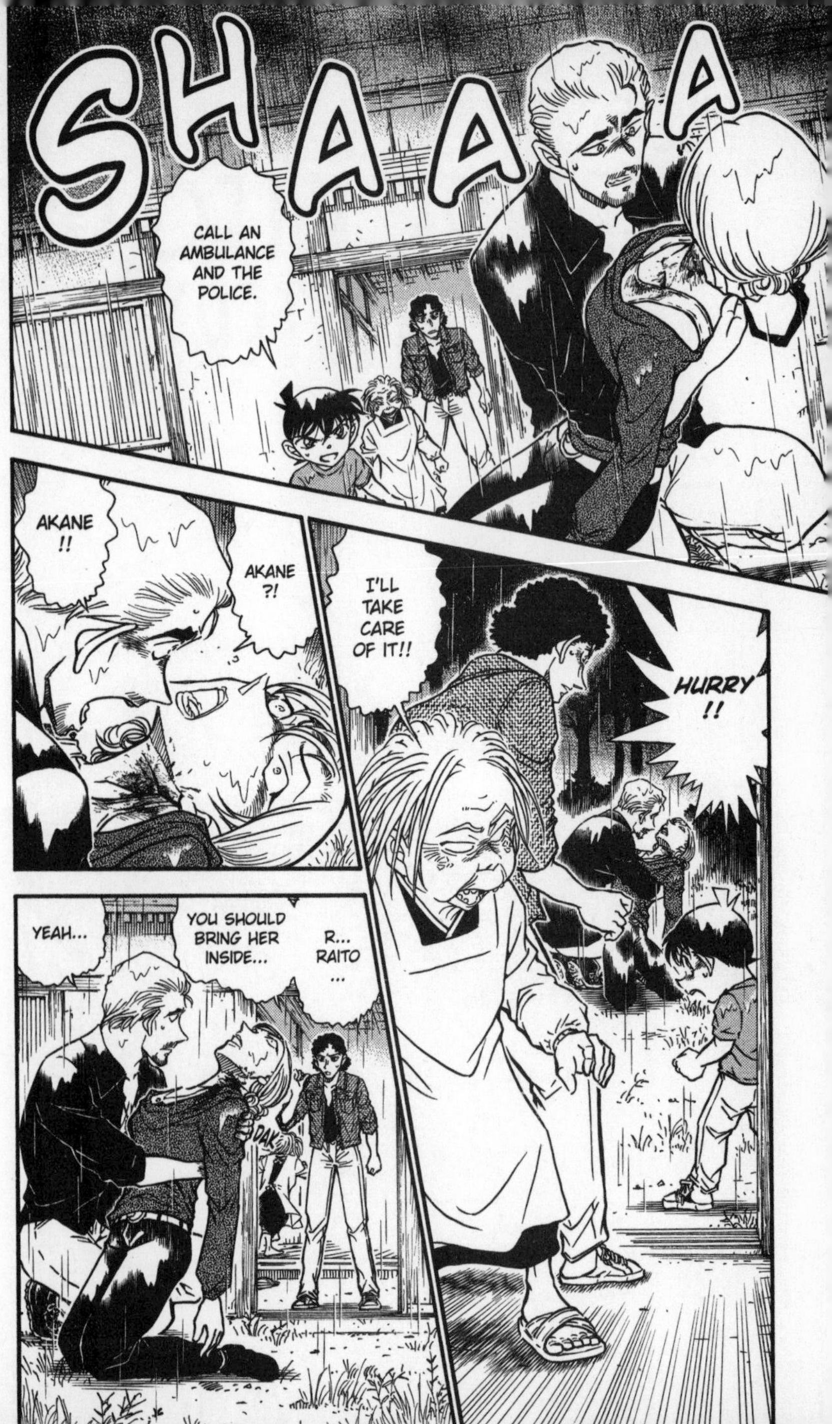
SHAAAA
CALL AN AMBULANCE AND THE POLICE.
HURRY!!
I'LL TAKE CARE OF IT!!
AKANE?!
AKANE!!
R... RAITO...
YOU SHOULD BRING HER INSIDE...
YEAH...
DAK

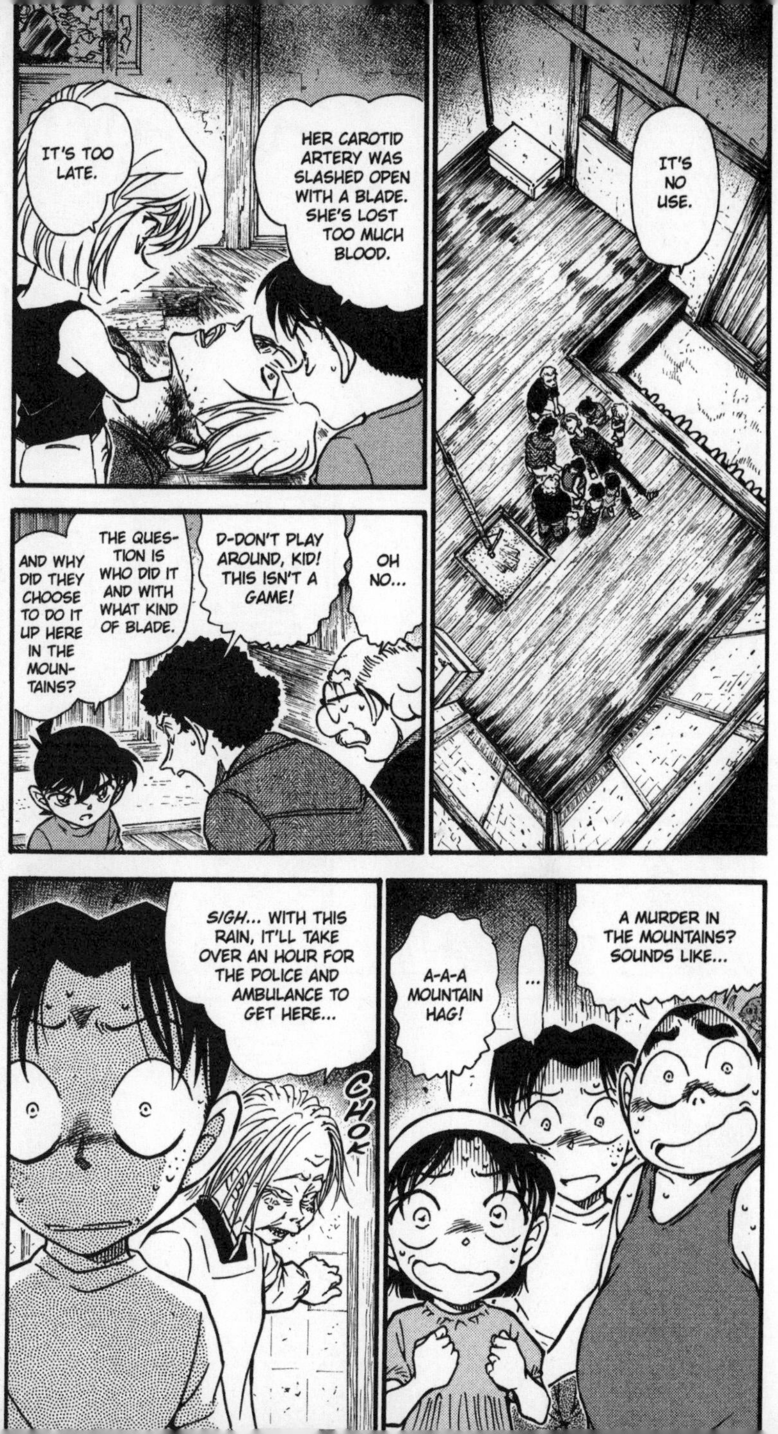
IT'S NO USE.
HER CAROTID ARTERY WAS SLASHED OPEN WITH A BLADE. SHE'S LOST TOO MUCH BLOOD.
IT'S TOO LATE.
OH NO...
D-DON'T PLAY AROUND, KID! THIS ISN'T A GAME!
THE QUESTION IS WHO DID IT AND WITH WHAT KIND OF BLADE.
AND WHY DID THEY CHOOSE TO DO IT UP HERE IN THE MOUNTAINS?
A MURDER IN THE MOUNTAINS? SOUNDS LIKE...
...
A-A-A MOUNTAIN HAG!
SIGH... WITH THIS RAIN, IT'LL TAKE OVER AN HOUR FOR THE POLICE AND AMBULANCE TO GET HERE...
CHOK

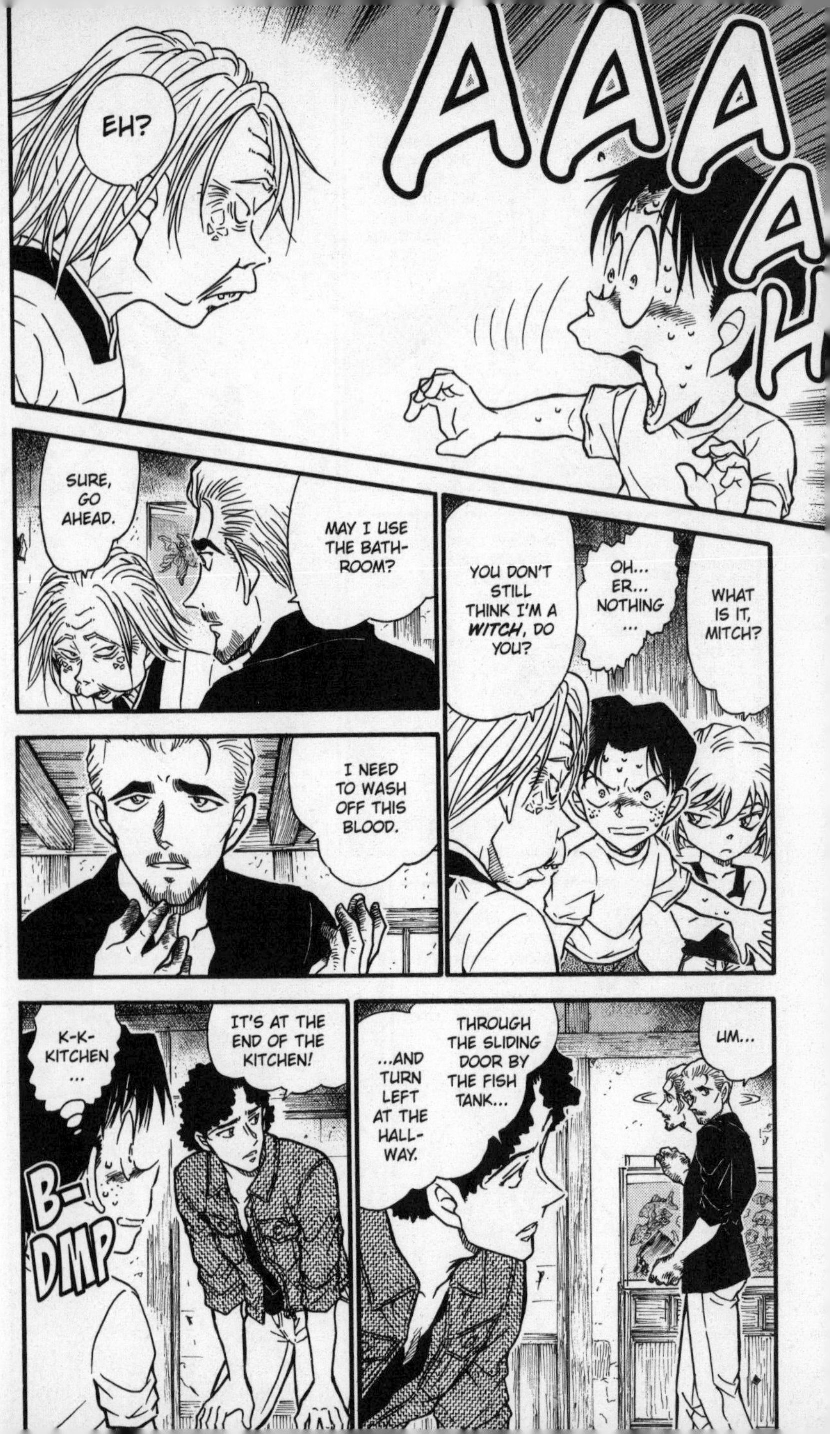
AAAAH
EH?
WHAT IS IT, MITCH?
OH... ER... NOTHING ...
YOU DON'T STILL THINK I'M A *WITCH*, DO YOU?
MAY I USE THE BATH-ROOM?
SURE, GO AHEAD.
I NEED TO WASH OFF THIS BLOOD.
UM...
THROUGH THE SLIDING DOOR BY THE FISH TANK...
...AND TURN LEFT AT THE HALL-WAY.
IT'S AT THE END OF THE KITCHEN!
K-K-KITCHEN ...
B-DMP

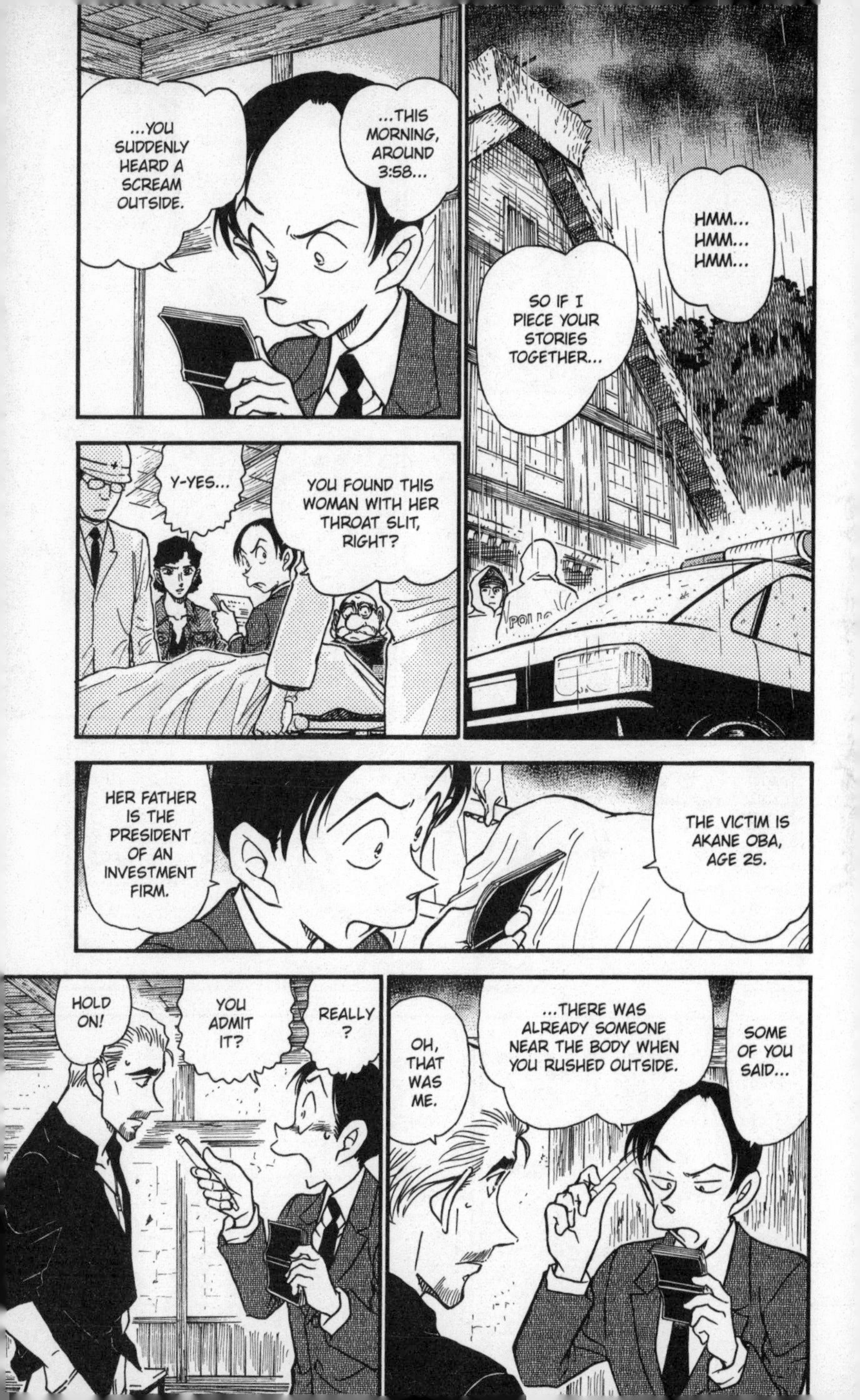
HMM... HMM... HMM...
SO IF I PIECE YOUR STORIES TOGETHER...
...THIS MORNING, AROUND 3:58...
...YOU SUDDENLY HEARD A SCREAM OUTSIDE.
YOU FOUND THIS WOMAN WITH HER THROAT SLIT, RIGHT?
Y-YES...
THE VICTIM IS AKANE OBA, AGE 25.
HER FATHER IS THE PRESIDENT OF AN INVESTMENT FIRM.
SOME OF YOU SAID...
...THERE WAS ALREADY SOMEONE NEAR THE BODY WHEN YOU RUSHED OUTSIDE.
OH, THAT WAS ME.
REALLY?
YOU ADMIT IT?
HOLD ON!

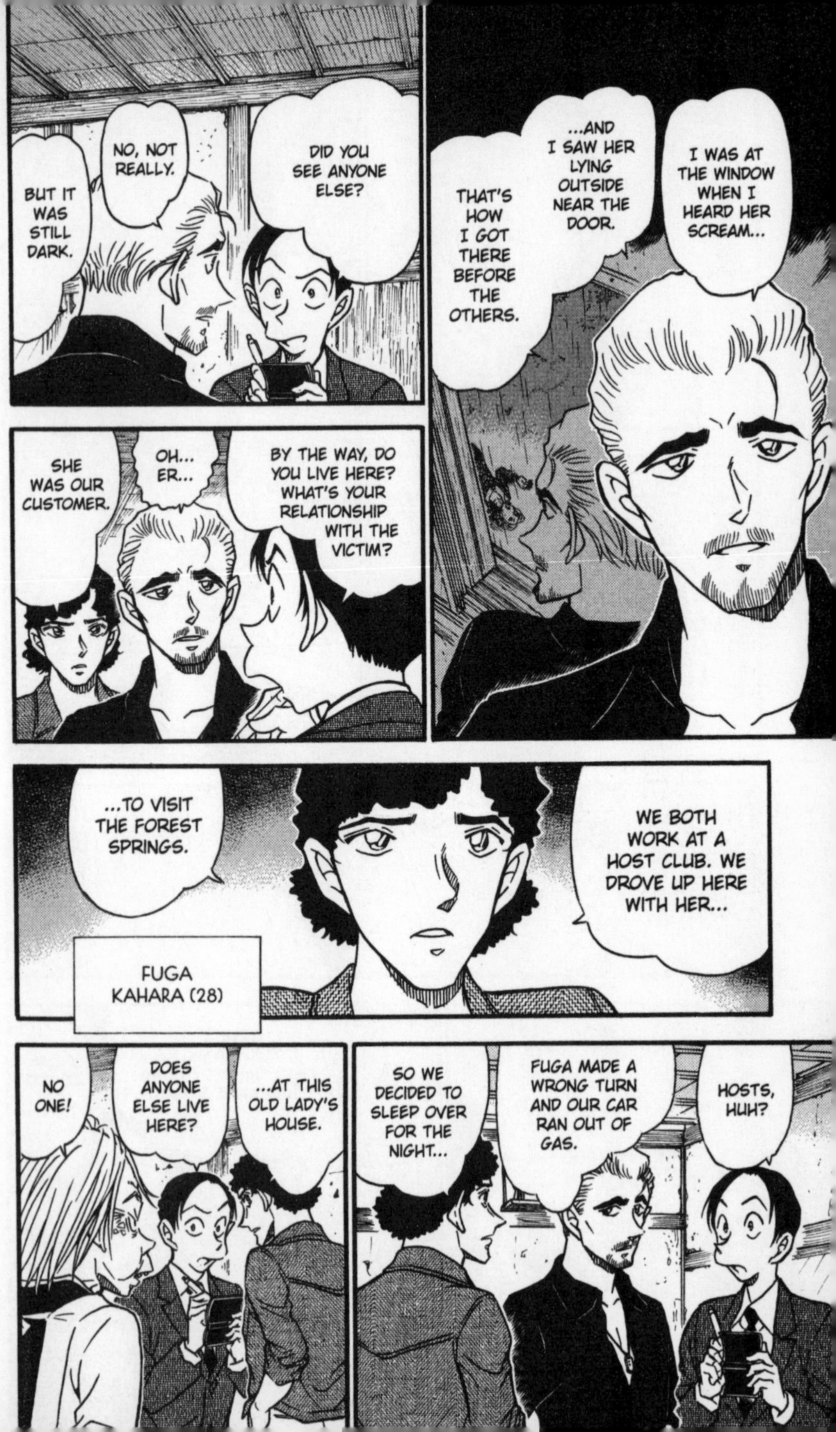
I WAS AT THE WINDOW WHEN I HEARD HER SCREAM...
...AND I SAW HER LYING OUTSIDE NEAR THE DOOR.
THAT'S HOW I GOT THERE BEFORE THE OTHERS.
DID YOU SEE ANYONE ELSE?
NO, NOT REALLY.
BUT IT WAS STILL DARK.
BY THE WAY, DO YOU LIVE HERE? WHAT'S YOUR RELATIONSHIP WITH THE VICTIM?
OH... ER...
SHE WAS OUR CUSTOMER.
WE BOTH WORK AT A HOST CLUB. WE DROVE UP HERE WITH HER...
...TO VISIT THE FOREST SPRINGS.
FUGA KAHARA (28)
HOSTS, HUH?
FUGA MADE A WRONG TURN AND OUR CAR RAN OUT OF GAS.
SO WE DECIDED TO SLEEP OVER FOR THE NIGHT...
...AT THIS OLD LADY'S HOUSE.
DOES ANYONE ELSE LIVE HERE?
NO ONE!

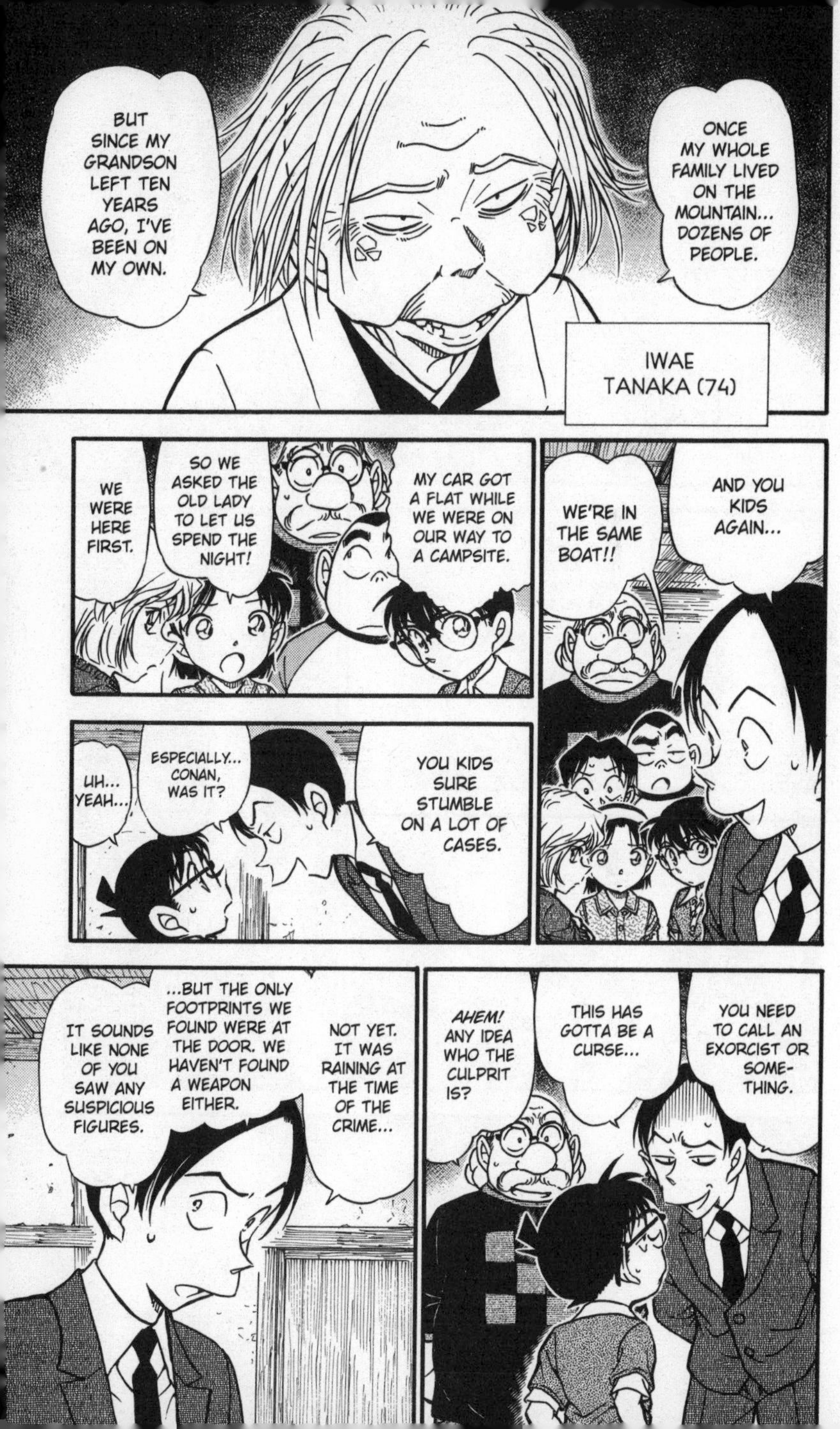
ONCE MY WHOLE FAMILY LIVED ON THE MOUNTAIN... DOZENS OF PEOPLE.
BUT SINCE MY GRANDSON LEFT TEN YEARS AGO, I'VE BEEN ON MY OWN.
IWAE TANAKA (74)
AND YOU KIDS AGAIN...
WE'RE IN THE SAME BOAT!!
MY CAR GOT A FLAT WHILE WE WERE ON OUR WAY TO A CAMPSITE.
SO WE ASKED THE OLD LADY TO LET US SPEND THE NIGHT!
WE WERE HERE FIRST.
YOU KIDS SURE STUMBLE ON A LOT OF CASES.
ESPECIALLY... CONAN, WAS IT?
UH... YEAH...
YOU NEED TO CALL AN EXORCIST OR SOME-THING.
THIS HAS GOTTA BE A CURSE...
AHEM! ANY IDEA WHO THE CULPRIT IS?
NOT YET. IT WAS RAINING AT THE TIME OF THE CRIME...
...BUT THE ONLY FOOTPRINTS WE FOUND WERE AT THE DOOR. WE HAVEN'T FOUND A WEAPON EITHER.
IT SOUNDS LIKE NONE OF YOU SAW ANY SUSPICIOUS FIGURES.

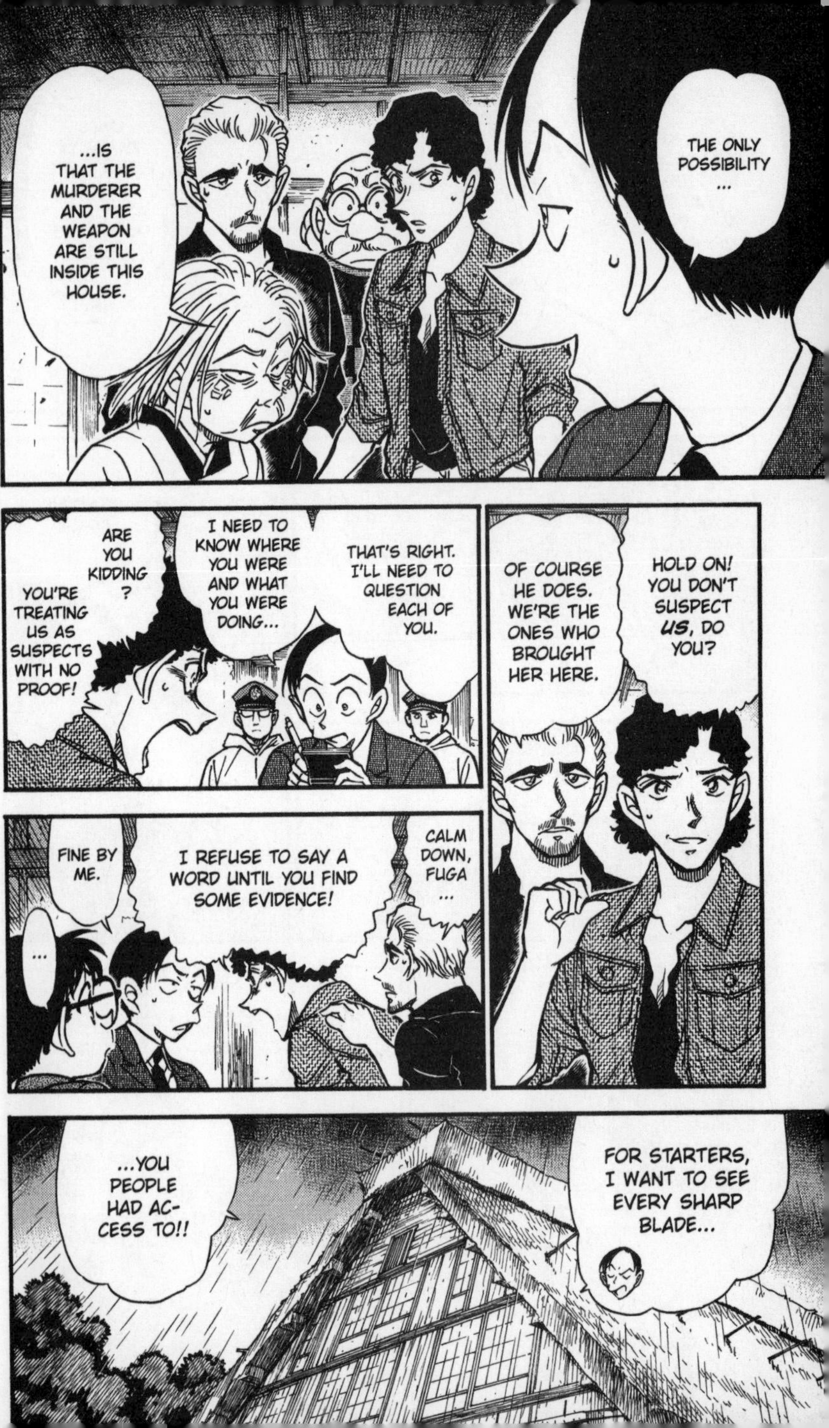
THE ONLY POSSIBILITY ...
...IS THAT THE MURDERER AND THE WEAPON ARE STILL INSIDE THIS HOUSE.
HOLD ON! YOU DON'T SUSPECT **US**, DO YOU?
OF COURSE HE DOES. WE'RE THE ONES WHO BROUGHT HER HERE.
THAT'S RIGHT. I'LL NEED TO QUESTION EACH OF YOU.
I NEED TO KNOW WHERE YOU WERE AND WHAT YOU WERE DOING...
ARE YOU KIDDING?
YOU'RE TREATING US AS SUSPECTS WITH NO PROOF!
CALM DOWN, FUGA ...
I REFUSE TO SAY A WORD UNTIL YOU FIND SOME EVIDENCE!
FINE BY ME.
...
FOR STARTERS, I WANT TO SEE EVERY SHARP BLADE...
...YOU PEOPLE HAD ACCESS TO!!

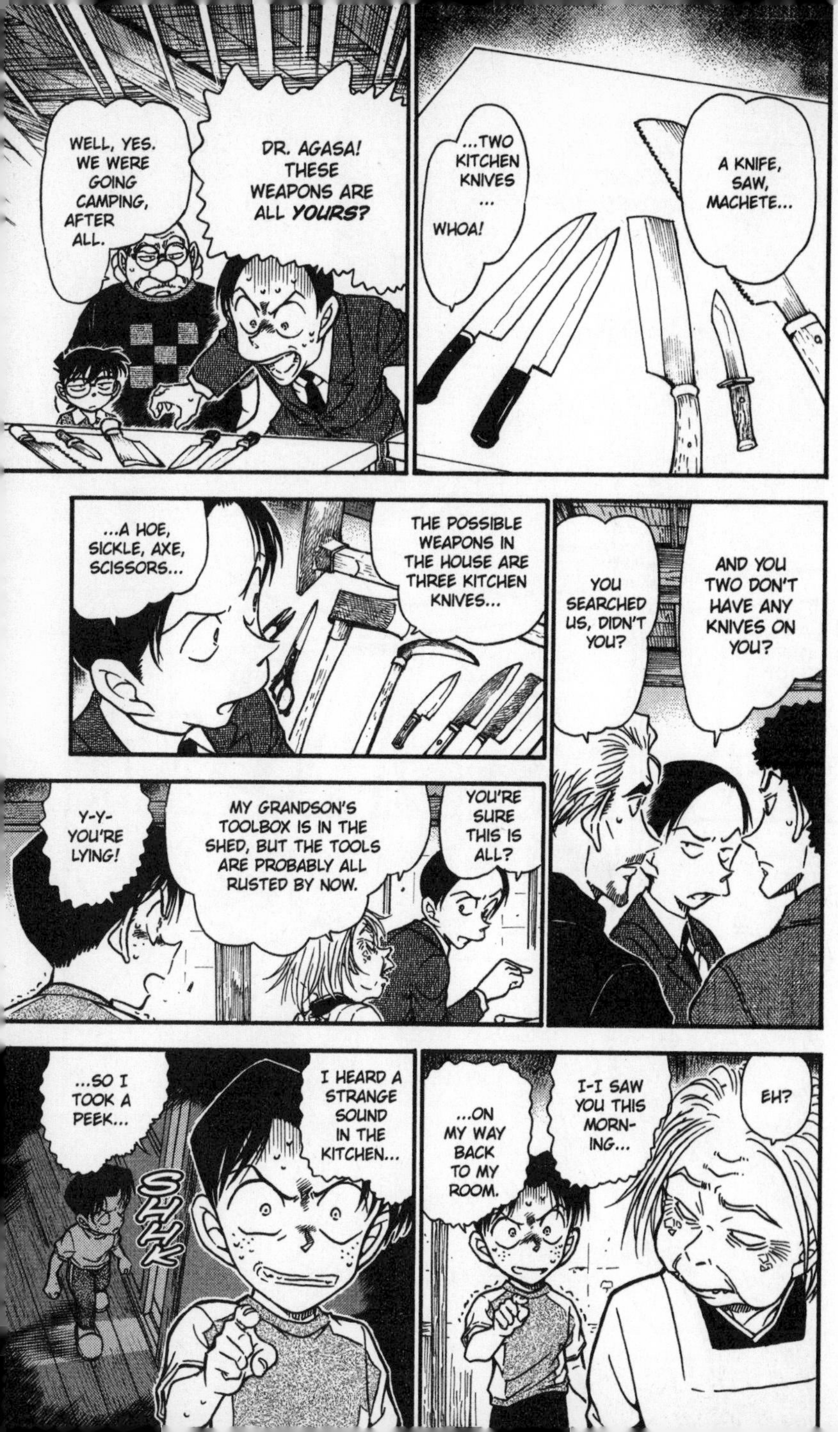
A KNIFE, SAW, MACHETE...
...TWO KITCHEN KNIVES ... WHOA!
DR. AGASA! THESE WEAPONS ARE ALL *YOURS?*
WELL, YES. WE WERE GOING CAMPING, AFTER ALL.
AND YOU TWO DON'T HAVE ANY KNIVES ON YOU?
YOU SEARCHED US, DIDN'T YOU?
THE POSSIBLE WEAPONS IN THE HOUSE ARE THREE KITCHEN KNIVES...
...A HOE, SICKLE, AXE, SCISSORS...
YOU'RE SURE THIS IS ALL?
MY GRANDSON'S TOOLBOX IS IN THE SHED, BUT THE TOOLS ARE PROBABLY ALL RUSTED BY NOW.
Y-Y-YOU'RE LYING!
EH?
I-I SAW YOU THIS MORNING...
...ON MY WAY BACK TO MY ROOM.
I HEARD A STRANGE SOUND IN THE KITCHEN...
SHHK
...SO I TOOK A PEEK...

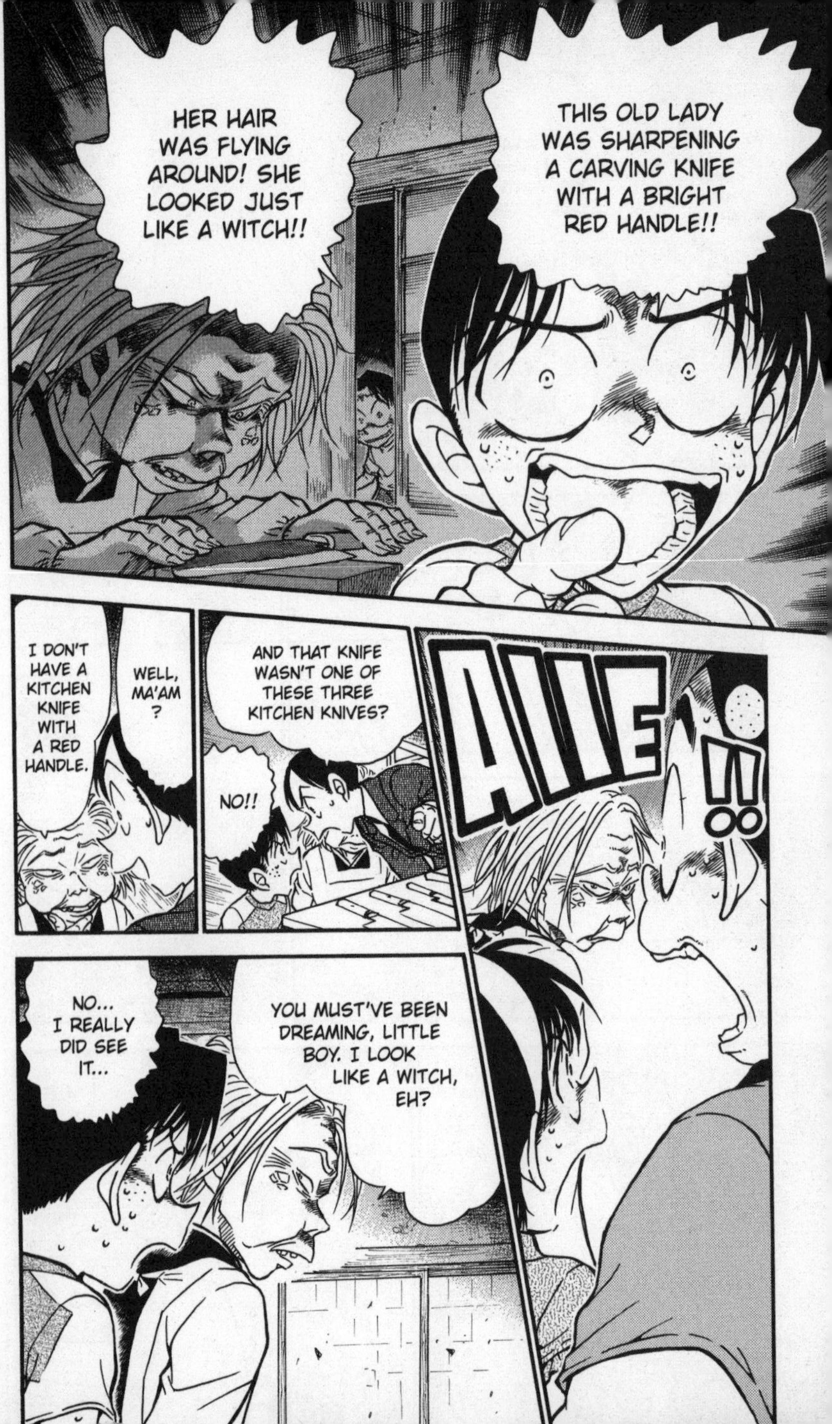
THIS OLD LADY WAS SHARPENING A CARVING KNIFE WITH A BRIGHT RED HANDLE!!
HER HAIR WAS FLYING AROUND! SHE LOOKED JUST LIKE A WITCH!!
AIIE!!
AND THAT KNIFE WASN'T ONE OF THESE THREE KITCHEN KNIVES?
NO!!
WELL, MA'AM ?
I DON'T HAVE A KITCHEN KNIFE WITH A RED HANDLE.
YOU MUST'VE BEEN DREAMING, LITTLE BOY. I LOOK LIKE A WITCH, EH?
NO... I REALLY DID SEE IT...

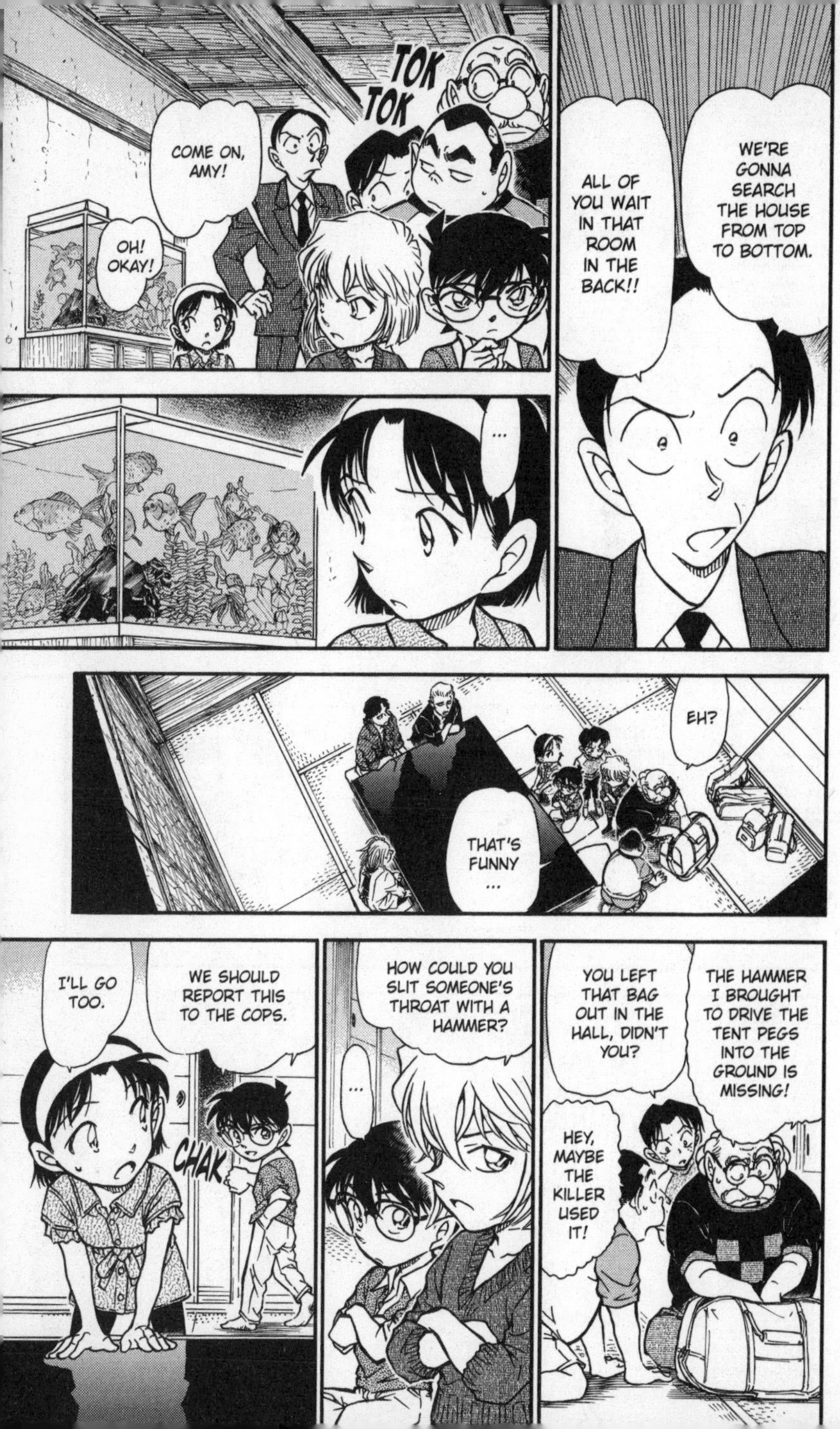
WE'RE GONNA SEARCH THE HOUSE FROM TOP TO BOTTOM.
ALL OF YOU WAIT IN THAT ROOM IN THE BACK!!
TOK TOK
COME ON, AMY!
OH! OKAY!
...
EH?
THAT'S FUNNY ...
THE HAMMER I BROUGHT TO DRIVE THE TENT PEGS INTO THE GROUND IS MISSING!
YOU LEFT THAT BAG OUT IN THE HALL, DIDN'T YOU?
HEY, MAYBE THE KILLER USED IT!
HOW COULD YOU SLIT SOMEONE'S THROAT WITH A HAMMER?
...
WE SHOULD REPORT THIS TO THE COPS.
CHAK
I'LL GO TOO.

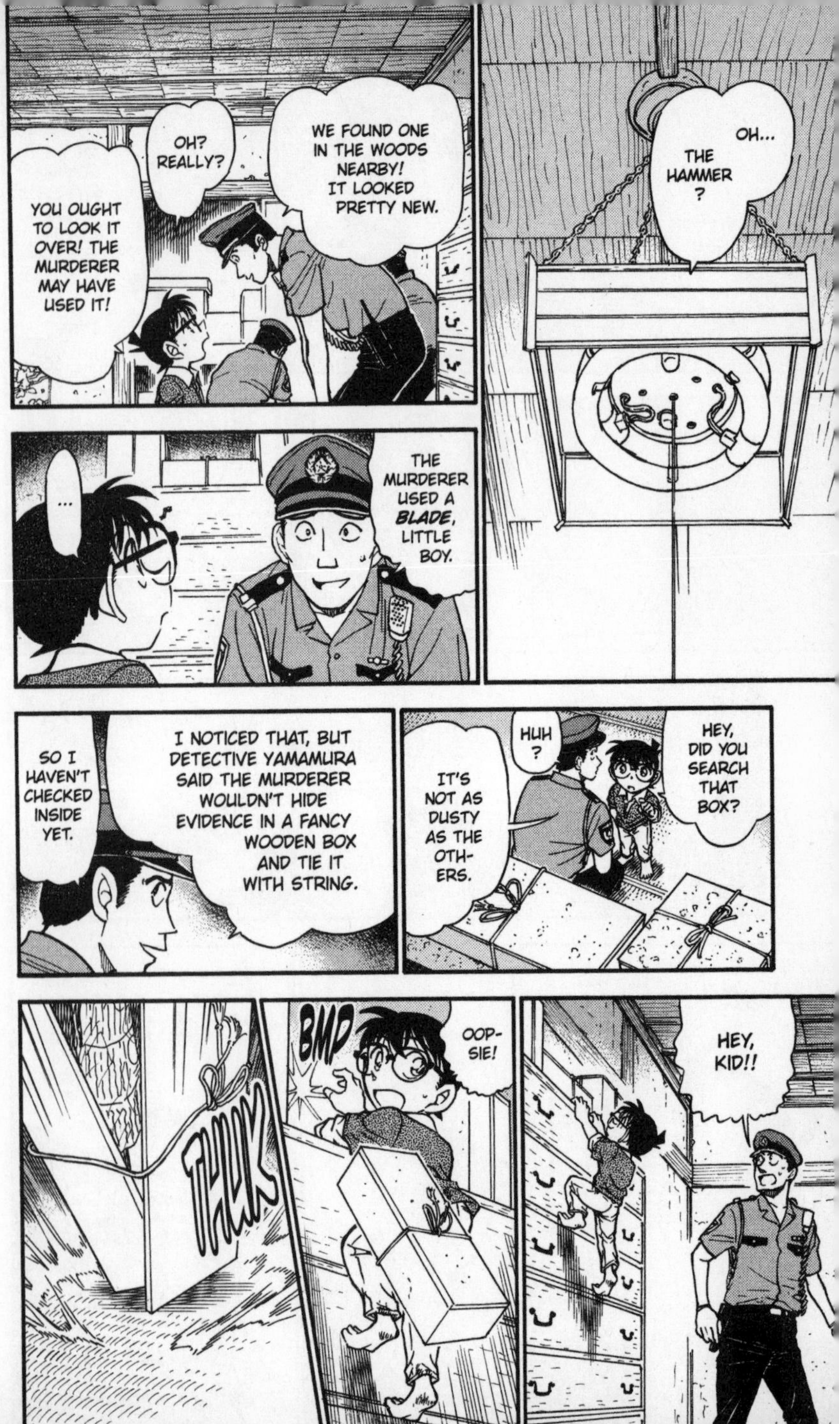
OH... THE HAMMER ?
WE FOUND ONE IN THE WOODS NEARBY! IT LOOKED PRETTY NEW.
OH? REALLY?
YOU OUGHT TO LOOK IT OVER! THE MURDERER MAY HAVE USED IT!
THE MURDERER USED A ***BLADE***, LITTLE BOY.
...
HEY, DID YOU SEARCH THAT BOX?
HUH ?
IT'S NOT AS DUSTY AS THE OTH-ERS.
I NOTICED THAT, BUT DETECTIVE YAMAMURA SAID THE MURDERER WOULDN'T HIDE EVIDENCE IN A FANCY WOODEN BOX AND TIE IT WITH STRING.
SO I HAVEN'T CHECKED INSIDE YET.
HEY, KID!!
OOP-SIE!
BMP
THUNK

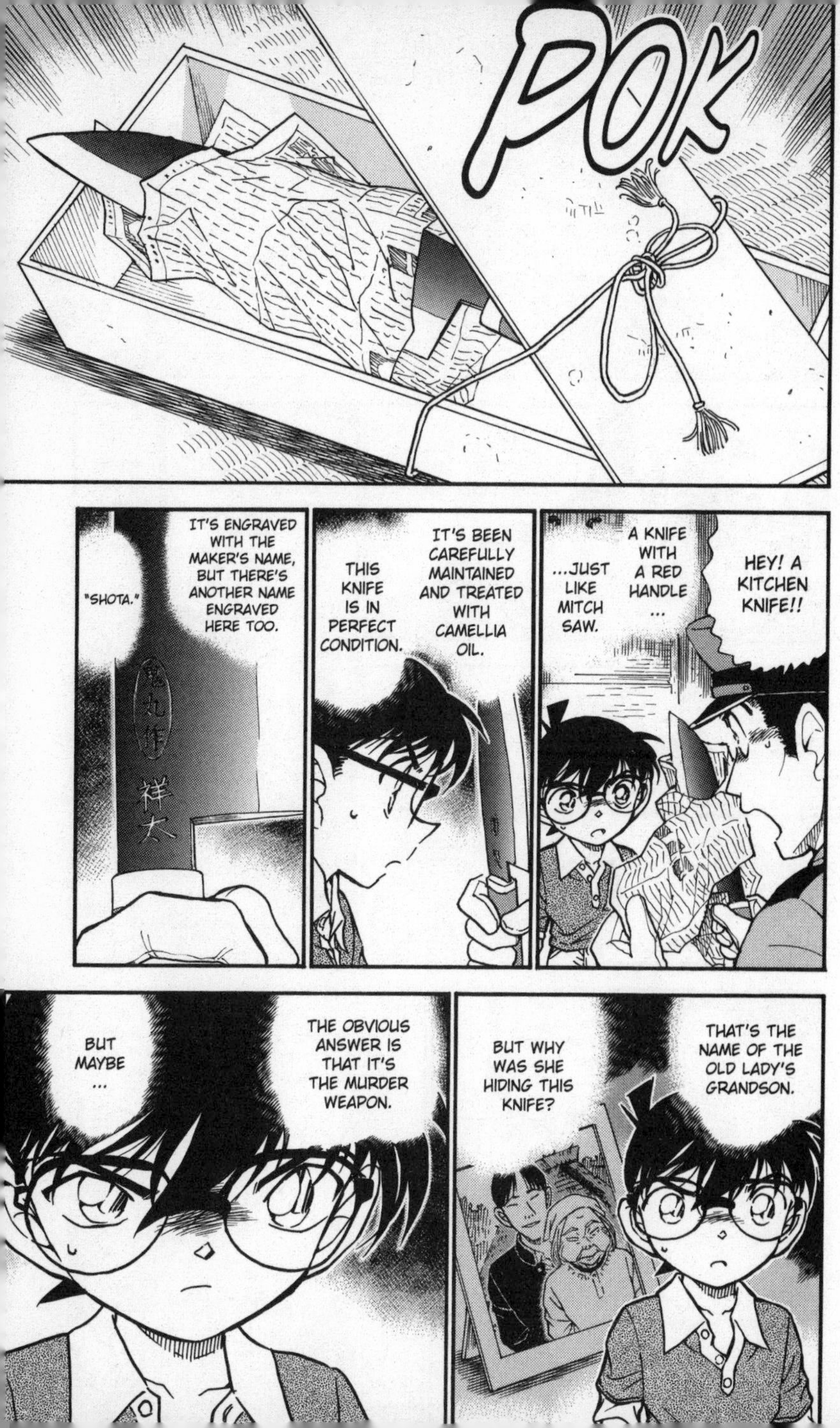
POK
HEY! A KITCHEN KNIFE!!
A KNIFE WITH A RED HANDLE ...
...JUST LIKE MITCH SAW.
IT'S BEEN CAREFULLY MAINTAINED AND TREATED WITH CAMELLIA OIL.
THIS KNIFE IS IN PERFECT CONDITION.
IT'S ENGRAVED WITH THE MAKER'S NAME, BUT THERE'S ANOTHER NAME ENGRAVED HERE TOO.
"SHOTA."
祥太
THAT'S THE NAME OF THE OLD LADY'S GRANDSON.
BUT WHY WAS SHE HIDING THIS KNIFE?
THE OBVIOUS ANSWER IS THAT IT'S THE MURDER WEAPON.
BUT MAYBE ...

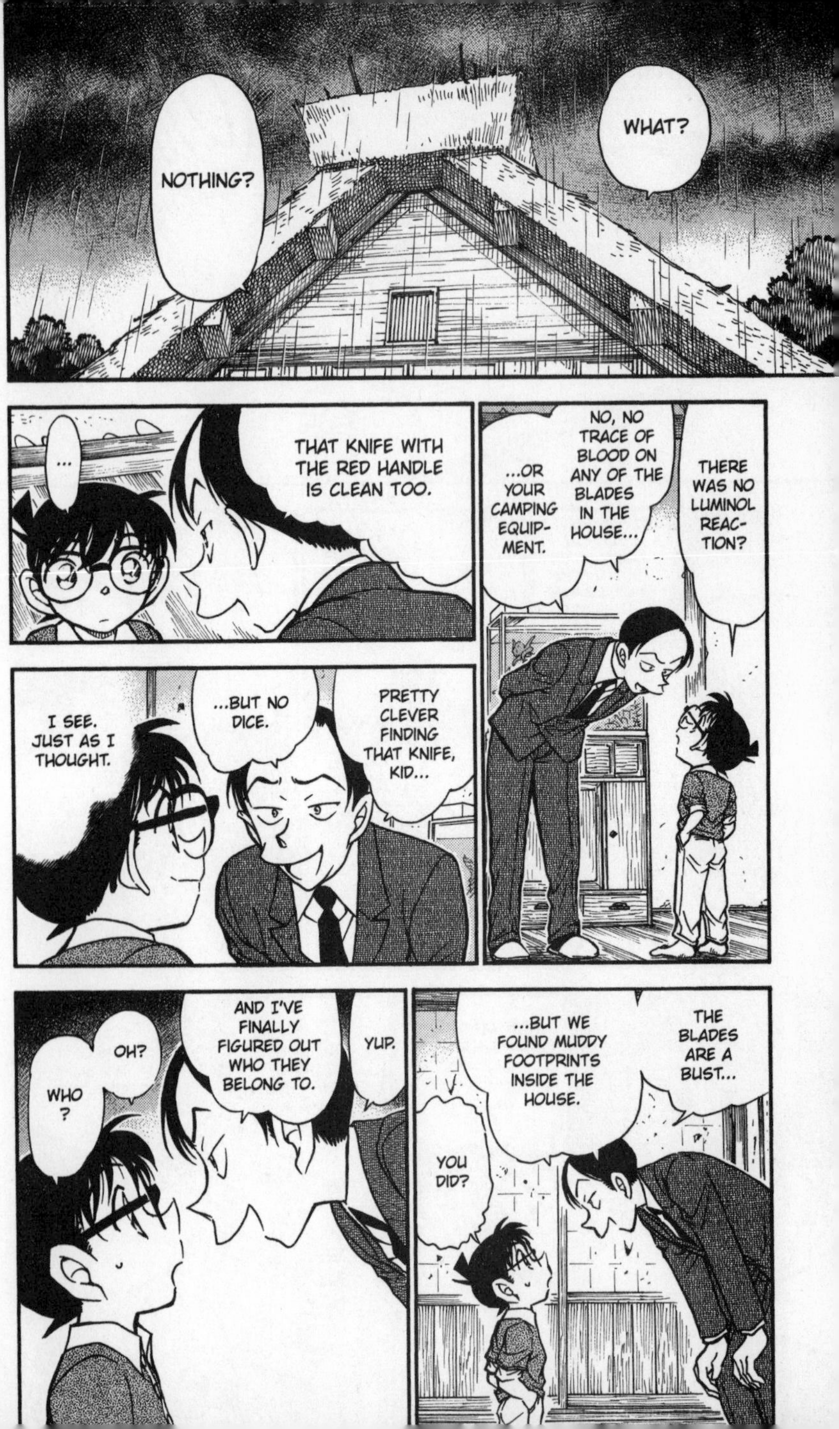
WHAT?
NOTHING?
THERE WAS NO LUMINOL REACTION?
NO, NO TRACE OF BLOOD ON ANY OF THE BLADES IN THE HOUSE...
...OR YOUR CAMPING EQUIPMENT.
THAT KNIFE WITH THE RED HANDLE IS CLEAN TOO.
...
PRETTY CLEVER FINDING THAT KNIFE, KID...
...BUT NO DICE.
I SEE. JUST AS I THOUGHT.
THE BLADES ARE A BUST...
...BUT WE FOUND MUDDY FOOTPRINTS INSIDE THE HOUSE.
YOU DID?
YUP.
AND I'VE FINALLY FIGURED OUT WHO THEY BELONG TO.
OH?
WHO?

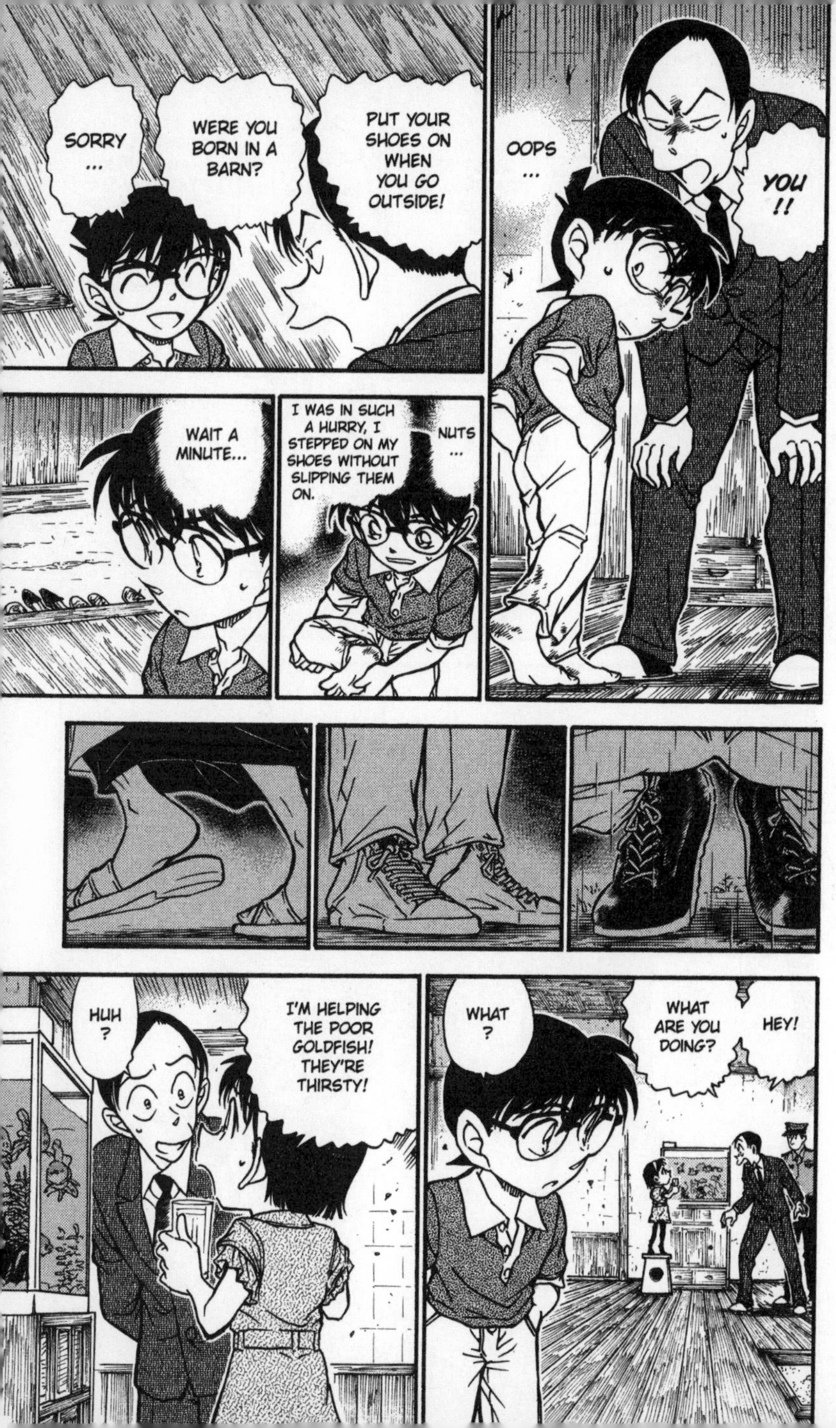
YOU !!
OOPS ...
PUT YOUR SHOES ON WHEN YOU GO OUTSIDE!
WERE YOU BORN IN A BARN?
SORRY ...
NUTS ...
I WAS IN SUCH A HURRY, I STEPPED ON MY SHOES WITHOUT SLIPPING THEM ON.
WAIT A MINUTE...
HEY!
WHAT ARE YOU DOING?
WHAT ?
I'M HELPING THE POOR GOLDFISH! THEY'RE THIRSTY!
HUH ?

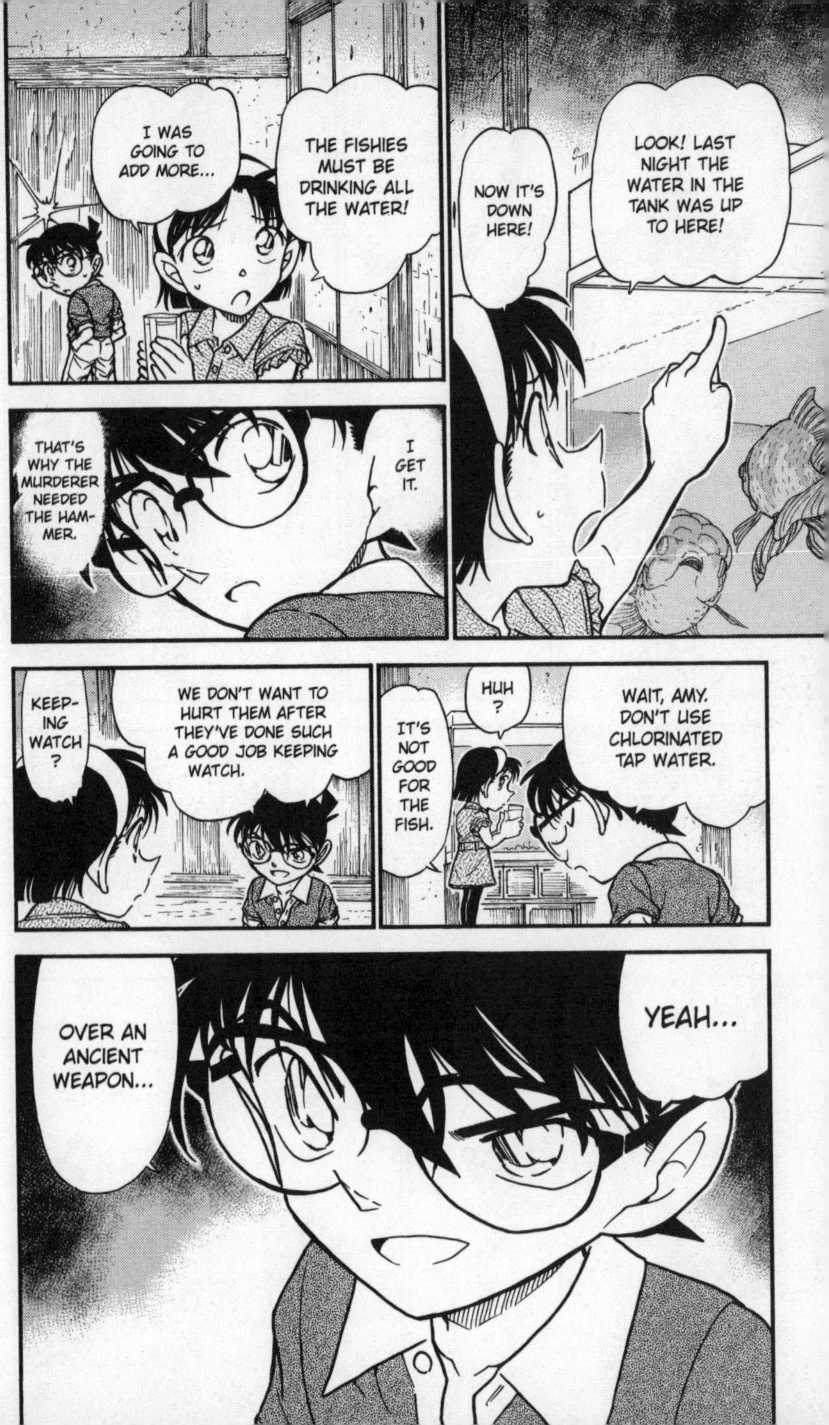
LOOK! LAST NIGHT THE WATER IN THE TANK WAS UP TO HERE!
NOW IT'S DOWN HERE!
THE FISHIES MUST BE DRINKING ALL THE WATER!
I WAS GOING TO ADD MORE...
I GET IT.
THAT'S WHY THE MURDERER NEEDED THE HAMMER.
WAIT, AMY. DON'T USE CHLORINATED TAP WATER.
HUH?
IT'S NOT GOOD FOR THE FISH.
WE DON'T WANT TO HURT THEM AFTER THEY'VE DONE SUCH A GOOD JOB KEEPING WATCH.
KEEPING WATCH?
YEAH...
OVER AN ANCIENT WEAPON...

THE WITCH LEGEND MYSTERY ③

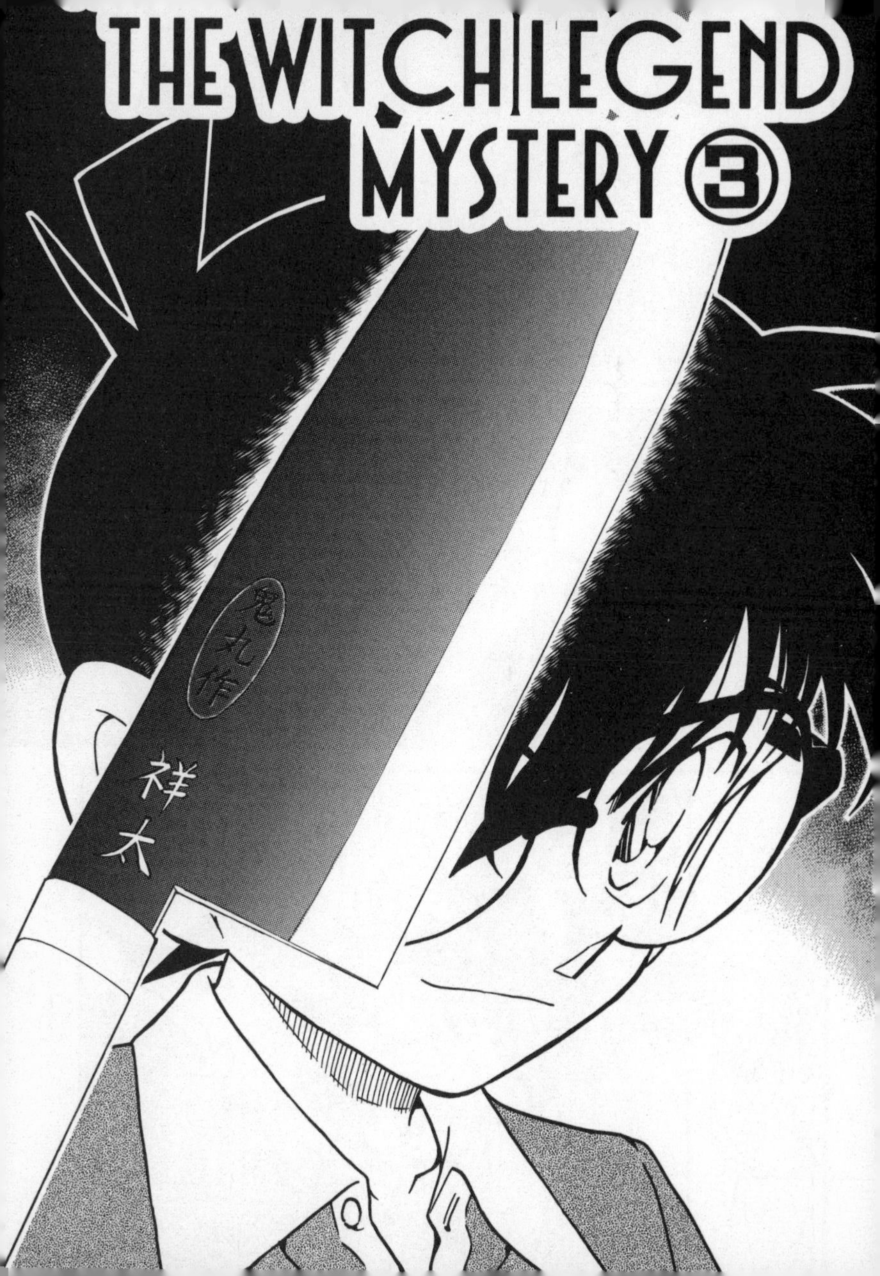
鬼丸作
祥太

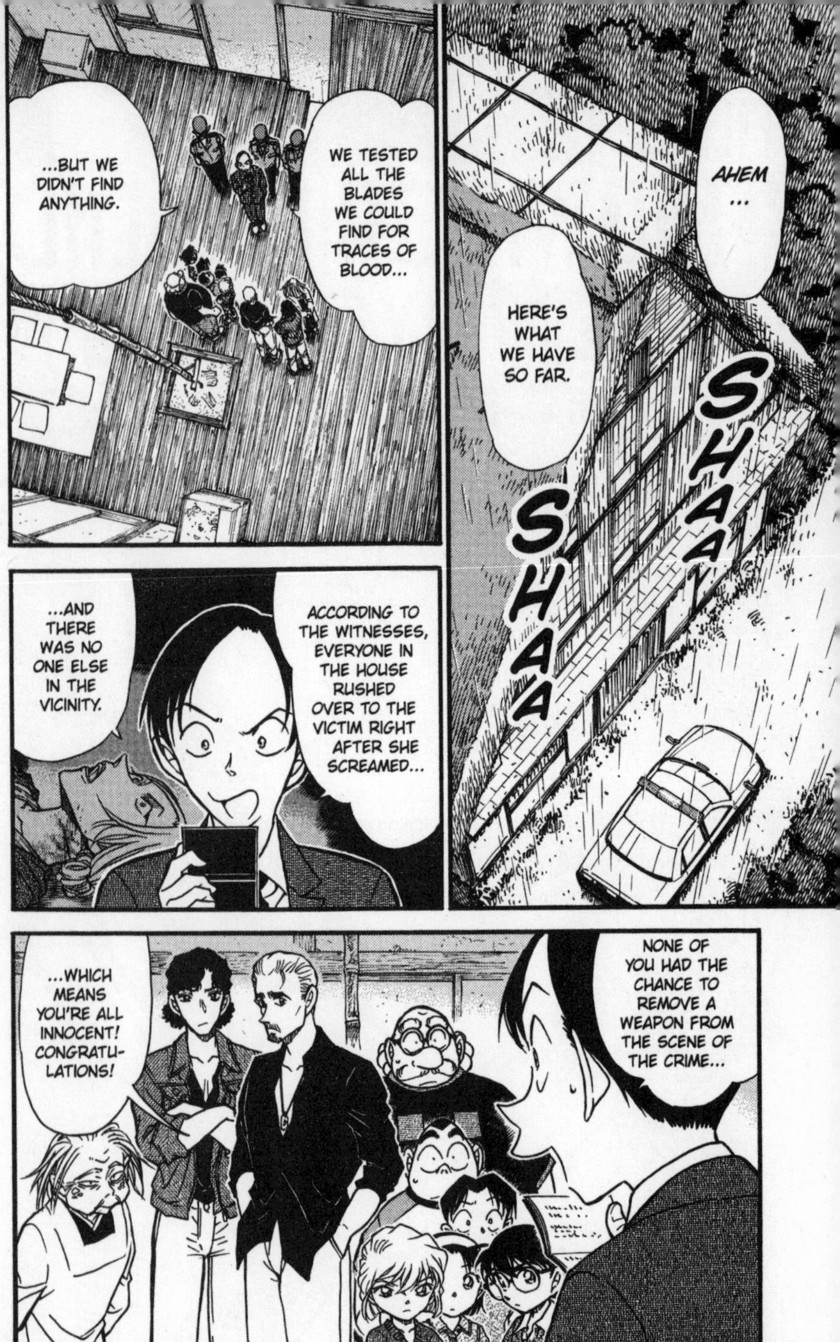
AHEM...
HERE'S WHAT WE HAVE SO FAR.
SHAA
SHAA
WE TESTED ALL THE BLADES WE COULD FIND FOR TRACES OF BLOOD...
...BUT WE DIDN'T FIND ANYTHING.
ACCORDING TO THE WITNESSES, EVERYONE IN THE HOUSE RUSHED OVER TO THE VICTIM RIGHT AFTER SHE SCREAMED...
...AND THERE WAS NO ONE ELSE IN THE VICINITY.
NONE OF YOU HAD THE CHANCE TO REMOVE A WEAPON FROM THE SCENE OF THE CRIME...
...WHICH MEANS YOU'RE ALL INNOCENT! CONGRATULATIONS!

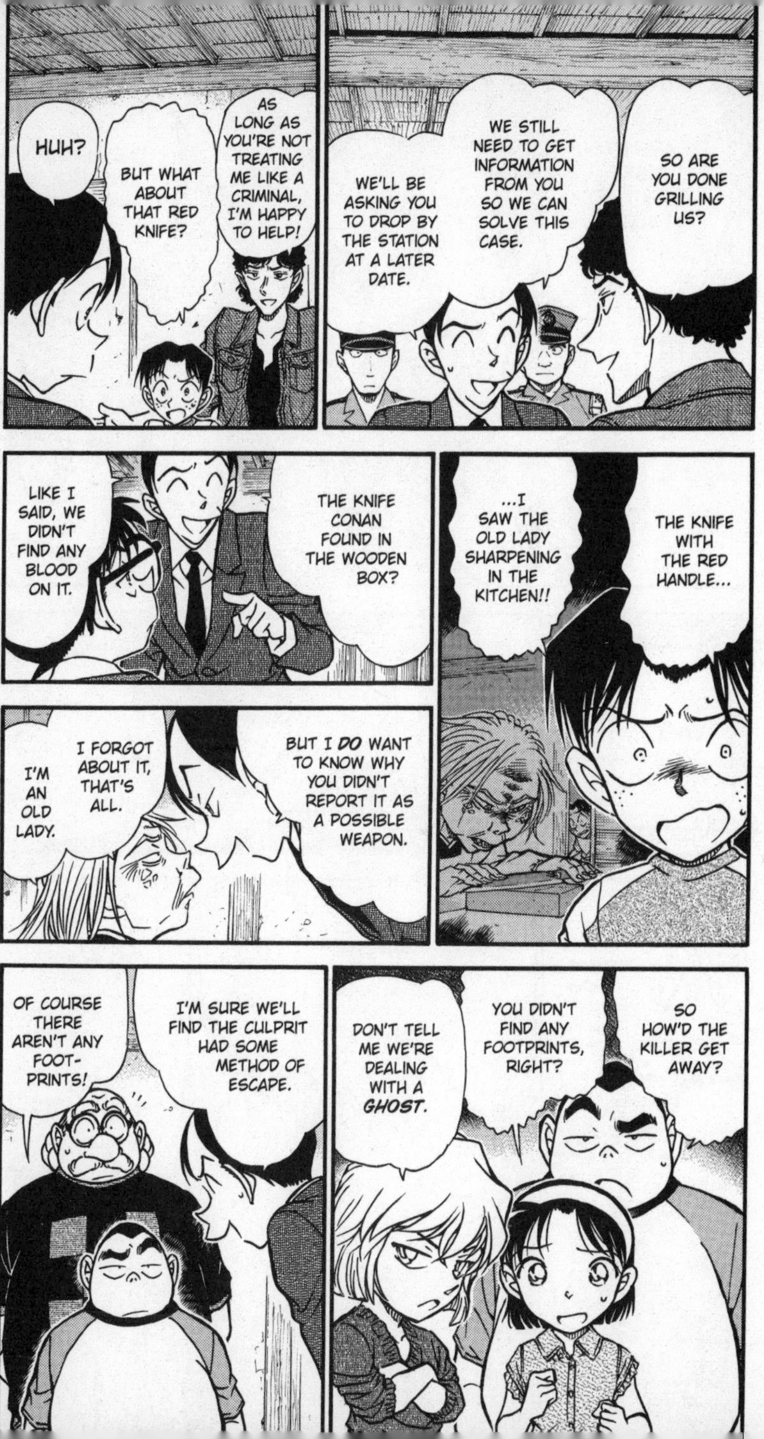
SO ARE YOU DONE GRILLING US?
WE STILL NEED TO GET INFORMATION FROM YOU SO WE CAN SOLVE THIS CASE.
WE'LL BE ASKING YOU TO DROP BY THE STATION AT A LATER DATE.
AS LONG AS YOU'RE NOT TREATING ME LIKE A CRIMINAL, I'M HAPPY TO HELP!
BUT WHAT ABOUT THAT RED KNIFE?
HUH?
THE KNIFE WITH THE RED HANDLE...
...I SAW THE OLD LADY SHARPENING IN THE KITCHEN!!
THE KNIFE CONAN FOUND IN THE WOODEN BOX?
LIKE I SAID, WE DIDN'T FIND ANY BLOOD ON IT.
BUT I *DO* WANT TO KNOW WHY YOU DIDN'T REPORT IT AS A POSSIBLE WEAPON.
I FORGOT ABOUT IT, THAT'S ALL.
I'M AN OLD LADY.
SO HOW'D THE KILLER GET AWAY?
YOU DIDN'T FIND ANY FOOTPRINTS, RIGHT?
DON'T TELL ME WE'RE DEALING WITH A *GHOST*.
I'M SURE WE'LL FIND THE CULPRIT HAD SOME METHOD OF ESCAPE.
OF COURSE THERE AREN'T ANY FOOT-PRINTS!

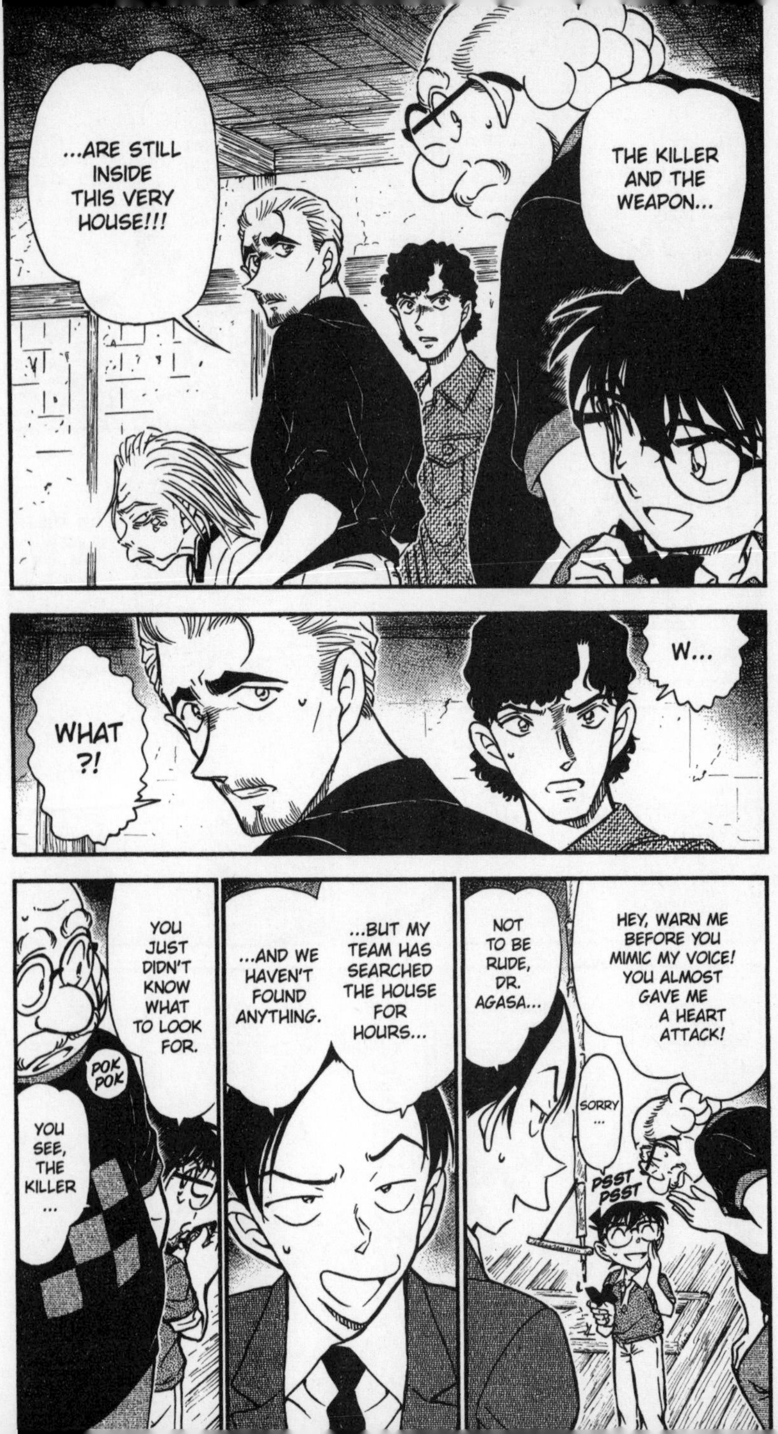
THE KILLER AND THE WEAPON...
...ARE STILL INSIDE THIS VERY HOUSE!!!
W...
WHAT ?!
HEY, WARN ME BEFORE YOU MIMIC MY VOICE! YOU ALMOST GAVE ME A HEART ATTACK!
NOT TO BE RUDE, DR. AGASA...
SORRY ...
PSST PSST
...BUT MY TEAM HAS SEARCHED THE HOUSE FOR HOURS...
...AND WE HAVEN'T FOUND ANYTHING.
YOU JUST DIDN'T KNOW WHAT TO LOOK FOR.
POK POK
YOU SEE, THE KILLER ...

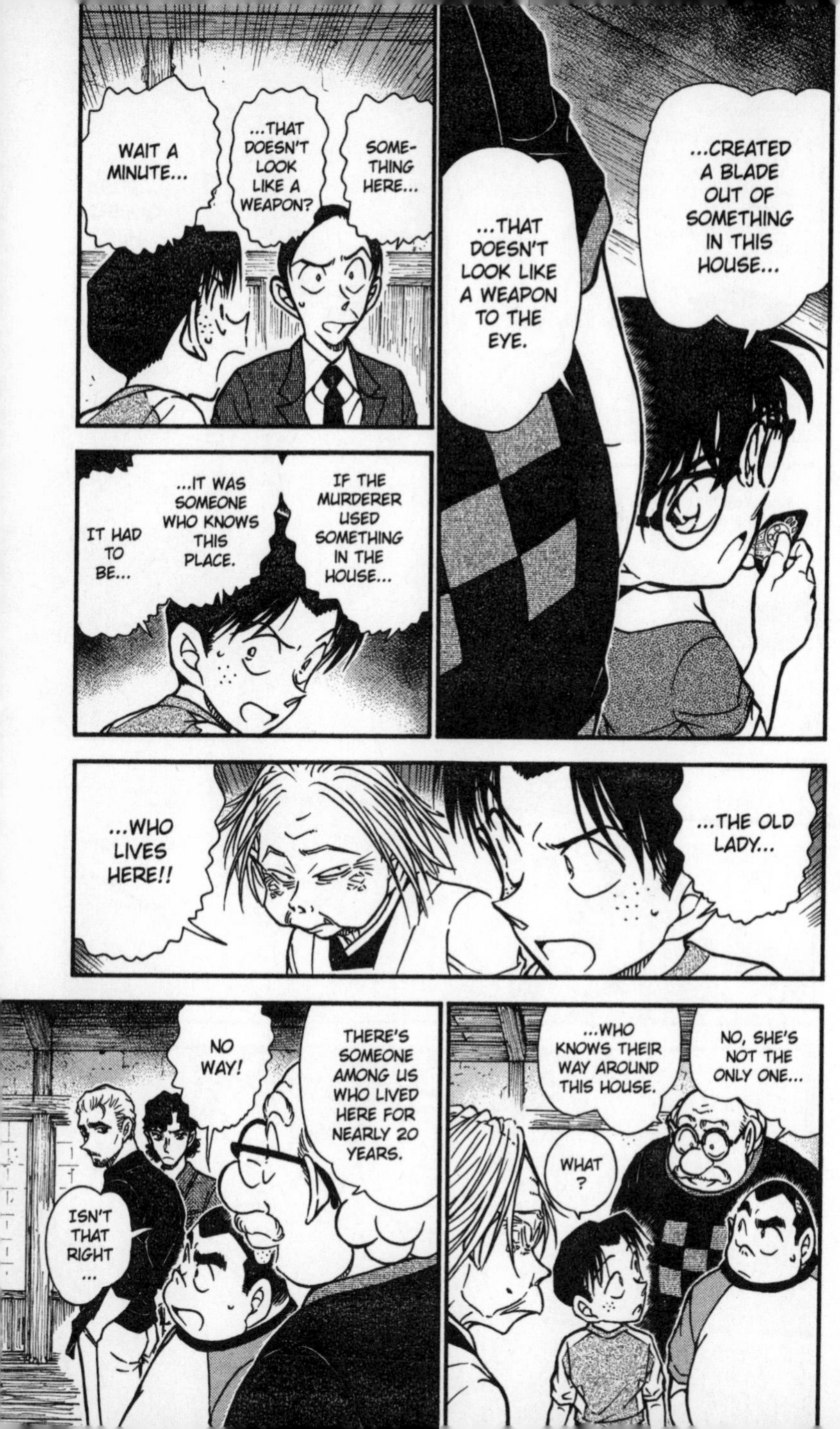
...CREATED A BLADE OUT OF SOMETHING IN THIS HOUSE...
...THAT DOESN'T LOOK LIKE A WEAPON TO THE EYE.
SOME-THING HERE...
...THAT DOESN'T LOOK LIKE A WEAPON?
WAIT A MINUTE...
IF THE MURDERER USED SOMETHING IN THE HOUSE...
...IT WAS SOMEONE WHO KNOWS THIS PLACE.
IT HAD TO BE...
...THE OLD LADY...
...WHO LIVES HERE!!
NO, SHE'S NOT THE ONLY ONE...
...WHO KNOWS THEIR WAY AROUND THIS HOUSE.
WHAT?
THERE'S SOMEONE AMONG US WHO LIVED HERE FOR NEARLY 20 YEARS.
NO WAY!
ISN'T THAT RIGHT...

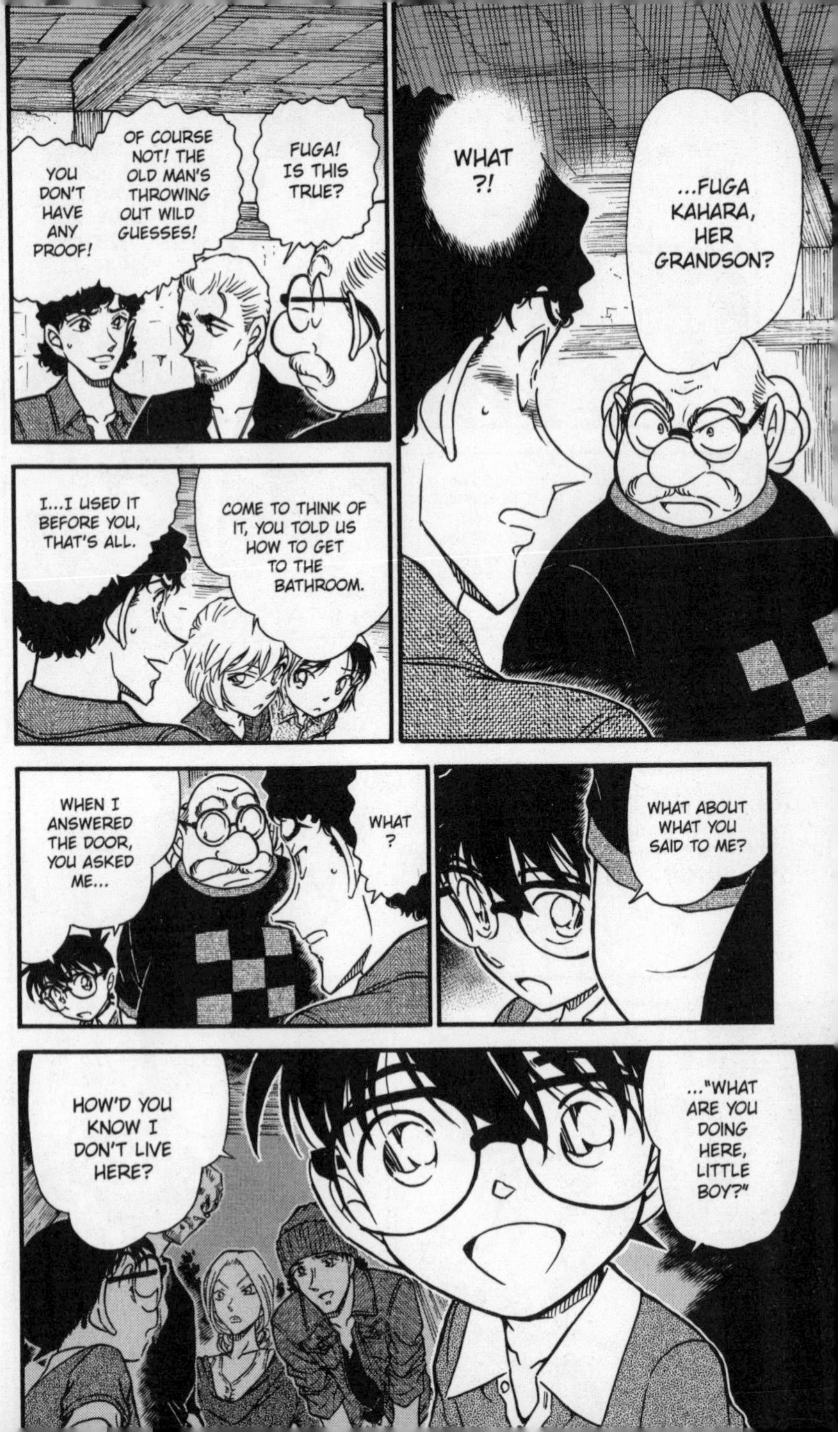
...FUGA KAHARA, HER GRANDSON?
WHAT ?!
FUGA! IS THIS TRUE?
OF COURSE NOT! THE OLD MAN'S THROWING OUT WILD GUESSES!
YOU DON'T HAVE ANY PROOF!
COME TO THINK OF IT, YOU TOLD US HOW TO GET TO THE BATHROOM.
I...I USED IT BEFORE YOU, THAT'S ALL.
WHAT ABOUT WHAT YOU SAID TO ME?
WHAT ?
WHEN I ANSWERED THE DOOR, YOU ASKED ME...
..."WHAT ARE YOU DOING HERE, LITTLE BOY?"
HOW'D YOU KNOW I DON'T LIVE HERE?

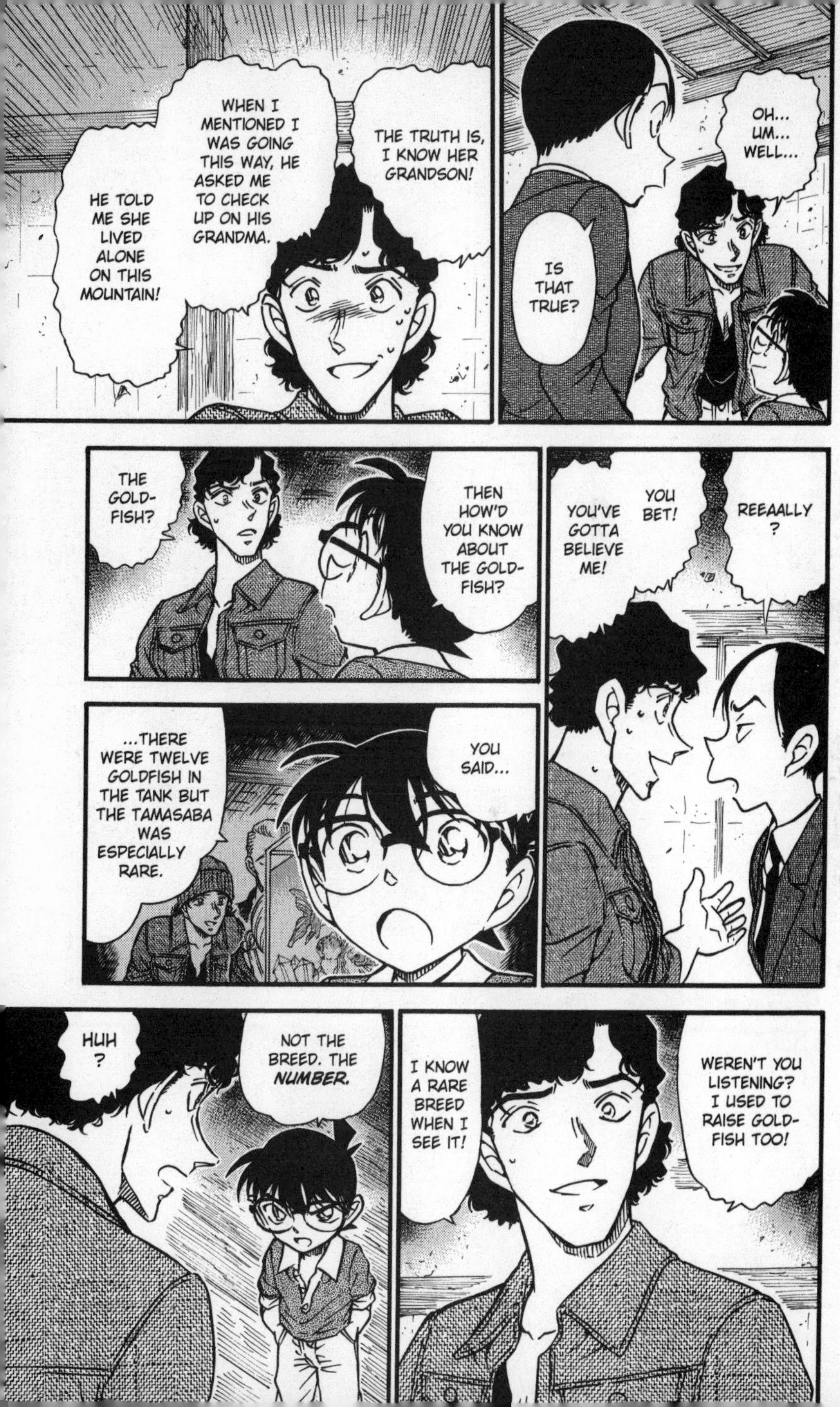
OH... UM... WELL...
IS THAT TRUE?
THE TRUTH IS, I KNOW HER GRANDSON!
WHEN I MENTIONED I WAS GOING THIS WAY, HE ASKED ME TO CHECK UP ON HIS GRANDMA.
HE TOLD ME SHE LIVED ALONE ON THIS MOUNTAIN!
REEAALLY?
YOU BET!
YOU'VE GOTTA BELIEVE ME!
THEN HOW'D YOU KNOW ABOUT THE GOLD-FISH?
THE GOLD-FISH?
YOU SAID...
...THERE WERE TWELVE GOLDFISH IN THE TANK BUT THE TAMASABA WAS ESPECIALLY RARE.
WEREN'T YOU LISTENING? I USED TO RAISE GOLD-FISH TOO!
I KNOW A RARE BREED WHEN I SEE IT!
NOT THE BREED. THE *NUMBER.*
HUH?

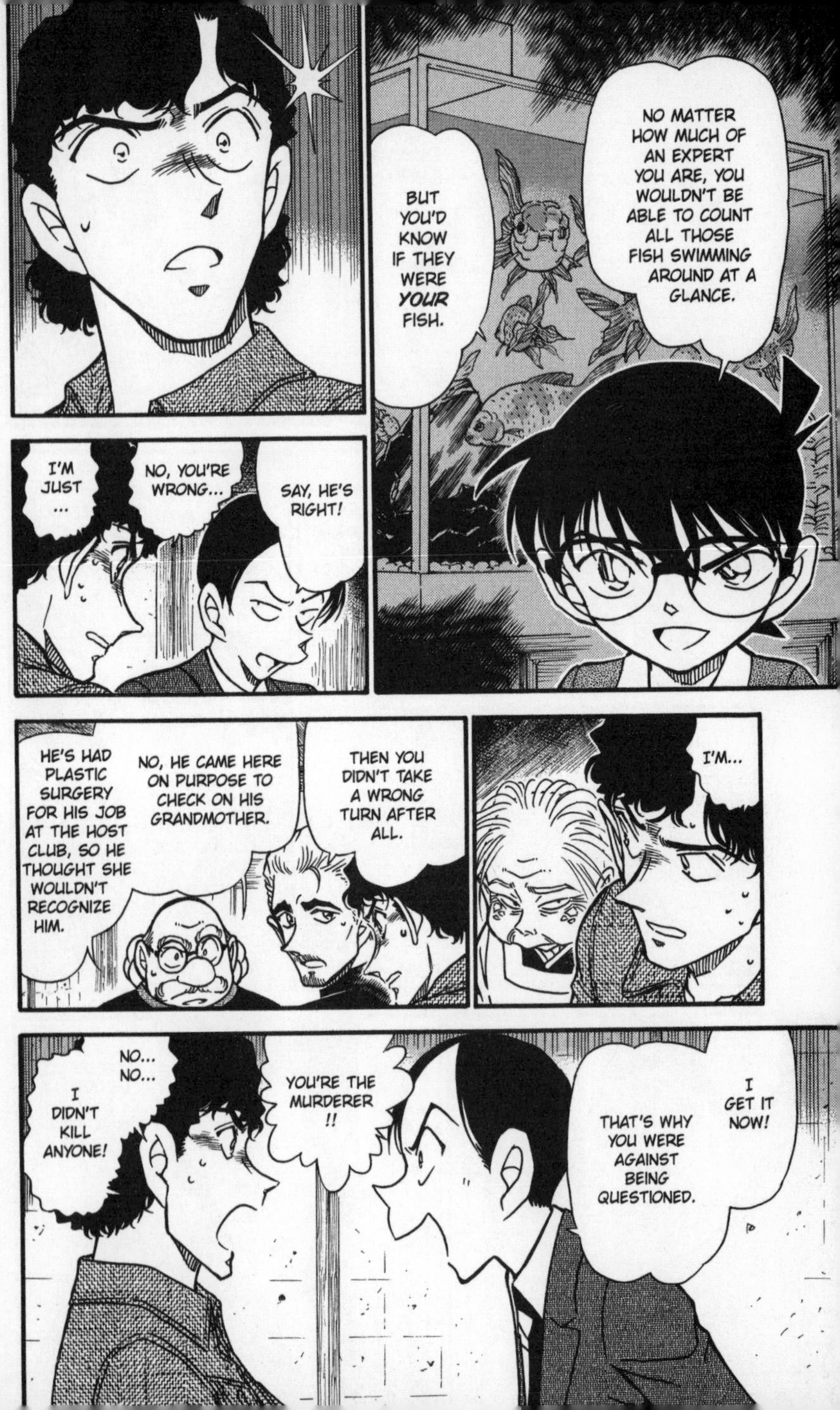
NO MATTER HOW MUCH OF AN EXPERT YOU ARE, YOU WOULDN'T BE ABLE TO COUNT ALL THOSE FISH SWIMMING AROUND AT A GLANCE.
BUT YOU'D KNOW IF THEY WERE *YOUR* FISH.
SAY, HE'S RIGHT!
NO, YOU'RE WRONG...
I'M JUST ...
I'M...
THEN YOU DIDN'T TAKE A WRONG TURN AFTER ALL.
NO, HE CAME HERE ON PURPOSE TO CHECK ON HIS GRANDMOTHER.
HE'S HAD PLASTIC SURGERY FOR HIS JOB AT THE HOST CLUB, SO HE THOUGHT SHE WOULDN'T RECOGNIZE HIM.
I GET IT NOW!
THAT'S WHY YOU WERE AGAINST BEING QUESTIONED.
YOU'RE THE MURDERER !!
NO... NO...
I DIDN'T KILL ANYONE!

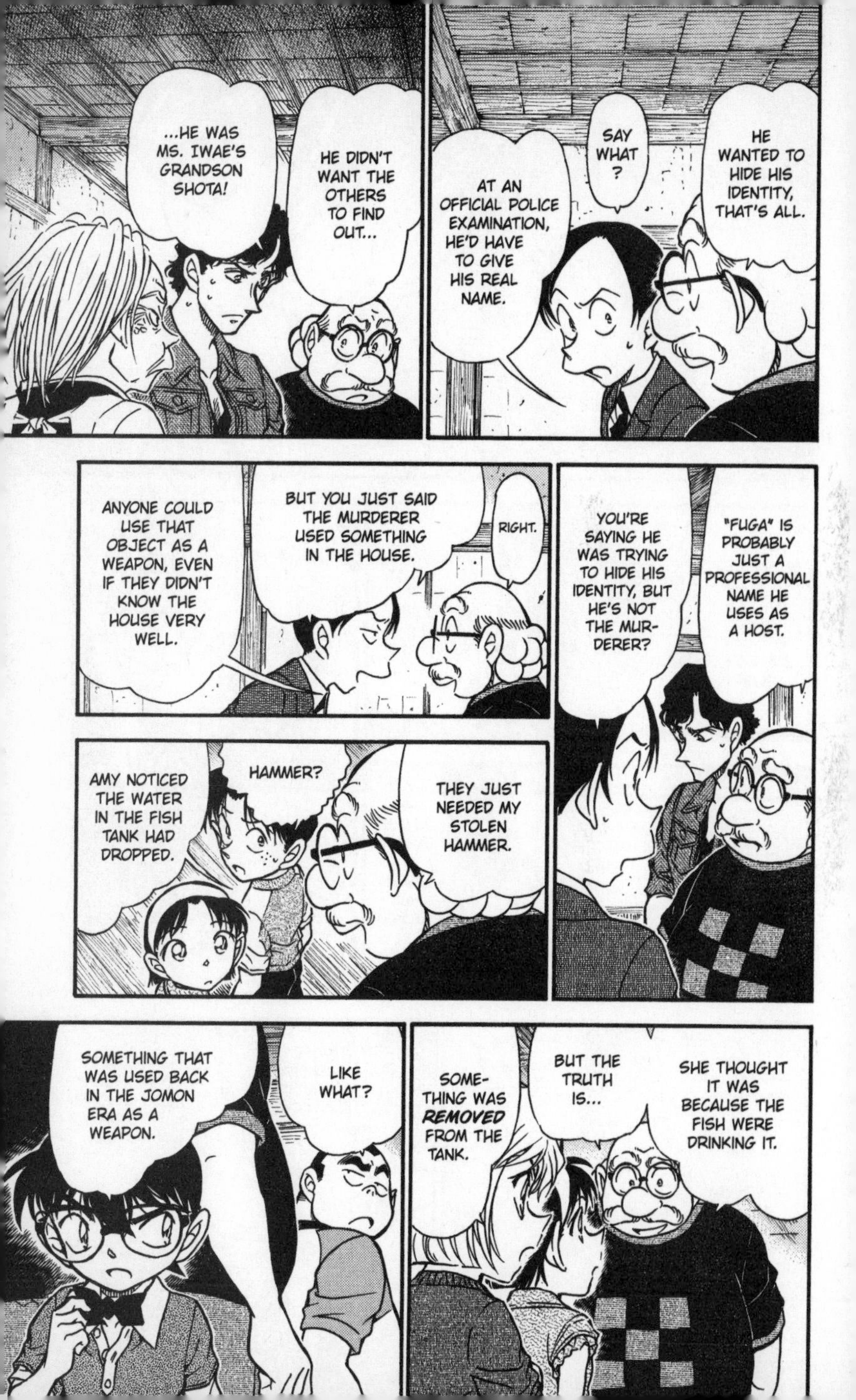
HE WANTED TO HIDE HIS IDENTITY, THAT'S ALL.
SAY WHAT?
AT AN OFFICIAL POLICE EXAMINATION, HE'D HAVE TO GIVE HIS REAL NAME.
HE DIDN'T WANT THE OTHERS TO FIND OUT...
...HE WAS MS. IWAE'S GRANDSON SHOTA!
"FUGA" IS PROBABLY JUST A PROFESSIONAL NAME HE USES AS A HOST.
YOU'RE SAYING HE WAS TRYING TO HIDE HIS IDENTITY, BUT HE'S NOT THE MUR-DERER?
RIGHT.
BUT YOU JUST SAID THE MURDERER USED SOMETHING IN THE HOUSE.
ANYONE COULD USE THAT OBJECT AS A WEAPON, EVEN IF THEY DIDN'T KNOW THE HOUSE VERY WELL.
THEY JUST NEEDED MY STOLEN HAMMER.
HAMMER?
AMY NOTICED THE WATER IN THE FISH TANK HAD DROPPED.
SHE THOUGHT IT WAS BECAUSE THE FISH WERE DRINKING IT.
BUT THE TRUTH IS...
SOME-THING WAS *REMOVED* FROM THE TANK.
LIKE WHAT?
SOMETHING THAT WAS USED BACK IN THE JOMON ERA AS A WEAPON.

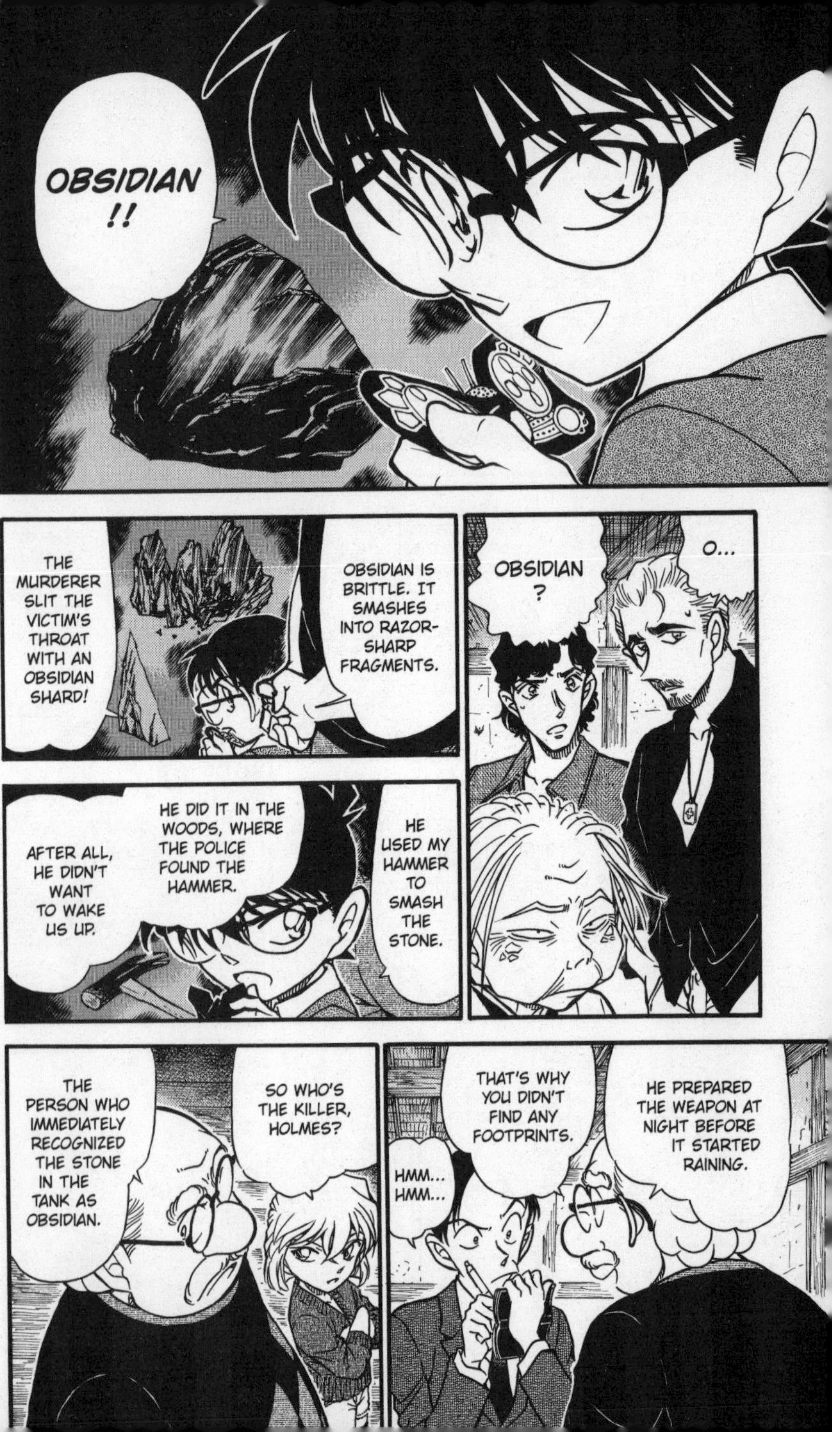
OBSIDIAN !!
O...
OBSIDIAN ?
OBSIDIAN IS BRITTLE. IT SMASHES INTO RAZOR-SHARP FRAGMENTS.
THE MURDERER SLIT THE VICTIM'S THROAT WITH AN OBSIDIAN SHARD!
HE USED MY HAMMER TO SMASH THE STONE.
HE DID IT IN THE WOODS, WHERE THE POLICE FOUND THE HAMMER.
AFTER ALL, HE DIDN'T WANT TO WAKE US UP.
HE PREPARED THE WEAPON AT NIGHT BEFORE IT STARTED RAINING.
THAT'S WHY YOU DIDN'T FIND ANY FOOTPRINTS.
HMM... HMM...
SO WHO'S THE KILLER, HOLMES?
THE PERSON WHO IMMEDIATELY RECOGNIZED THE STONE IN THE TANK AS OBSIDIAN.

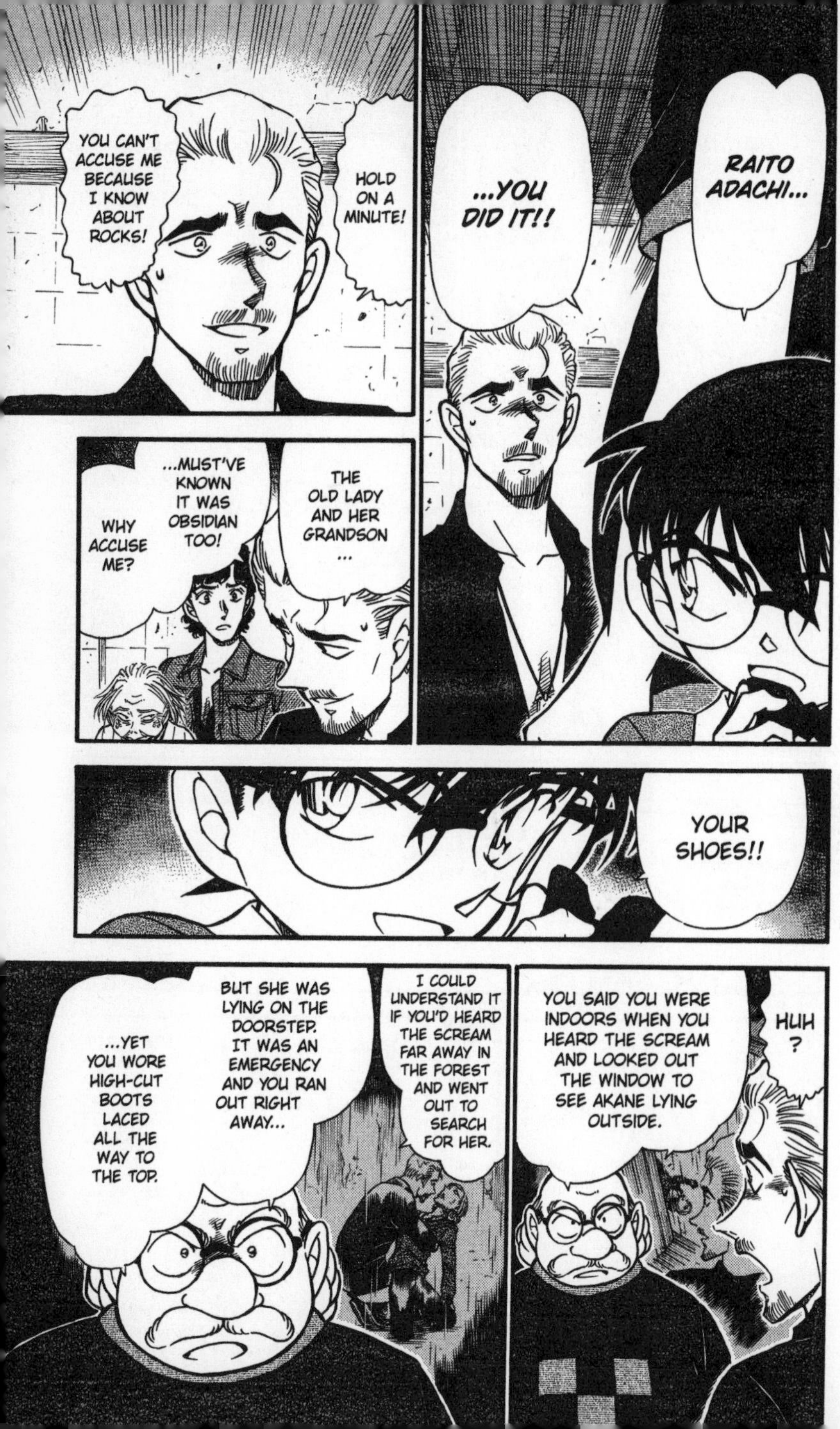
RAITO ADACHI...
...YOU DID IT!!
HOLD ON A MINUTE!
YOU CAN'T ACCUSE ME BECAUSE I KNOW ABOUT ROCKS!
THE OLD LADY AND HER GRANDSON ...
...MUST'VE KNOWN IT WAS OBSIDIAN TOO!
WHY ACCUSE ME?
YOUR SHOES!!
HUH?
YOU SAID YOU WERE INDOORS WHEN YOU HEARD THE SCREAM AND LOOKED OUT THE WINDOW TO SEE AKANE LYING OUTSIDE.
I COULD UNDERSTAND IT IF YOU'D HEARD THE SCREAM FAR AWAY IN THE FOREST AND WENT OUT TO SEARCH FOR HER.
BUT SHE WAS LYING ON THE DOORSTEP. IT WAS AN EMERGENCY AND YOU RAN OUT RIGHT AWAY...
...YET YOU WORE HIGH-CUT BOOTS LACED ALL THE WAY TO THE TOP.

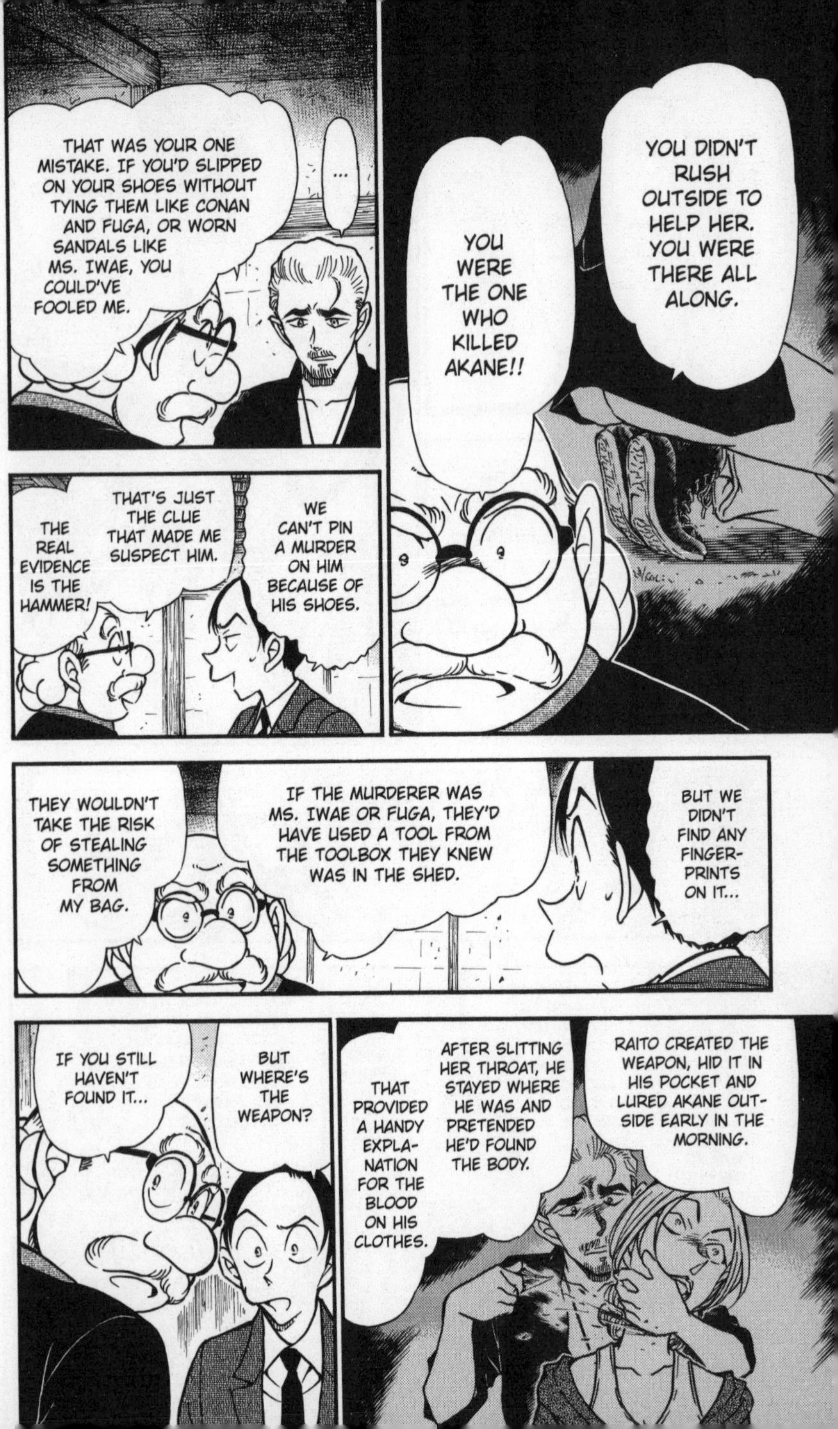
YOU DIDN'T RUSH OUTSIDE TO HELP HER. YOU WERE THERE ALL ALONG.
YOU WERE THE ONE WHO KILLED AKANE!!
...
THAT WAS YOUR ONE MISTAKE. IF YOU'D SLIPPED ON YOUR SHOES WITHOUT TYING THEM LIKE CONAN AND FUGA, OR WORN SANDALS LIKE MS. IWAE, YOU COULD'VE FOOLED ME.
WE CAN'T PIN A MURDER ON HIM BECAUSE OF HIS SHOES.
THAT'S JUST THE CLUE THAT MADE ME SUSPECT HIM.
THE REAL EVIDENCE IS THE HAMMER!
BUT WE DIDN'T FIND ANY FINGER-PRINTS ON IT...
IF THE MURDERER WAS MS. IWAE OR FUGA, THEY'D HAVE USED A TOOL FROM THE TOOLBOX THEY KNEW WAS IN THE SHED.
THEY WOULDN'T TAKE THE RISK OF STEALING SOMETHING FROM MY BAG.
RAITO CREATED THE WEAPON, HID IT IN HIS POCKET AND LURED AKANE OUT-SIDE EARLY IN THE MORNING.
AFTER SLITTING HER THROAT, HE STAYED WHERE HE WAS AND PRETENDED HE'D FOUND THE BODY.
THAT PROVIDED A HANDY EXPLA-NATION FOR THE BLOOD ON HIS CLOTHES.
BUT WHERE'S THE WEAPON?
IF YOU STILL HAVEN'T FOUND IT...

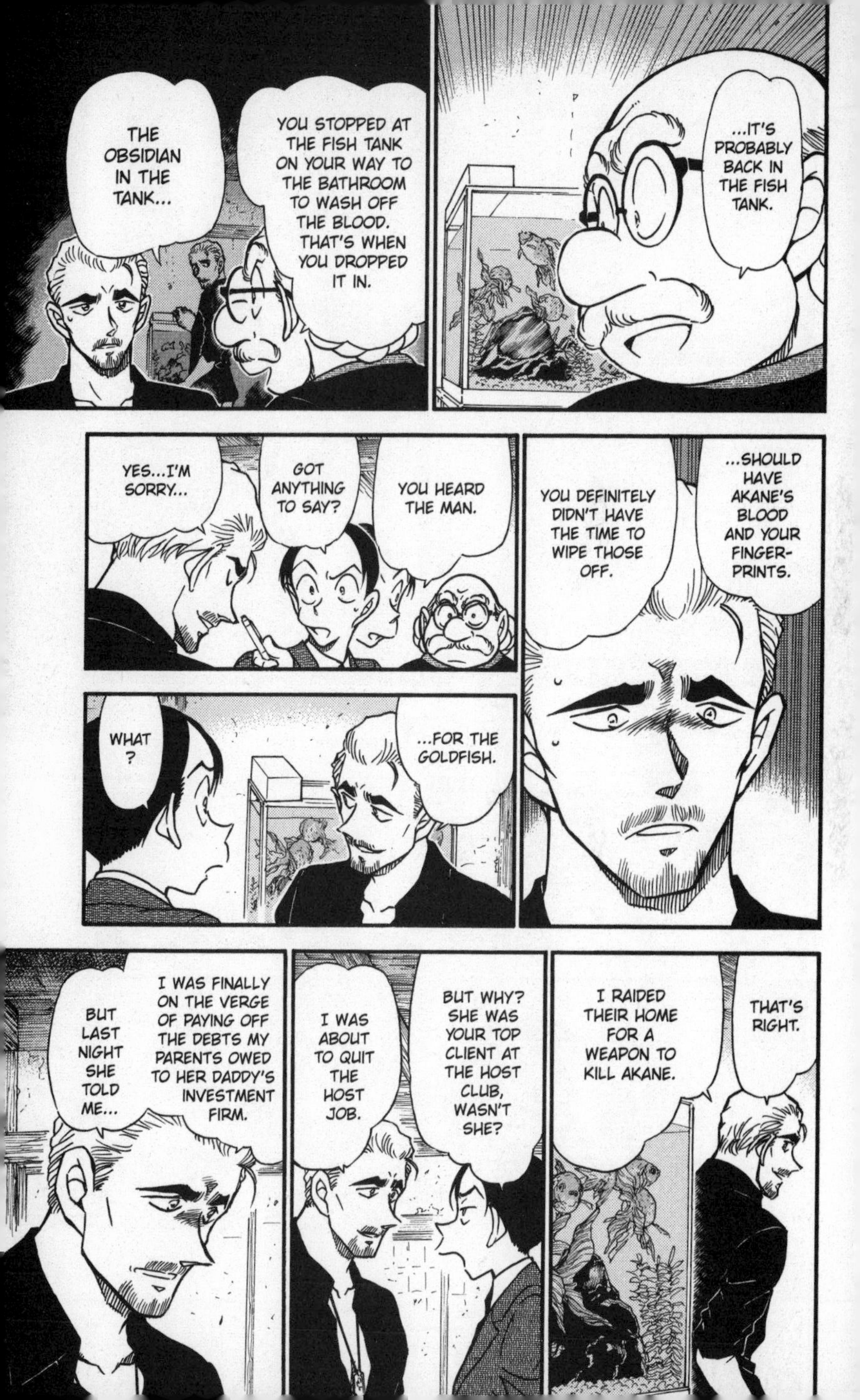
...IT'S PROBABLY BACK IN THE FISH TANK.
YOU STOPPED AT THE FISH TANK ON YOUR WAY TO THE BATHROOM TO WASH OFF THE BLOOD. THAT'S WHEN YOU DROPPED IT IN.
THE OBSIDIAN IN THE TANK...
...SHOULD HAVE AKANE'S BLOOD AND YOUR FINGER-PRINTS.
YOU DEFINITELY DIDN'T HAVE THE TIME TO WIPE THOSE OFF.
YOU HEARD THE MAN.
GOT ANYTHING TO SAY?
YES...I'M SORRY...
...FOR THE GOLDFISH.
WHAT?
THAT'S RIGHT.
I RAIDED THEIR HOME FOR A WEAPON TO KILL AKANE.
BUT WHY? SHE WAS YOUR TOP CLIENT AT THE HOST CLUB, WASN'T SHE?
I WAS ABOUT TO QUIT THE HOST JOB.
I WAS FINALLY ON THE VERGE OF PAYING OFF THE DEBTS MY PARENTS OWED TO HER DADDY'S INVESTMENT FIRM.
BUT LAST NIGHT SHE TOLD ME...

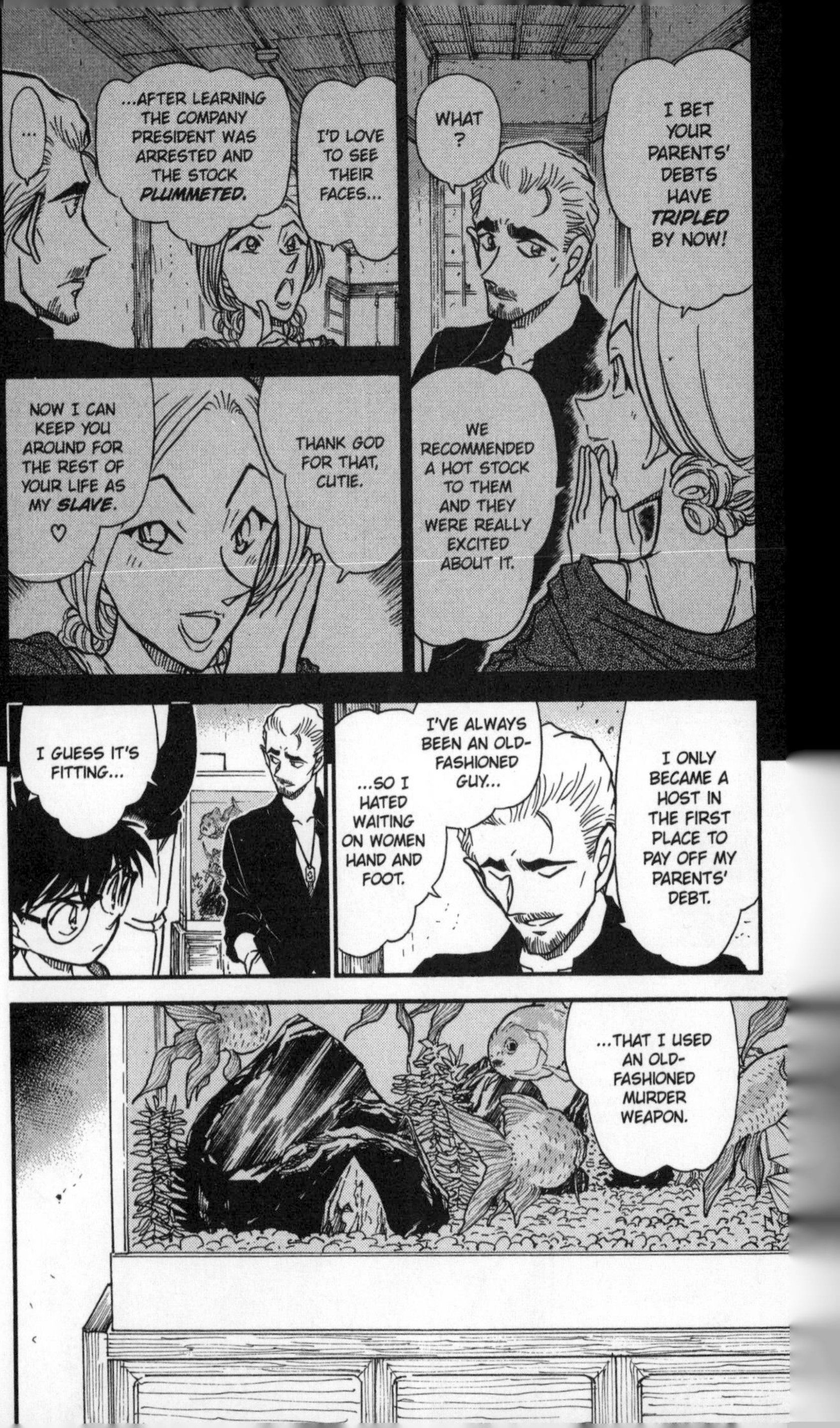
WHAT?
I BET YOUR PARENTS' DEBTS HAVE *TRIPLED* BY NOW!
WE RECOMMENDED A HOT STOCK TO THEM AND THEY WERE REALLY EXCITED ABOUT IT.
...AFTER LEARNING THE COMPANY PRESIDENT WAS ARRESTED AND THE STOCK *PLUMMETED.*
I'D LOVE TO SEE THEIR FACES...
...
THANK GOD FOR THAT, CUTIE.
NOW I CAN KEEP YOU AROUND FOR THE REST OF YOUR LIFE AS MY *SLAVE.* ♡
I ONLY BECAME A HOST IN THE FIRST PLACE TO PAY OFF MY PARENTS' DEBT.
I'VE ALWAYS BEEN AN OLD-FASHIONED GUY...
...SO I HATED WAITING ON WOMEN HAND AND FOOT.
I GUESS IT'S FITTING...
...THAT I USED AN OLD-FASHIONED MURDER WEAPON.

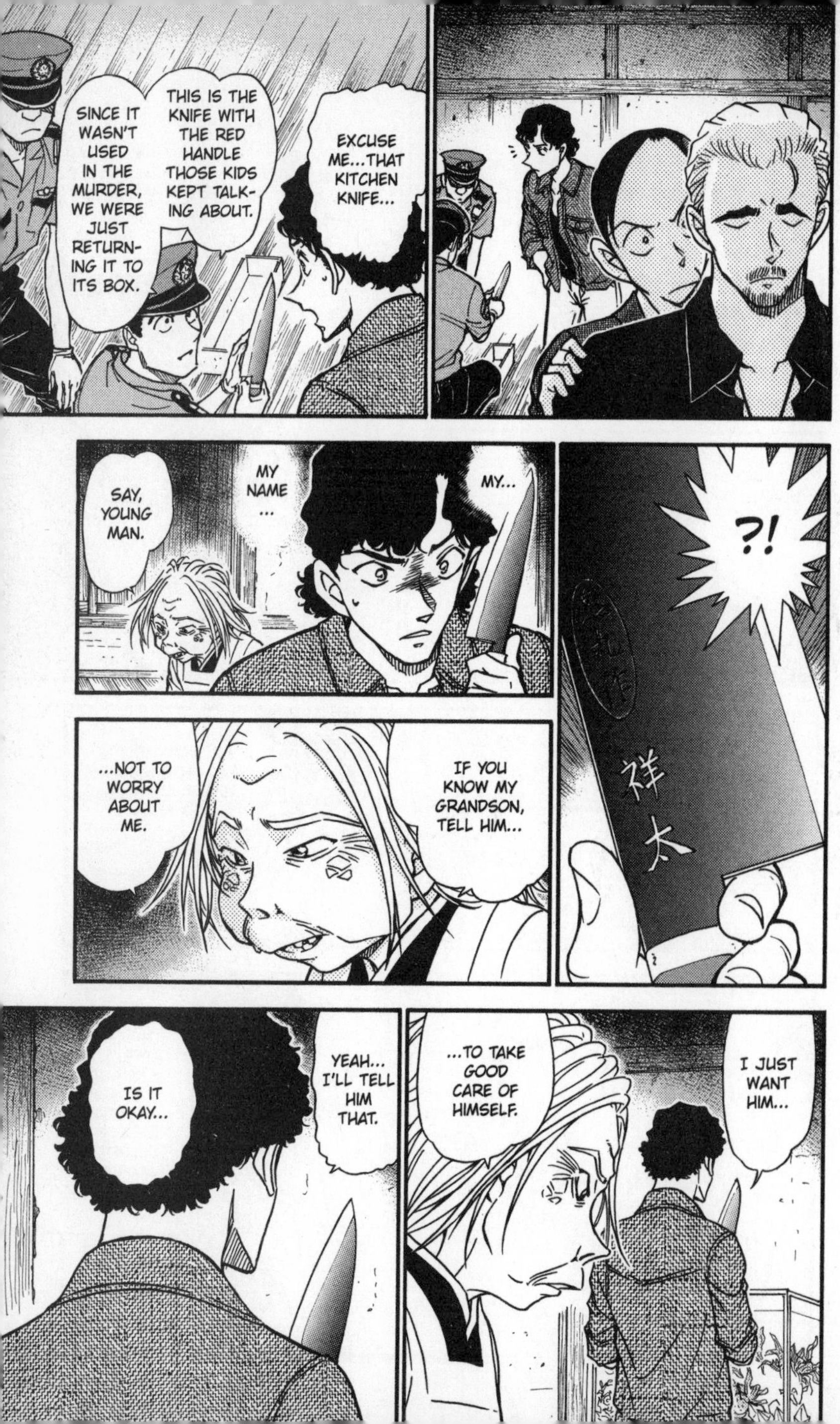
EXCUSE ME...THAT KITCHEN KNIFE...
THIS IS THE KNIFE WITH THE RED HANDLE THOSE KIDS KEPT TALKING ABOUT.
SINCE IT WASN'T USED IN THE MURDER, WE WERE JUST RETURNING IT TO ITS BOX.
?!
祥太
MY...
MY NAME ...
SAY, YOUNG MAN.
IF YOU KNOW MY GRANDSON, TELL HIM...
...NOT TO WORRY ABOUT ME.
I JUST WANT HIM...
...TO TAKE GOOD CARE OF HIMSELF.
YEAH... I'LL TELL HIM THAT.
IS IT OKAY...

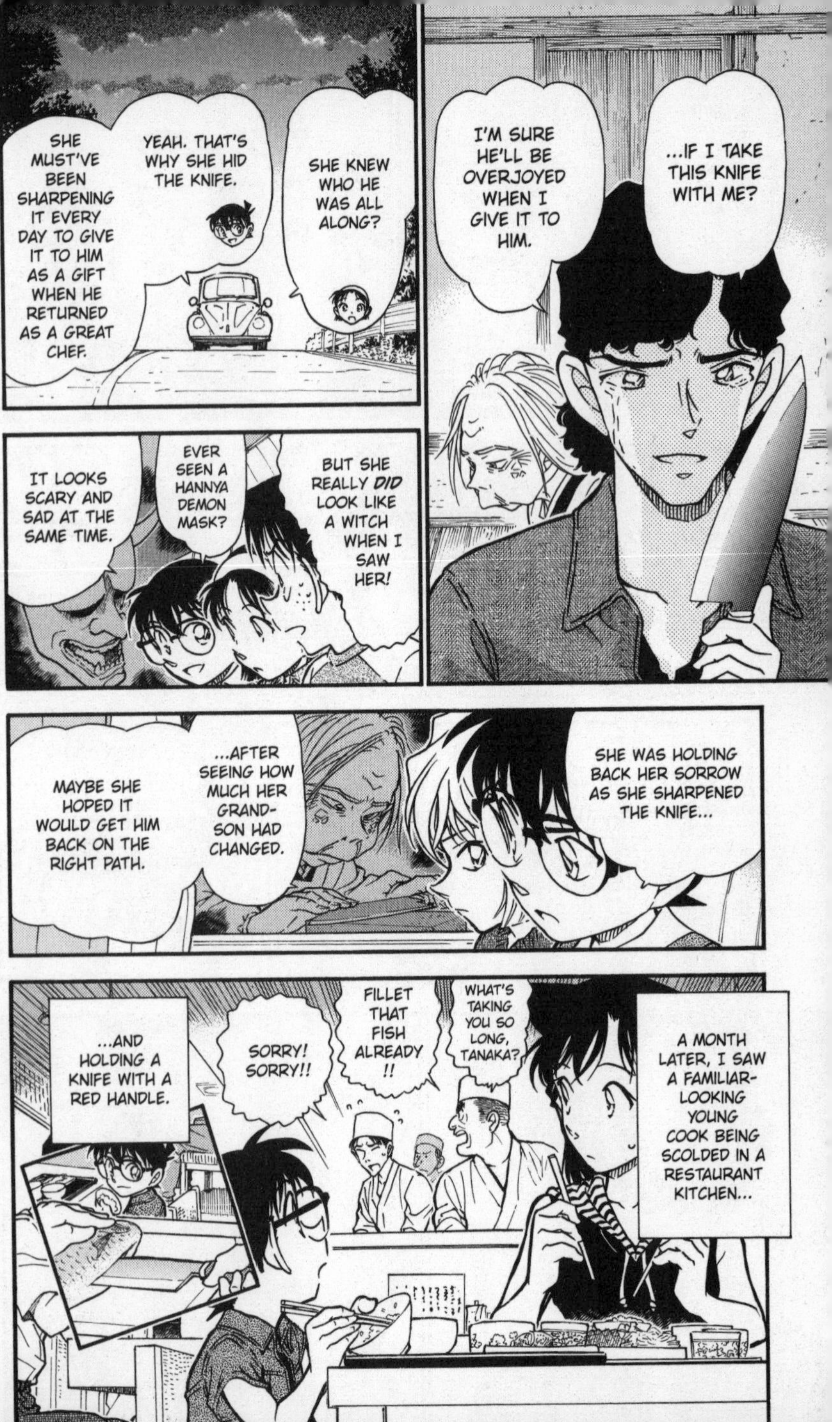
...IF I TAKE THIS KNIFE WITH ME?
I'M SURE HE'LL BE OVERJOYED WHEN I GIVE IT TO HIM.
SHE KNEW WHO HE WAS ALL ALONG?
YEAH. THAT'S WHY SHE HID THE KNIFE.
SHE MUST'VE BEEN SHARPENING IT EVERY DAY TO GIVE IT TO HIM AS A GIFT WHEN HE RETURNED AS A GREAT CHEF.
BUT SHE REALLY DID LOOK LIKE A WITCH WHEN I SAW HER!
EVER SEEN A HANNYA DEMON MASK?
IT LOOKS SCARY AND SAD AT THE SAME TIME.
SHE WAS HOLDING BACK HER SORROW AS SHE SHARPENED THE KNIFE...
...AFTER SEEING HOW MUCH HER GRAND-SON HAD CHANGED.
MAYBE SHE HOPED IT WOULD GET HIM BACK ON THE RIGHT PATH.
A MONTH LATER, I SAW A FAMILIAR-LOOKING YOUNG COOK BEING SCOLDED IN A RESTAURANT KITCHEN...
WHAT'S TAKING YOU SO LONG, TANAKA?
FILLET THAT FISH ALREADY!!
SORRY! SORRY!!
...AND HOLDING A KNIFE WITH A RED HANDLE.

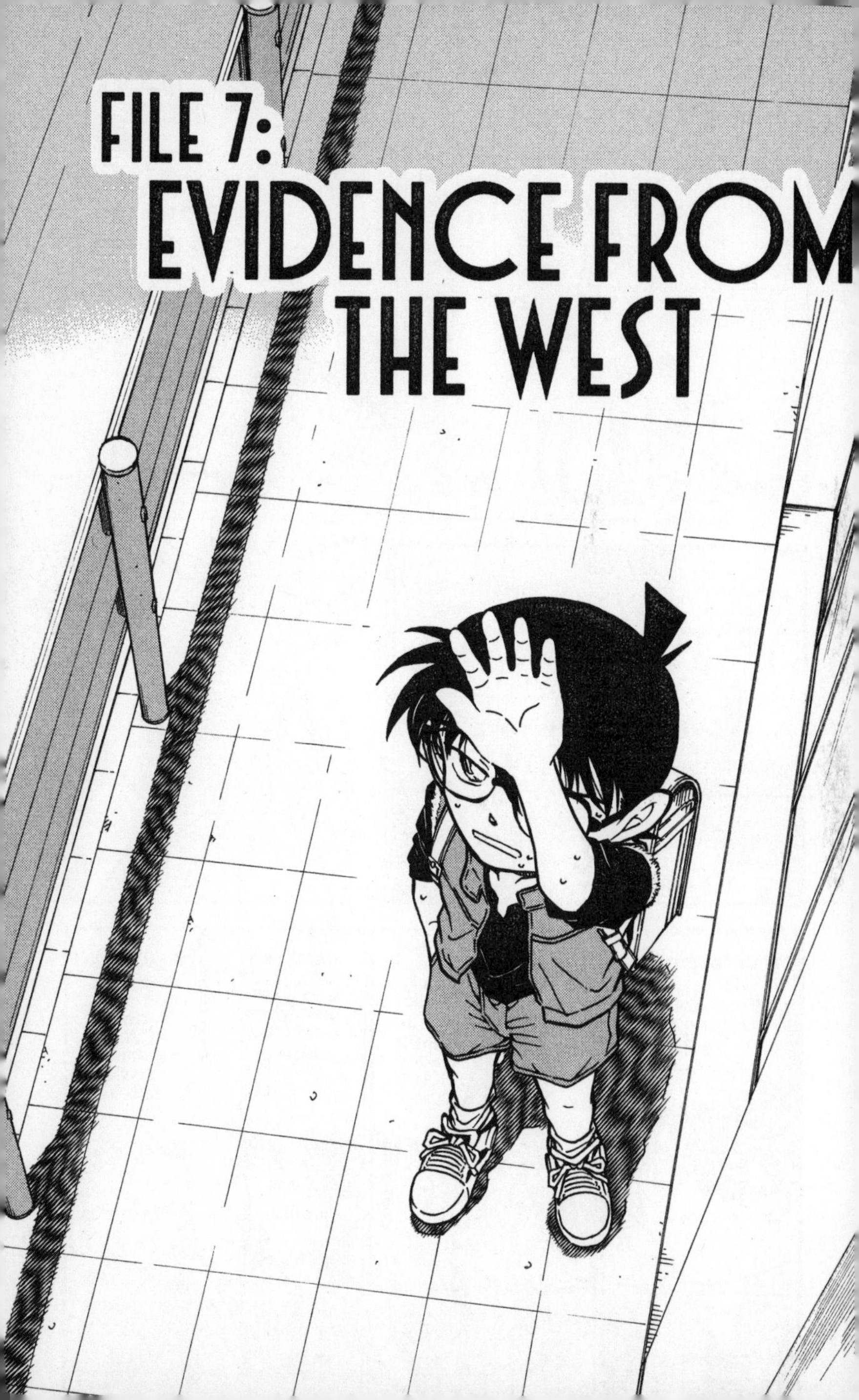
FILE 7:
EVIDENCE FROM THE WEST

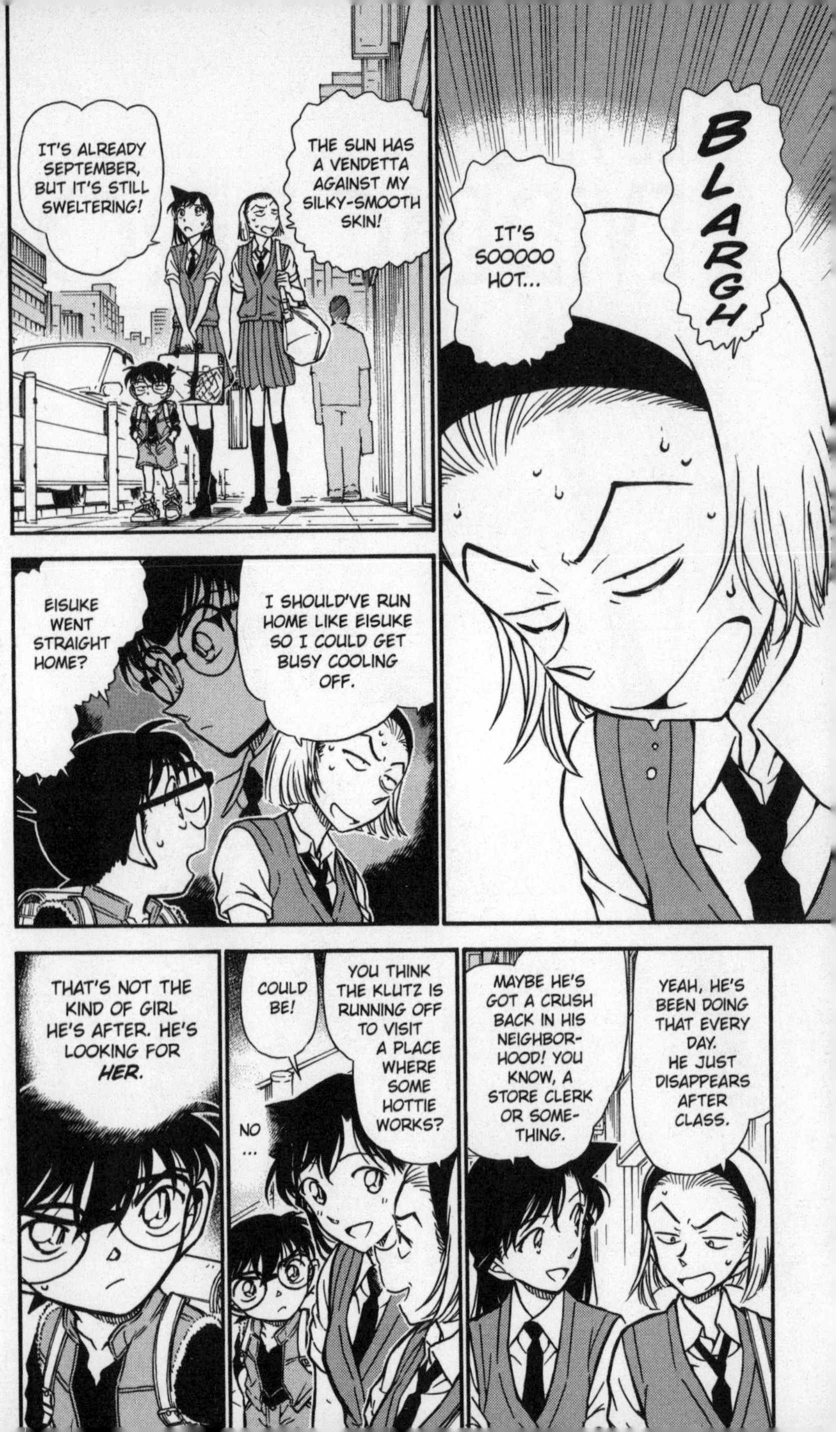
BLARGH
IT'S SOOOOO HOT...
THE SUN HAS A VENDETTA AGAINST MY SILKY-SMOOTH SKIN!
IT'S ALREADY SEPTEMBER, BUT IT'S STILL SWELTERING!
I SHOULD'VE RUN HOME LIKE EISUKE SO I COULD GET BUSY COOLING OFF.
EISUKE WENT STRAIGHT HOME?
YEAH, HE'S BEEN DOING THAT EVERY DAY. HE JUST DISAPPEARS AFTER CLASS.
MAYBE HE'S GOT A CRUSH BACK IN HIS NEIGHBOR-HOOD! YOU KNOW, A STORE CLERK OR SOME-THING.
YOU THINK THE KLUTZ IS RUNNING OFF TO VISIT A PLACE WHERE SOME HOTTIE WORKS?
COULD BE!
NO ...
THAT'S NOT THE KIND OF GIRL HE'S AFTER. HE'S LOOKING FOR **HER**.

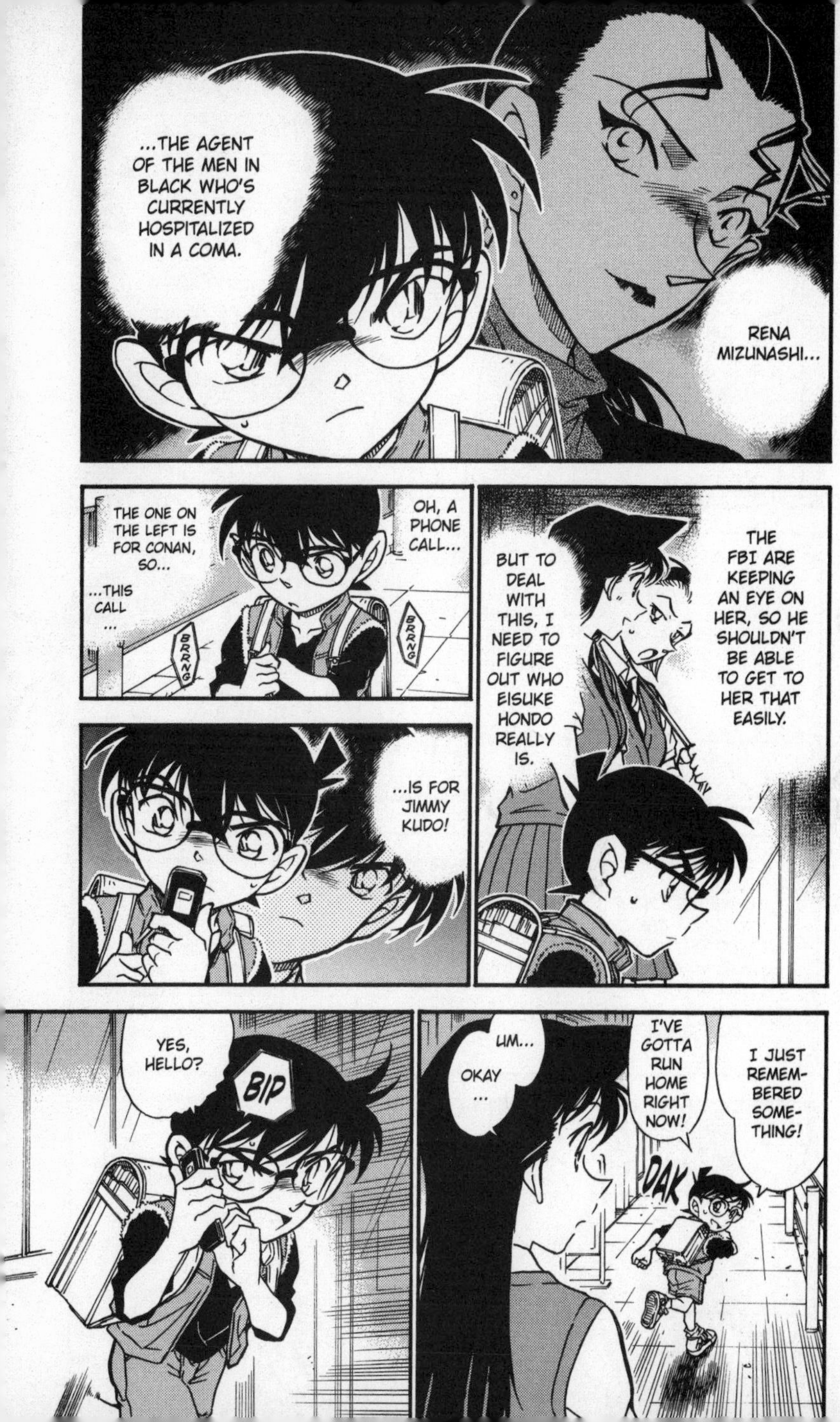
RENA MIZUNASHI...
...THE AGENT OF THE MEN IN BLACK WHO'S CURRENTLY HOSPITALIZED IN A COMA.
THE FBI ARE KEEPING AN EYE ON HER, SO HE SHOULDN'T BE ABLE TO GET TO HER THAT EASILY.
BUT TO DEAL WITH THIS, I NEED TO FIGURE OUT WHO EISUKE HONDO REALLY IS.
OH, A PHONE CALL...
BRRNG
THE ONE ON THE LEFT IS FOR CONAN, SO...
...THIS CALL ...
BRRNG
...IS FOR JIMMY KUDO!
I JUST REMEM-BERED SOME-THING!
I'VE GOTTA RUN HOME RIGHT NOW!
UM... OKAY ...
DAK
YES, HELLO?
BIP

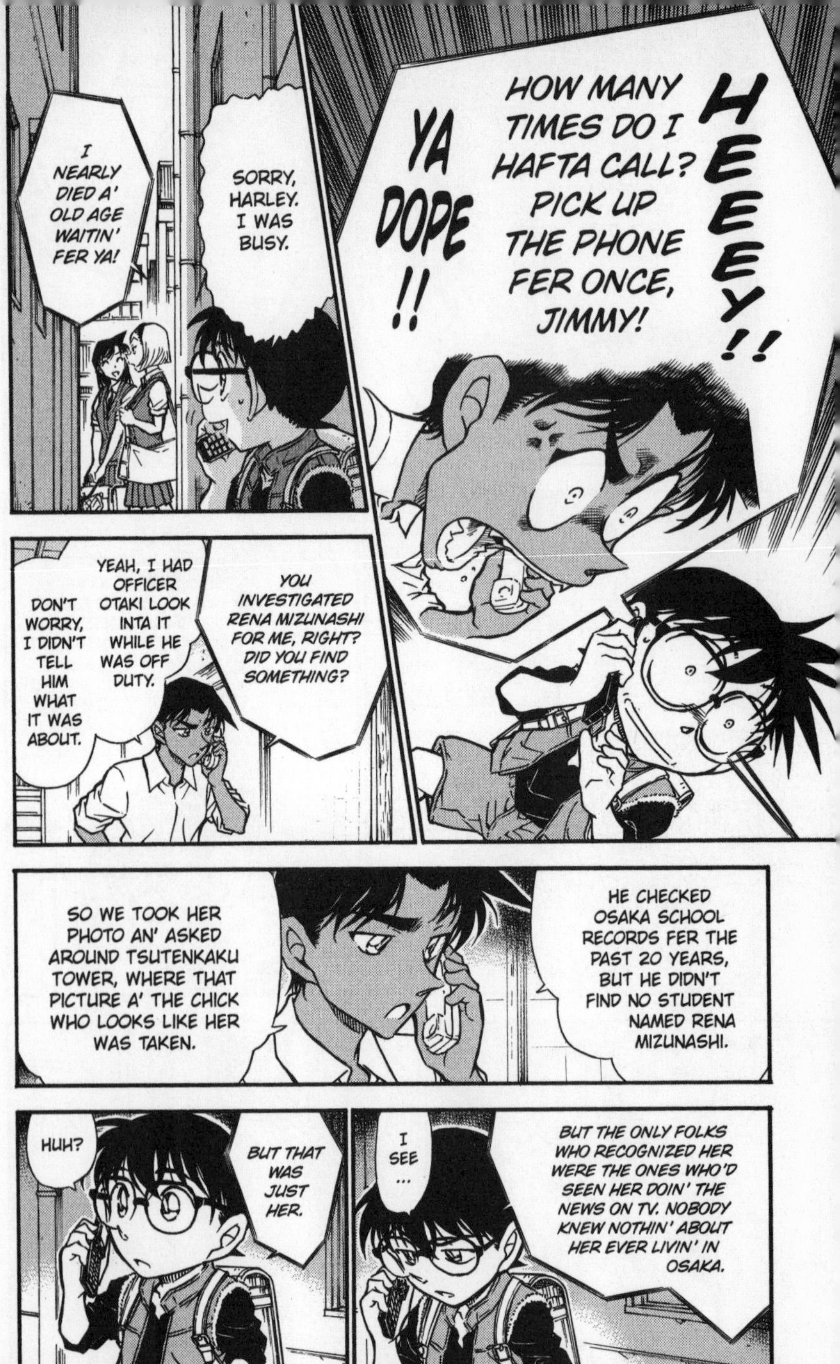
HEEEY!!
HOW MANY TIMES DO I HAFTA CALL? PICK UP THE PHONE FER ONCE, JIMMY!
YA DOPE!!
SORRY, HARLEY. I WAS BUSY.
I NEARLY DIED A' OLD AGE WAITIN' FER YA!
YOU INVESTIGATED RENA MIZUNASHI FOR ME, RIGHT? DID YOU FIND SOMETHING?
YEAH, I HAD OFFICER OTAKI LOOK INTA IT WHILE HE WAS OFF DUTY.
DON'T WORRY, I DIDN'T TELL HIM WHAT IT WAS ABOUT.
HE CHECKED OSAKA SCHOOL RECORDS FER THE PAST 20 YEARS, BUT HE DIDN'T FIND NO STUDENT NAMED RENA MIZUNASHI.
SO WE TOOK HER PHOTO AN' ASKED AROUND TSUTENKAKU TOWER, WHERE THAT PICTURE A' THE CHICK WHO LOOKS LIKE HER WAS TAKEN.
BUT THE ONLY FOLKS WHO RECOGNIZED HER WERE THE ONES WHO'D SEEN HER DOIN' THE NEWS ON TV. NOBODY KNEW NOTHIN' ABOUT HER EVER LIVIN' IN OSAKA.
I SEE ...
BUT THAT WAS JUST HER.
HUH?

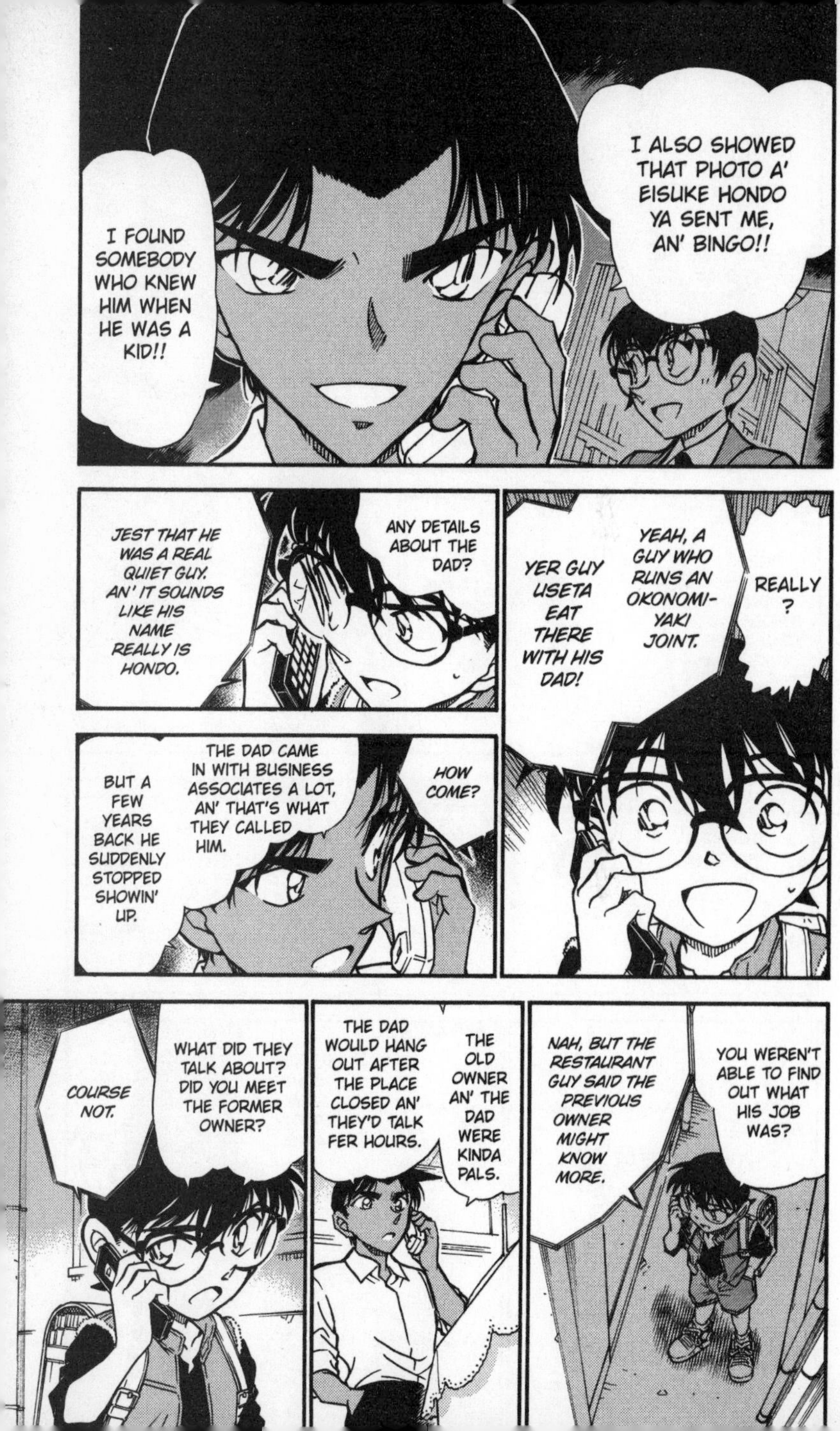
I ALSO SHOWED THAT PHOTO A' EISUKE HONDO YA SENT ME, AN' BINGO!!
I FOUND SOMEBODY WHO KNEW HIM WHEN HE WAS A KID!!
REALLY?
YEAH, A GUY WHO RUNS AN OKONOMI-YAKI JOINT.
YER GUY USETA EAT THERE WITH HIS DAD!
ANY DETAILS ABOUT THE DAD?
JEST THAT HE WAS A REAL QUIET GUY. AN' IT SOUNDS LIKE HIS NAME REALLY IS HONDO.
HOW COME?
THE DAD CAME IN WITH BUSINESS ASSOCIATES A LOT, AN' THAT'S WHAT THEY CALLED HIM.
BUT A FEW YEARS BACK HE SUDDENLY STOPPED SHOWIN' UP.
YOU WEREN'T ABLE TO FIND OUT WHAT HIS JOB WAS?
NAH, BUT THE RESTAURANT GUY SAID THE PREVIOUS OWNER MIGHT KNOW MORE.
THE OLD OWNER AN' THE DAD WERE KINDA PALS.
THE DAD WOULD HANG OUT AFTER THE PLACE CLOSED AN' THEY'D TALK FER HOURS.
WHAT DID THEY TALK ABOUT? DID YOU MEET THE FORMER OWNER?
COURSE NOT.

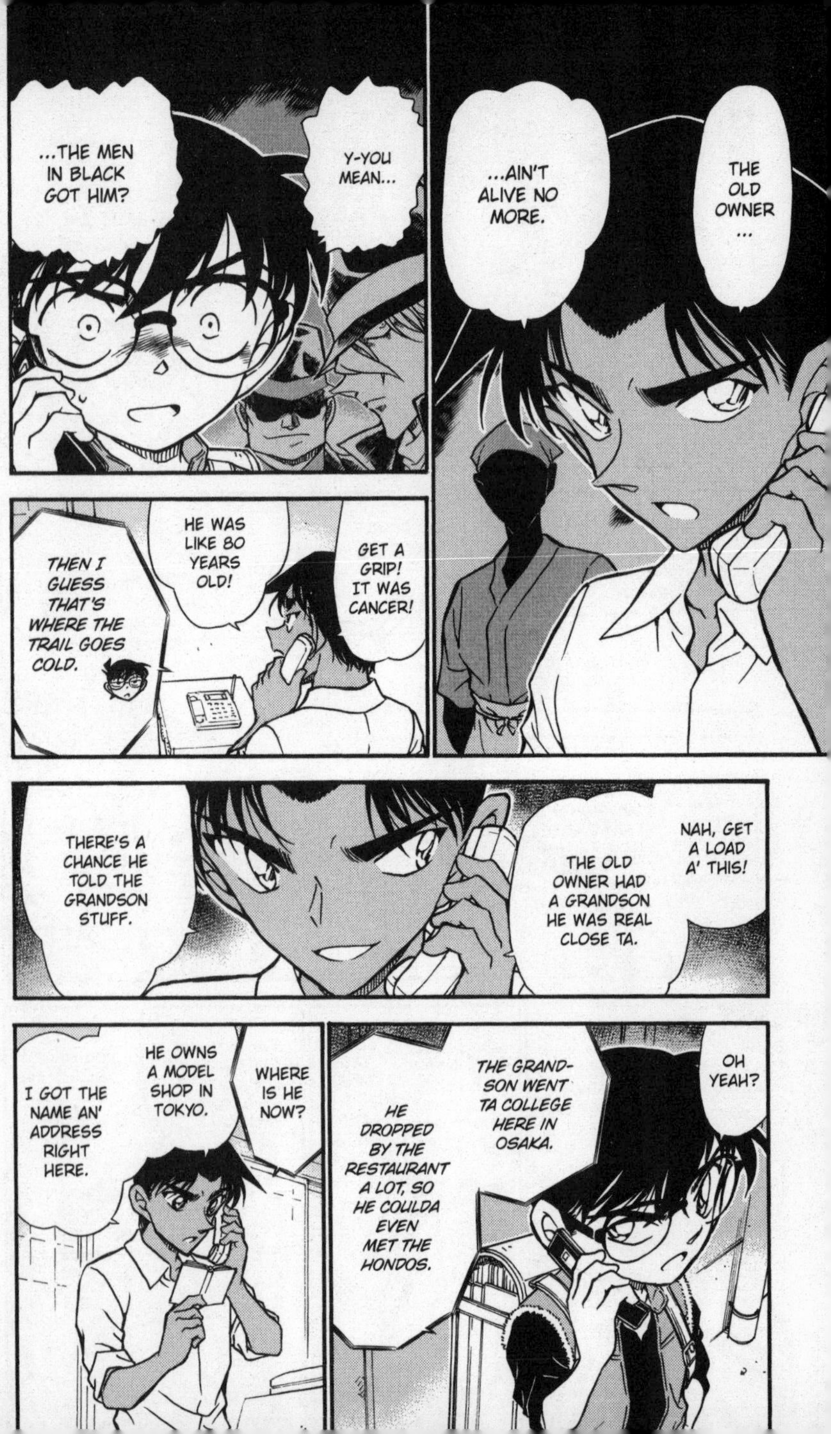
THE OLD OWNER ...
...AIN'T ALIVE NO MORE.
Y-YOU MEAN...
...THE MEN IN BLACK GOT HIM?
GET A GRIP! IT WAS CANCER!
HE WAS LIKE 80 YEARS OLD!
THEN I GUESS THAT'S WHERE THE TRAIL GOES COLD.
NAH, GET A LOAD A' THIS!
THE OLD OWNER HAD A GRANDSON HE WAS REAL CLOSE TA.
THERE'S A CHANCE HE TOLD THE GRANDSON STUFF.
OH YEAH?
THE GRAND-SON WENT TA COLLEGE HERE IN OSAKA.
HE DROPPED BY THE RESTAURANT A LOT, SO HE COULDA EVEN MET THE HONDOS.
WHERE IS HE NOW?
HE OWNS A MODEL SHOP IN TOKYO.
I GOT THE NAME AN' ADDRESS RIGHT HERE.

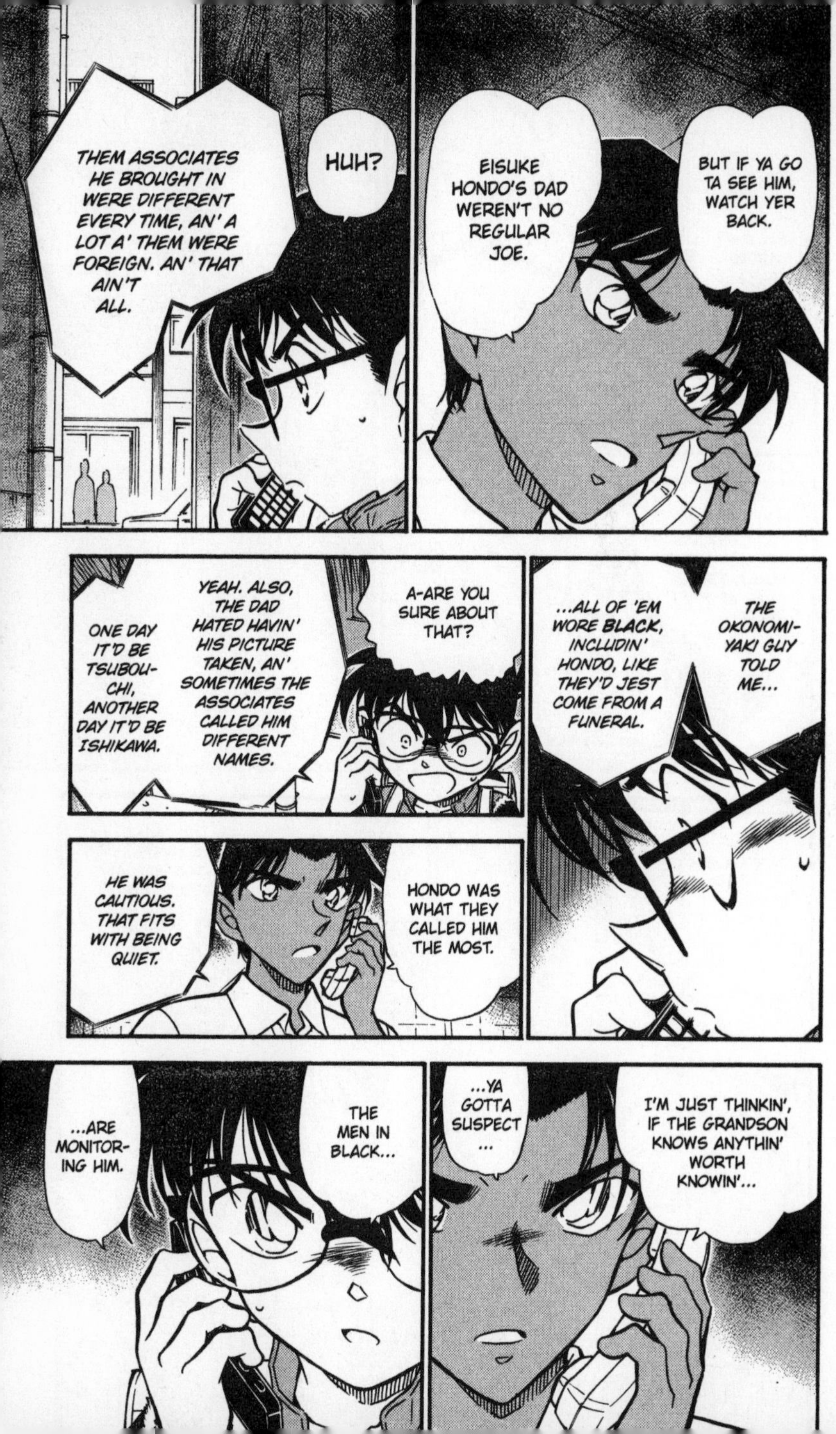
BUT IF YA GO TA SEE HIM, WATCH YER BACK.
EISUKE HONDO'S DAD WEREN'T NO REGULAR JOE.
HUH?
THEM ASSOCIATES HE BROUGHT IN WERE DIFFERENT EVERY TIME, AN' A LOT A' THEM WERE FOREIGN. AN' THAT AIN'T ALL.
THE OKONOMI-YAKI GUY TOLD ME...
...ALL OF 'EM WORE BLACK, INCLUDIN' HONDO, LIKE THEY'D JEST COME FROM A FUNERAL.
A-ARE YOU SURE ABOUT THAT?
YEAH. ALSO, THE DAD HATED HAVIN' HIS PICTURE TAKEN, AN' SOMETIMES THE ASSOCIATES CALLED HIM DIFFERENT NAMES.
ONE DAY IT'D BE TSUBOU-CHI, ANOTHER DAY IT'D BE ISHIKAWA.
HONDO WAS WHAT THEY CALLED HIM THE MOST.
HE WAS CAUTIOUS. THAT FITS WITH BEING QUIET.
I'M JUST THINKIN', IF THE GRANDSON KNOWS ANYTHIN' WORTH KNOWIN'...
...YA GOTTA SUSPECT ...
THE MEN IN BLACK...
...ARE MONITOR-ING HIM.

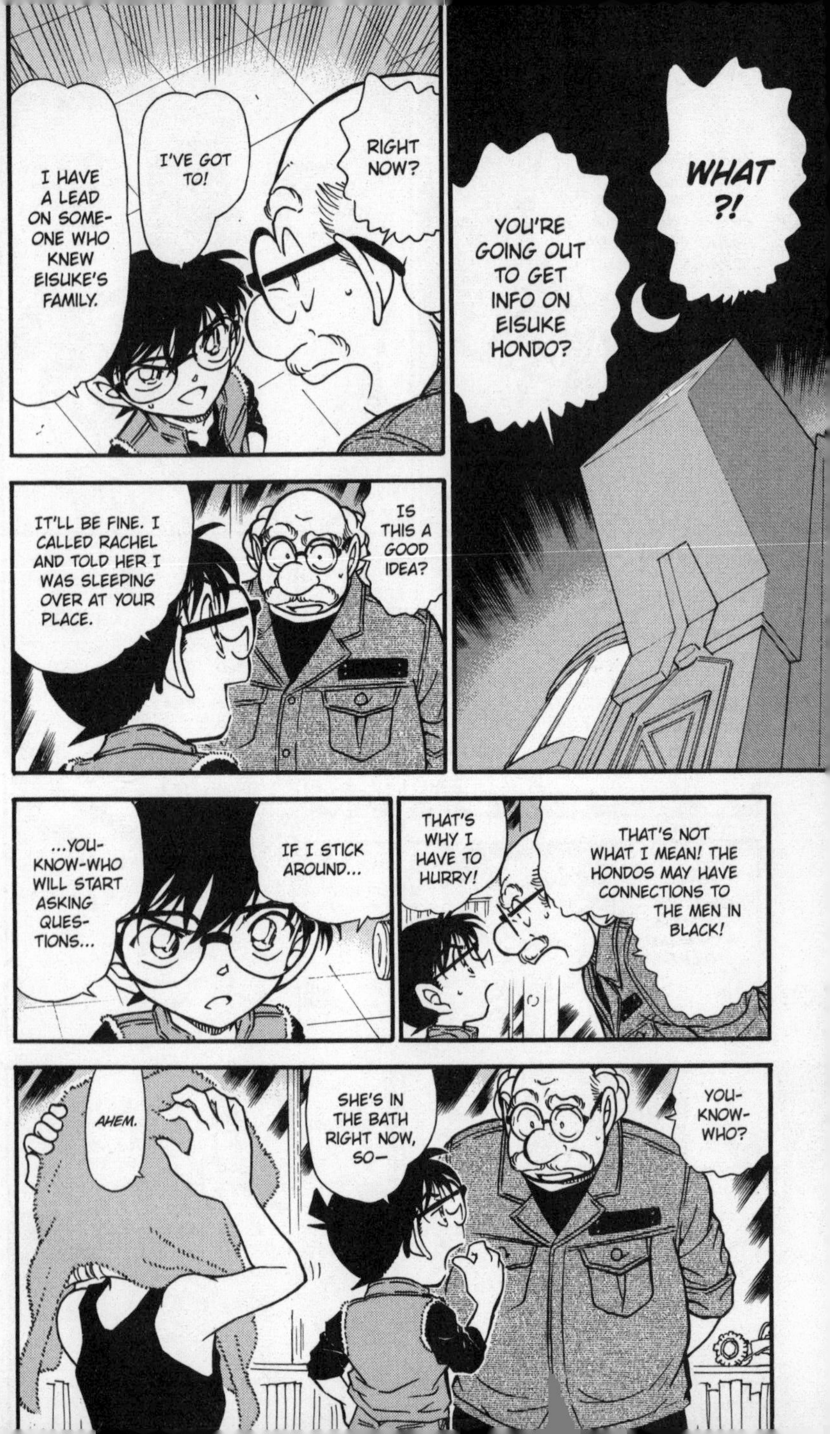
WHAT ?!
YOU'RE GOING OUT TO GET INFO ON EISUKE HONDO?
RIGHT NOW?
I'VE GOT TO!
I HAVE A LEAD ON SOME-ONE WHO KNEW EISUKE'S FAMILY.
IS THIS A GOOD IDEA?
IT'LL BE FINE. I CALLED RACHEL AND TOLD HER I WAS SLEEPING OVER AT YOUR PLACE.
THAT'S NOT WHAT I MEAN! THE HONDOS MAY HAVE CONNECTIONS TO THE MEN IN BLACK!
THAT'S WHY I HAVE TO HURRY!
IF I STICK AROUND...
...YOU-KNOW-WHO WILL START ASKING QUES-TIONS...
YOU-KNOW-WHO?
SHE'S IN THE BATH RIGHT NOW, SO—
AHEM.

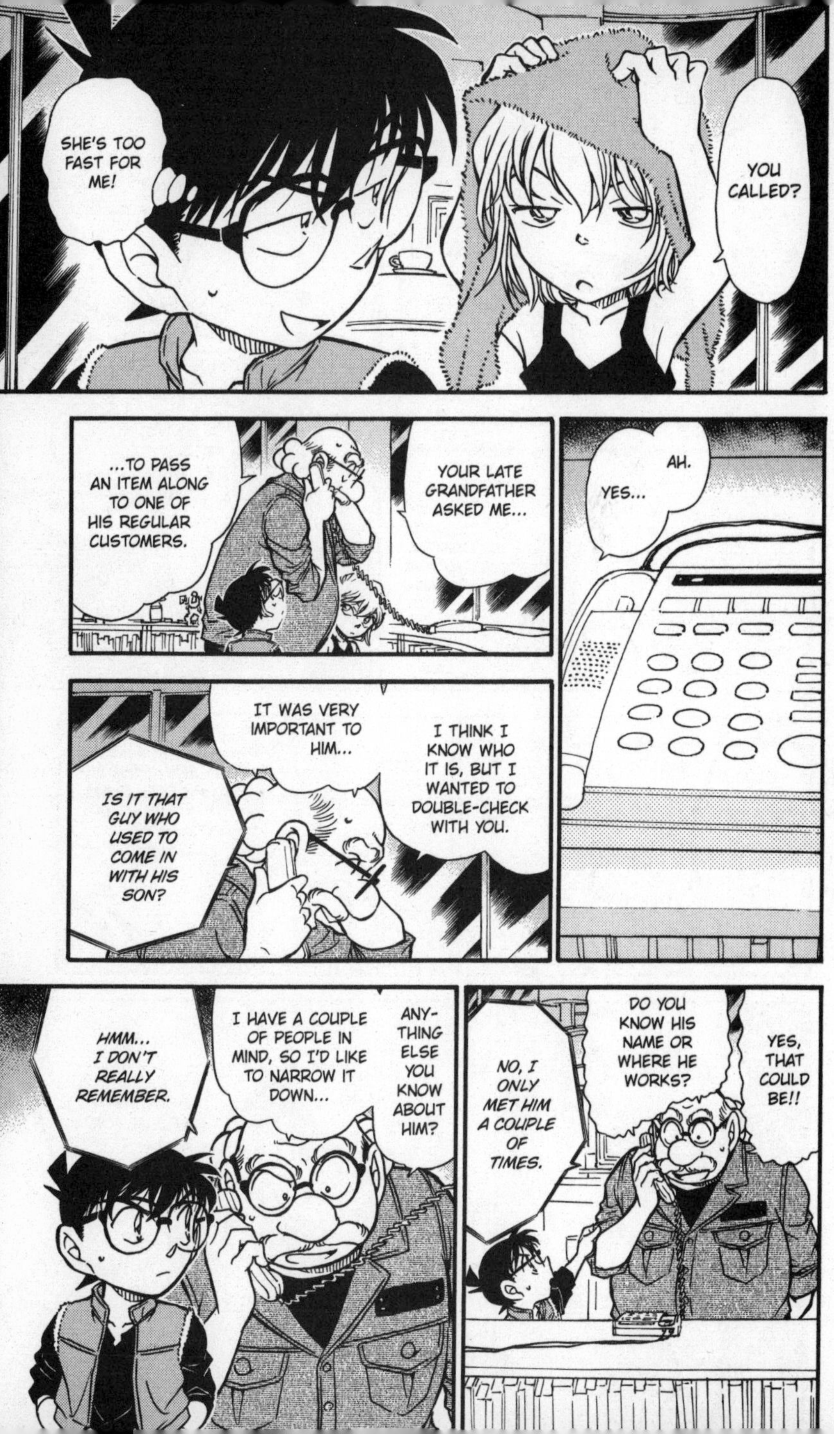
YOU CALLED?
SHE'S TOO FAST FOR ME!
AH. YES...
YOUR LATE GRANDFATHER ASKED ME...
...TO PASS AN ITEM ALONG TO ONE OF HIS REGULAR CUSTOMERS.
IT WAS VERY IMPORTANT TO HIM...
I THINK I KNOW WHO IT IS, BUT I WANTED TO DOUBLE-CHECK WITH YOU.
IS IT THAT GUY WHO USED TO COME IN WITH HIS SON?
YES, THAT COULD BE!!
DO YOU KNOW HIS NAME OR WHERE HE WORKS?
NO, I ONLY MET HIM A COUPLE OF TIMES.
ANYTHING ELSE YOU KNOW ABOUT HIM?
I HAVE A COUPLE OF PEOPLE IN MIND, SO I'D LIKE TO NARROW IT DOWN...
HMM... I DON'T REALLY REMEMBER.

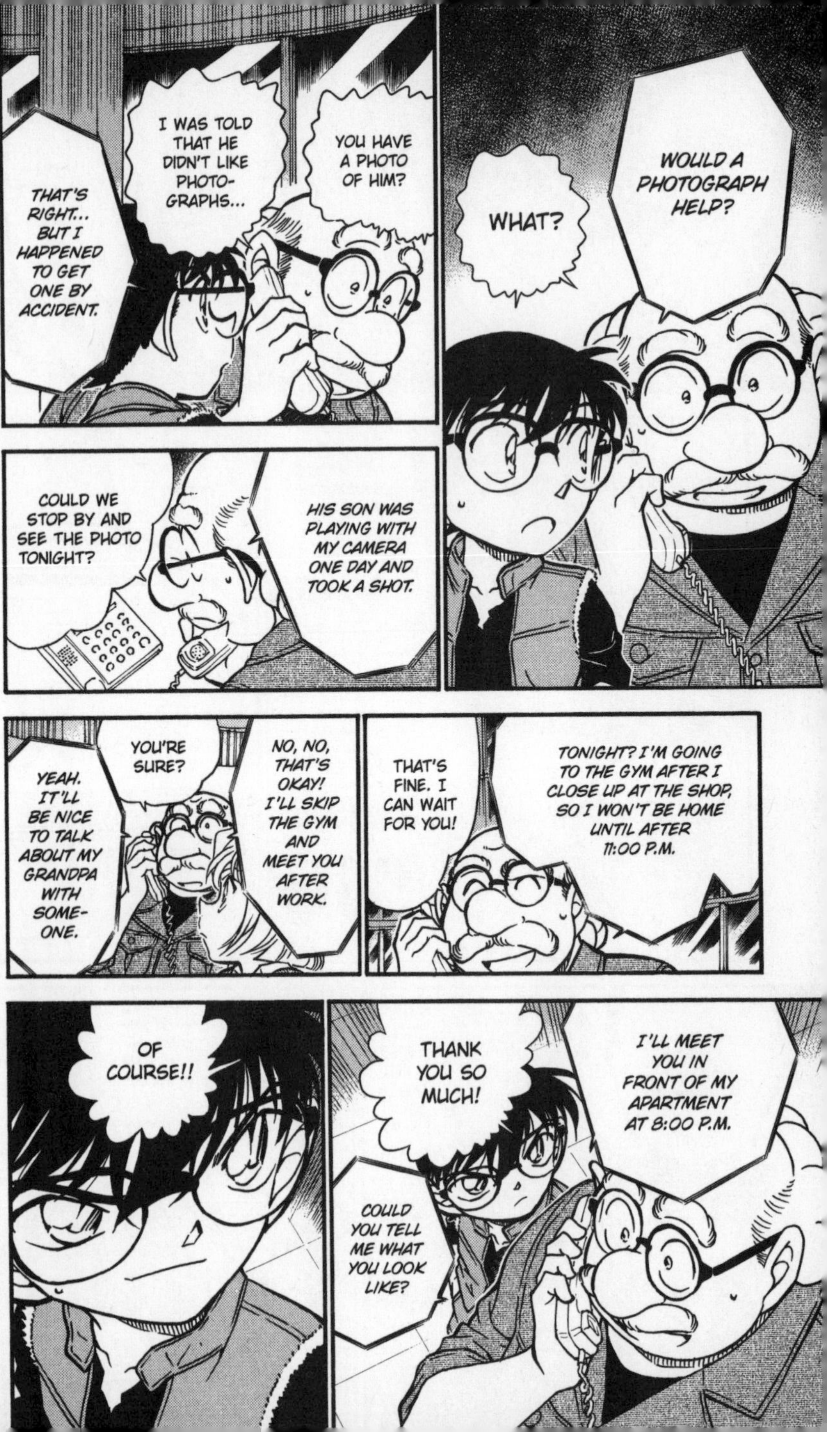
WOULD A PHOTOGRAPH HELP?
WHAT?
YOU HAVE A PHOTO OF HIM?
I WAS TOLD THAT HE DIDN'T LIKE PHOTO-GRAPHS...
THAT'S RIGHT... BUT I HAPPENED TO GET ONE BY ACCIDENT.
HIS SON WAS PLAYING WITH MY CAMERA ONE DAY AND TOOK A SHOT.
COULD WE STOP BY AND SEE THE PHOTO TONIGHT?
TONIGHT? I'M GOING TO THE GYM AFTER I CLOSE UP AT THE SHOP, SO I WON'T BE HOME UNTIL AFTER 11:00 P.M.
THAT'S FINE. I CAN WAIT FOR YOU!
NO, NO, THAT'S OKAY! I'LL SKIP THE GYM AND MEET YOU AFTER WORK.
YOU'RE SURE?
YEAH. IT'LL BE NICE TO TALK ABOUT MY GRANDPA WITH SOME-ONE.
I'LL MEET YOU IN FRONT OF MY APARTMENT AT 8:00 P.M.
THANK YOU SO MUCH!
COULD YOU TELL ME WHAT YOU LOOK LIKE?
OF COURSE!!

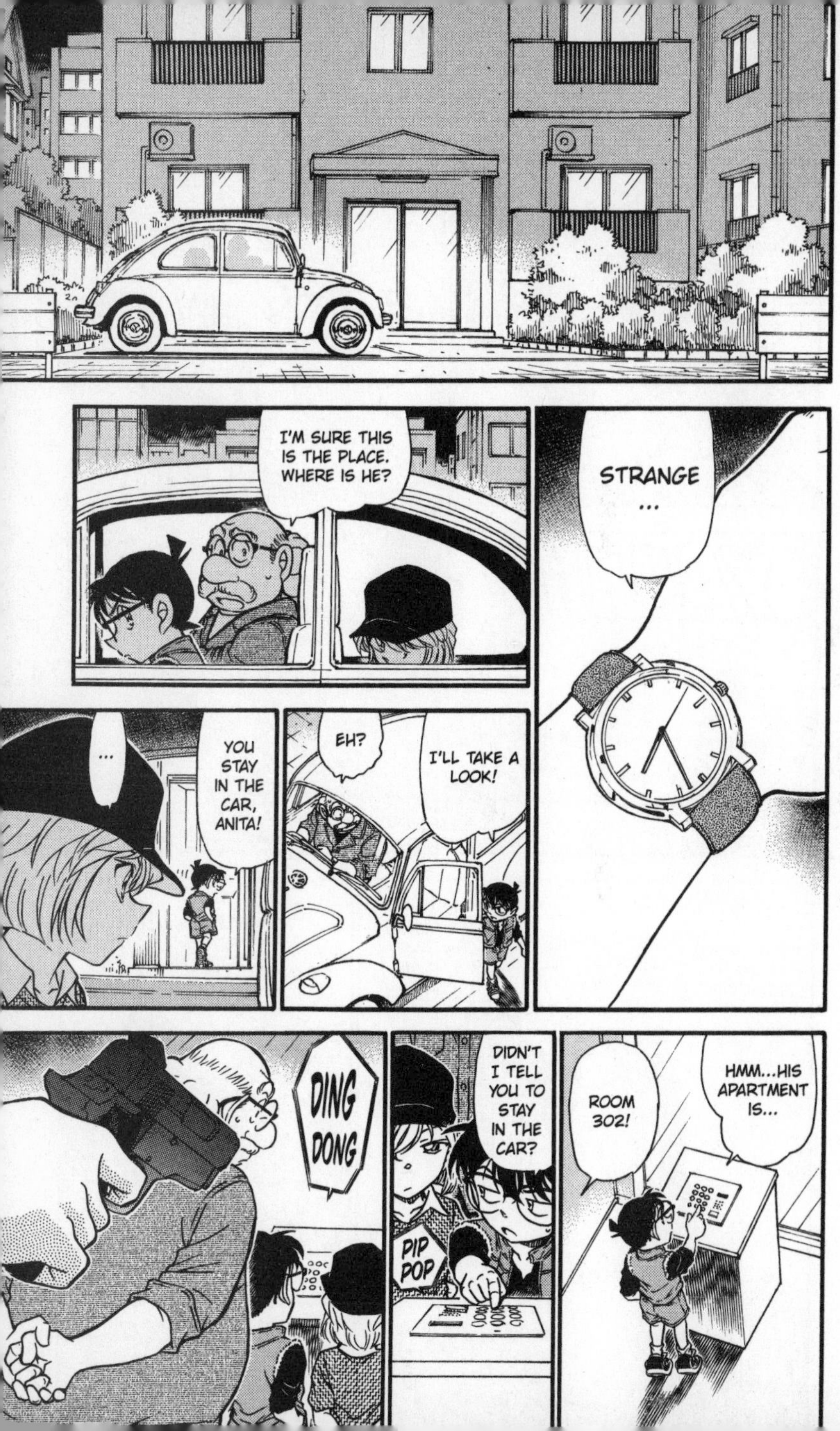
STRANGE ...
I'M SURE THIS IS THE PLACE. WHERE IS HE?
I'LL TAKE A LOOK!
EH?
YOU STAY IN THE CAR, ANITA!
...
HMM...HIS APARTMENT IS...
ROOM 302!
DIDN'T I TELL YOU TO STAY IN THE CAR?
PIP POP
DING DONG

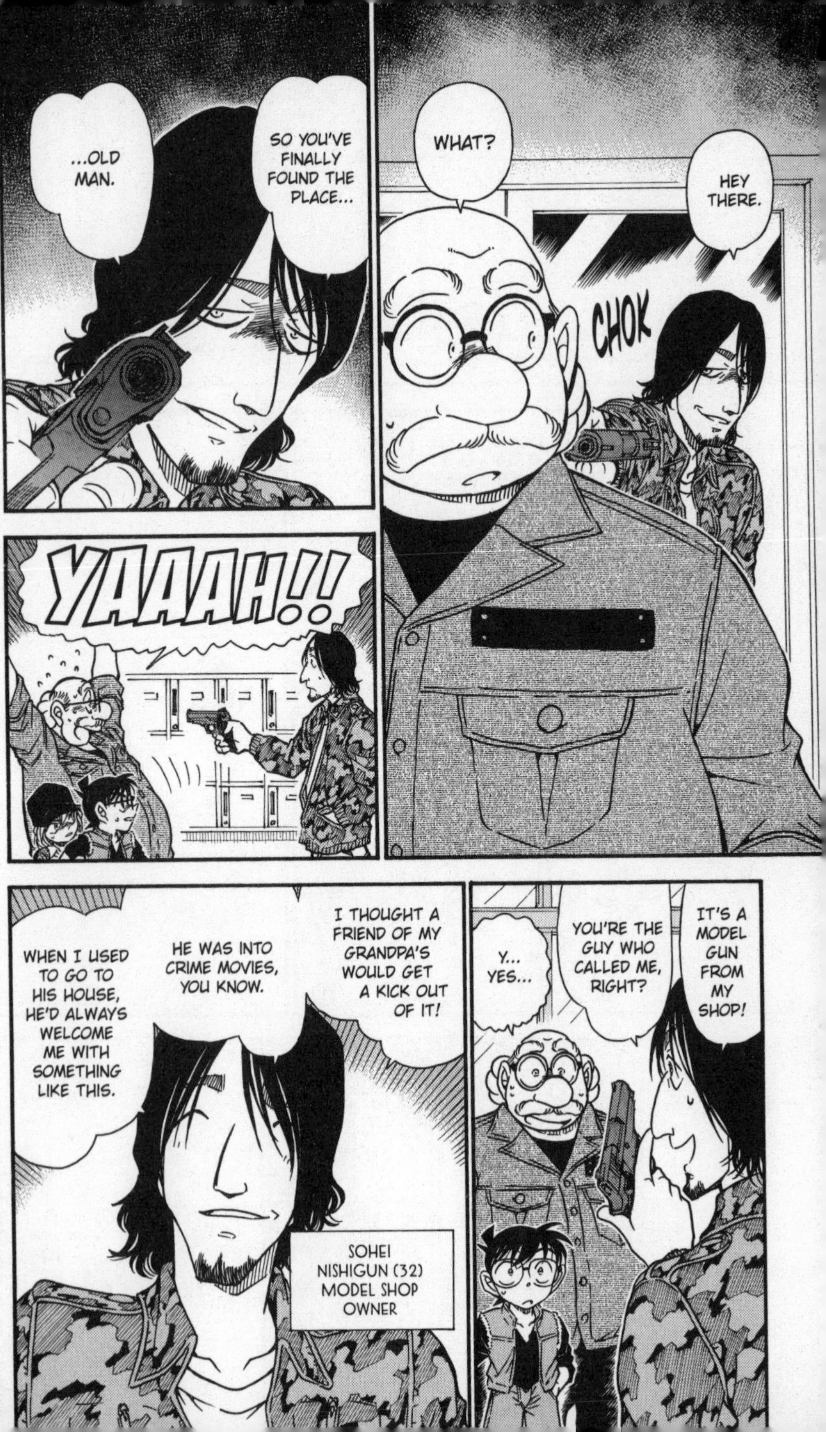
HEY THERE.
CHOK
WHAT?
SO YOU'VE FINALLY FOUND THE PLACE...
...OLD MAN.
YAAAH!!
IT'S A MODEL GUN FROM MY SHOP!
YOU'RE THE GUY WHO CALLED ME, RIGHT?
Y... YES...
I THOUGHT A FRIEND OF MY GRANDPA'S WOULD GET A KICK OUT OF IT!
HE WAS INTO CRIME MOVIES, YOU KNOW.
WHEN I USED TO GO TO HIS HOUSE, HE'D ALWAYS WELCOME ME WITH SOMETHING LIKE THIS.
SOHEI NISHIGUN (32) MODEL SHOP OWNER

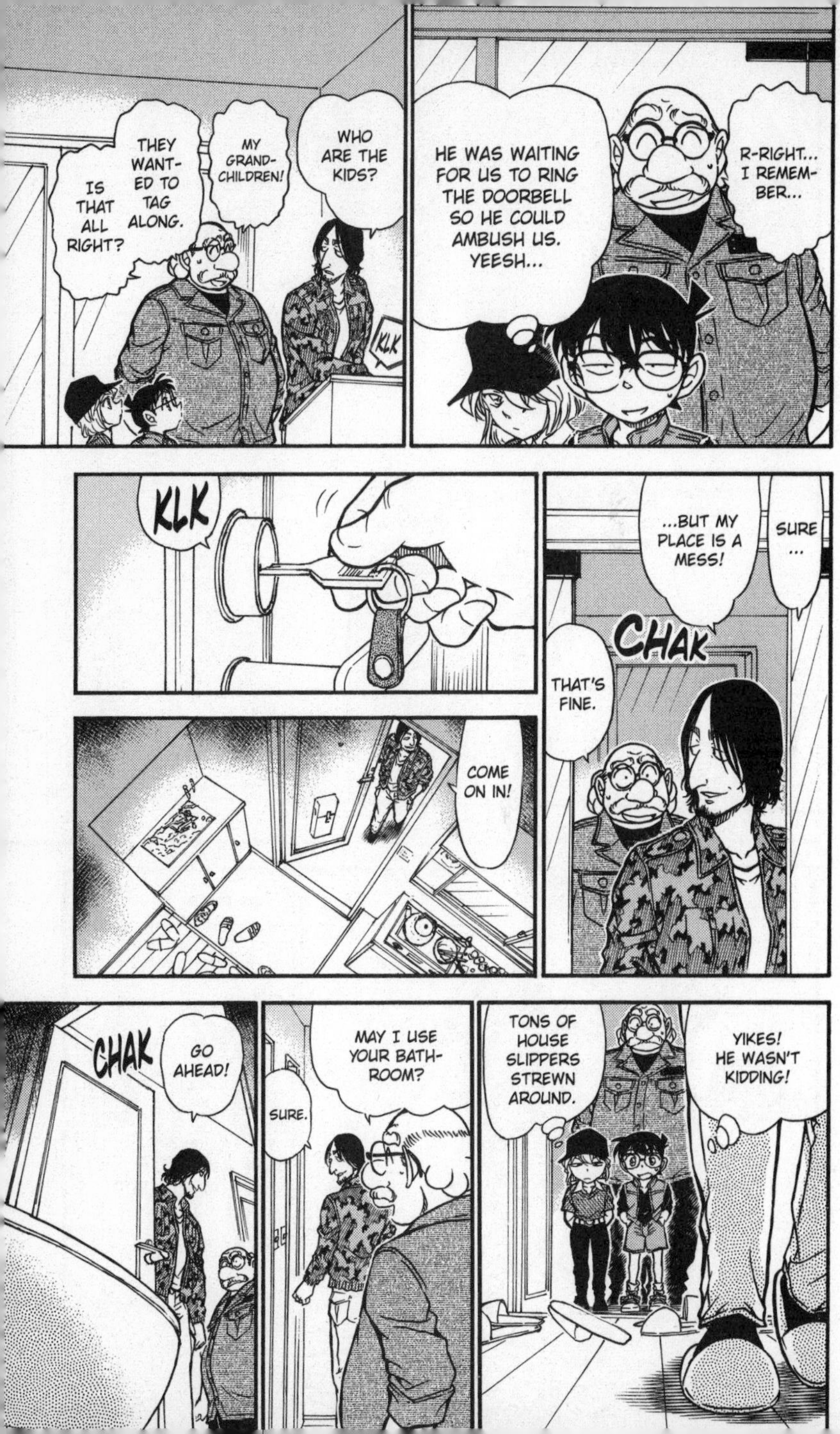
R-RIGHT... I REMEMBER...
HE WAS WAITING FOR US TO RING THE DOORBELL SO HE COULD AMBUSH US. YEESH...
WHO ARE THE KIDS?
MY GRAND-CHILDREN!
THEY WANT-ED TO TAG ALONG.
IS THAT ALL RIGHT?
KLK
SURE...
...BUT MY PLACE IS A MESS!
CHAK
THAT'S FINE.
KLK
COME ON IN!
YIKES! HE WASN'T KIDDING!
TONS OF HOUSE SLIPPERS STREWN AROUND.
MAY I USE YOUR BATH-ROOM?
SURE.
GO AHEAD!
CHAK

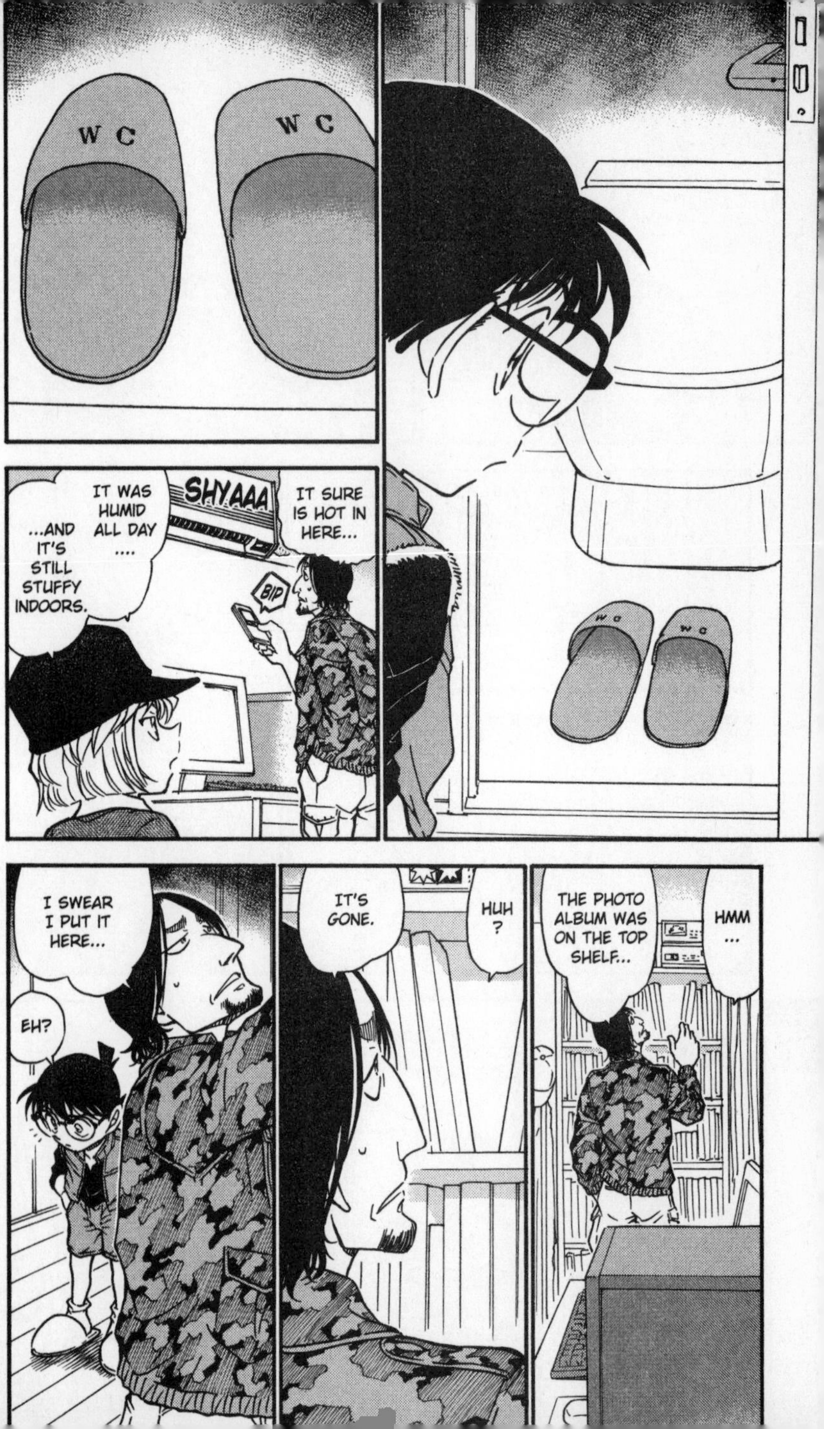
W C
W C
W C
W C
IT SURE IS HOT IN HERE...
SHYAAA
IT WAS HUMID ALL DAY ....
...AND IT'S STILL STUFFY INDOORS.
BIP
HMM ...
THE PHOTO ALBUM WAS ON THE TOP SHELF...
HUH ?
IT'S GONE.
I SWEAR I PUT IT HERE...
EH?

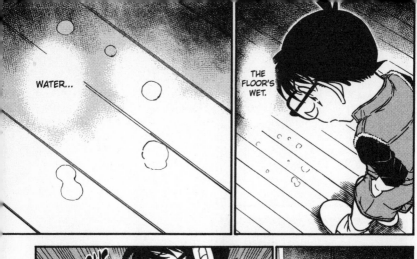

WATER...

THE FLOOR'S WET.

SHF SHF

HEY, YEAH!

HEY, DO YOU SAVE YOUR PHOTOS ON YOUR COMPUTER?

A DAMP TISSUE...

WHAT?

KLIK KLIK

JUST WAIT A SECOND...

VWOON

KLIK

I'LL SHOW YOU.

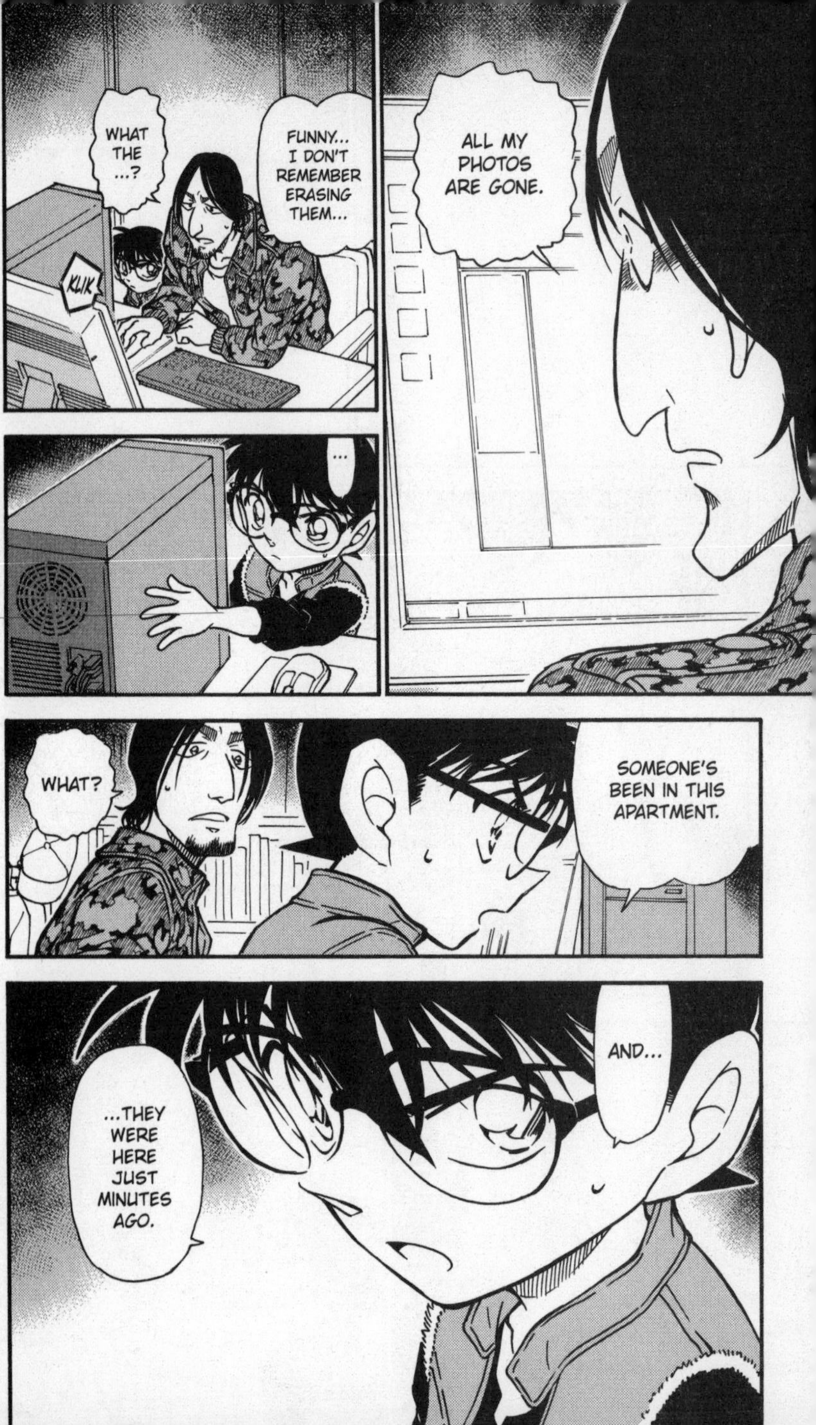
ALL MY PHOTOS ARE GONE.
FUNNY... I DON'T REMEMBER ERASING THEM...
WHAT THE ...?
KLIK
...
SOMEONE'S BEEN IN THIS APARTMENT.
WHAT?
AND...
...THEY WERE HERE JUST MINUTES AGO.

FILE 8: LOCATION OF THE PHOTOGRAPH

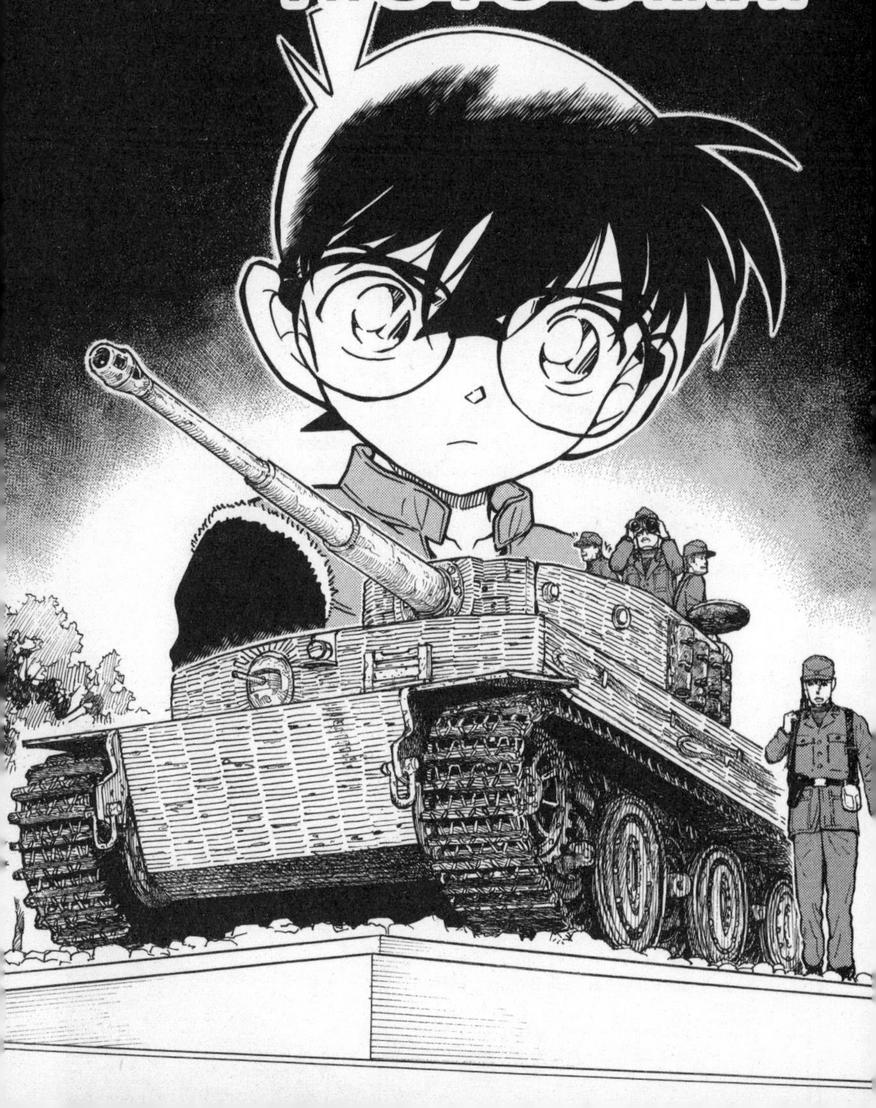

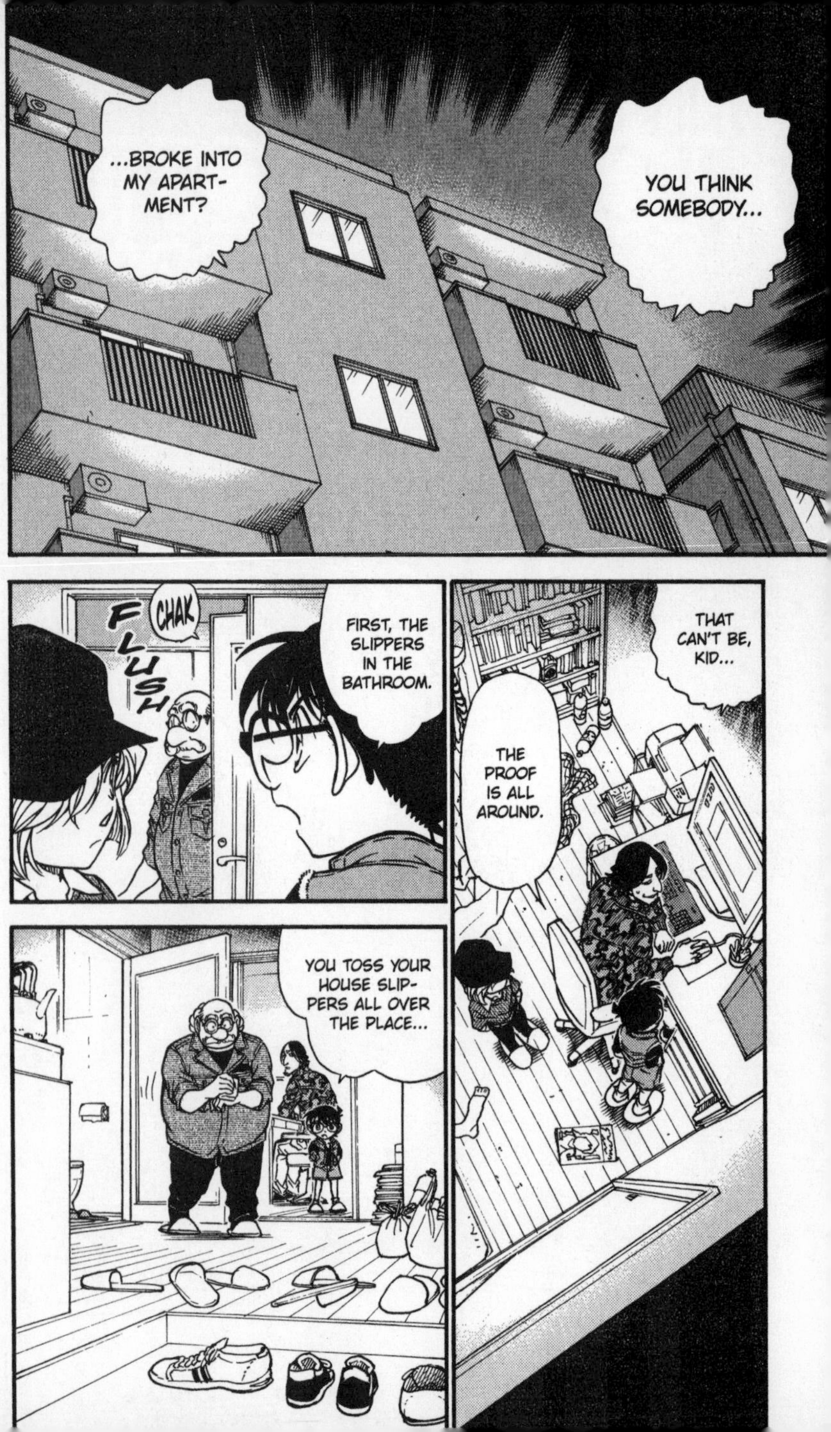
YOU THINK SOMEBODY...
...BROKE INTO MY APART-MENT?
THAT CAN'T BE, KID...
THE PROOF IS ALL AROUND.
FIRST, THE SLIPPERS IN THE BATHROOM.
CHAK
FLUSH
YOU TOSS YOUR HOUSE SLIP-PERS ALL OVER THE PLACE...

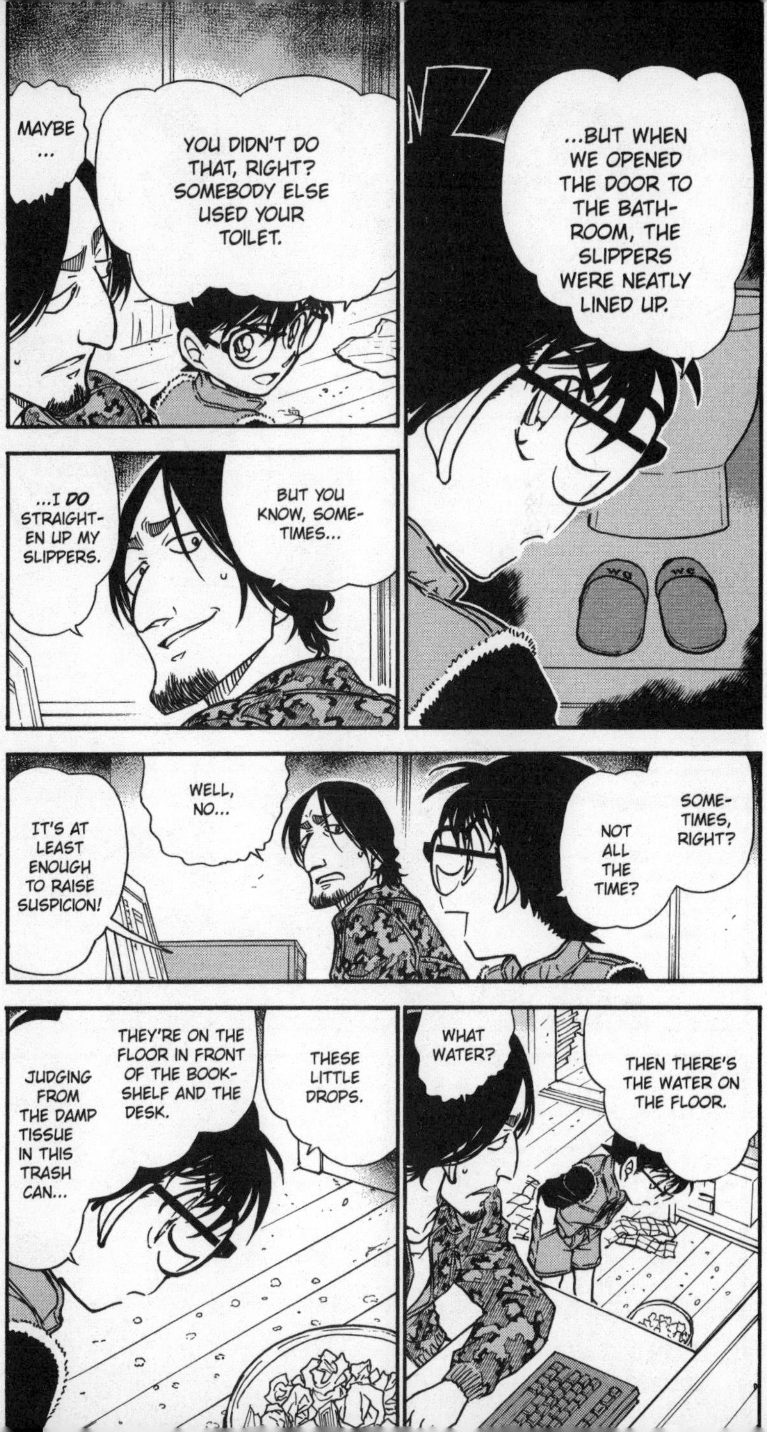
...BUT WHEN WE OPENED THE DOOR TO THE BATH-ROOM, THE SLIPPERS WERE NEATLY LINED UP.
YOU DIDN'T DO THAT, RIGHT? SOMEBODY ELSE USED YOUR TOILET.
MAYBE ...
BUT YOU KNOW, SOME-TIMES...
...I DO STRAIGHT-EN UP MY SLIPPERS.
SOME-TIMES, RIGHT?
NOT ALL THE TIME?
WELL, NO...
IT'S AT LEAST ENOUGH TO RAISE SUSPICION!
THEN THERE'S THE WATER ON THE FLOOR.
WHAT WATER?
THESE LITTLE DROPS.
THEY'RE ON THE FLOOR IN FRONT OF THE BOOK-SHELF AND THE DESK.
JUDGING FROM THE DAMP TISSUE IN THIS TRASH CAN...

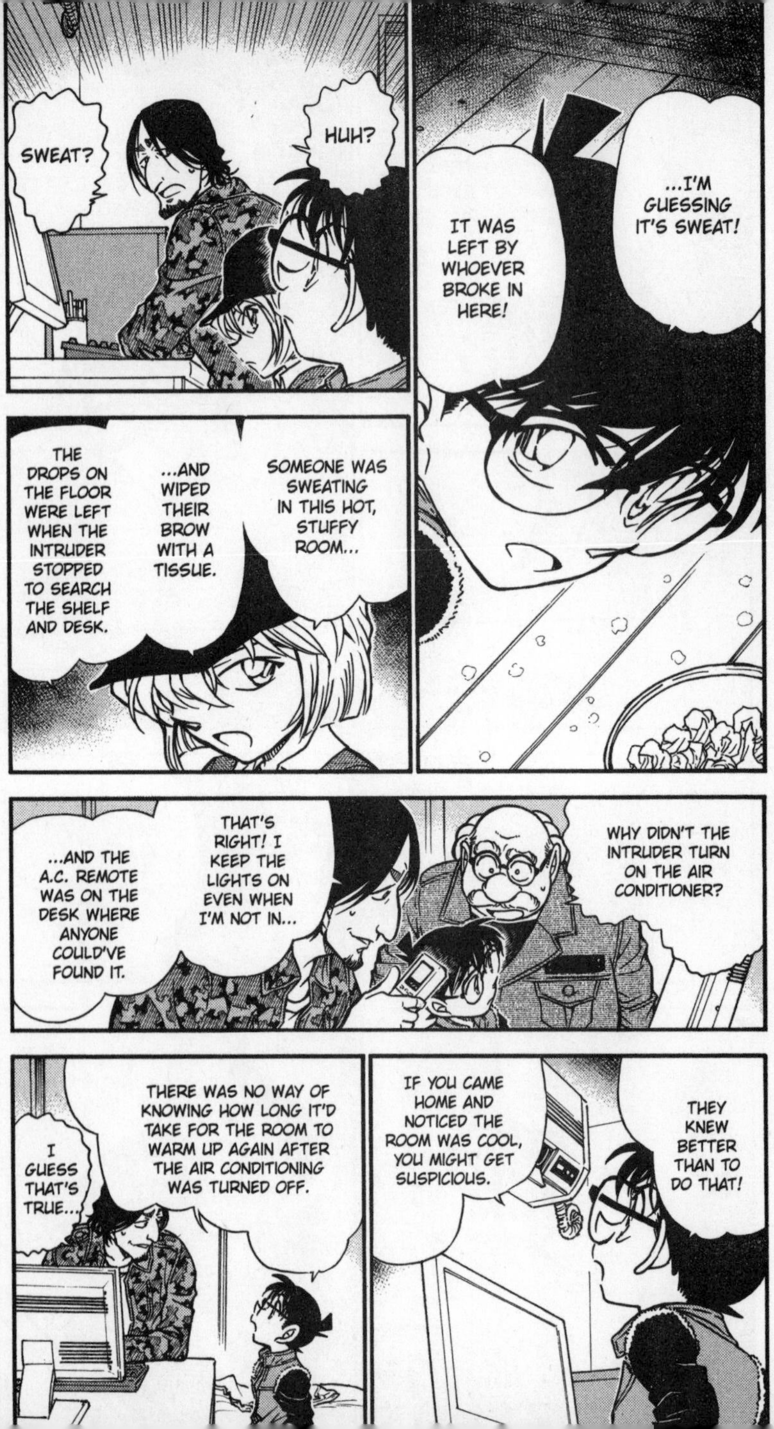
...I'M GUESSING IT'S SWEAT!
IT WAS LEFT BY WHOEVER BROKE IN HERE!
HUH?
SWEAT?
SOMEONE WAS SWEATING IN THIS HOT, STUFFY ROOM...
...AND WIPED THEIR BROW WITH A TISSUE.
THE DROPS ON THE FLOOR WERE LEFT WHEN THE INTRUDER STOPPED TO SEARCH THE SHELF AND DESK.
WHY DIDN'T THE INTRUDER TURN ON THE AIR CONDITIONER?
THAT'S RIGHT! I KEEP THE LIGHTS ON EVEN WHEN I'M NOT IN...
...AND THE A.C. REMOTE WAS ON THE DESK WHERE ANYONE COULD'VE FOUND IT.
THEY KNEW BETTER THAN TO DO THAT!
IF YOU CAME HOME AND NOTICED THE ROOM WAS COOL, YOU MIGHT GET SUSPICIOUS.
THERE WAS NO WAY OF KNOWING HOW LONG IT'D TAKE FOR THE ROOM TO WARM UP AGAIN AFTER THE AIR CONDITIONING WAS TURNED OFF.
I GUESS THAT'S TRUE...

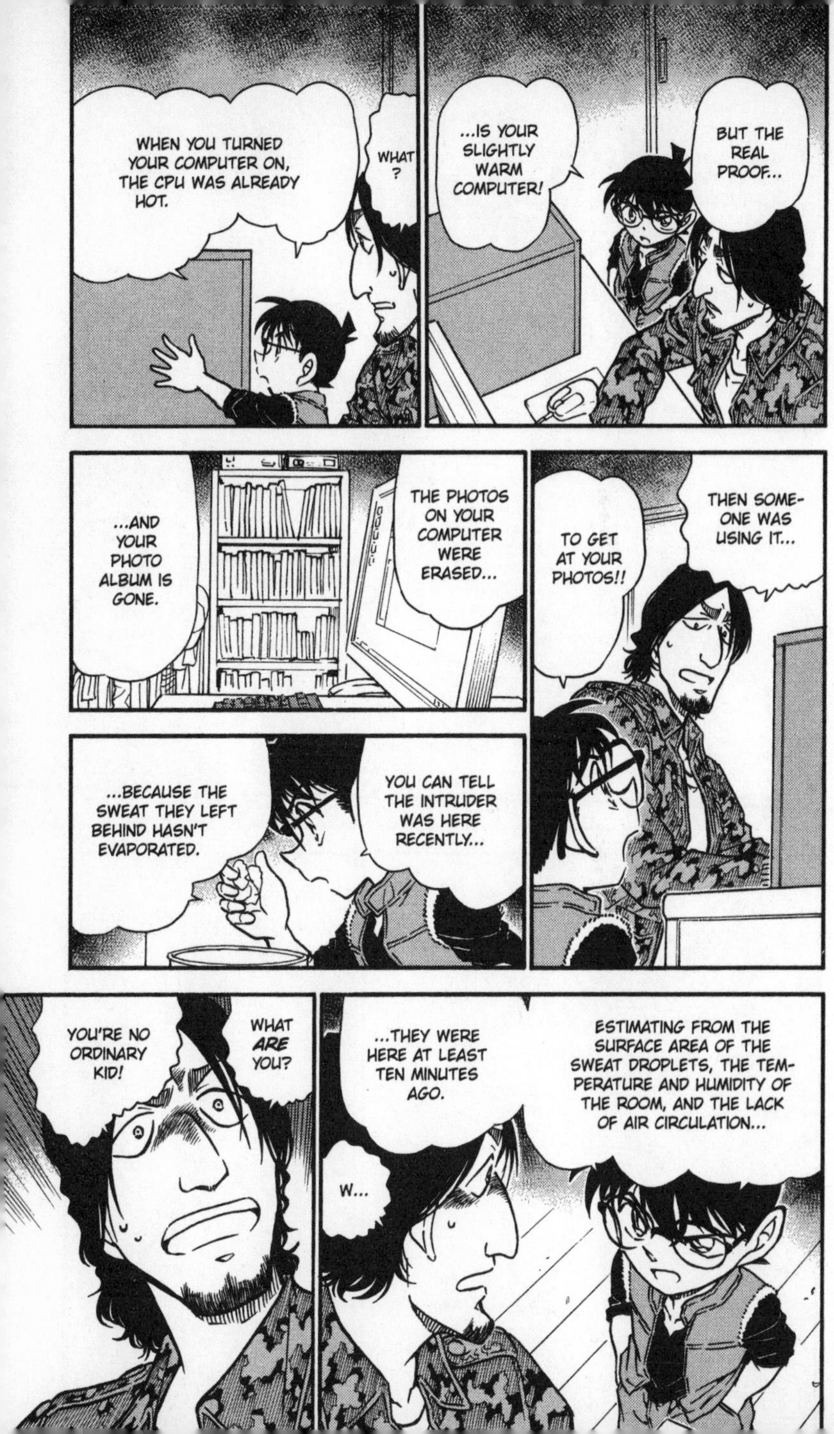
BUT THE REAL PROOF...
...IS YOUR SLIGHTLY WARM COMPUTER!
WHAT?
WHEN YOU TURNED YOUR COMPUTER ON, THE CPU WAS ALREADY HOT.
THEN SOME-ONE WAS USING IT...
TO GET AT YOUR PHOTOS!!
THE PHOTOS ON YOUR COMPUTER WERE ERASED...
...AND YOUR PHOTO ALBUM IS GONE.
YOU CAN TELL THE INTRUDER WAS HERE RECENTLY...
...BECAUSE THE SWEAT THEY LEFT BEHIND HASN'T EVAPORATED.
ESTIMATING FROM THE SURFACE AREA OF THE SWEAT DROPLETS, THE TEM-PERATURE AND HUMIDITY OF THE ROOM, AND THE LACK OF AIR CIRCULATION...
...THEY WERE HERE AT LEAST TEN MINUTES AGO.
W...
WHAT *ARE* YOU?
YOU'RE NO ORDINARY KID!

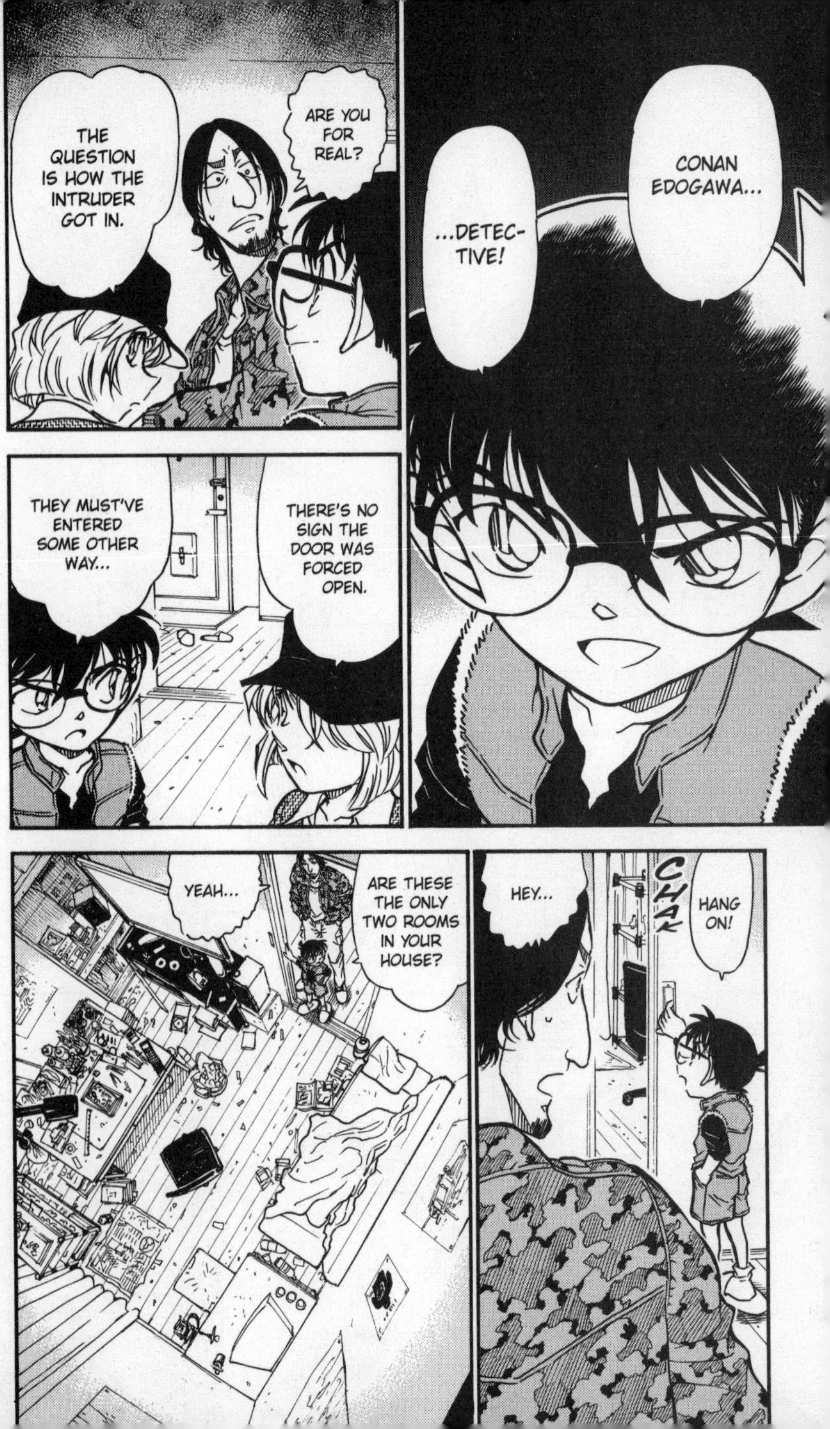
CONAN EDOGAWA...
...DETECTIVE!
ARE YOU FOR REAL?
THE QUESTION IS HOW THE INTRUDER GOT IN.
THERE'S NO SIGN THE DOOR WAS FORCED OPEN.
THEY MUST'VE ENTERED SOME OTHER WAY...
HANG ON!
CHAK
HEY...
ARE THESE THE ONLY TWO ROOMS IN YOUR HOUSE?
YEAH...

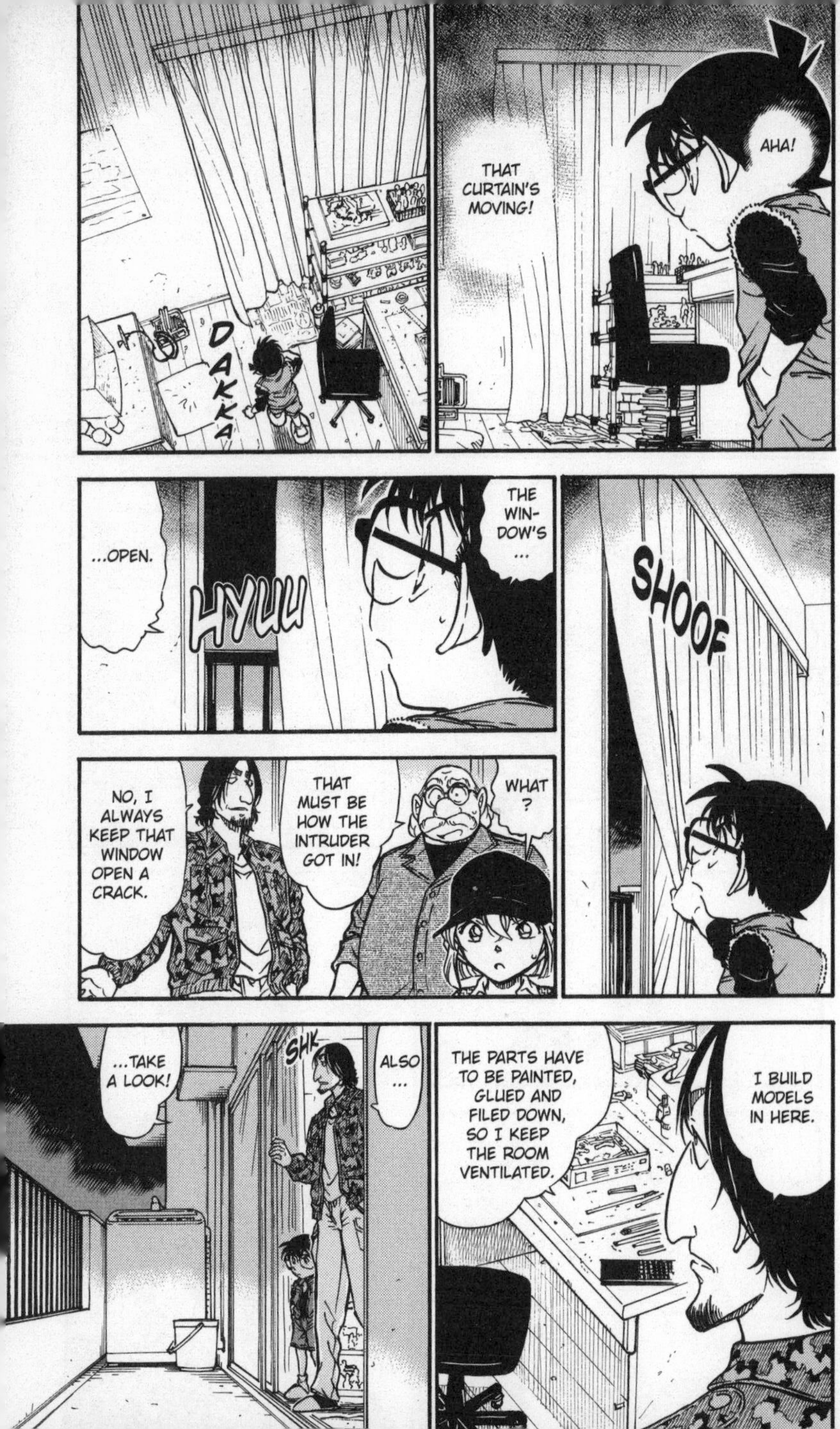
AHA!
THAT CURTAIN'S MOVING!
DAKKA
SHOOF
THE WIN-DOW'S ...
...OPEN.
HYUU
WHAT?
THAT MUST BE HOW THE INTRUDER GOT IN!
NO, I ALWAYS KEEP THAT WINDOW OPEN A CRACK.
I BUILD MODELS IN HERE.
THE PARTS HAVE TO BE PAINTED, GLUED AND FILED DOWN, SO I KEEP THE ROOM VENTILATED.
ALSO ...
SHK
...TAKE A LOOK!

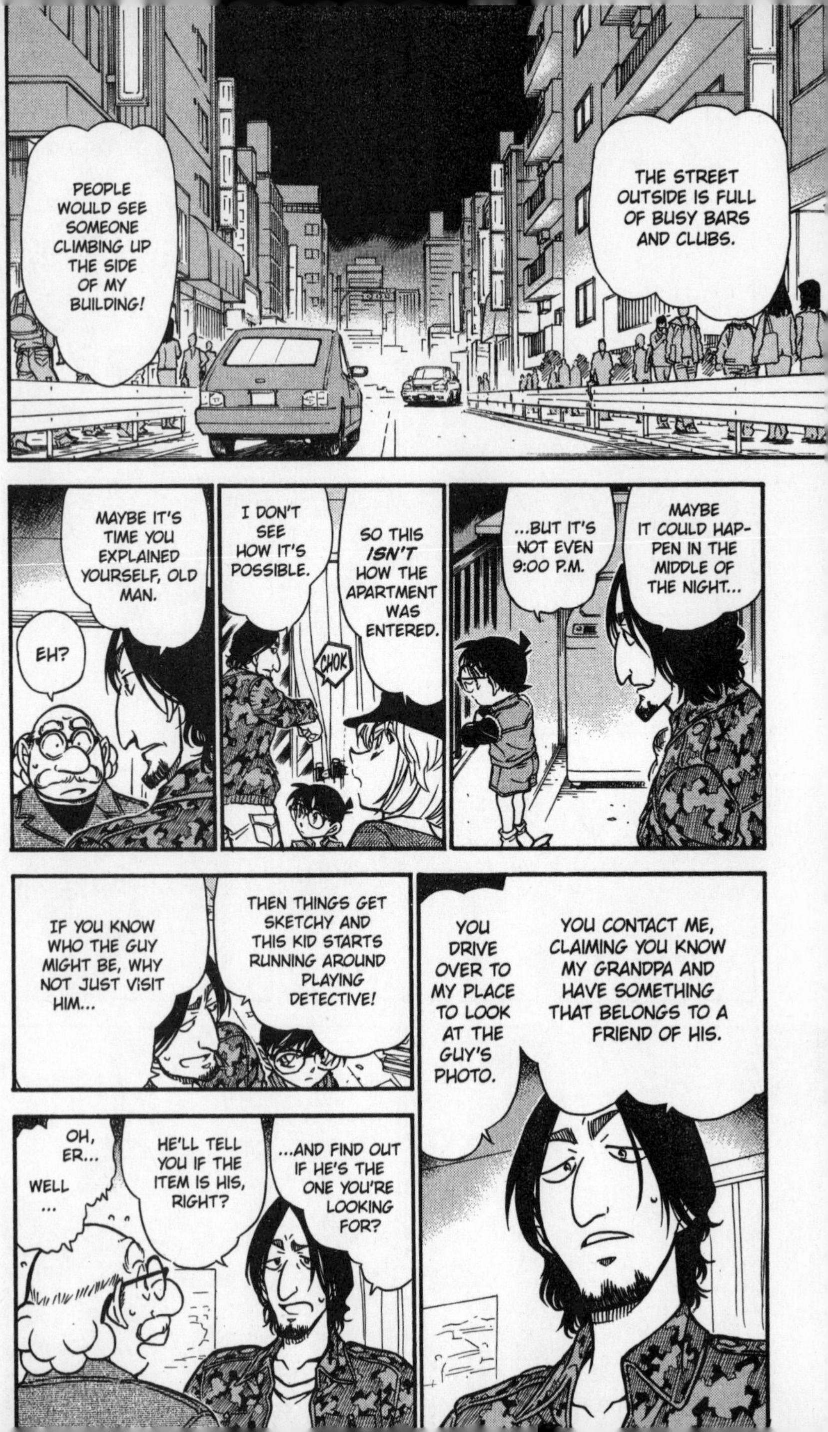
THE STREET OUTSIDE IS FULL OF BUSY BARS AND CLUBS.
PEOPLE WOULD SEE SOMEONE CLIMBING UP THE SIDE OF MY BUILDING!
MAYBE IT COULD HAPPEN IN THE MIDDLE OF THE NIGHT...
...BUT IT'S NOT EVEN 9:00 P.M.
SO THIS ISN'T HOW THE APARTMENT WAS ENTERED.
I DON'T SEE HOW IT'S POSSIBLE.
CHOK
MAYBE IT'S TIME YOU EXPLAINED YOURSELF, OLD MAN.
EH?
YOU CONTACT ME, CLAIMING YOU KNOW MY GRANDPA AND HAVE SOMETHING THAT BELONGS TO A FRIEND OF HIS.
YOU DRIVE OVER TO MY PLACE TO LOOK AT THE GUY'S PHOTO.
THEN THINGS GET SKETCHY AND THIS KID STARTS RUNNING AROUND PLAYING DETECTIVE!
IF YOU KNOW WHO THE GUY MIGHT BE, WHY NOT JUST VISIT HIM...
...AND FIND OUT IF HE'S THE ONE YOU'RE LOOKING FOR?
HE'LL TELL YOU IF THE ITEM IS HIS, RIGHT?
OH, ER...
WELL ...

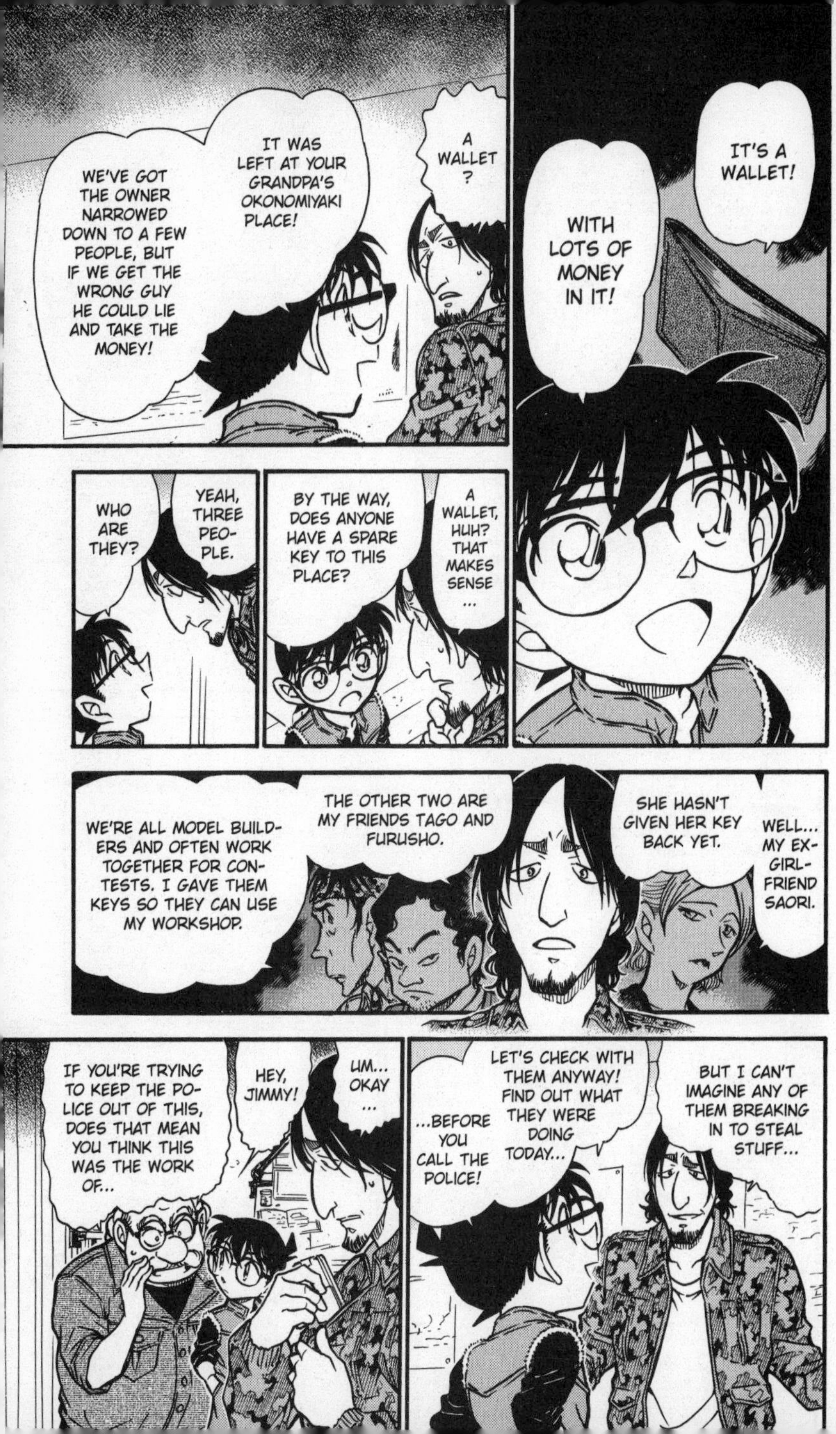
IT'S A WALLET!
WITH LOTS OF MONEY IN IT!
A WALLET?
IT WAS LEFT AT YOUR GRANDPA'S OKONOMIYAKI PLACE!
WE'VE GOT THE OWNER NARROWED DOWN TO A FEW PEOPLE, BUT IF WE GET THE WRONG GUY HE COULD LIE AND TAKE THE MONEY!
A WALLET, HUH? THAT MAKES SENSE...
BY THE WAY, DOES ANYONE HAVE A SPARE KEY TO THIS PLACE?
YEAH, THREE PEO-PLE.
WHO ARE THEY?
WELL... MY EX-GIRL-FRIEND SAORI.
SHE HASN'T GIVEN HER KEY BACK YET.
THE OTHER TWO ARE MY FRIENDS TAGO AND FURUSHO.
WE'RE ALL MODEL BUILD-ERS AND OFTEN WORK TOGETHER FOR CON-TESTS. I GAVE THEM KEYS SO THEY CAN USE MY WORKSHOP.
BUT I CAN'T IMAGINE ANY OF THEM BREAKING IN TO STEAL STUFF...
LET'S CHECK WITH THEM ANYWAY! FIND OUT WHAT THEY WERE DOING TODAY...
...BEFORE YOU CALL THE POLICE!
UM... OKAY...
HEY, JIMMY!
IF YOU'RE TRYING TO KEEP THE PO-LICE OUT OF THIS, DOES THAT MEAN YOU THINK THIS WAS THE WORK OF...

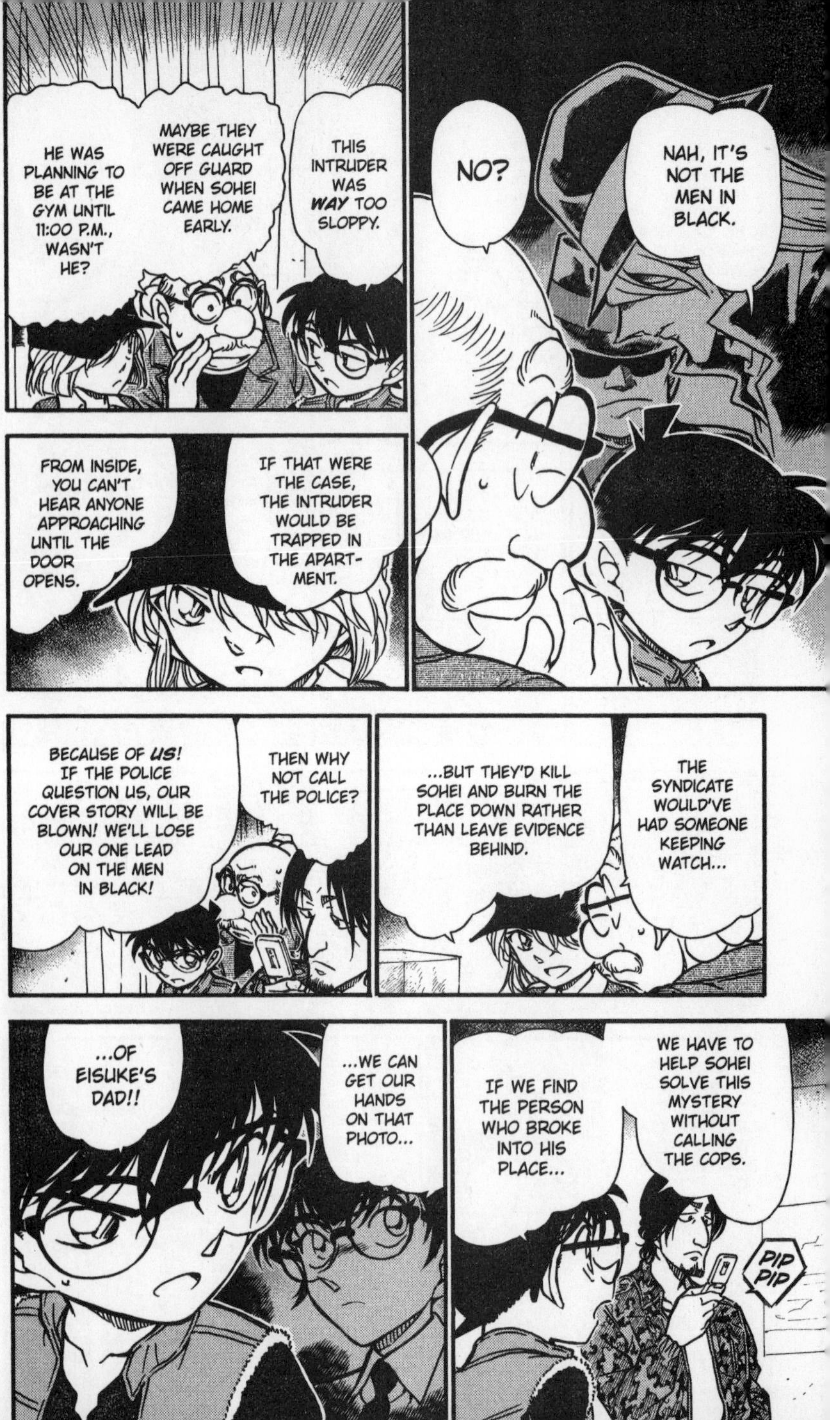
NAH, IT'S NOT THE MEN IN BLACK.
NO?
THIS INTRUDER WAS WAY TOO SLOPPY.
MAYBE THEY WERE CAUGHT OFF GUARD WHEN SOHEI CAME HOME EARLY.
HE WAS PLANNING TO BE AT THE GYM UNTIL 11:00 P.M., WASN'T HE?
IF THAT WERE THE CASE, THE INTRUDER WOULD BE TRAPPED IN THE APART-MENT.
FROM INSIDE, YOU CAN'T HEAR ANYONE APPROACHING UNTIL THE DOOR OPENS.
THE SYNDICATE WOULD'VE HAD SOMEONE KEEPING WATCH...
...BUT THEY'D KILL SOHEI AND BURN THE PLACE DOWN RATHER THAN LEAVE EVIDENCE BEHIND.
THEN WHY NOT CALL THE POLICE?
BECAUSE OF US! IF THE POLICE QUESTION US, OUR COVER STORY WILL BE BLOWN! WE'LL LOSE OUR ONE LEAD ON THE MEN IN BLACK!
WE HAVE TO HELP SOHEI SOLVE THIS MYSTERY WITHOUT CALLING THE COPS.
IF WE FIND THE PERSON WHO BROKE INTO HIS PLACE...
PIP PIP
...WE CAN GET OUR HANDS ON THAT PHOTO...
...OF EISUKE'S DAD!!

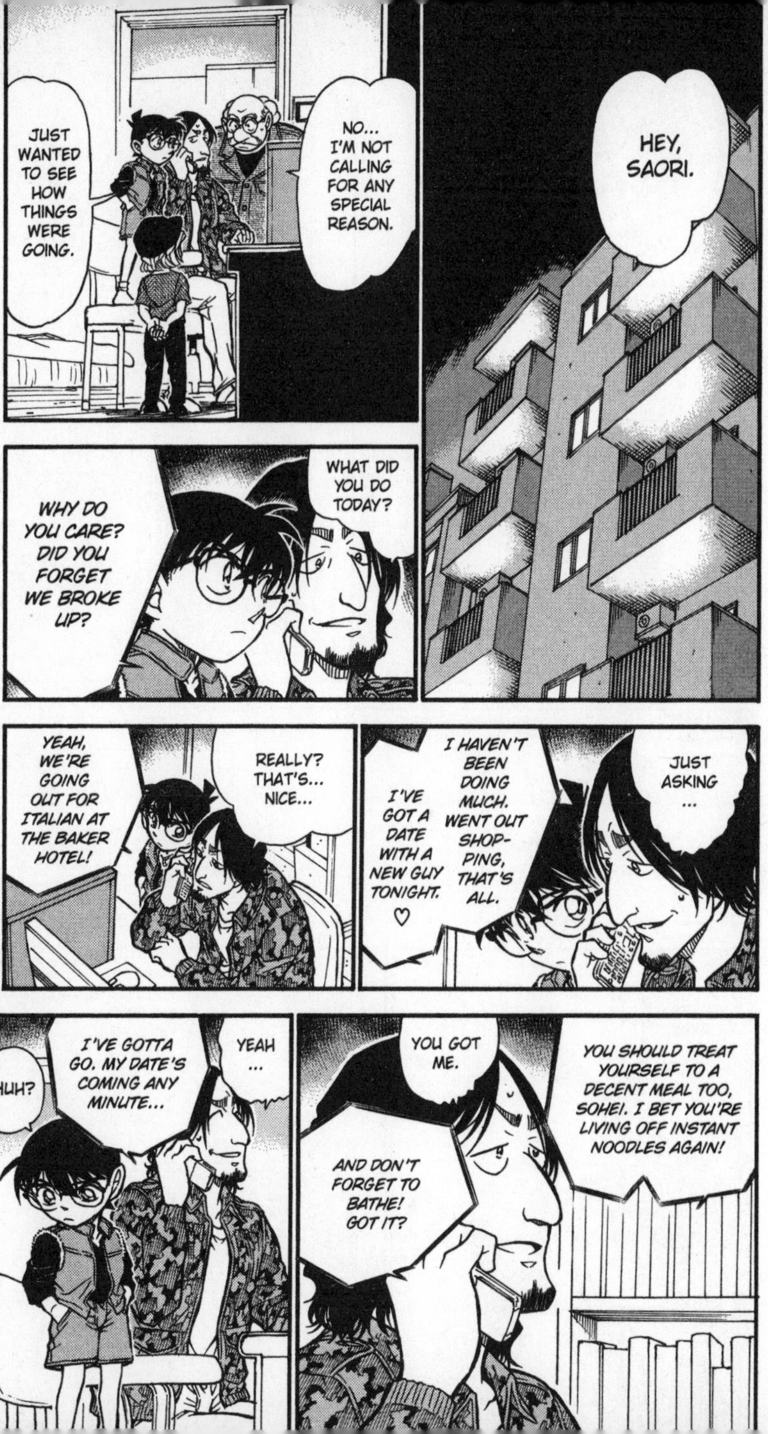
HEY, SAORI.
NO... I'M NOT CALLING FOR ANY SPECIAL REASON.
JUST WANTED TO SEE HOW THINGS WERE GOING.
WHAT DID YOU DO TODAY?
WHY DO YOU CARE? DID YOU FORGET WE BROKE UP?
JUST ASKING ...
I HAVEN'T BEEN DOING MUCH. WENT OUT SHOPPING, THAT'S ALL.
I'VE GOT A DATE WITH A NEW GUY TONIGHT. ♡
REALLY? THAT'S... NICE...
YEAH, WE'RE GOING OUT FOR ITALIAN AT THE BAKER HOTEL!
YOU SHOULD TREAT YOURSELF TO A DECENT MEAL TOO, SOHEI. I BET YOU'RE LIVING OFF INSTANT NOODLES AGAIN!
YOU GOT ME.
AND DON'T FORGET TO BATHE! GOT IT?
YEAH ...
I'VE GOTTA GO. MY DATE'S COMING ANY MINUTE...
HUH?

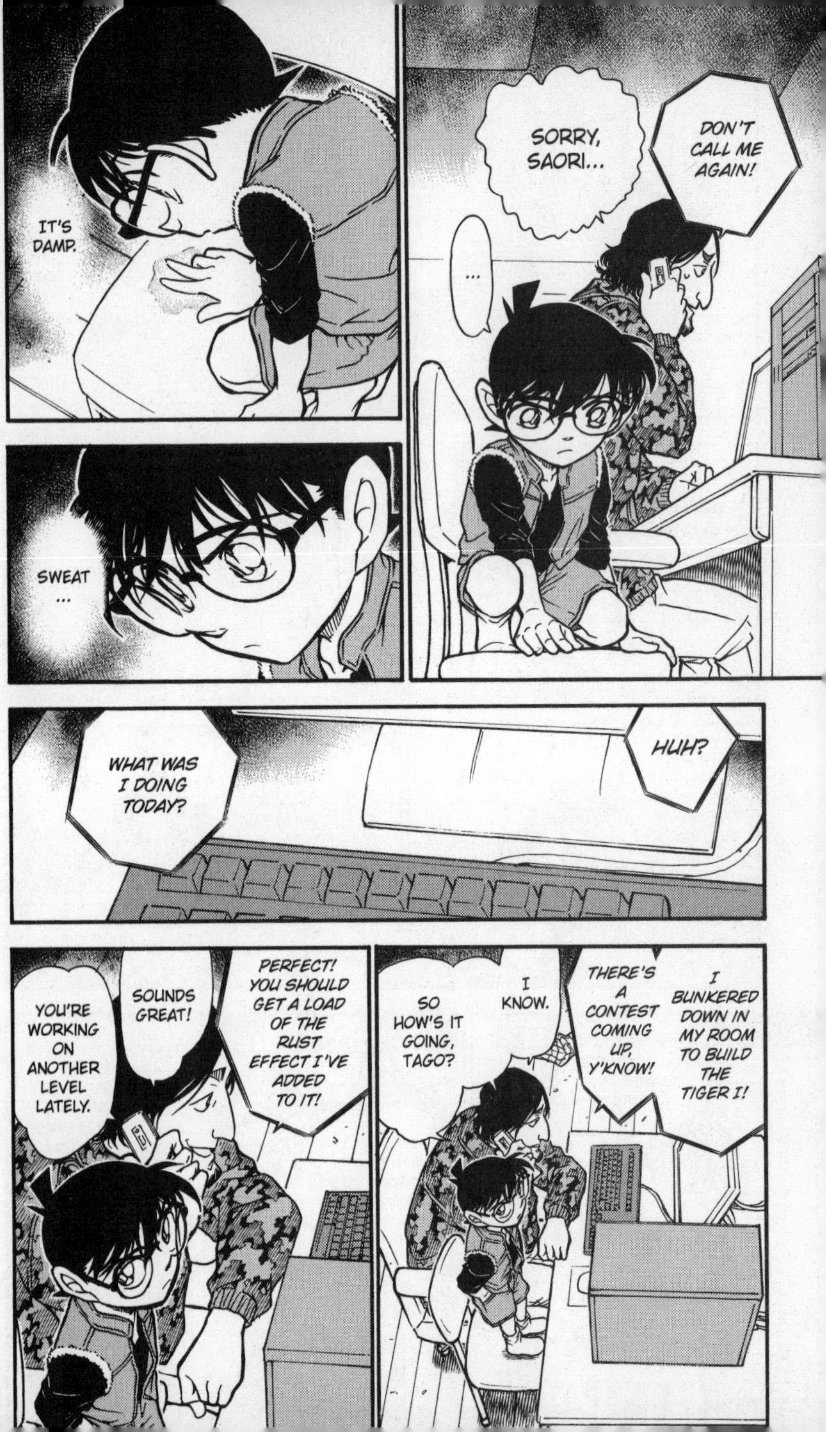
DON'T CALL ME AGAIN!
SORRY, SAORI...
...
IT'S DAMP.
SWEAT ...
HUH?
WHAT WAS I DOING TODAY?
I BUNKERED DOWN IN MY ROOM TO BUILD THE TIGER I!
THERE'S A CONTEST COMING UP, Y'KNOW!
I KNOW.
SO HOW'S IT GOING, TAGO?
PERFECT! YOU SHOULD GET A LOAD OF THE RUST EFFECT I'VE ADDED TO IT!
SOUNDS GREAT!
YOU'RE WORKING ON ANOTHER LEVEL LATELY.

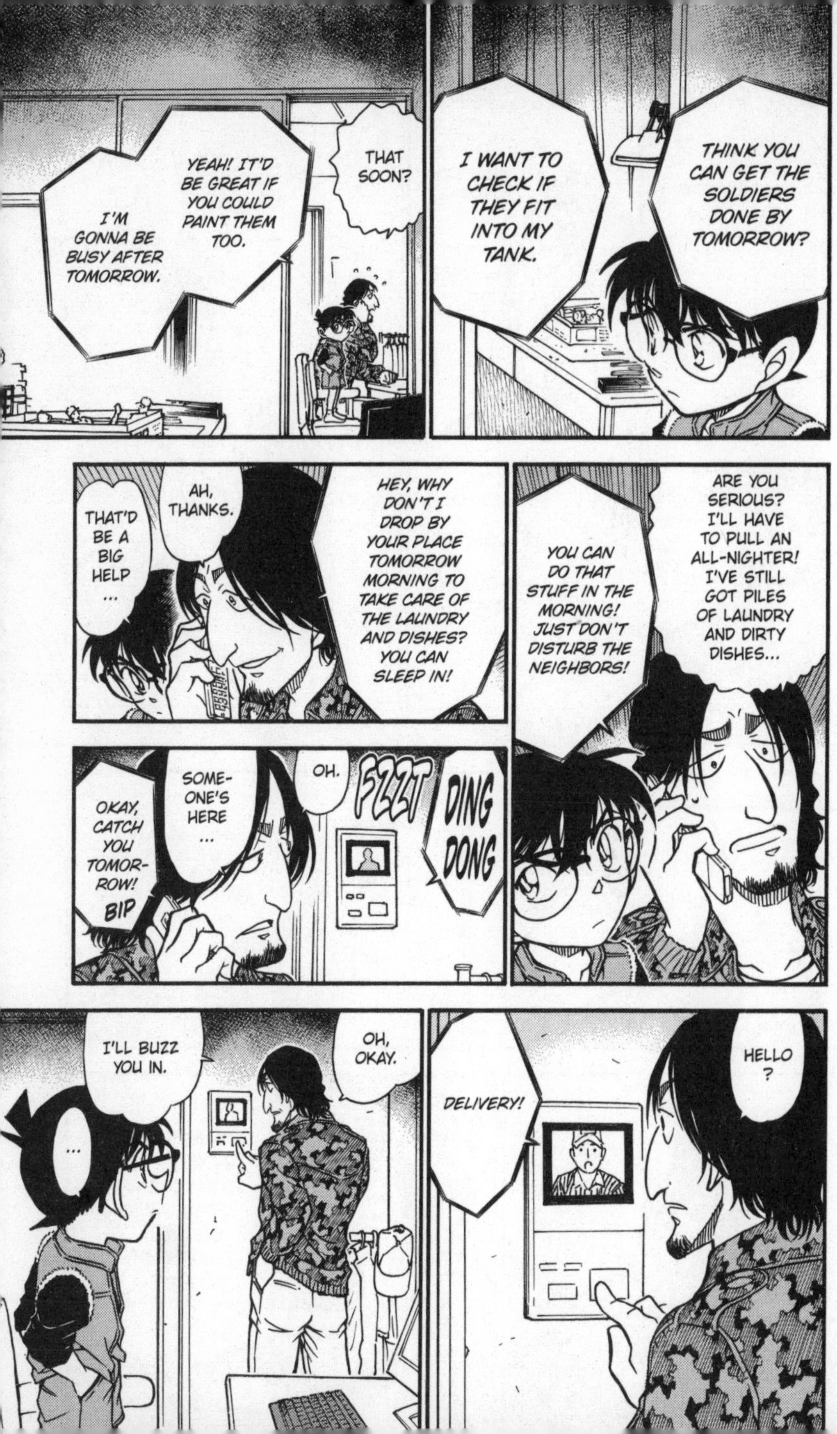
THINK YOU CAN GET THE SOLDIERS DONE BY TOMORROW?
I WANT TO CHECK IF THEY FIT INTO MY TANK.
THAT SOON?
YEAH! IT'D BE GREAT IF YOU COULD PAINT THEM TOO.
I'M GONNA BE BUSY AFTER TOMORROW.
ARE YOU SERIOUS? I'LL HAVE TO PULL AN ALL-NIGHTER! I'VE STILL GOT PILES OF LAUNDRY AND DIRTY DISHES...
YOU CAN DO THAT STUFF IN THE MORNING! JUST DON'T DISTURB THE NEIGHBORS!
HEY, WHY DON'T I DROP BY YOUR PLACE TOMORROW MORNING TO TAKE CARE OF THE LAUNDRY AND DISHES? YOU CAN SLEEP IN!
AH, THANKS.
THAT'D BE A BIG HELP ...
DING DONG
FZZT
OH.
SOME-ONE'S HERE ...
OKAY, CATCH YOU TOMOR-ROW!
BIP
HELLO ?
DELIVERY!
OH, OKAY.
I'LL BUZZ YOU IN.
...

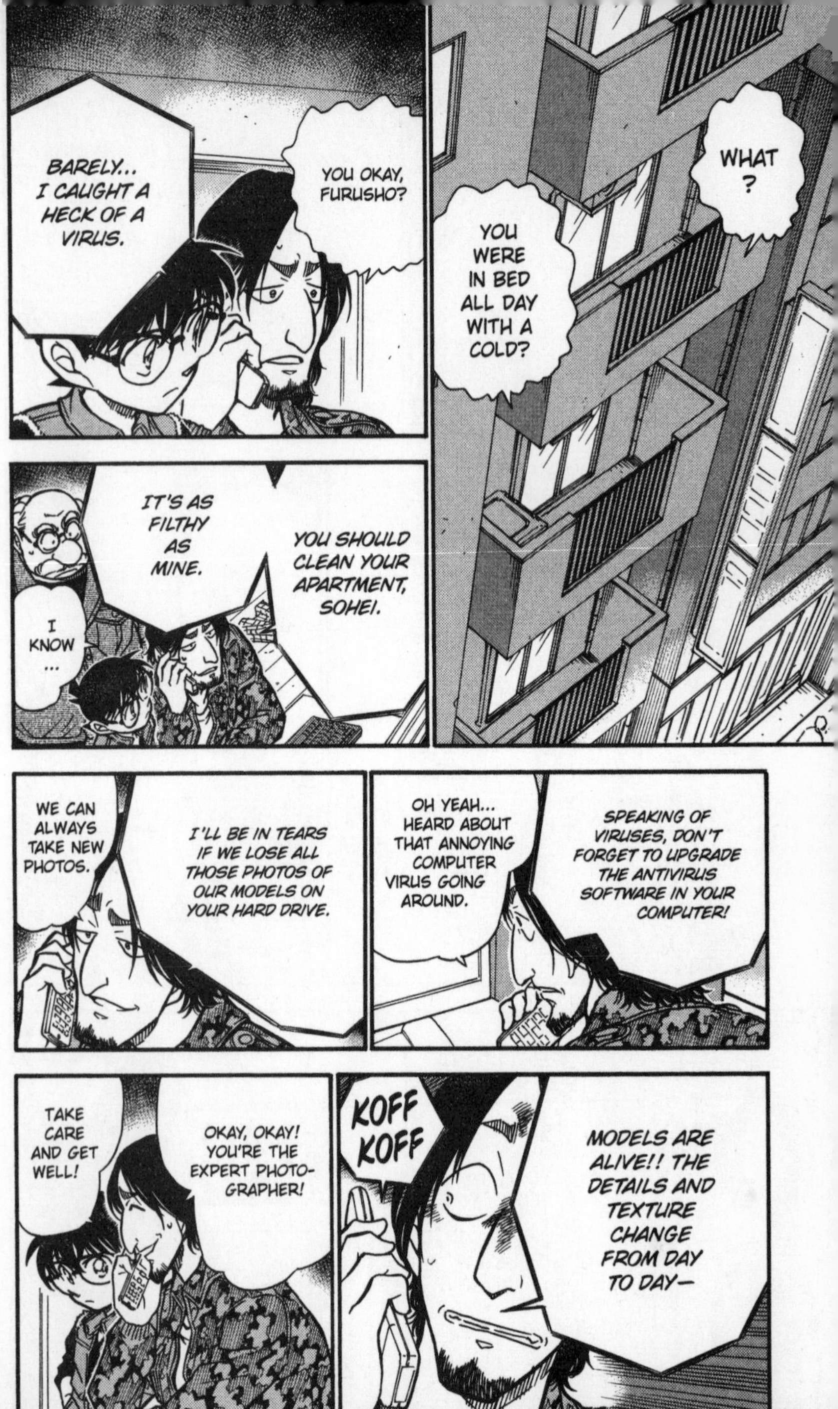
WHAT?
YOU WERE IN BED ALL DAY WITH A COLD?
YOU OKAY, FURUSHO?
BARELY... I CAUGHT A HECK OF A VIRUS.
YOU SHOULD CLEAN YOUR APARTMENT, SOHEI.
IT'S AS FILTHY AS MINE.
I KNOW...
SPEAKING OF VIRUSES, DON'T FORGET TO UPGRADE THE ANTIVIRUS SOFTWARE IN YOUR COMPUTER!
OH YEAH... HEARD ABOUT THAT ANNOYING COMPUTER VIRUS GOING AROUND.
I'LL BE IN TEARS IF WE LOSE ALL THOSE PHOTOS OF OUR MODELS ON YOUR HARD DRIVE.
WE CAN ALWAYS TAKE NEW PHOTOS.
MODELS ARE ALIVE!! THE DETAILS AND TEXTURE CHANGE FROM DAY TO DAY—
KOFF KOFF
OKAY, OKAY! YOU'RE THE EXPERT PHOTO-GRAPHER!
TAKE CARE AND GET WELL!

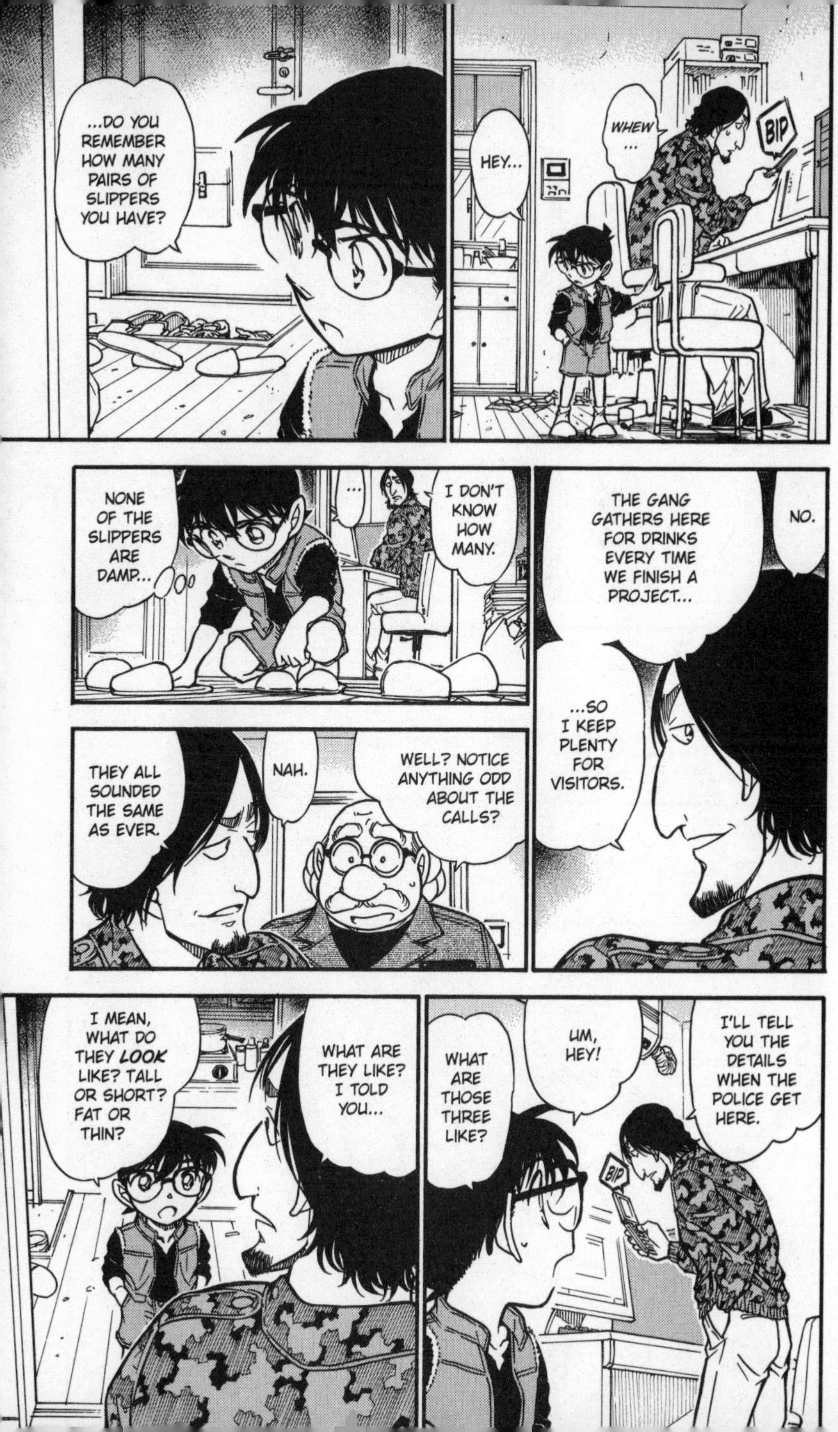
WHEW ...
BIP
HEY...
...DO YOU REMEMBER HOW MANY PAIRS OF SLIPPERS YOU HAVE?
NO.
THE GANG GATHERS HERE FOR DRINKS EVERY TIME WE FINISH A PROJECT...
...SO I KEEP PLENTY FOR VISITORS.
I DON'T KNOW HOW MANY.
...
NONE OF THE SLIPPERS ARE DAMP...
WELL? NOTICE ANYTHING ODD ABOUT THE CALLS?
NAH.
THEY ALL SOUNDED THE SAME AS EVER.
I'LL TELL YOU THE DETAILS WHEN THE POLICE GET HERE.
BIP
UM, HEY!
WHAT ARE THOSE THREE LIKE?
WHAT ARE THEY LIKE? I TOLD YOU...
I MEAN, WHAT DO THEY *LOOK* LIKE? TALL OR SHORT? FAT OR THIN?

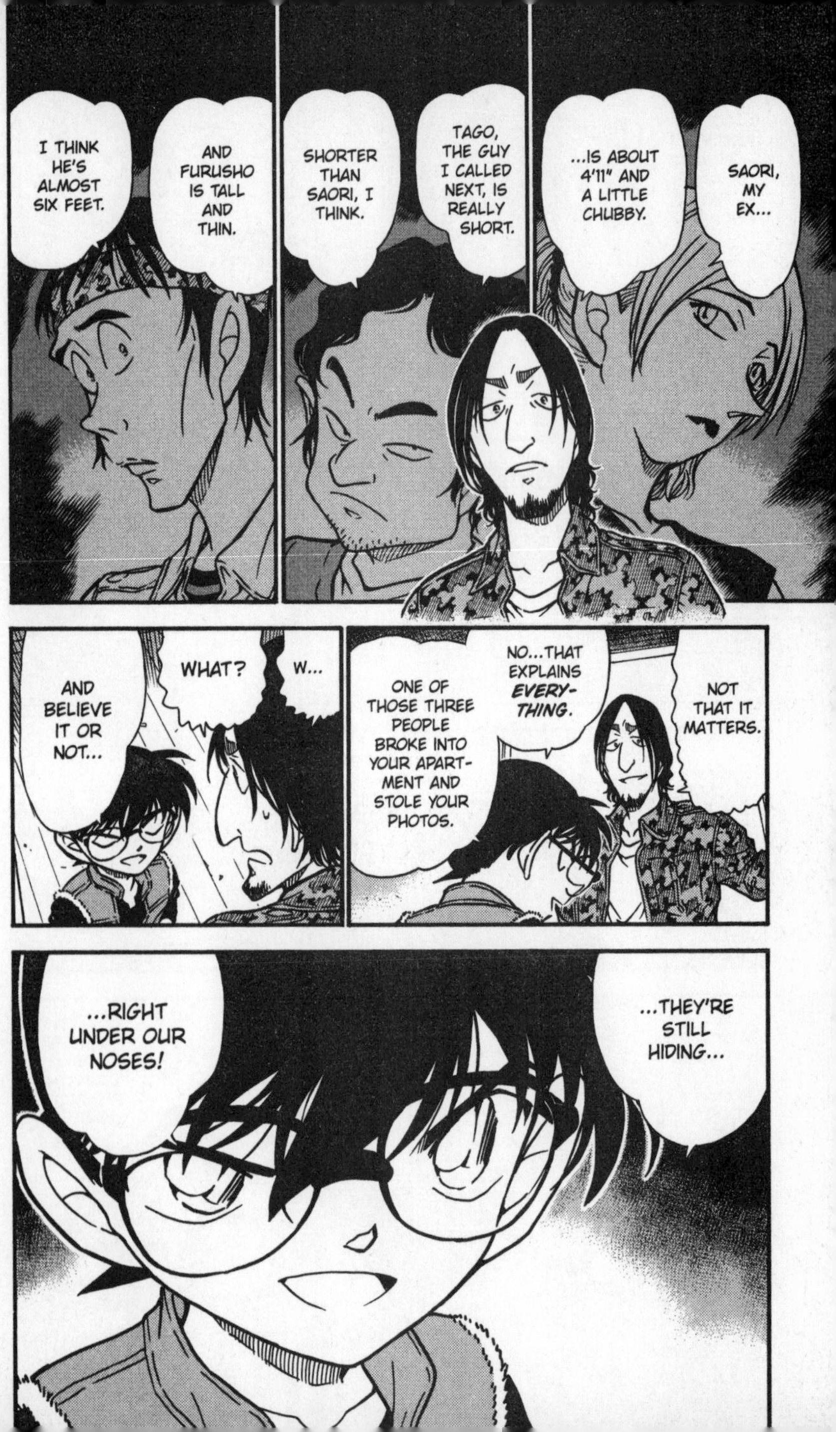
SAORI, MY EX...
...IS ABOUT 4'11" AND A LITTLE CHUBBY.
TAGO, THE GUY I CALLED NEXT, IS REALLY SHORT.
SHORTER THAN SAORI, I THINK.
AND FURUSHO IS TALL AND THIN.
I THINK HE'S ALMOST SIX FEET.
NOT THAT IT MATTERS.
NO...THAT EXPLAINS *EVERYTHING*.
ONE OF THOSE THREE PEOPLE BROKE INTO YOUR APARTMENT AND STOLE YOUR PHOTOS.
W...
WHAT?
AND BELIEVE IT OR NOT...
...THEY'RE STILL HIDING...
...RIGHT UNDER OUR NOSES!

FILE 9: THE COMPANY

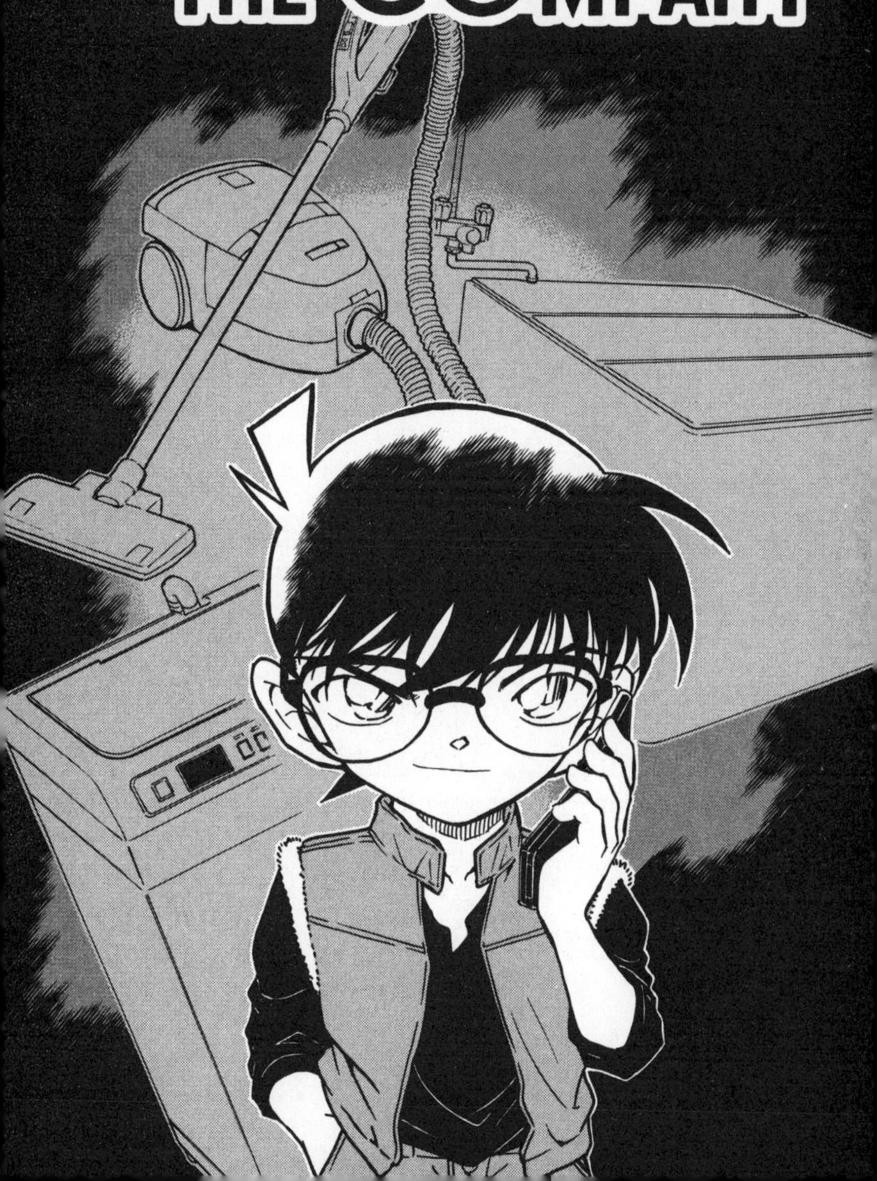

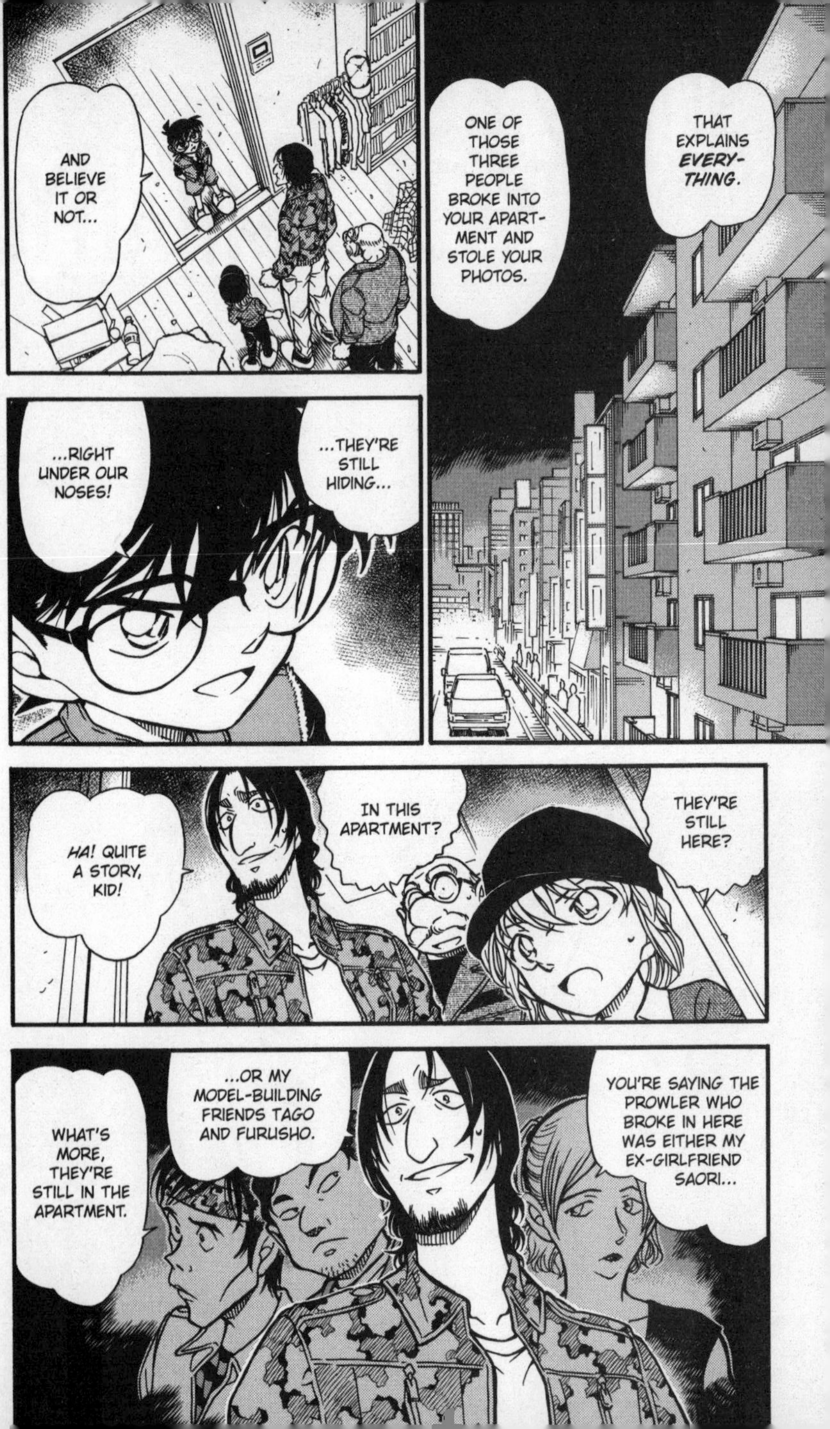

THAT EXPLAINS EVERYTHING.
ONE OF THOSE THREE PEOPLE BROKE INTO YOUR APARTMENT AND STOLE YOUR PHOTOS.
AND BELIEVE IT OR NOT...
...THEY'RE STILL HIDING...
...RIGHT UNDER OUR NOSES!
THEY'RE STILL HERE?
IN THIS APARTMENT?
HA! QUITE A STORY, KID!
YOU'RE SAYING THE PROWLER WHO BROKE IN HERE WAS EITHER MY EX-GIRLFRIEND SAORI...
...OR MY MODEL-BUILDING FRIENDS TAGO AND FURUSHO.
WHAT'S MORE, THEY'RE STILL IN THE APARTMENT.

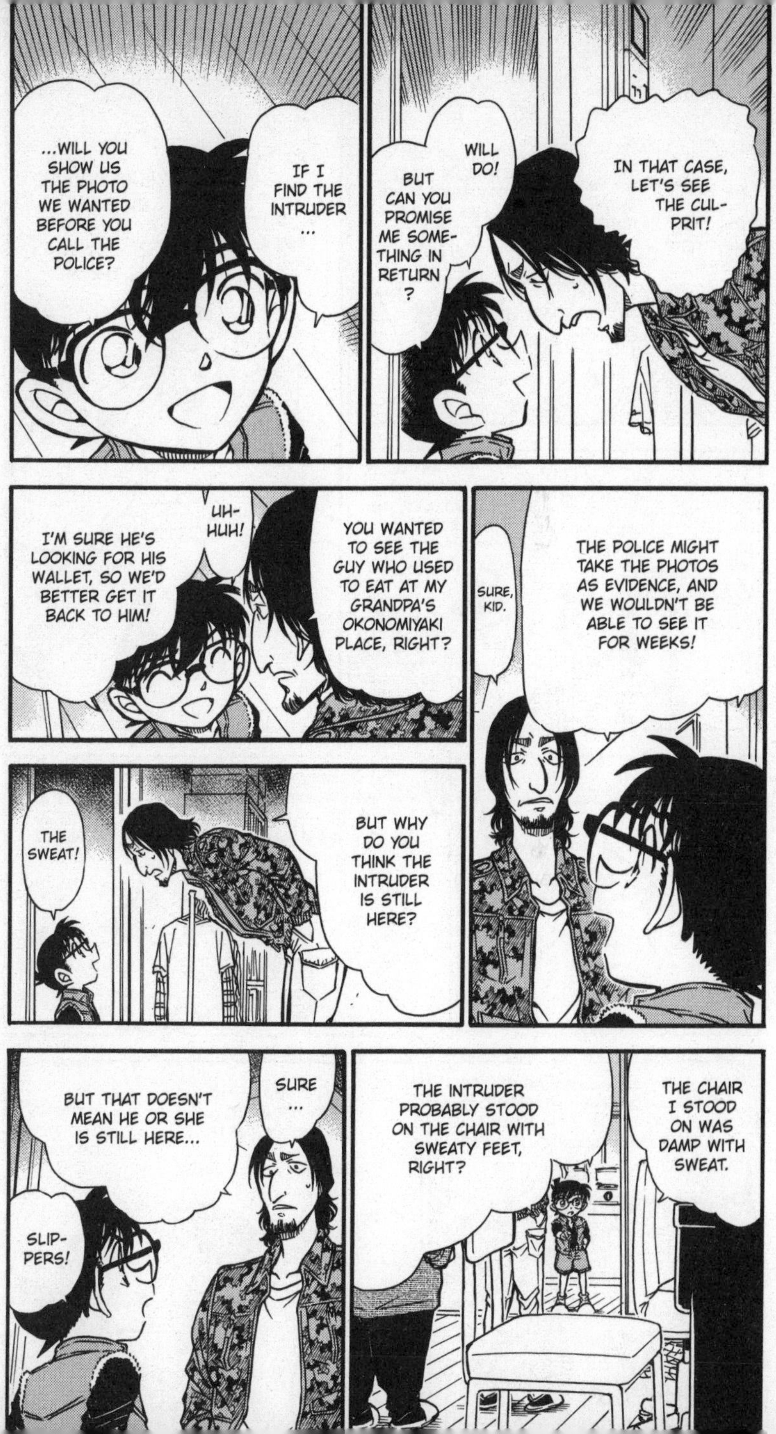
IN THAT CASE, LET'S SEE THE CUL-PRIT!
WILL DO!
BUT CAN YOU PROMISE ME SOME-THING IN RETURN?
IF I FIND THE INTRUDER...
...WILL YOU SHOW US THE PHOTO WE WANTED BEFORE YOU CALL THE POLICE?
THE POLICE MIGHT TAKE THE PHOTOS AS EVIDENCE, AND WE WOULDN'T BE ABLE TO SEE IT FOR WEEKS!
SURE, KID.
YOU WANTED TO SEE THE GUY WHO USED TO EAT AT MY GRANDPA'S OKONOMIYAKI PLACE, RIGHT?
UH-HUH!
I'M SURE HE'S LOOKING FOR HIS WALLET, SO WE'D BETTER GET IT BACK TO HIM!
BUT WHY DO YOU THINK THE INTRUDER IS STILL HERE?
THE SWEAT!
THE CHAIR I STOOD ON WAS DAMP WITH SWEAT.
THE INTRUDER PROBABLY STOOD ON THE CHAIR WITH SWEATY FEET, RIGHT?
SURE...
BUT THAT DOESN'T MEAN HE OR SHE IS STILL HERE...
SLIP-PERS!

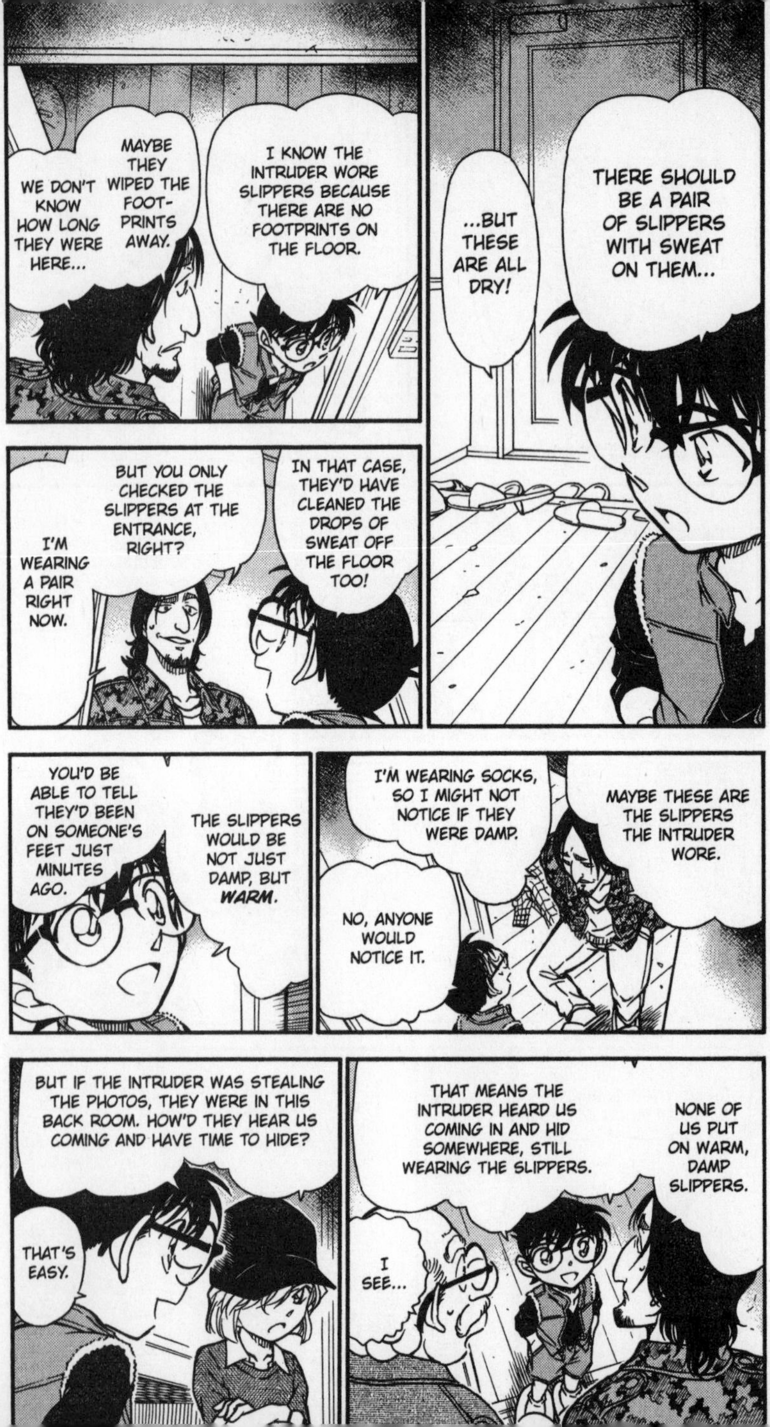
THERE SHOULD BE A PAIR OF SLIPPERS WITH SWEAT ON THEM...
...BUT THESE ARE ALL DRY!
I KNOW THE INTRUDER WORE SLIPPERS BECAUSE THERE ARE NO FOOTPRINTS ON THE FLOOR.
MAYBE THEY WIPED THE FOOT-PRINTS AWAY.
WE DON'T KNOW HOW LONG THEY WERE HERE...
IN THAT CASE, THEY'D HAVE CLEANED THE DROPS OF SWEAT OFF THE FLOOR TOO!
BUT YOU ONLY CHECKED THE SLIPPERS AT THE ENTRANCE, RIGHT?
I'M WEARING A PAIR RIGHT NOW.
MAYBE THESE ARE THE SLIPPERS THE INTRUDER WORE.
I'M WEARING SOCKS, SO I MIGHT NOT NOTICE IF THEY WERE DAMP.
NO, ANYONE WOULD NOTICE IT.
THE SLIPPERS WOULD BE NOT JUST DAMP, BUT ***WARM***.
YOU'D BE ABLE TO TELL THEY'D BEEN ON SOMEONE'S FEET JUST MINUTES AGO.
NONE OF US PUT ON WARM, DAMP SLIPPERS.
THAT MEANS THE INTRUDER HEARD US COMING IN AND HID SOMEWHERE, STILL WEARING THE SLIPPERS.
I SEE...
BUT IF THE INTRUDER WAS STEALING THE PHOTOS, THEY WERE IN THIS BACK ROOM. HOW'D THEY HEAR US COMING AND HAVE TIME TO HIDE?
THAT'S EASY.

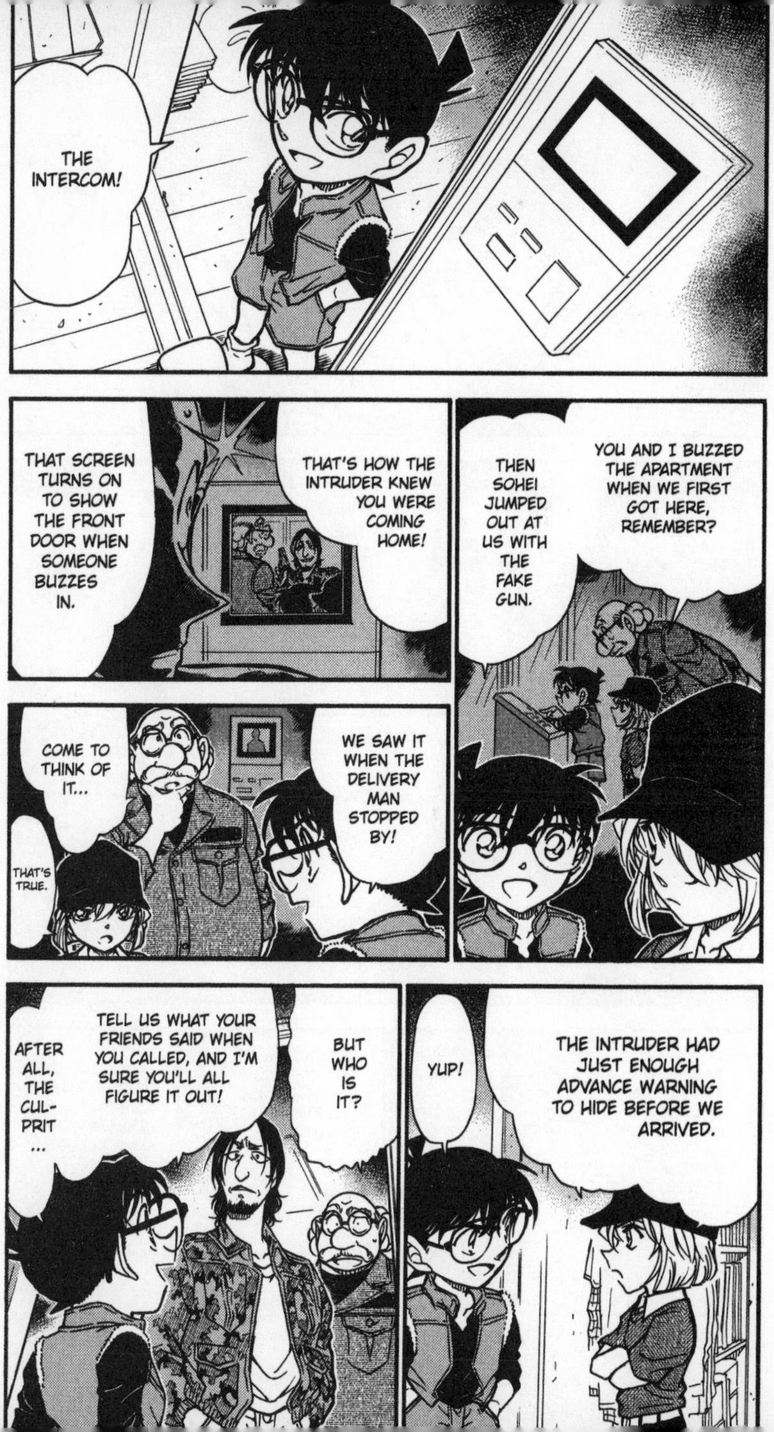
THE INTERCOM!
YOU AND I BUZZED THE APARTMENT WHEN WE FIRST GOT HERE, REMEMBER?
THEN SOHEI JUMPED OUT AT US WITH THE FAKE GUN.
THAT'S HOW THE INTRUDER KNEW YOU WERE COMING HOME!
THAT SCREEN TURNS ON TO SHOW THE FRONT DOOR WHEN SOMEONE BUZZES IN.
WE SAW IT WHEN THE DELIVERY MAN STOPPED BY!
COME TO THINK OF IT...
THAT'S TRUE.
THE INTRUDER HAD JUST ENOUGH ADVANCE WARNING TO HIDE BEFORE WE ARRIVED.
YUP!
BUT WHO IS IT?
TELL US WHAT YOUR FRIENDS SAID WHEN YOU CALLED, AND I'M SURE YOU'LL ALL FIGURE IT OUT!
AFTER ALL, THE CUL-PRIT ...

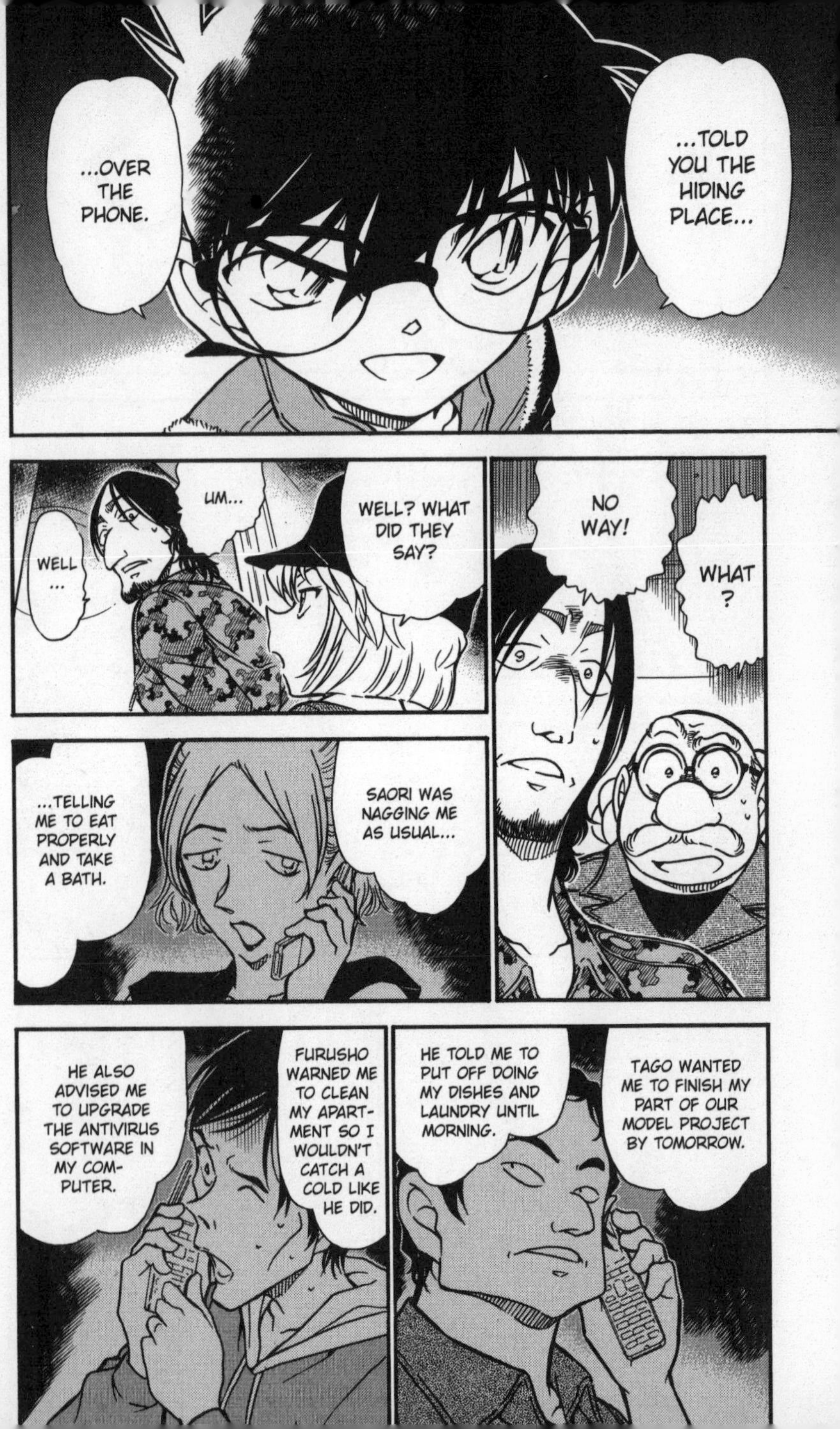
...TOLD YOU THE HIDING PLACE...
...OVER THE PHONE.
NO WAY!
WHAT ?
WELL? WHAT DID THEY SAY?
UM...
WELL ...
SAORI WAS NAGGING ME AS USUAL...
...TELLING ME TO EAT PROPERLY AND TAKE A BATH.
TAGO WANTED ME TO FINISH MY PART OF OUR MODEL PROJECT BY TOMORROW.
HE TOLD ME TO PUT OFF DOING MY DISHES AND LAUNDRY UNTIL MORNING.
FURUSHO WARNED ME TO CLEAN MY APART-MENT SO I WOULDN'T CATCH A COLD LIKE HE DID.
HE ALSO ADVISED ME TO UPGRADE THE ANTIVIRUS SOFTWARE IN MY COM-PUTER.

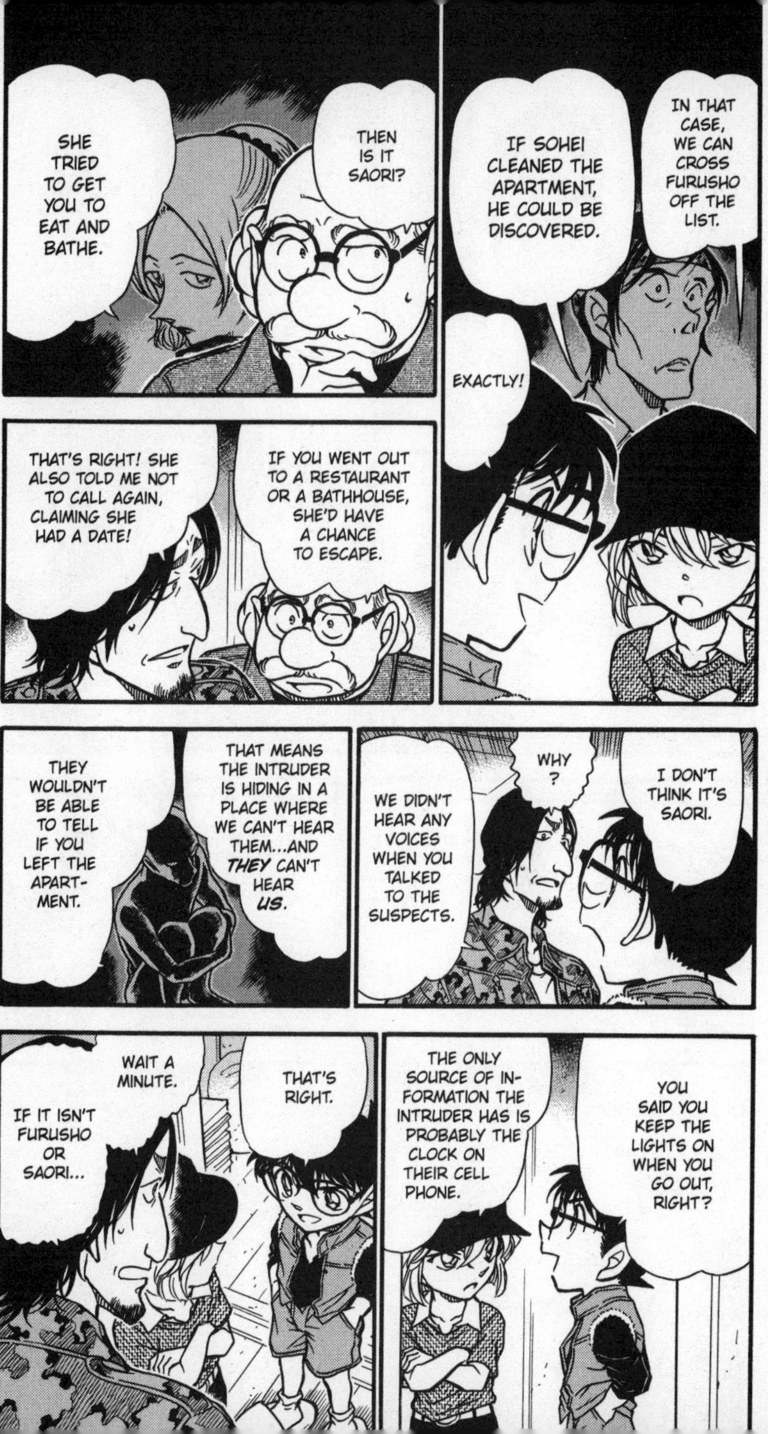

IN THAT CASE, WE CAN CROSS FURUSHO OFF THE LIST.
IF SOHEI CLEANED THE APARTMENT, HE COULD BE DISCOVERED.
EXACTLY!
THEN IS IT SAORI?
SHE TRIED TO GET YOU TO EAT AND BATHE.
IF YOU WENT OUT TO A RESTAURANT OR A BATHHOUSE, SHE'D HAVE A CHANCE TO ESCAPE.
THAT'S RIGHT! SHE ALSO TOLD ME NOT TO CALL AGAIN, CLAIMING SHE HAD A DATE!
I DON'T THINK IT'S SAORI.
WHY?
WE DIDN'T HEAR ANY VOICES WHEN YOU TALKED TO THE SUSPECTS.
THAT MEANS THE INTRUDER IS HIDING IN A PLACE WHERE WE CAN'T HEAR THEM...AND *THEY* CAN'T HEAR *US*.
THEY WOULDN'T BE ABLE TO TELL IF YOU LEFT THE APART-MENT.
YOU SAID YOU KEEP THE LIGHTS ON WHEN YOU GO OUT, RIGHT?
THE ONLY SOURCE OF IN-FORMATION THE INTRUDER HAS IS PROBABLY THE CLOCK ON THEIR CELL PHONE.
THAT'S RIGHT.
WAIT A MINUTE.
IF IT ISN'T FURUSHO OR SAORI...

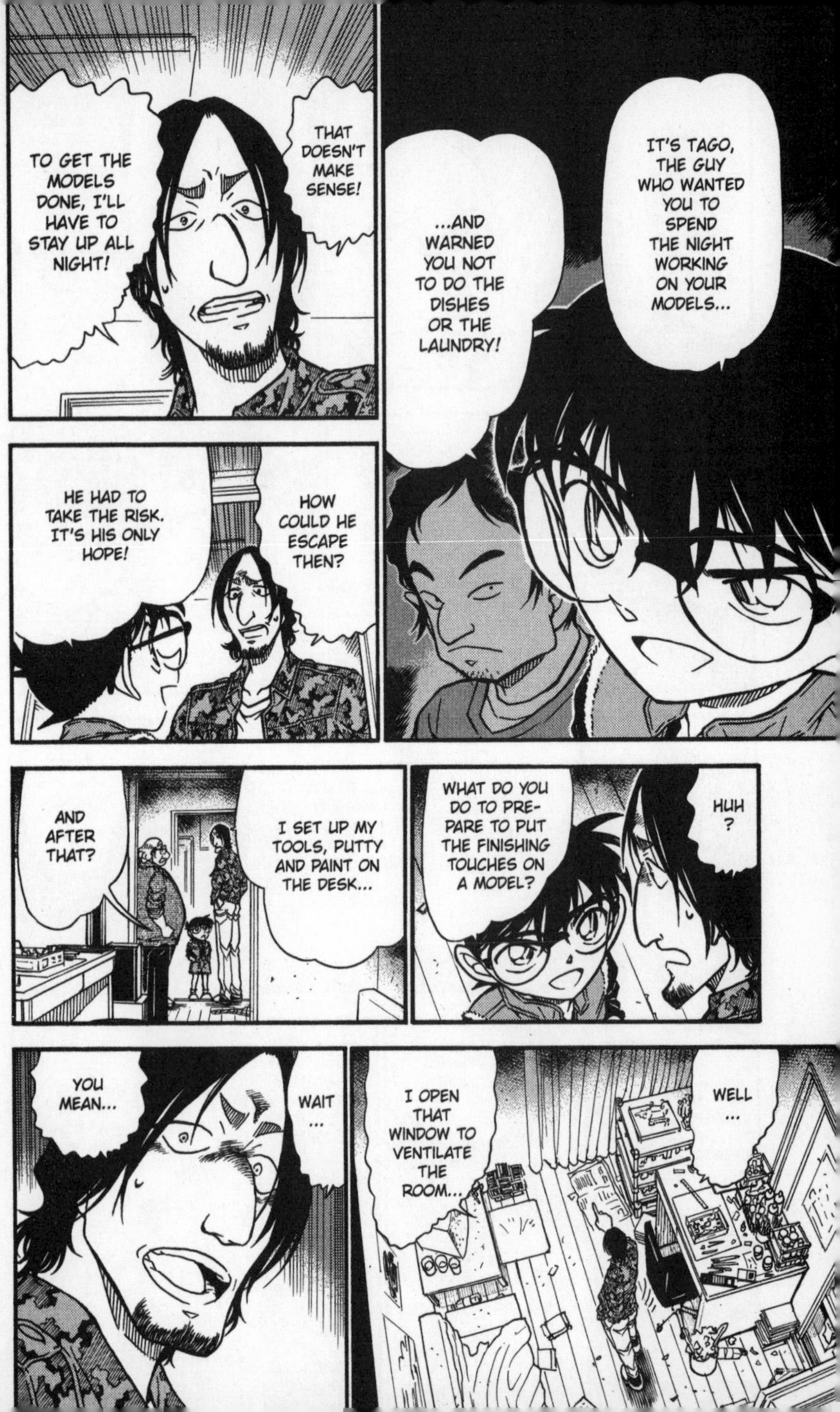
IT'S TAGO, THE GUY WHO WANTED YOU TO SPEND THE NIGHT WORKING ON YOUR MODELS...
...AND WARNED YOU NOT TO DO THE DISHES OR THE LAUNDRY!
THAT DOESN'T MAKE SENSE!
TO GET THE MODELS DONE, I'LL HAVE TO STAY UP ALL NIGHT!
HOW COULD HE ESCAPE THEN?
HE HAD TO TAKE THE RISK. IT'S HIS ONLY HOPE!
HUH?
WHAT DO YOU DO TO PRE-PARE TO PUT THE FINISHING TOUCHES ON A MODEL?
I SET UP MY TOOLS, PUTTY AND PAINT ON THE DESK...
AND AFTER THAT?
WELL...
I OPEN THAT WINDOW TO VENTILATE THE ROOM...
WAIT...
YOU MEAN...

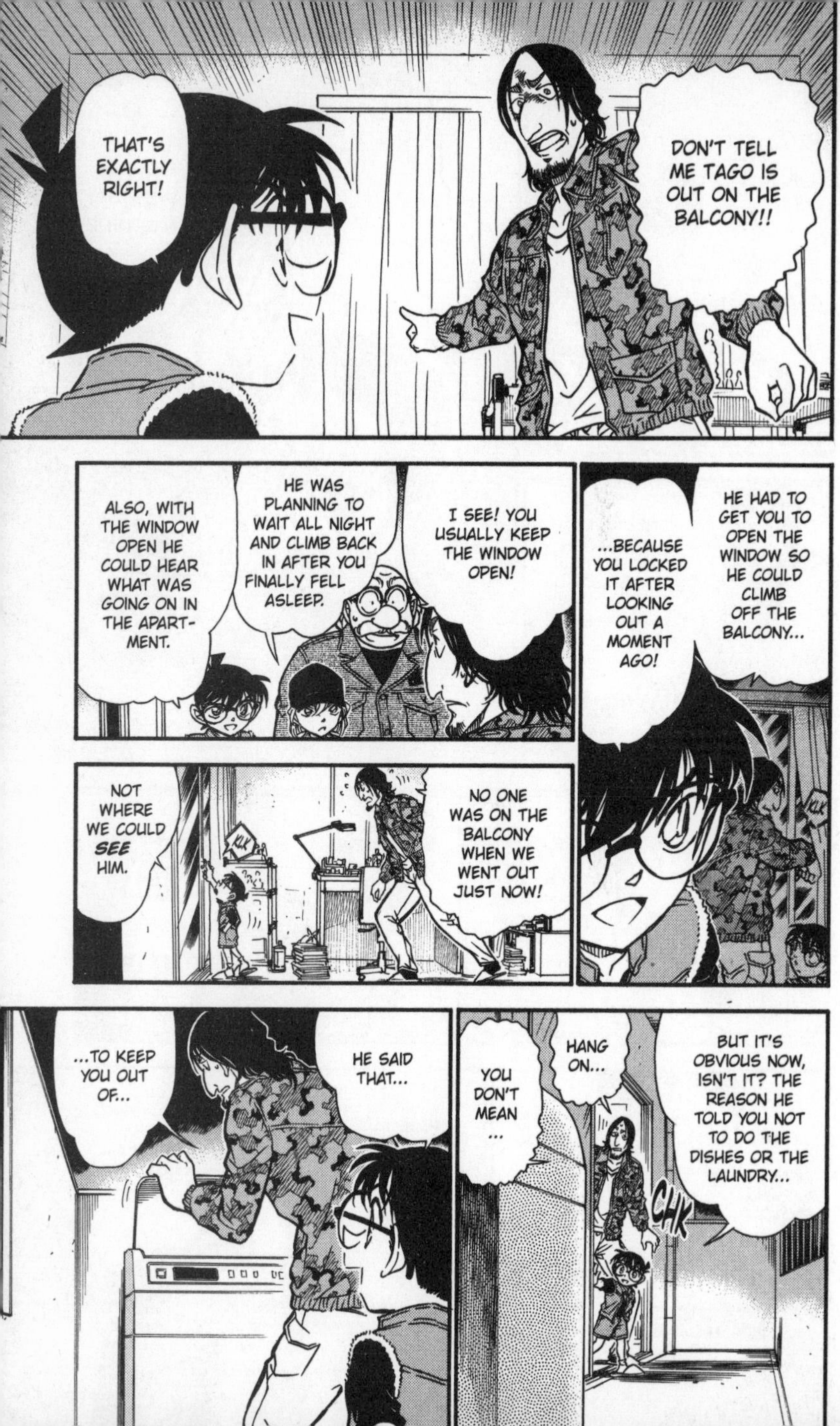

DON'T TELL ME TAGO IS OUT ON THE BALCONY!!
THAT'S EXACTLY RIGHT!
HE HAD TO GET YOU TO OPEN THE WINDOW SO HE COULD CLIMB OFF THE BALCONY...
...BECAUSE YOU LOCKED IT AFTER LOOKING OUT A MOMENT AGO!
KLK
I SEE! YOU USUALLY KEEP THE WINDOW OPEN!
HE WAS PLANNING TO WAIT ALL NIGHT AND CLIMB BACK IN AFTER YOU FINALLY FELL ASLEEP.
ALSO, WITH THE WINDOW OPEN HE COULD HEAR WHAT WAS GOING ON IN THE APART-MENT.
NO ONE WAS ON THE BALCONY WHEN WE WENT OUT JUST NOW!
KLK
NOT WHERE WE COULD *SEE* HIM.
BUT IT'S OBVIOUS NOW, ISN'T IT? THE REASON HE TOLD YOU NOT TO DO THE DISHES OR THE LAUNDRY...
HANG ON...
YOU DON'T MEAN ...
CHK
HE SAID THAT...
...TO KEEP YOU OUT OF...

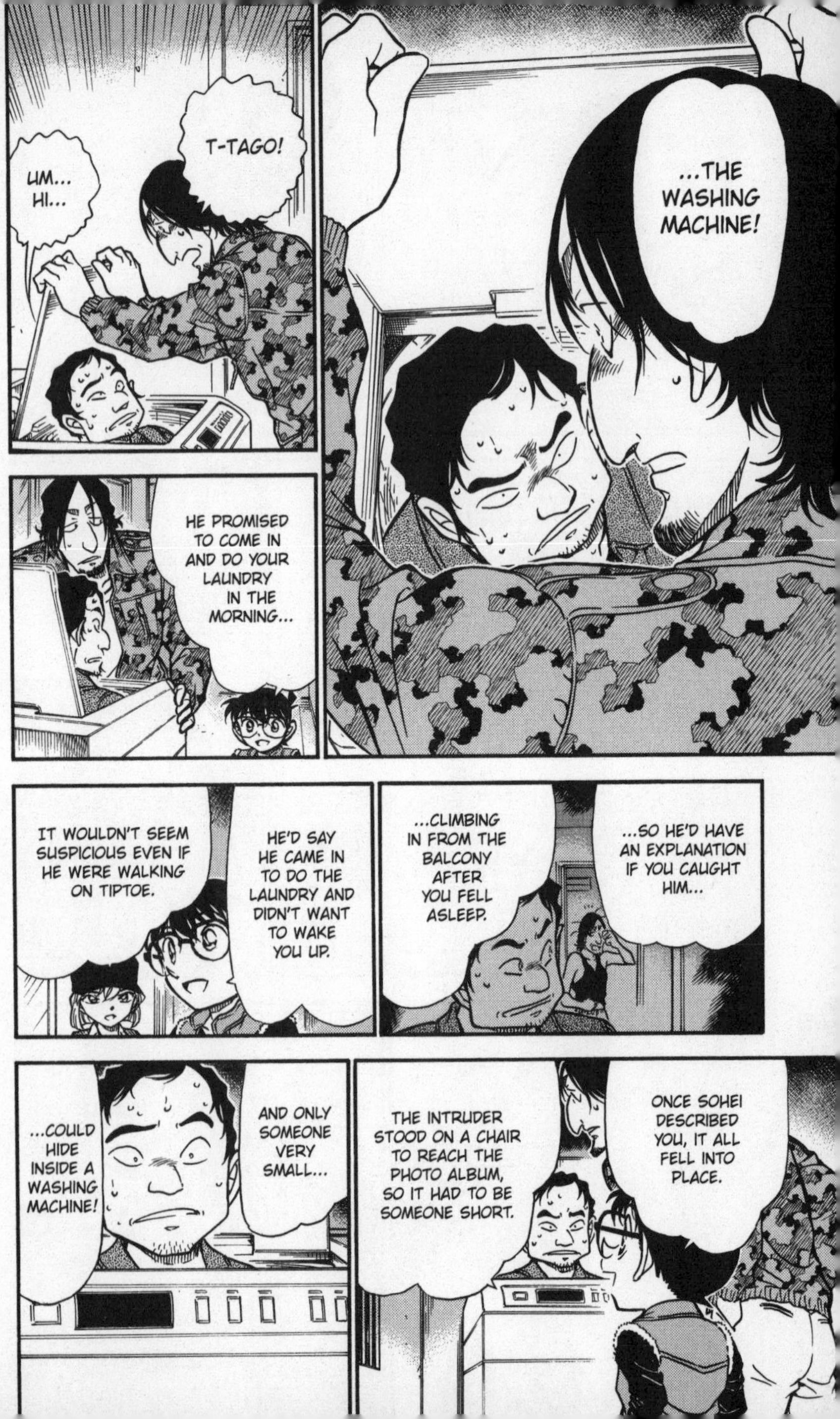
...THE WASHING MACHINE!
T-TAGO!
UM... HI...
HE PROMISED TO COME IN AND DO YOUR LAUNDRY IN THE MORNING...
...SO HE'D HAVE AN EXPLANATION IF YOU CAUGHT HIM...
...CLIMBING IN FROM THE BALCONY AFTER YOU FELL ASLEEP.
HE'D SAY HE CAME IN TO DO THE LAUNDRY AND DIDN'T WANT TO WAKE YOU UP.
IT WOULDN'T SEEM SUSPICIOUS EVEN IF HE WERE WALKING ON TIPTOE.
ONCE SOHEI DESCRIBED YOU, IT ALL FELL INTO PLACE.
THE INTRUDER STOOD ON A CHAIR TO REACH THE PHOTO ALBUM, SO IT HAD TO BE SOMEONE SHORT.
AND ONLY SOMEONE VERY SMALL...
...COULD HIDE INSIDE A WASHING MACHINE!

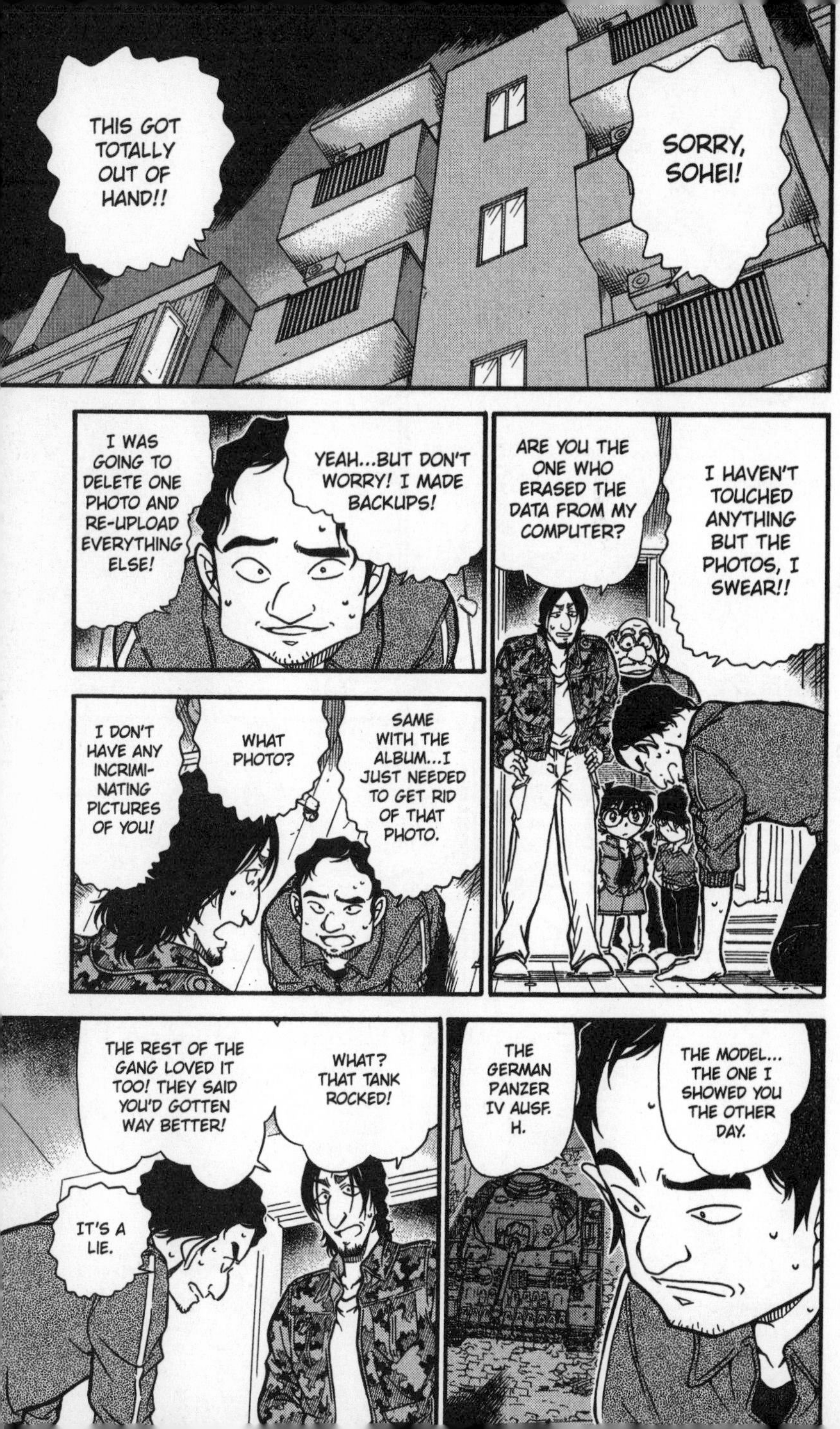
SORRY, SOHEI!
THIS GOT TOTALLY OUT OF HAND!!
ARE YOU THE ONE WHO ERASED THE DATA FROM MY COMPUTER?
I HAVEN'T TOUCHED ANYTHING BUT THE PHOTOS, I SWEAR!!
YEAH...BUT DON'T WORRY! I MADE BACKUPS!
I WAS GOING TO DELETE ONE PHOTO AND RE-UPLOAD EVERYTHING ELSE!
SAME WITH THE ALBUM...I JUST NEEDED TO GET RID OF THAT PHOTO.
WHAT PHOTO?
I DON'T HAVE ANY INCRIMINATING PICTURES OF YOU!
THE MODEL... THE ONE I SHOWED YOU THE OTHER DAY.
THE GERMAN PANZER IV AUSF. H.
WHAT? THAT TANK ROCKED!
THE REST OF THE GANG LOVED IT TOO! THEY SAID YOU'D GOTTEN WAY BETTER!
IT'S A LIE.

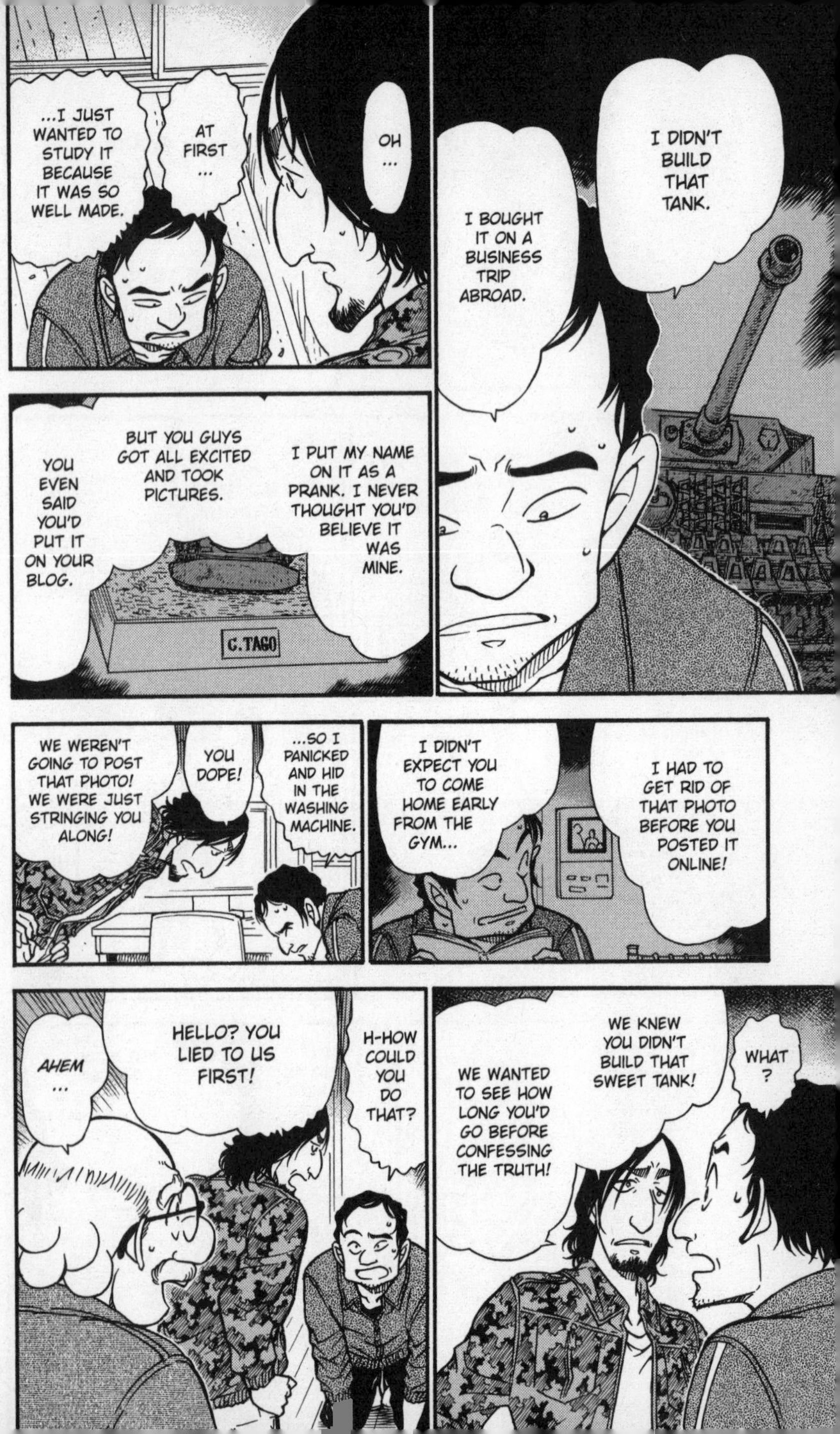
I DIDN'T BUILD THAT TANK.
I BOUGHT IT ON A BUSINESS TRIP ABROAD.
OH...
AT FIRST...
...I JUST WANTED TO STUDY IT BECAUSE IT WAS SO WELL MADE.
I PUT MY NAME ON IT AS A PRANK. I NEVER THOUGHT YOU'D BELIEVE IT WAS MINE.
BUT YOU GUYS GOT ALL EXCITED AND TOOK PICTURES.
YOU EVEN SAID YOU'D PUT IT ON YOUR BLOG.
C.TAGO
I HAD TO GET RID OF THAT PHOTO BEFORE YOU POSTED IT ONLINE!
I DIDN'T EXPECT YOU TO COME HOME EARLY FROM THE GYM...
...SO I PANICKED AND HID IN THE WASHING MACHINE.
YOU DOPE!
WE WEREN'T GOING TO POST THAT PHOTO! WE WERE JUST STRINGING YOU ALONG!
WHAT?
WE KNEW YOU DIDN'T BUILD THAT SWEET TANK!
WE WANTED TO SEE HOW LONG YOU'D GO BEFORE CONFESSING THE TRUTH!
H-HOW COULD YOU DO THAT?
HELLO? YOU LIED TO US FIRST!
AHEM...

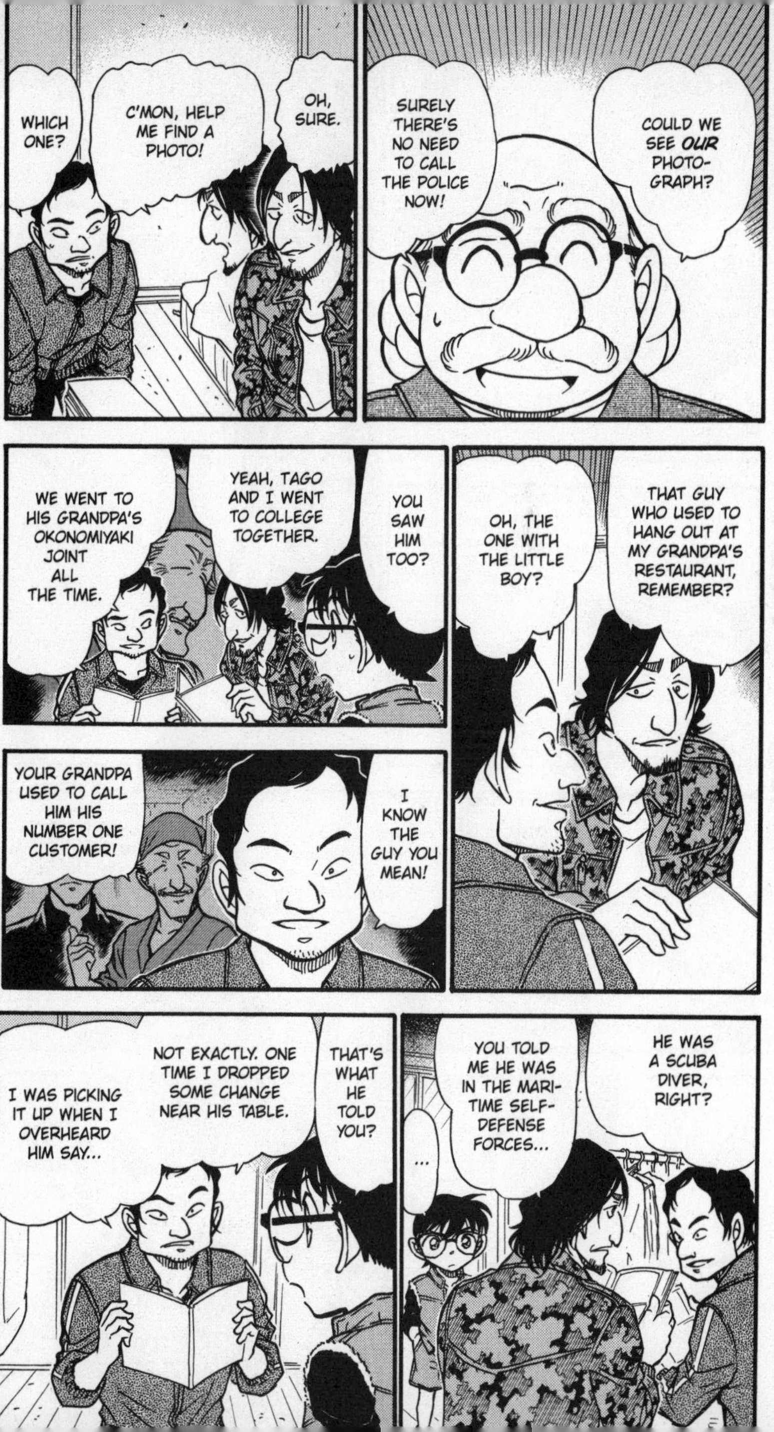
COULD WE SEE ***OUR*** PHOTOGRAPH?
SURELY THERE'S NO NEED TO CALL THE POLICE NOW!
OH, SURE.
C'MON, HELP ME FIND A PHOTO!
WHICH ONE?
THAT GUY WHO USED TO HANG OUT AT MY GRANDPA'S RESTAURANT, REMEMBER?
OH, THE ONE WITH THE LITTLE BOY?
YOU SAW HIM TOO?
YEAH, TAGO AND I WENT TO COLLEGE TOGETHER.
WE WENT TO HIS GRANDPA'S OKONOMIYAKI JOINT ALL THE TIME.
I KNOW THE GUY YOU MEAN!
YOUR GRANDPA USED TO CALL HIM HIS NUMBER ONE CUSTOMER!
HE WAS A SCUBA DIVER, RIGHT?
YOU TOLD ME HE WAS IN THE MARITIME SELF-DEFENSE FORCES...
...
THAT'S WHAT HE TOLD YOU?
NOT EXACTLY. ONE TIME I DROPPED SOME CHANGE NEAR HIS TABLE.
I WAS PICKING IT UP WHEN I OVERHEARD HIM SAY...

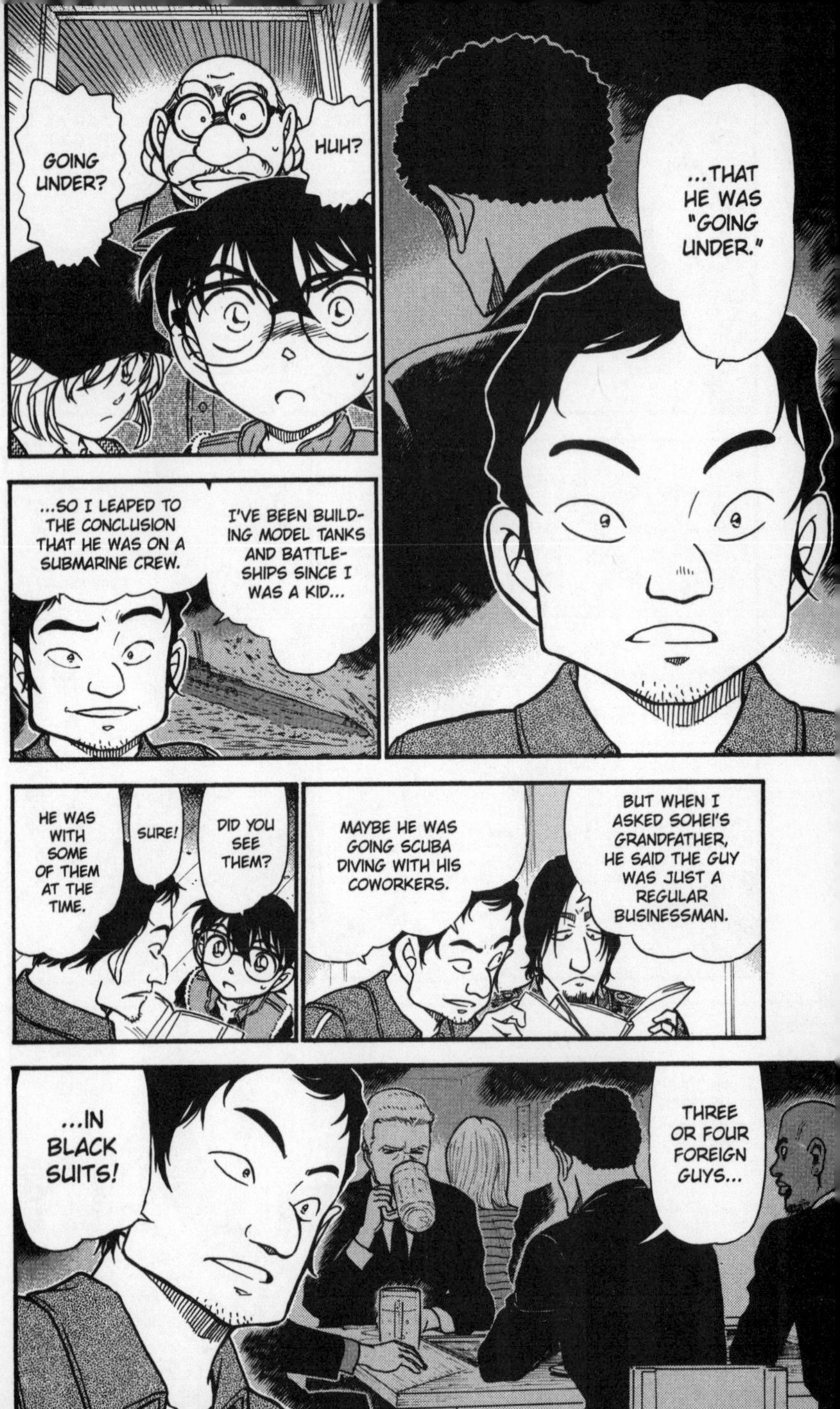
...THAT HE WAS "GOING UNDER."
HUH?
GOING UNDER?
I'VE BEEN BUILDING MODEL TANKS AND BATTLESHIPS SINCE I WAS A KID...
...SO I LEAPED TO THE CONCLUSION THAT HE WAS ON A SUBMARINE CREW.
BUT WHEN I ASKED SOHEI'S GRANDFATHER, HE SAID THE GUY WAS JUST A REGULAR BUSINESSMAN.
MAYBE HE WAS GOING SCUBA DIVING WITH HIS COWORKERS.
DID YOU SEE THEM?
SURE!
HE WAS WITH SOME OF THEM AT THE TIME.
THREE OR FOUR FOREIGN GUYS...
...IN BLACK SUITS!

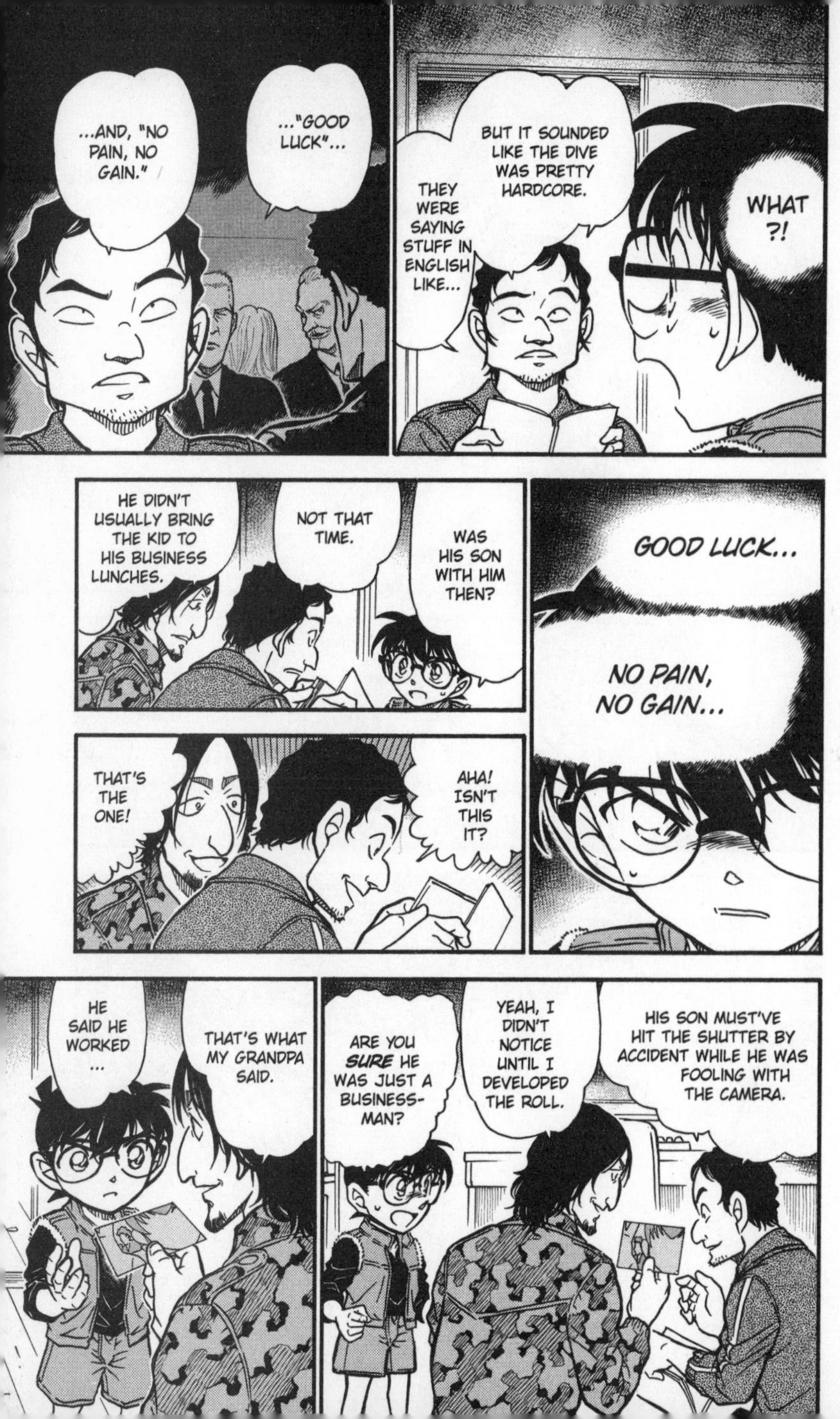
BUT IT SOUNDED LIKE THE DIVE WAS PRETTY HARDCORE.
THEY WERE SAYING STUFF IN ENGLISH LIKE...
WHAT ?!
..."GOOD LUCK"...
...AND, "NO PAIN, NO GAIN."
GOOD LUCK...
NO PAIN, NO GAIN...
WAS HIS SON WITH HIM THEN?
NOT THAT TIME.
HE DIDN'T USUALLY BRING THE KID TO HIS BUSINESS LUNCHES.
AHA! ISN'T THIS IT?
THAT'S THE ONE!
HIS SON MUST'VE HIT THE SHUTTER BY ACCIDENT WHILE HE WAS FOOLING WITH THE CAMERA.
YEAH, I DIDN'T NOTICE UNTIL I DEVELOPED THE ROLL.
ARE YOU *SURE* HE WAS JUST A BUSINESS-MAN?
THAT'S WHAT MY GRANDPA SAID.
HE SAID HE WORKED ...

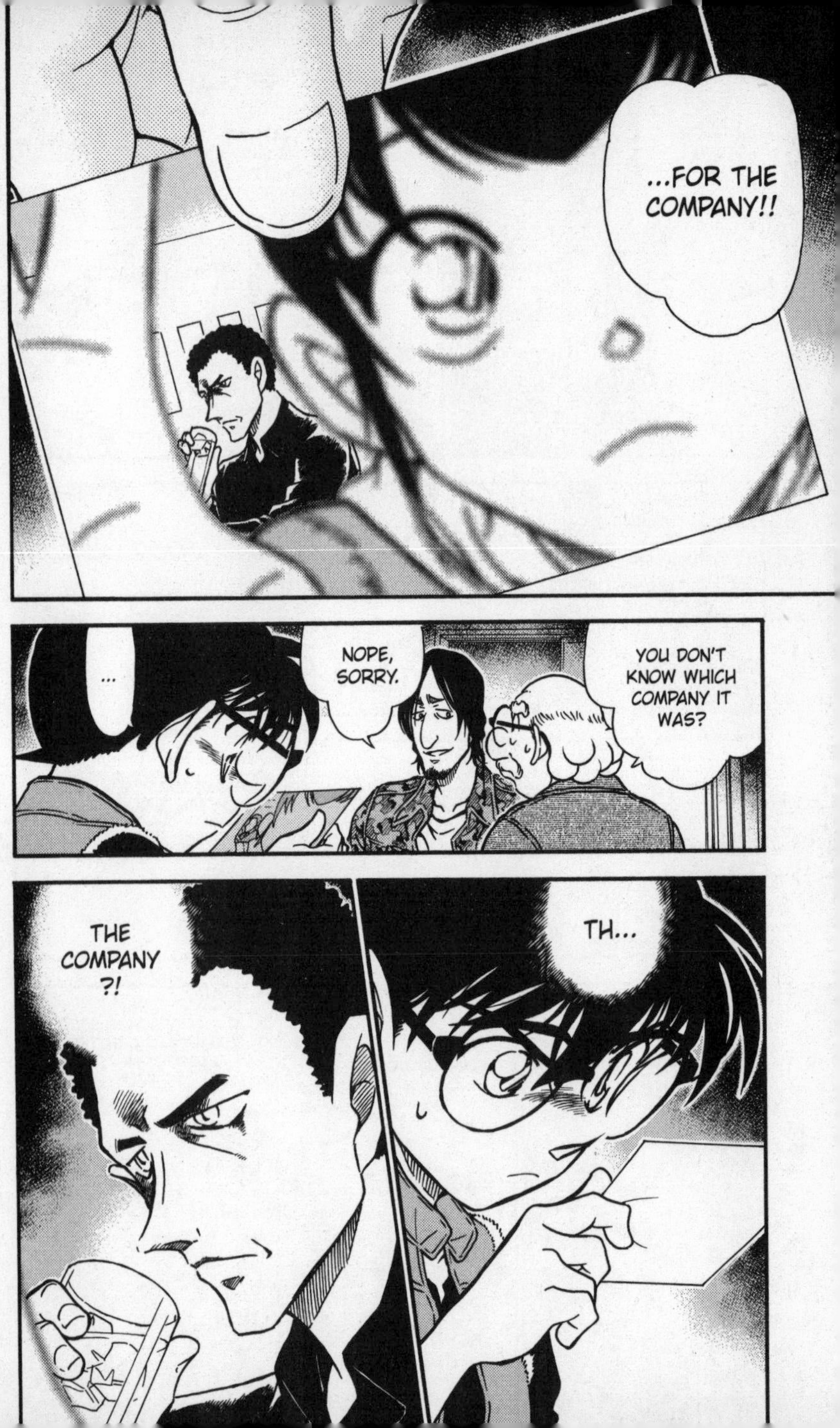
...FOR THE COMPANY!!
YOU DON'T KNOW WHICH COMPANY IT WAS?
NOPE, SORRY.
...
TH...
THE COMPANY ?!

FILE 10: WRONG NUMBER

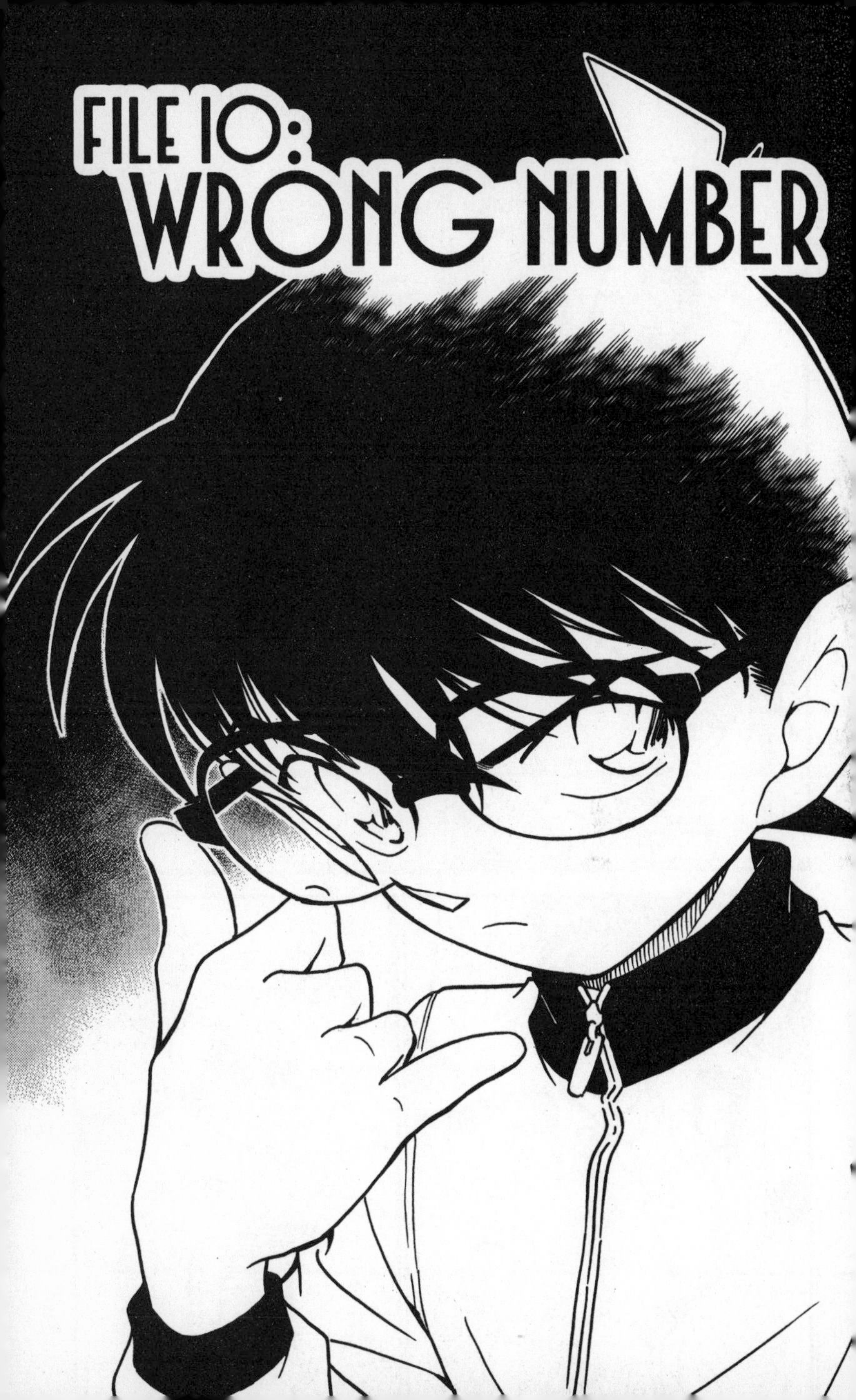

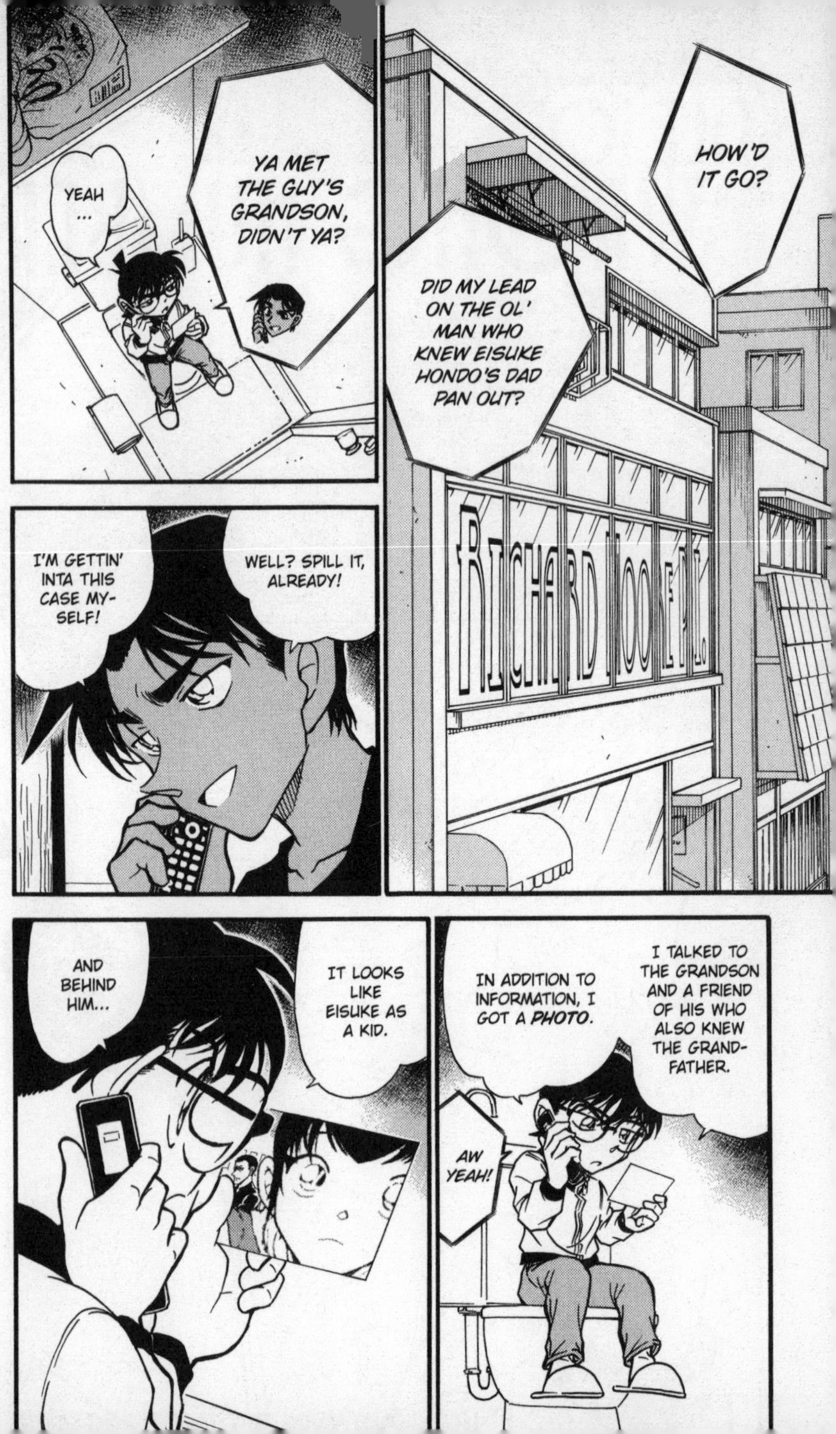
HOW'D IT GO?
DID MY LEAD ON THE OL' MAN WHO KNEW EISUKE HONDO'S DAD PAN OUT?
YA MET THE GUY'S GRANDSON, DIDN'T YA?
YEAH ...
WELL? SPILL IT, ALREADY!
I'M GETTIN' INTA THIS CASE MY-SELF!
I TALKED TO THE GRANDSON AND A FRIEND OF HIS WHO ALSO KNEW THE GRAND-FATHER.
IN ADDITION TO INFORMATION, I GOT A ***PHOTO***.
AW YEAH!
IT LOOKS LIKE EISUKE AS A KID.
AND BEHIND HIM...

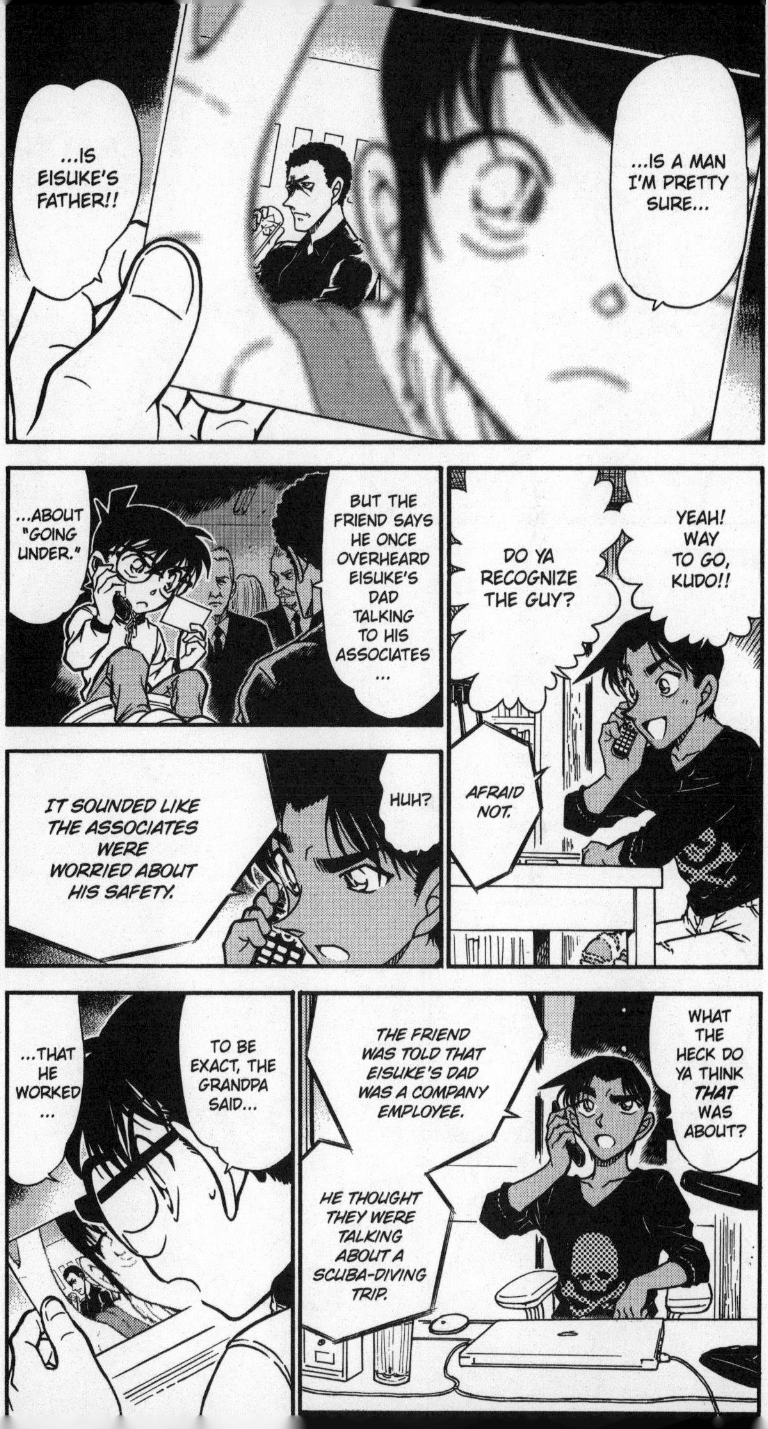
...IS A MAN I'M PRETTY SURE...
...IS EISUKE'S FATHER!!
YEAH! WAY TO GO, KUDO!!
DO YA RECOGNIZE THE GUY?
AFRAID NOT.
BUT THE FRIEND SAYS HE ONCE OVERHEARD EISUKE'S DAD TALKING TO HIS ASSOCIATES ...
...ABOUT "GOING UNDER."
HUH?
IT SOUNDED LIKE THE ASSOCIATES WERE WORRIED ABOUT HIS SAFETY.
WHAT THE HECK DO YA THINK *THAT* WAS ABOUT?
THE FRIEND WAS TOLD THAT EISUKE'S DAD WAS A COMPANY EMPLOYEE.
HE THOUGHT THEY WERE TALKING ABOUT A SCUBA-DIVING TRIP.
TO BE EXACT, THE GRANDPA SAID...
...THAT HE WORKED ...

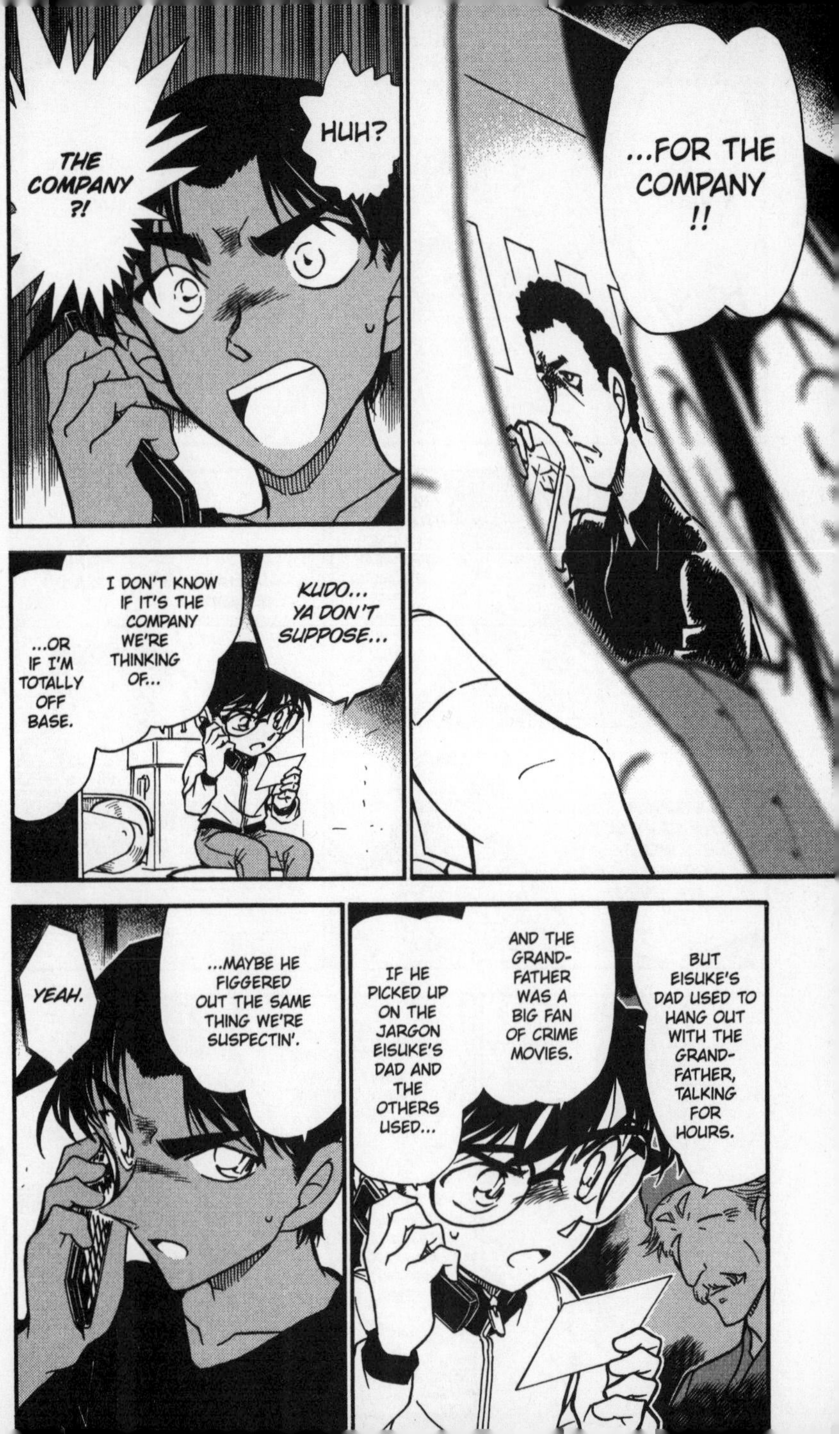
...FOR THE COMPANY !!
HUH?
THE COMPANY ?!
KUDO... YA DON'T SUPPOSE...
I DON'T KNOW IF IT'S THE COMPANY WE'RE THINKING OF...
...OR IF I'M TOTALLY OFF BASE.
BUT EISUKE'S DAD USED TO HANG OUT WITH THE GRANDFATHER, TALKING FOR HOURS.
AND THE GRANDFATHER WAS A BIG FAN OF CRIME MOVIES.
IF HE PICKED UP ON THE JARGON EISUKE'S DAD AND THE OTHERS USED...
...MAYBE HE FIGGERED OUT THE SAME THING WE'RE SUSPECTIN'.
YEAH.

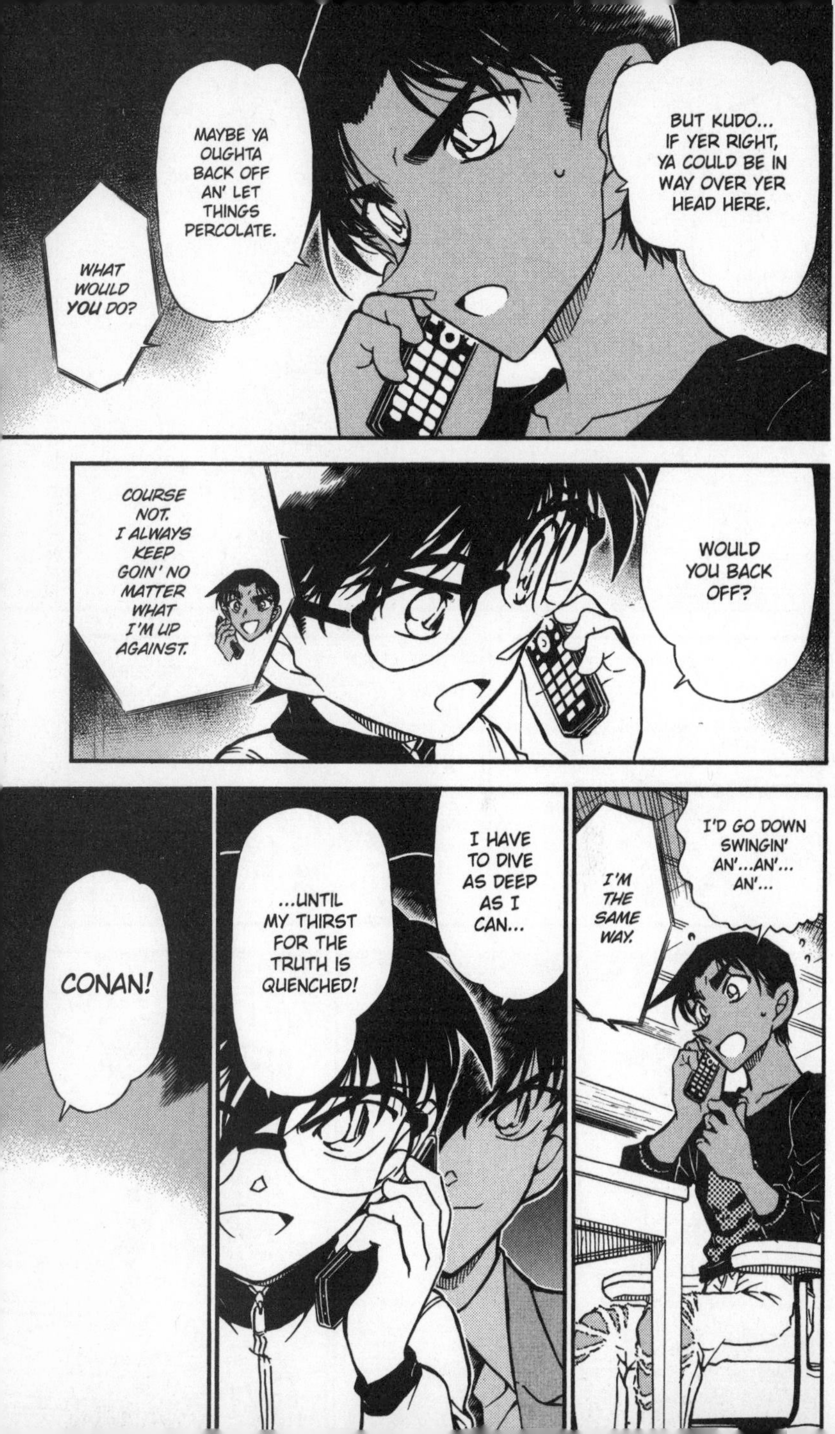
BUT KUDO... IF YER RIGHT, YA COULD BE IN WAY OVER YER HEAD HERE.
MAYBE YA OUGHTA BACK OFF AN' LET THINGS PERCOLATE.
WHAT WOULD YOU DO?
WOULD YOU BACK OFF?
COURSE NOT. I ALWAYS KEEP GOIN' NO MATTER WHAT I'M UP AGAINST.
I'D GO DOWN SWINGIN' AN'...AN'... AN'...
I'M THE SAME WAY.
I HAVE TO DIVE AS DEEP AS I CAN...
...UNTIL MY THIRST FOR THE TRUTH IS QUENCHED!
CONAN!

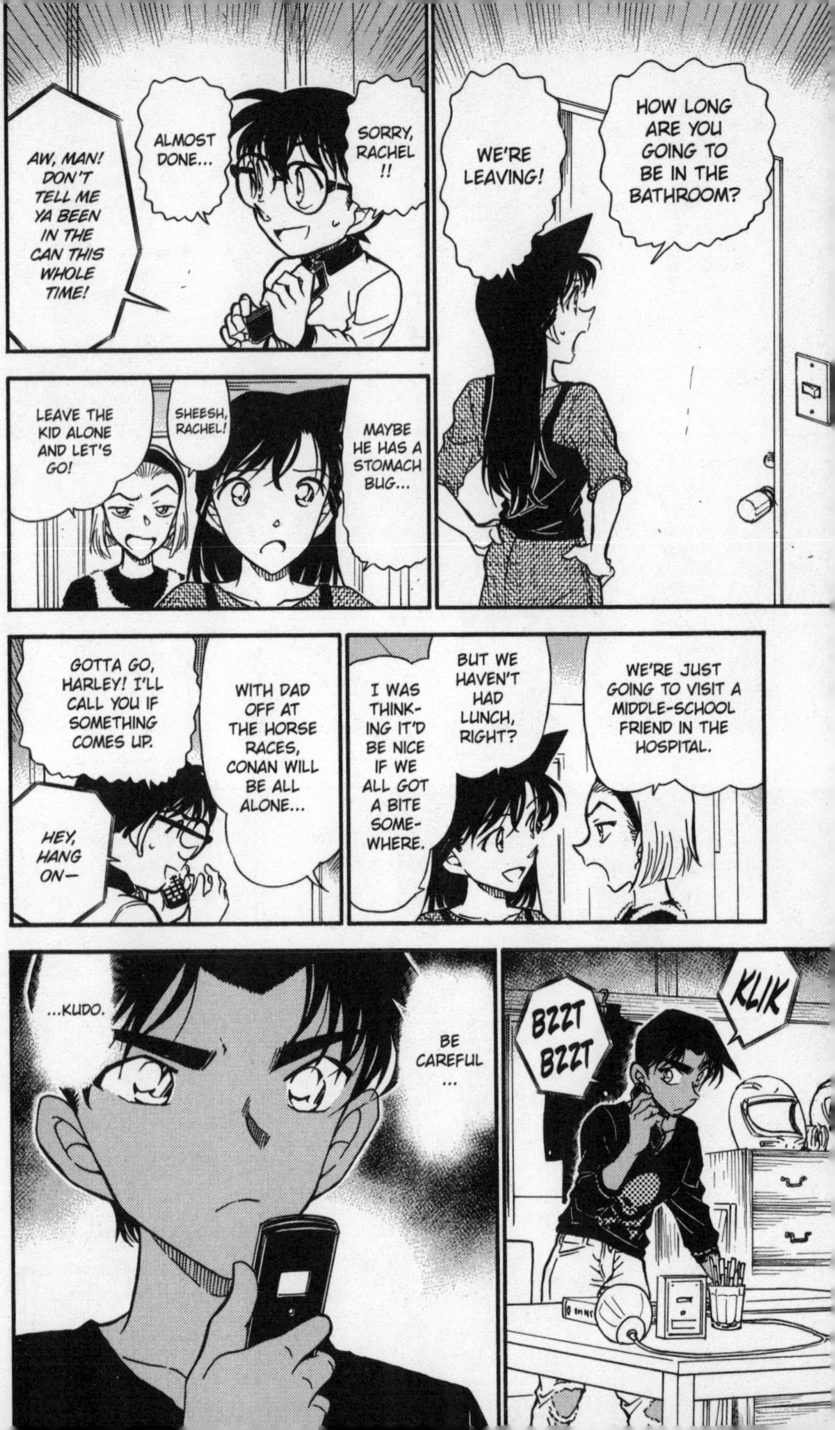
HOW LONG ARE YOU GOING TO BE IN THE BATHROOM?
WE'RE LEAVING!
SORRY, RACHEL !!
ALMOST DONE...
AW, MAN! DON'T TELL ME YA BEEN IN THE CAN THIS WHOLE TIME!
MAYBE HE HAS A STOMACH BUG...
SHEESH, RACHEL!
LEAVE THE KID ALONE AND LET'S GO!
WE'RE JUST GOING TO VISIT A MIDDLE-SCHOOL FRIEND IN THE HOSPITAL.
BUT WE HAVEN'T HAD LUNCH, RIGHT?
I WAS THINKING IT'D BE NICE IF WE ALL GOT A BITE SOMEWHERE.
WITH DAD OFF AT THE HORSE RACES, CONAN WILL BE ALL ALONE...
GOTTA GO, HARLEY! I'LL CALL YOU IF SOMETHING COMES UP.
HEY, HANG ON—
KLIK
BZZT BZZT
BE CAREFUL ...
...KUDO.

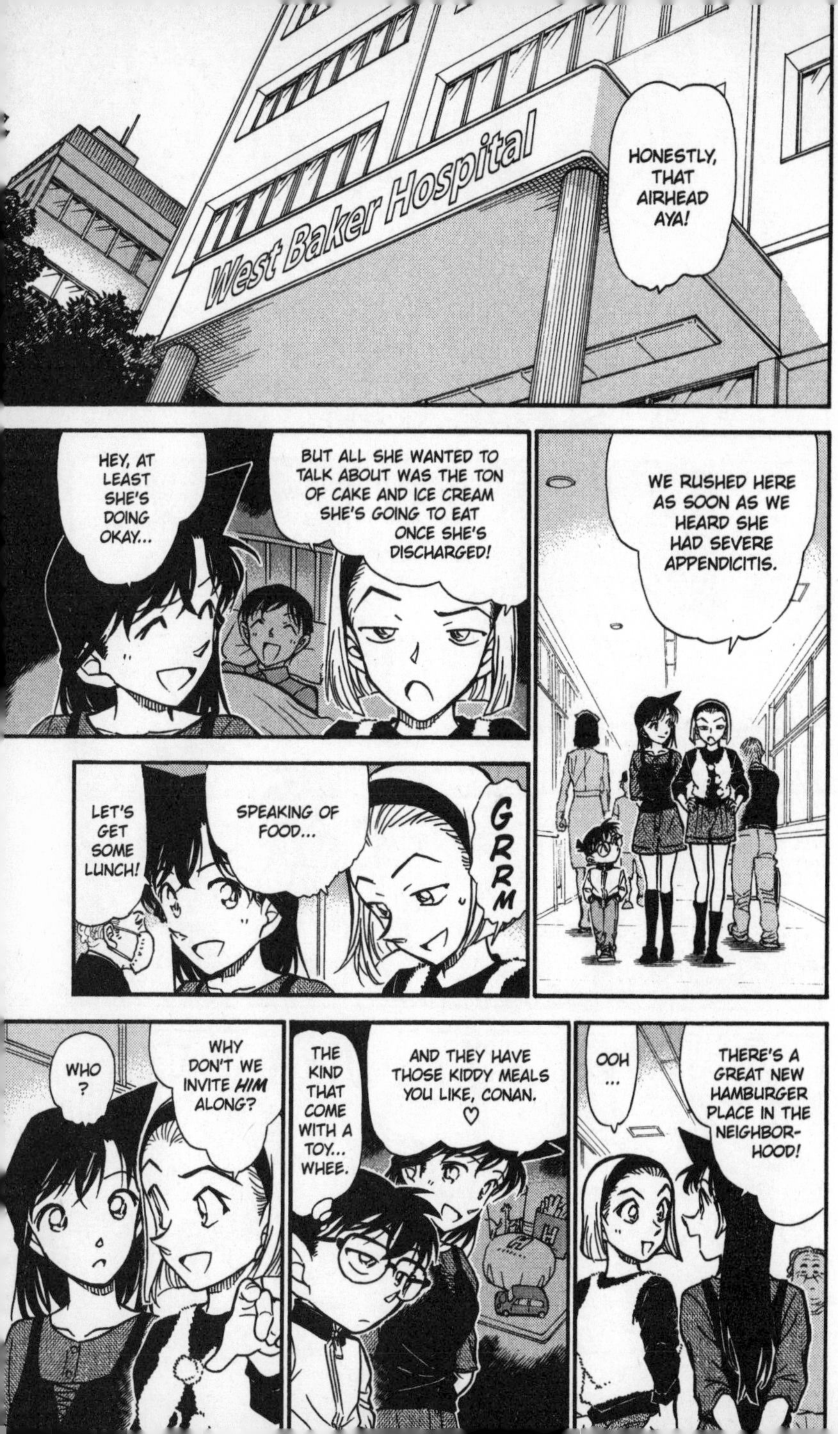
West Baker Hospital
HONESTLY, THAT AIRHEAD AYA!
WE RUSHED HERE AS SOON AS WE HEARD SHE HAD SEVERE APPENDICITIS.
BUT ALL SHE WANTED TO TALK ABOUT WAS THE TON OF CAKE AND ICE CREAM SHE'S GOING TO EAT ONCE SHE'S DISCHARGED!
HEY, AT LEAST SHE'S DOING OKAY...
GRRM
SPEAKING OF FOOD...
LET'S GET SOME LUNCH!
THERE'S A GREAT NEW HAMBURGER PLACE IN THE NEIGHBOR-HOOD!
OOH...
AND THEY HAVE THOSE KIDDY MEALS YOU LIKE, CONAN. ♡
THE KIND THAT COME WITH A TOY... WHEE.
WHY DON'T WE INVITE *HIM* ALONG?
WHO?

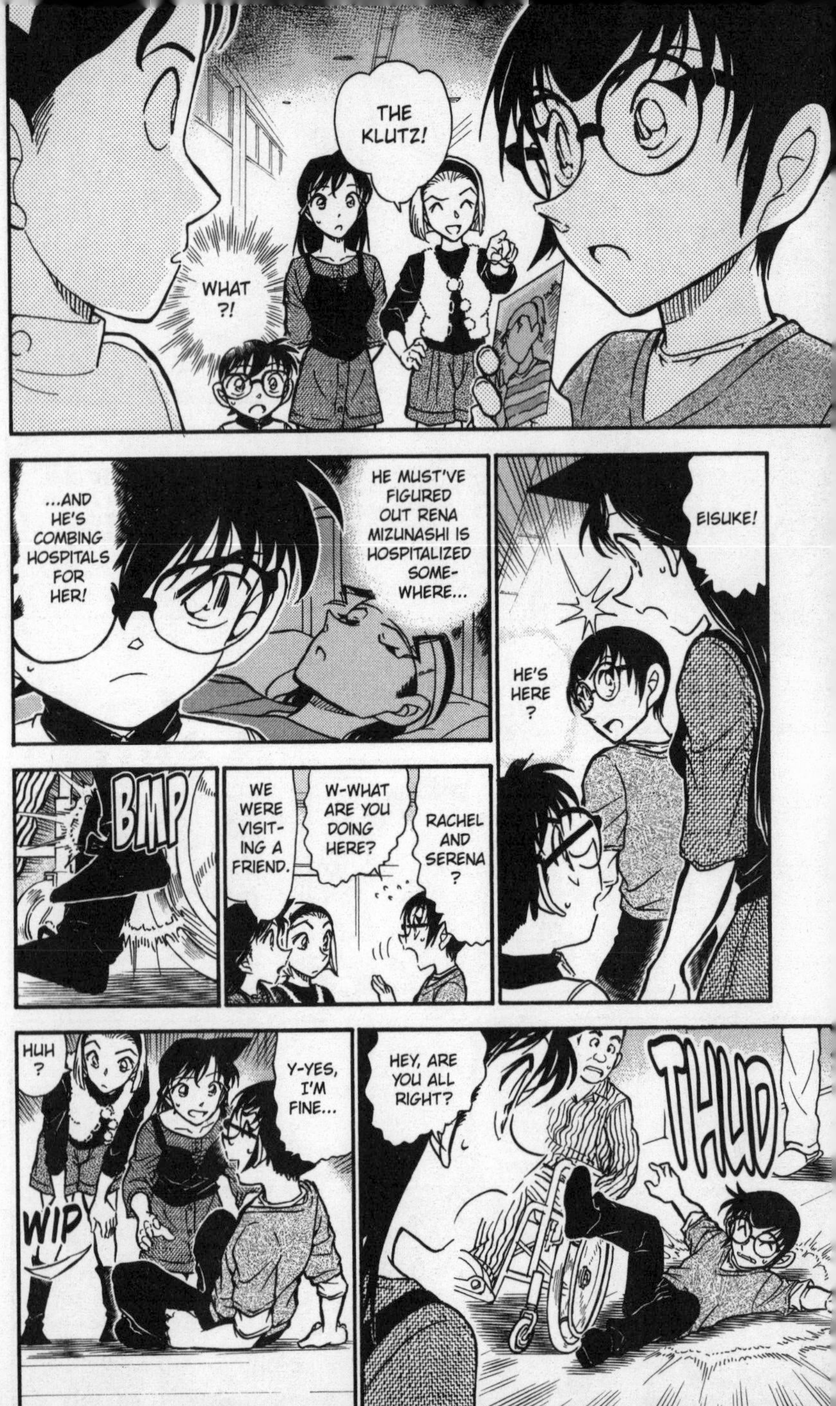
THE KLUTZ!
WHAT ?!
EISUKE!
HE'S HERE ?
HE MUST'VE FIGURED OUT RENA MIZUNASHI IS HOSPITALIZED SOME-WHERE...
...AND HE'S COMBING HOSPITALS FOR HER!
RACHEL AND SERENA ?
W-WHAT ARE YOU DOING HERE?
WE WERE VISITING A FRIEND.
BMP
THUD
HEY, ARE YOU ALL RIGHT?
Y-YES, I'M FINE...
HUH ?
WIP

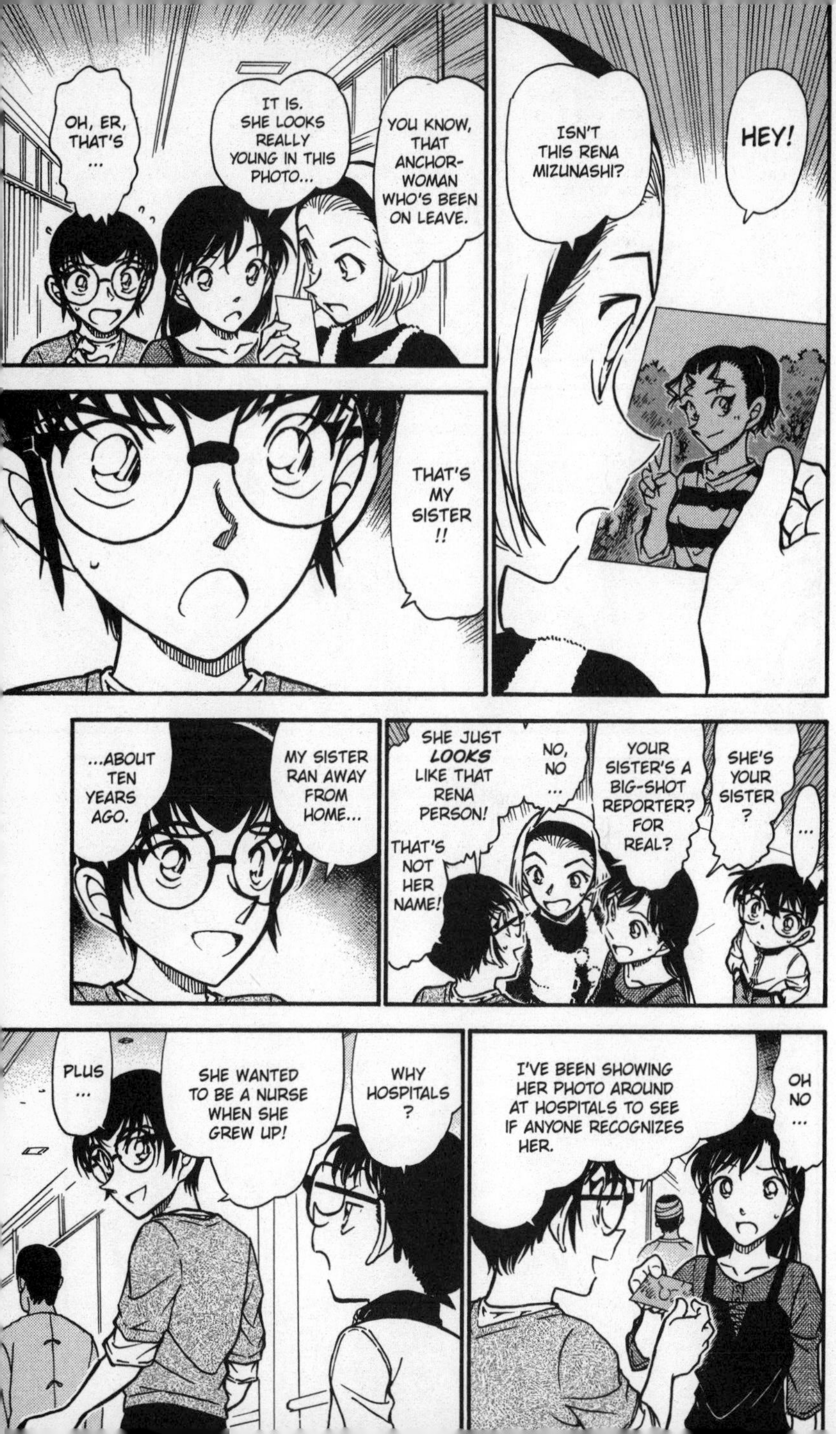
HEY!
ISN'T THIS RENA MIZUNASHI?
YOU KNOW, THAT ANCHOR-WOMAN WHO'S BEEN ON LEAVE.
IT IS. SHE LOOKS REALLY YOUNG IN THIS PHOTO...
OH, ER, THAT'S ...
THAT'S MY SISTER !!
SHE'S YOUR SISTER ?
...
YOUR SISTER'S A BIG-SHOT REPORTER? FOR REAL?
NO, NO ...
SHE JUST ***LOOKS*** LIKE THAT RENA PERSON!
THAT'S NOT HER NAME!
MY SISTER RAN AWAY FROM HOME...
...ABOUT TEN YEARS AGO.
OH NO ...
I'VE BEEN SHOWING HER PHOTO AROUND AT HOSPITALS TO SEE IF ANYONE RECOGNIZES HER.
WHY HOSPITALS ?
PLUS ...
SHE WANTED TO BE A NURSE WHEN SHE GREW UP!

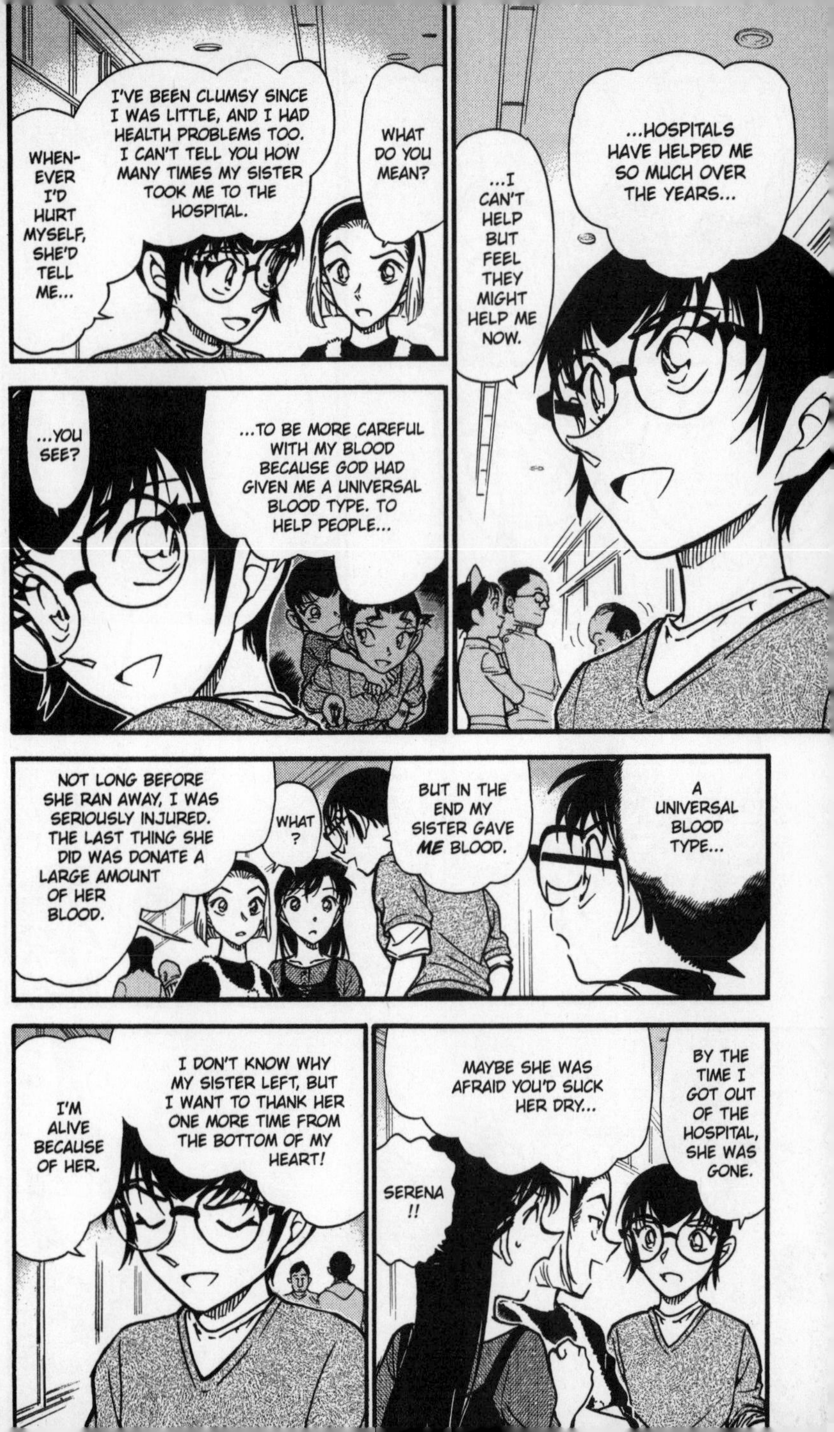
...HOSPITALS HAVE HELPED ME SO MUCH OVER THE YEARS...
...I CAN'T HELP BUT FEEL THEY MIGHT HELP ME NOW.
WHAT DO YOU MEAN?
I'VE BEEN CLUMSY SINCE I WAS LITTLE, AND I HAD HEALTH PROBLEMS TOO. I CAN'T TELL YOU HOW MANY TIMES MY SISTER TOOK ME TO THE HOSPITAL.
WHENEVER I'D HURT MYSELF, SHE'D TELL ME...
...TO BE MORE CAREFUL WITH MY BLOOD BECAUSE GOD HAD GIVEN ME A UNIVERSAL BLOOD TYPE. TO HELP PEOPLE...
...YOU SEE?
A UNIVERSAL BLOOD TYPE...
BUT IN THE END MY SISTER GAVE *ME* BLOOD.
WHAT?
NOT LONG BEFORE SHE RAN AWAY, I WAS SERIOUSLY INJURED. THE LAST THING SHE DID WAS DONATE A LARGE AMOUNT OF HER BLOOD.
BY THE TIME I GOT OUT OF THE HOSPITAL, SHE WAS GONE.
MAYBE SHE WAS AFRAID YOU'D SUCK HER DRY...
SERENA!!
I DON'T KNOW WHY MY SISTER LEFT, BUT I WANT TO THANK HER ONE MORE TIME FROM THE BOTTOM OF MY HEART!
I'M ALIVE BECAUSE OF HER.

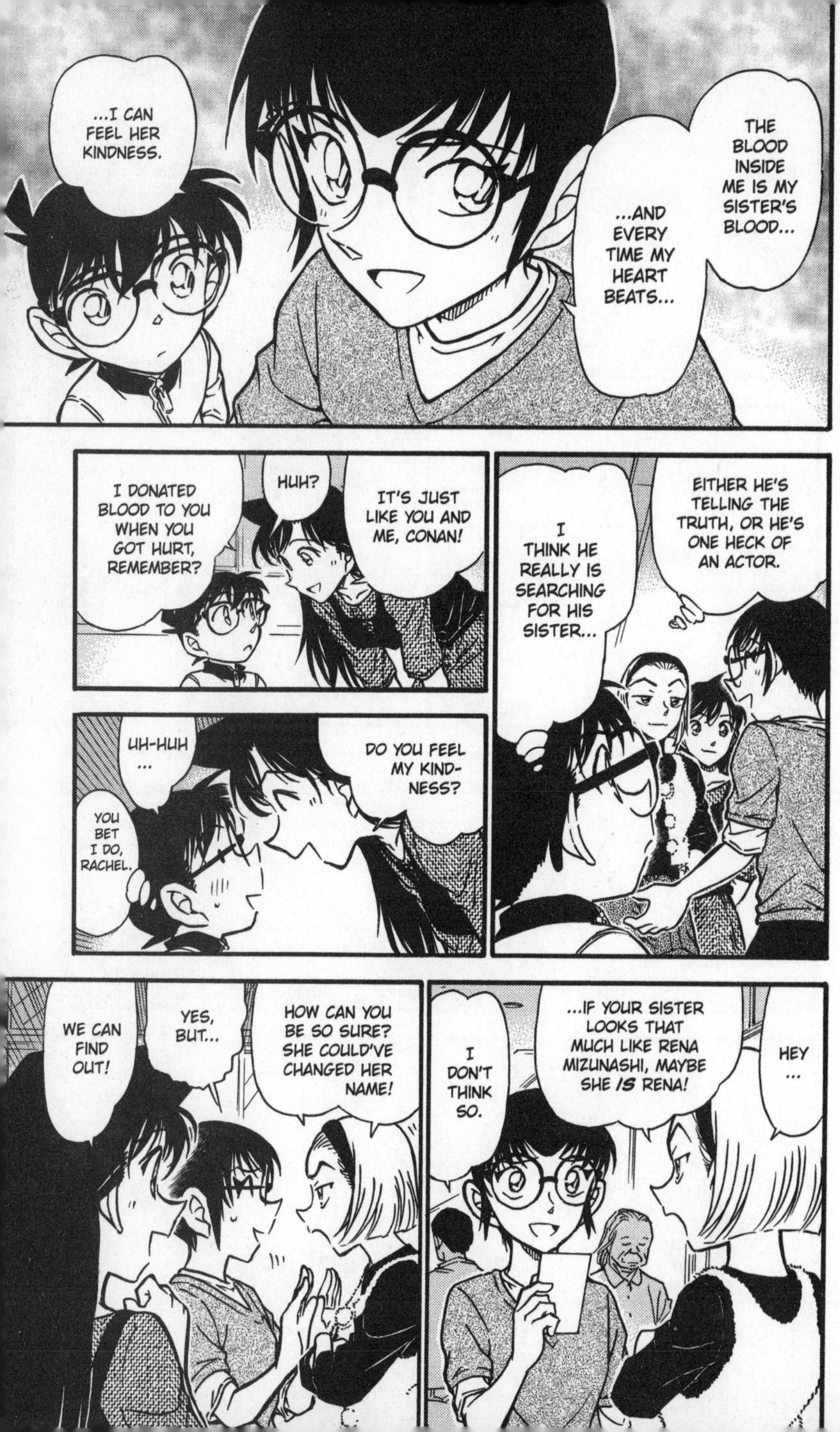
THE BLOOD INSIDE ME IS MY SISTER'S BLOOD...
...AND EVERY TIME MY HEART BEATS...
...I CAN FEEL HER KINDNESS.
EITHER HE'S TELLING THE TRUTH, OR HE'S ONE HECK OF AN ACTOR.
I THINK HE REALLY IS SEARCHING FOR HIS SISTER...
IT'S JUST LIKE YOU AND ME, CONAN!
HUH?
I DONATED BLOOD TO YOU WHEN YOU GOT HURT, REMEMBER?
DO YOU FEEL MY KIND-NESS?
UH-HUH ...
YOU BET I DO, RACHEL.
HEY ...
...IF YOUR SISTER LOOKS THAT MUCH LIKE RENA MIZUNASHI, MAYBE SHE *IS* RENA!
I DON'T THINK SO.
HOW CAN YOU BE SO SURE? SHE COULD'VE CHANGED HER NAME!
YES, BUT...
WE CAN FIND OUT!

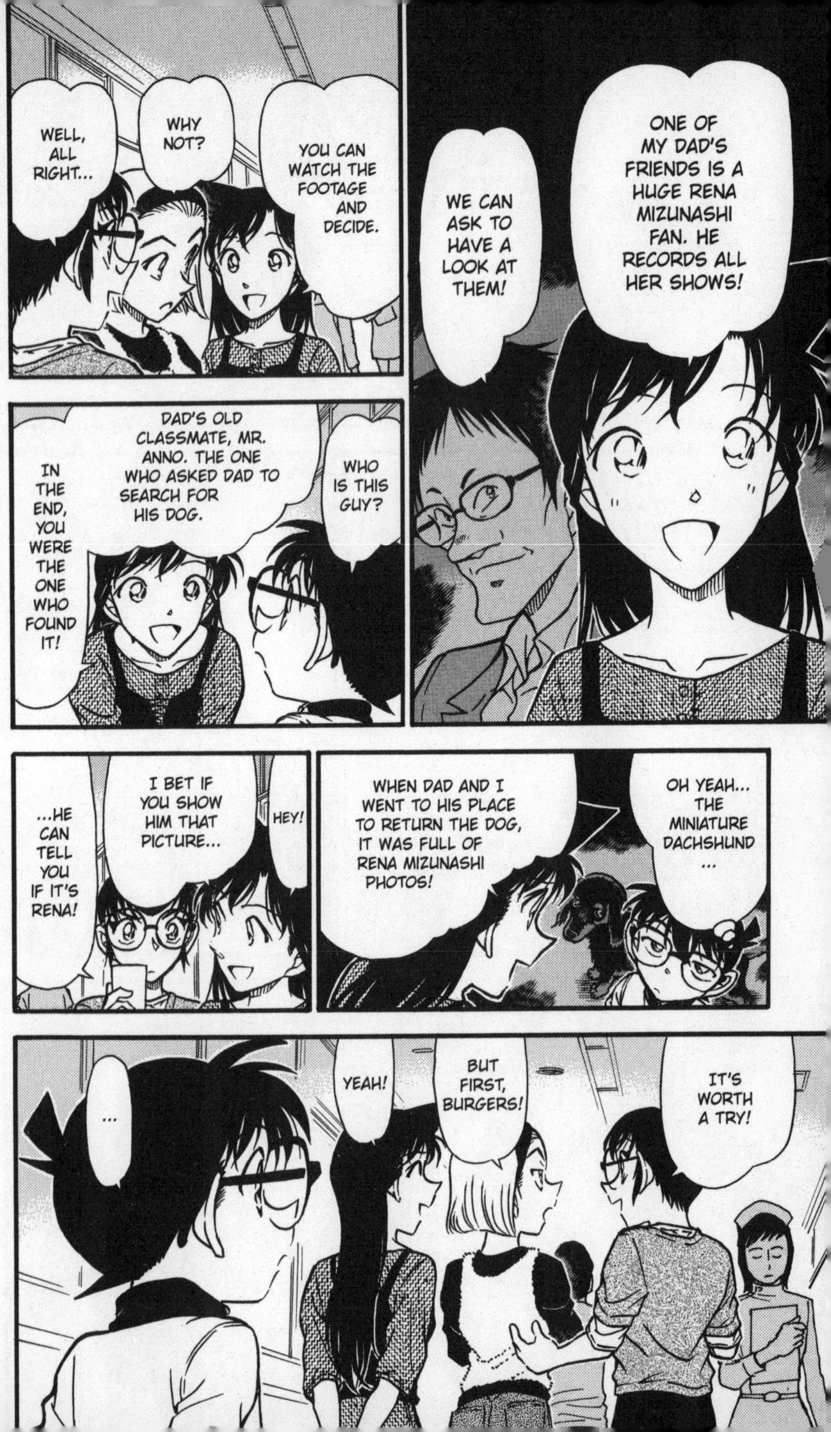
ONE OF MY DAD'S FRIENDS IS A HUGE RENA MIZUNASHI FAN. HE RECORDS ALL HER SHOWS!
WE CAN ASK TO HAVE A LOOK AT THEM!
YOU CAN WATCH THE FOOTAGE AND DECIDE.
WHY NOT?
WELL, ALL RIGHT...
WHO IS THIS GUY?
DAD'S OLD CLASSMATE, MR. ANNO. THE ONE WHO ASKED DAD TO SEARCH FOR HIS DOG.
IN THE END, YOU WERE THE ONE WHO FOUND IT!
OH YEAH... THE MINIATURE DACHSHUND ...
WHEN DAD AND I WENT TO HIS PLACE TO RETURN THE DOG, IT WAS FULL OF RENA MIZUNASHI PHOTOS!
HEY!
I BET IF YOU SHOW HIM THAT PICTURE...
...HE CAN TELL YOU IF IT'S RENA!
IT'S WORTH A TRY!
BUT FIRST, BURGERS!
YEAH!
...

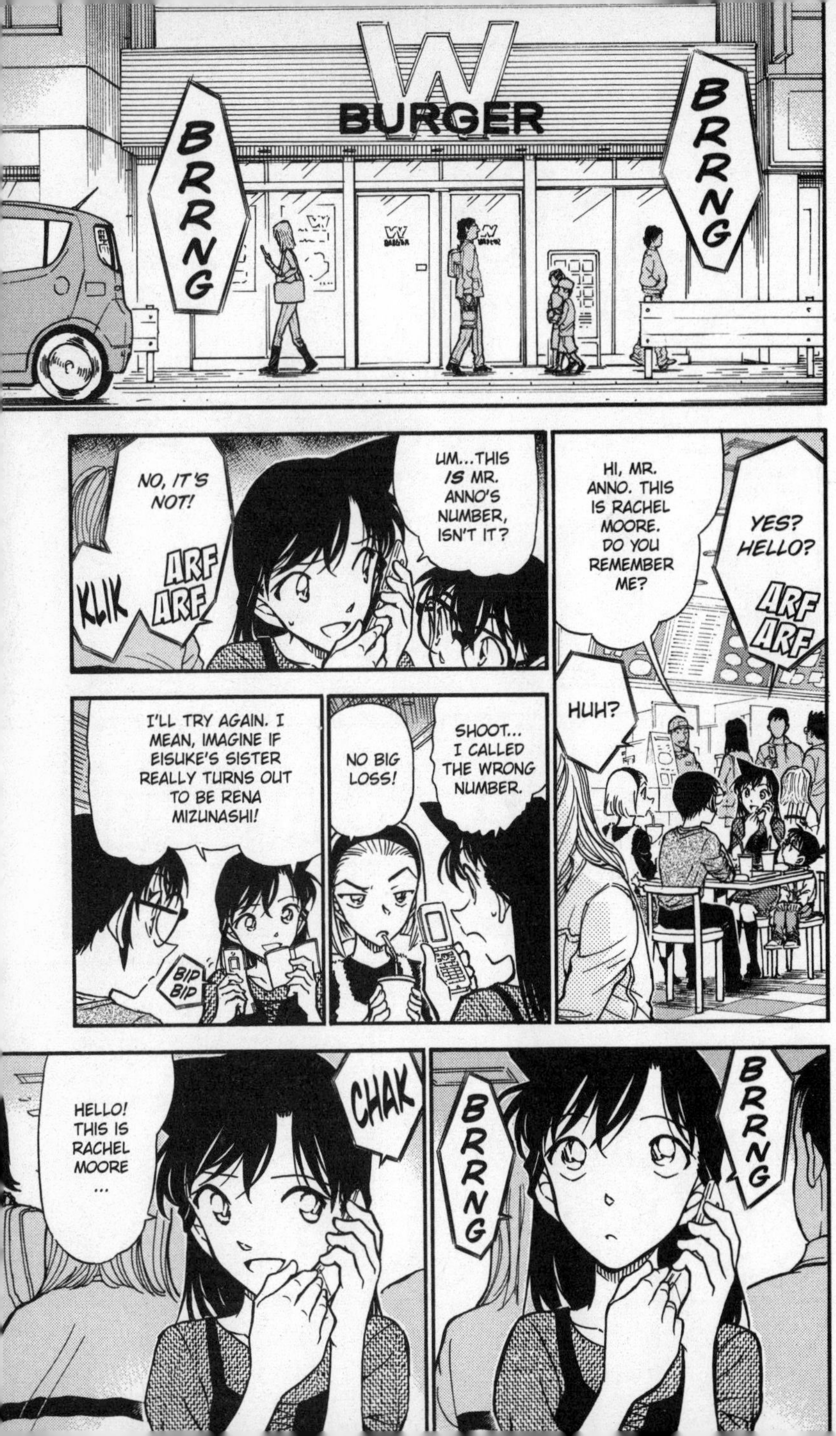
W BURGER
BRRNG
BRRNG
YES? HELLO?
ARF ARF
HI, MR. ANNO. THIS IS RACHEL MOORE. DO YOU REMEMBER ME?
HUH?
UM...THIS *IS* MR. ANNO'S NUMBER, ISN'T IT?
NO, IT'S NOT!
ARF ARF
KLIK
SHOOT... I CALLED THE WRONG NUMBER.
NO BIG LOSS!
I'LL TRY AGAIN. I MEAN, IMAGINE IF EISUKE'S SISTER REALLY TURNS OUT TO BE RENA MIZUNASHI!
BIP BIP
BRRNG
BRRNG
CHAK
HELLO! THIS IS RACHEL MOORE ...

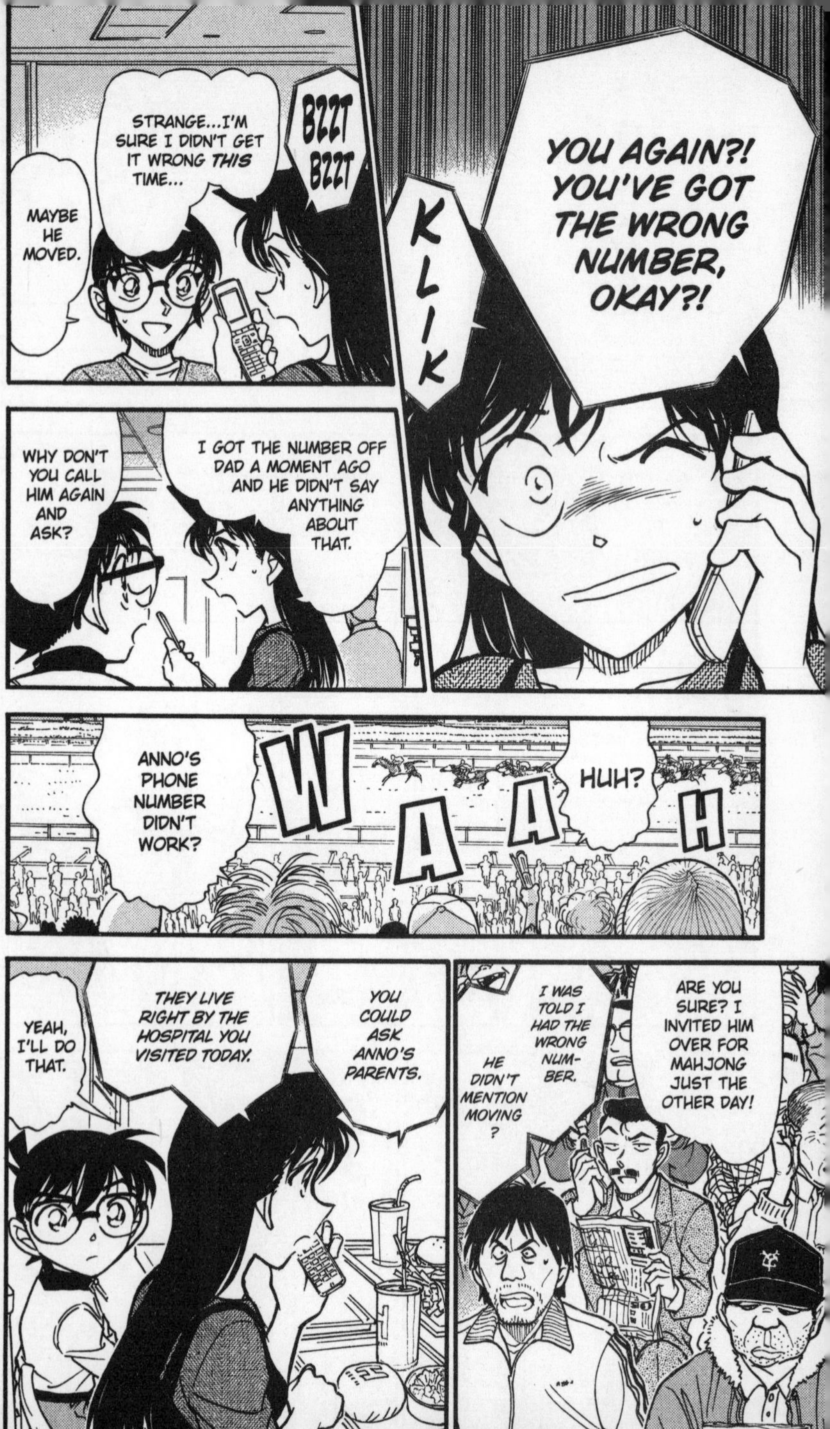
YOU AGAIN?! YOU'VE GOT THE WRONG NUMBER, OKAY?!
KLIK
BZZT BZZT
STRANGE...I'M SURE I DIDN'T GET IT WRONG *THIS* TIME...
MAYBE HE MOVED.
I GOT THE NUMBER OFF DAD A MOMENT AGO AND HE DIDN'T SAY ANYTHING ABOUT THAT.
WHY DON'T YOU CALL HIM AGAIN AND ASK?
HUH?
WAAH
ANNO'S PHONE NUMBER DIDN'T WORK?
ARE YOU SURE? I INVITED HIM OVER FOR MAHJONG JUST THE OTHER DAY!
I WAS TOLD I HAD THE WRONG NUM-BER.
HE DIDN'T MENTION MOVING?
YOU COULD ASK ANNO'S PARENTS.
THEY LIVE RIGHT BY THE HOSPITAL YOU VISITED TODAY.
YEAH, I'LL DO THAT.

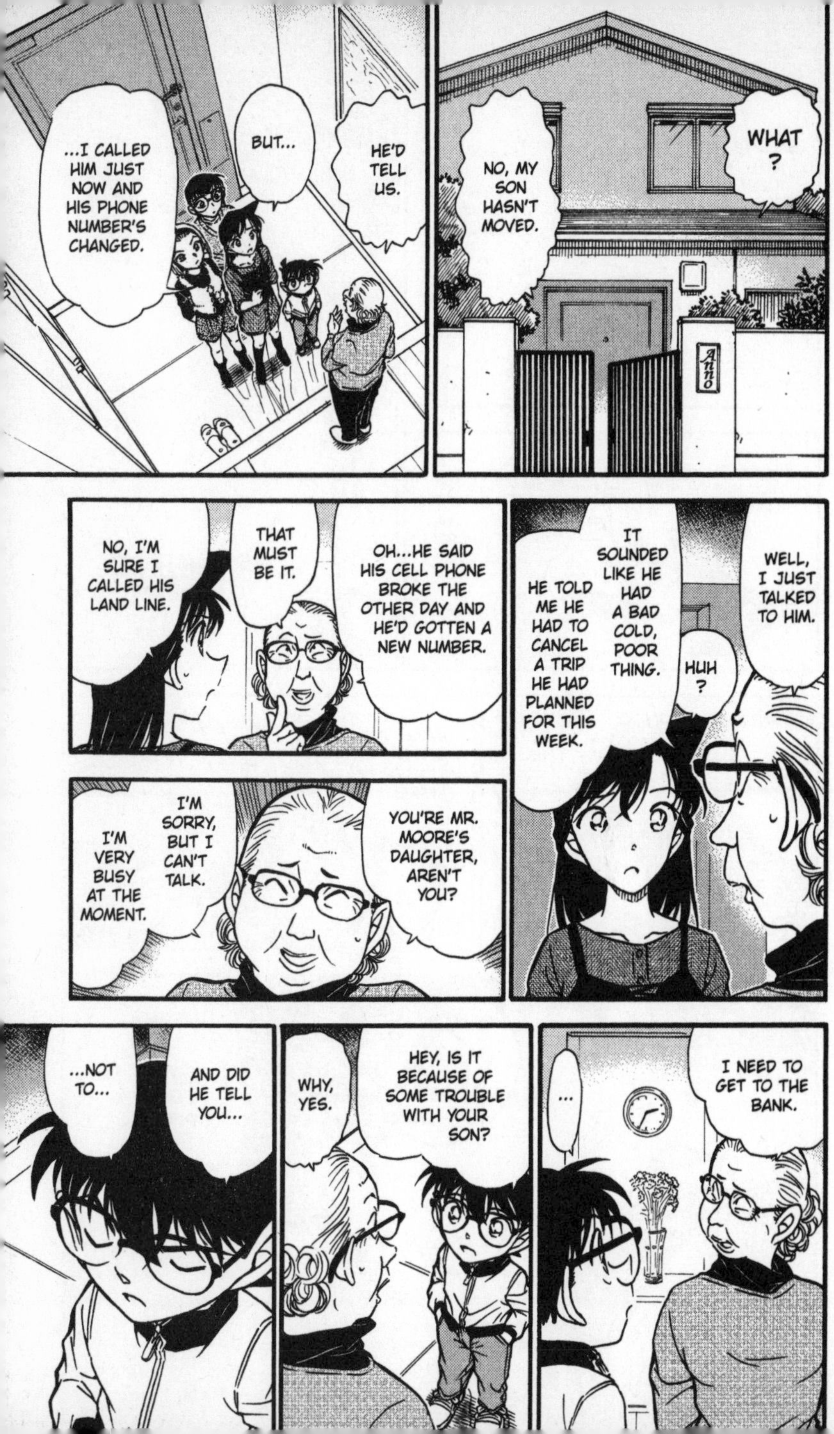
WHAT ?
NO, MY SON HASN'T MOVED.
HE'D TELL US.
BUT...
...I CALLED HIM JUST NOW AND HIS PHONE NUMBER'S CHANGED.
Anno
WELL, I JUST TALKED TO HIM.
HUH ?
IT SOUNDED LIKE HE HAD A BAD COLD, POOR THING.
HE TOLD ME HE HAD TO CANCEL A TRIP HE HAD PLANNED FOR THIS WEEK.
OH...HE SAID HIS CELL PHONE BROKE THE OTHER DAY AND HE'D GOTTEN A NEW NUMBER.
THAT MUST BE IT.
NO, I'M SURE I CALLED HIS LAND LINE.
YOU'RE MR. MOORE'S DAUGHTER, AREN'T YOU?
I'M SORRY, BUT I CAN'T TALK.
I'M VERY BUSY AT THE MOMENT.
I NEED TO GET TO THE BANK.
...
HEY, IS IT BECAUSE OF SOME TROUBLE WITH YOUR SON?
WHY, YES.
AND DID HE TELL YOU...
...NOT TO...

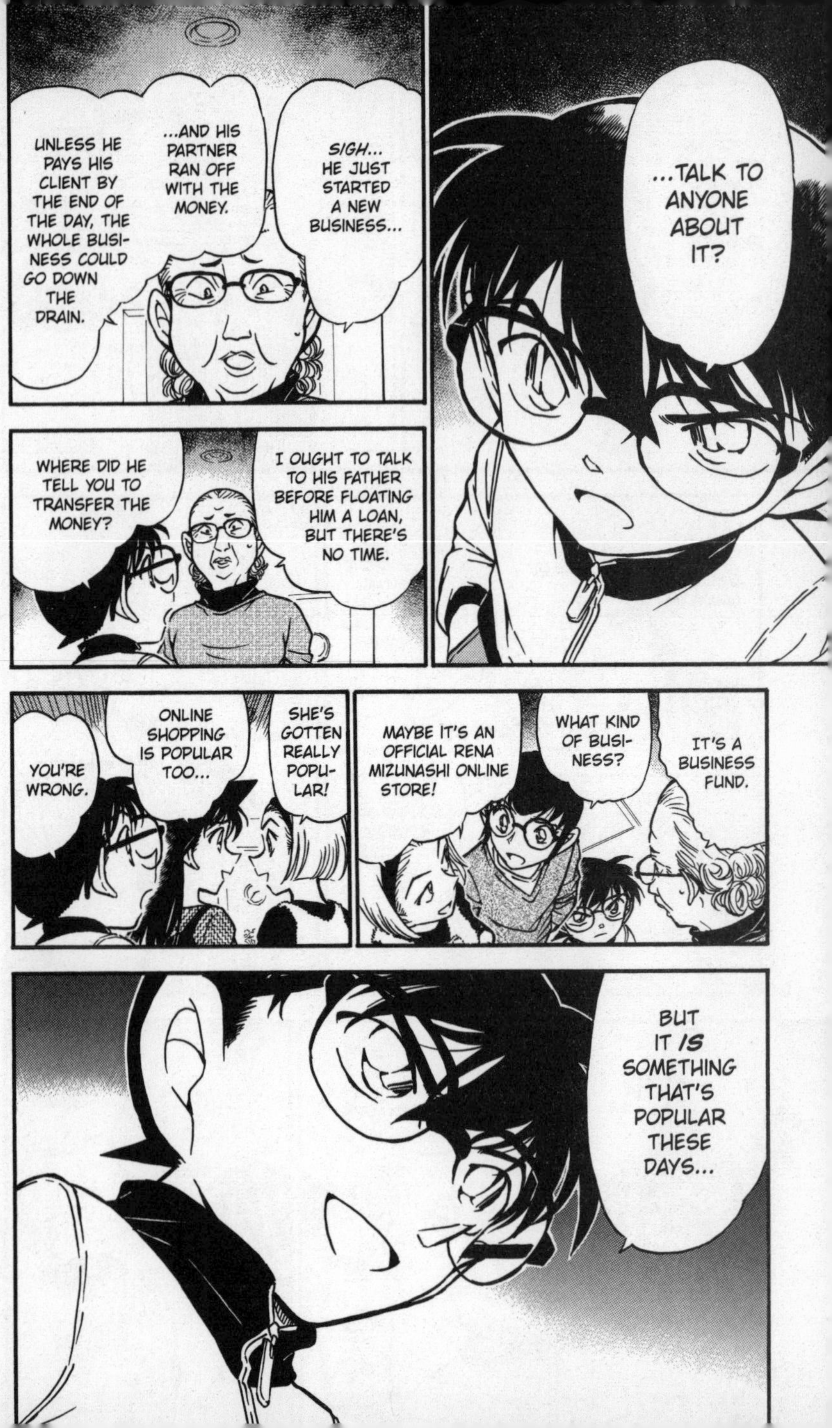
...TALK TO ANYONE ABOUT IT?
SIGH... HE JUST STARTED A NEW BUSINESS...
...AND HIS PARTNER RAN OFF WITH THE MONEY.
UNLESS HE PAYS HIS CLIENT BY THE END OF THE DAY, THE WHOLE BUSINESS COULD GO DOWN THE DRAIN.
I OUGHT TO TALK TO HIS FATHER BEFORE FLOATING HIM A LOAN, BUT THERE'S NO TIME.
WHERE DID HE TELL YOU TO TRANSFER THE MONEY?
IT'S A BUSINESS FUND.
WHAT KIND OF BUSINESS?
MAYBE IT'S AN OFFICIAL RENA MIZUNASHI ONLINE STORE!
SHE'S GOTTEN REALLY POPULAR!
ONLINE SHOPPING IS POPULAR TOO...
YOU'RE WRONG.
BUT IT *IS* SOMETHING THAT'S POPULAR THESE DAYS...

BLOOD WILL TELL

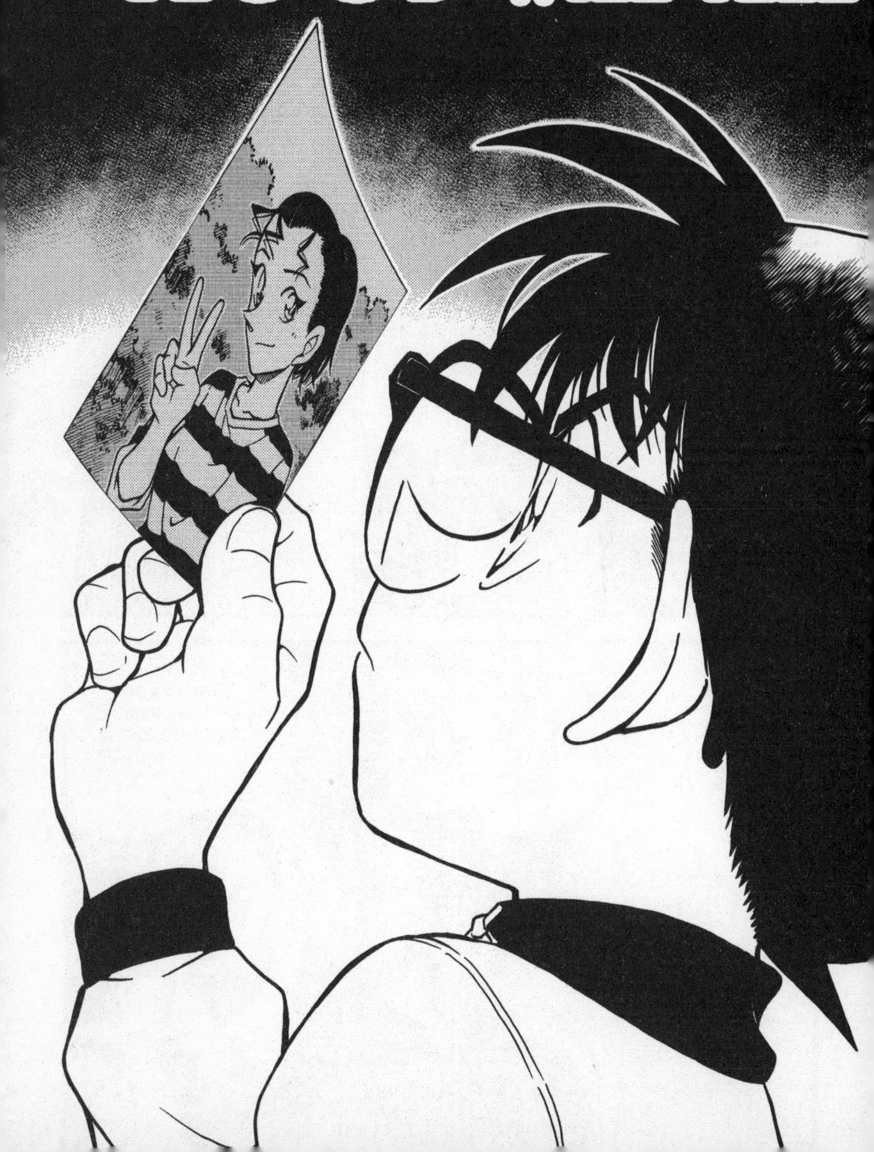

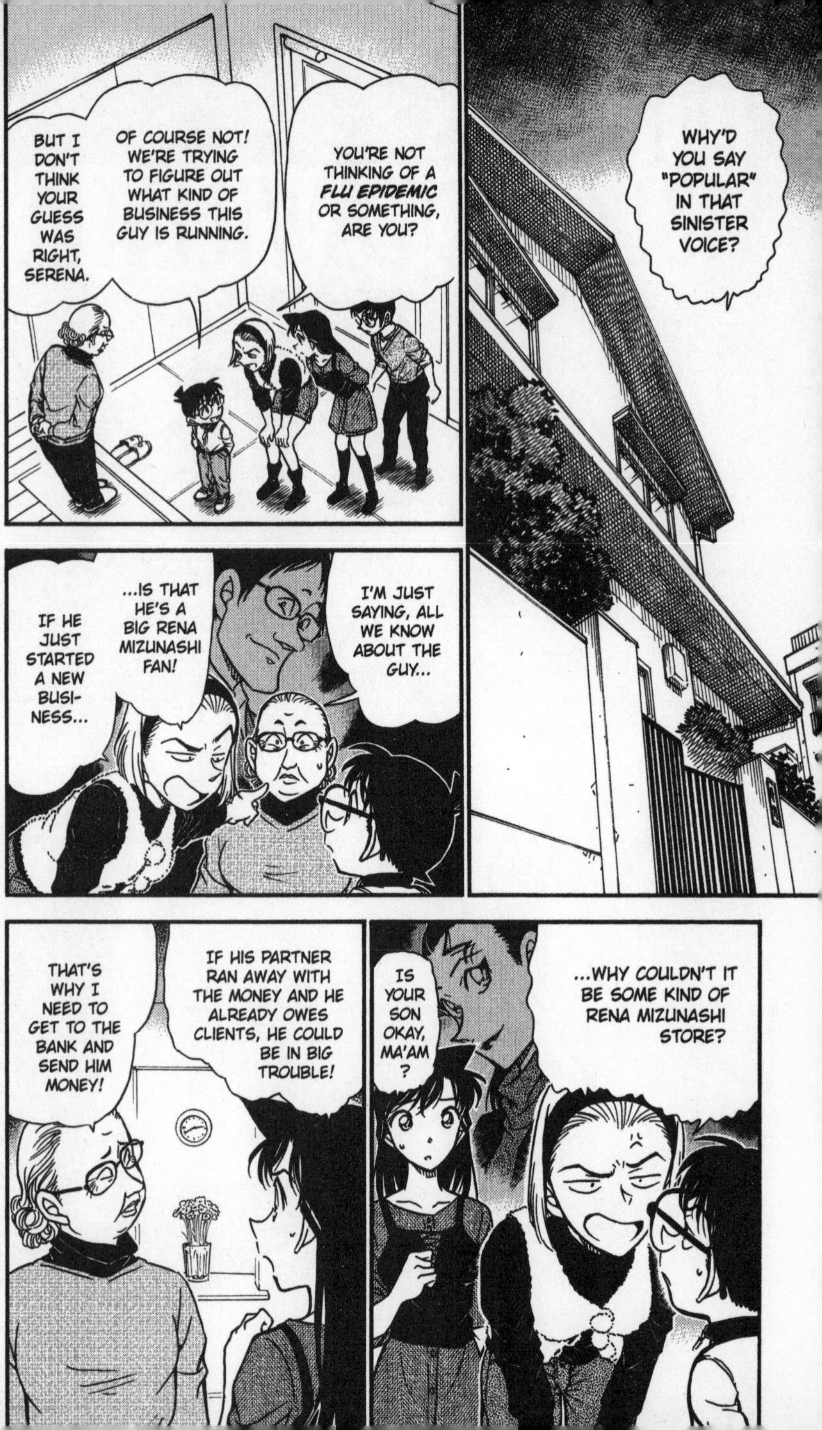
WHY'D YOU SAY "POPULAR" IN THAT SINISTER VOICE?
YOU'RE NOT THINKING OF A *FLU EPIDEMIC* OR SOMETHING, ARE YOU?
OF COURSE NOT! WE'RE TRYING TO FIGURE OUT WHAT KIND OF BUSINESS THIS GUY IS RUNNING.
BUT I DON'T THINK YOUR GUESS WAS RIGHT, SERENA.
I'M JUST SAYING, ALL WE KNOW ABOUT THE GUY...
...IS THAT HE'S A BIG RENA MIZUNASHI FAN!
IF HE JUST STARTED A NEW BUSI-NESS...
...WHY COULDN'T IT BE SOME KIND OF RENA MIZUNASHI STORE?
IS YOUR SON OKAY, MA'AM?
IF HIS PARTNER RAN AWAY WITH THE MONEY AND HE ALREADY OWES CLIENTS, HE COULD BE IN BIG TROUBLE!
THAT'S WHY I NEED TO GET TO THE BANK AND SEND HIM MONEY!

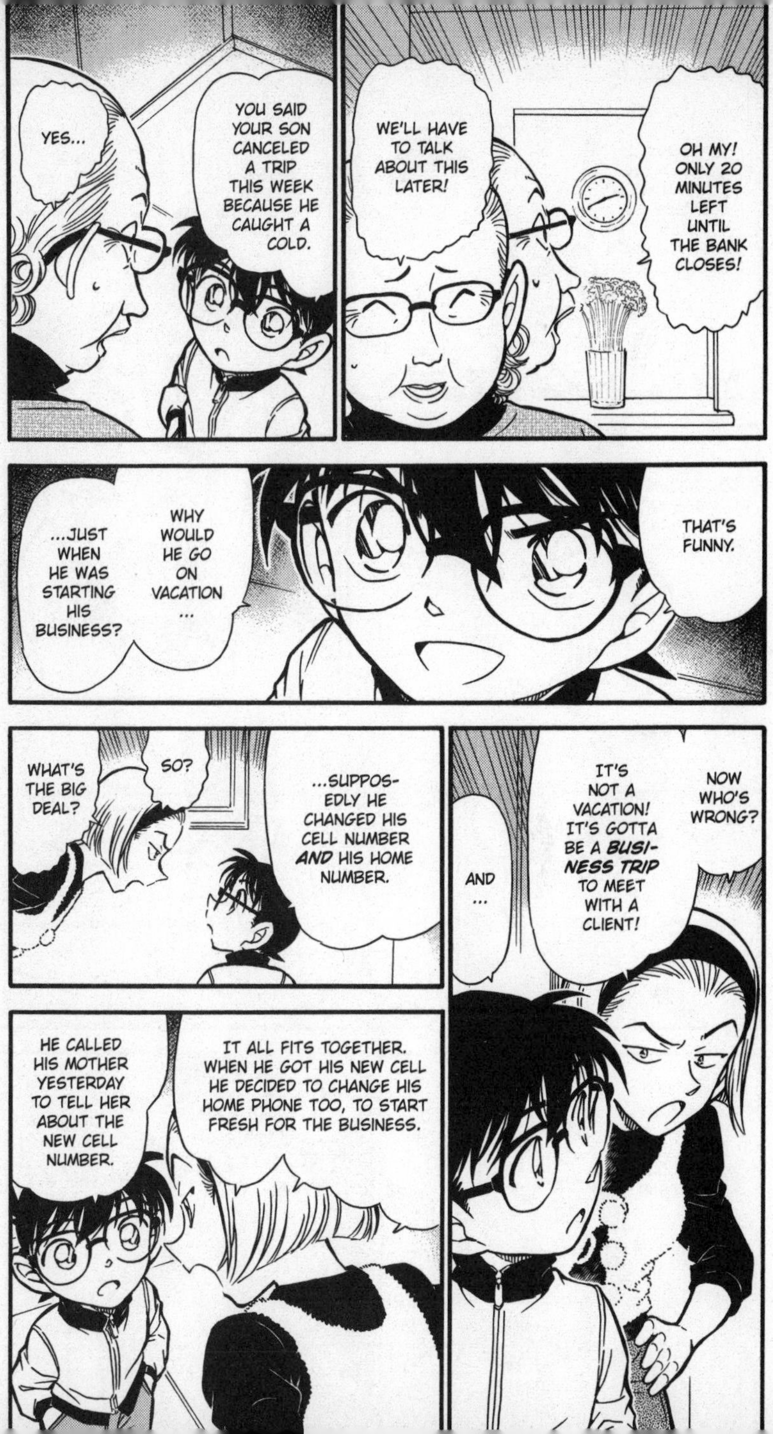
OH MY! ONLY 20 MINUTES LEFT UNTIL THE BANK CLOSES!
WE'LL HAVE TO TALK ABOUT THIS LATER!
YOU SAID YOUR SON CANCELED A TRIP THIS WEEK BECAUSE HE CAUGHT A COLD.
YES...
THAT'S FUNNY.
WHY WOULD HE GO ON VACATION ...
...JUST WHEN HE WAS STARTING HIS BUSINESS?
NOW WHO'S WRONG?
IT'S NOT A VACATION! IT'S GOTTA BE A ***BUSINESS TRIP*** TO MEET WITH A CLIENT!
AND ...
...SUPPOSEDLY HE CHANGED HIS CELL NUMBER ***AND*** HIS HOME NUMBER.
SO?
WHAT'S THE BIG DEAL?
IT ALL FITS TOGETHER. WHEN HE GOT HIS NEW CELL HE DECIDED TO CHANGE HIS HOME PHONE TOO, TO START FRESH FOR THE BUSINESS.
HE CALLED HIS MOTHER YESTERDAY TO TELL HER ABOUT THE NEW CELL NUMBER.

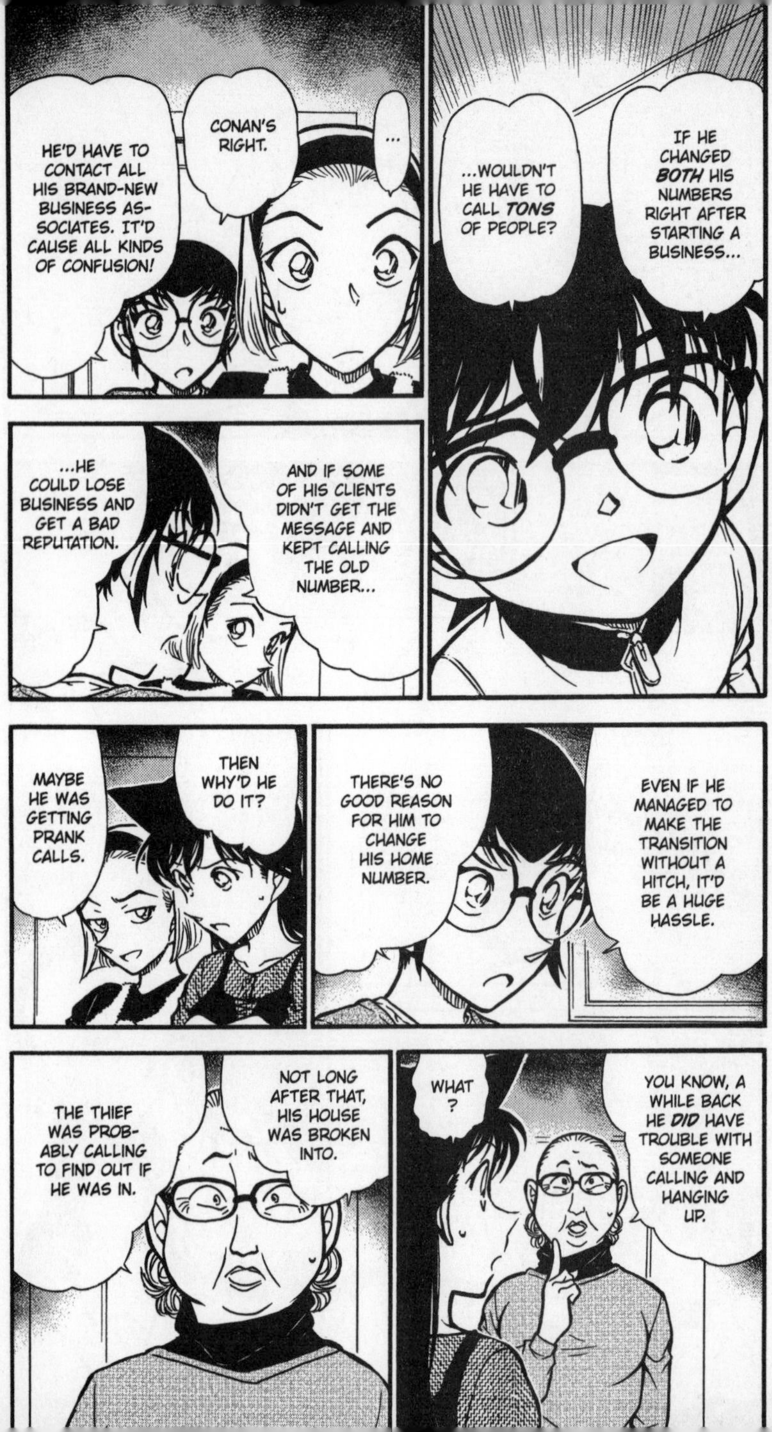
IF HE CHANGED **BOTH** HIS NUMBERS RIGHT AFTER STARTING A BUSINESS...
...WOULDN'T HE HAVE TO CALL **TONS** OF PEOPLE?
...
CONAN'S RIGHT.
HE'D HAVE TO CONTACT ALL HIS BRAND-NEW BUSINESS AS-SOCIATES. IT'D CAUSE ALL KINDS OF CONFUSION!
AND IF SOME OF HIS CLIENTS DIDN'T GET THE MESSAGE AND KEPT CALLING THE OLD NUMBER...
...HE COULD LOSE BUSINESS AND GET A BAD REPUTATION.
EVEN IF HE MANAGED TO MAKE THE TRANSITION WITHOUT A HITCH, IT'D BE A HUGE HASSLE.
THERE'S NO GOOD REASON FOR HIM TO CHANGE HIS HOME NUMBER.
THEN WHY'D HE DO IT?
MAYBE HE WAS GETTING PRANK CALLS.
YOU KNOW, A WHILE BACK HE **DID** HAVE TROUBLE WITH SOMEONE CALLING AND HANGING UP.
WHAT?
NOT LONG AFTER THAT, HIS HOUSE WAS BROKEN INTO.
THE THIEF WAS PROB-ABLY CALLING TO FIND OUT IF HE WAS IN.

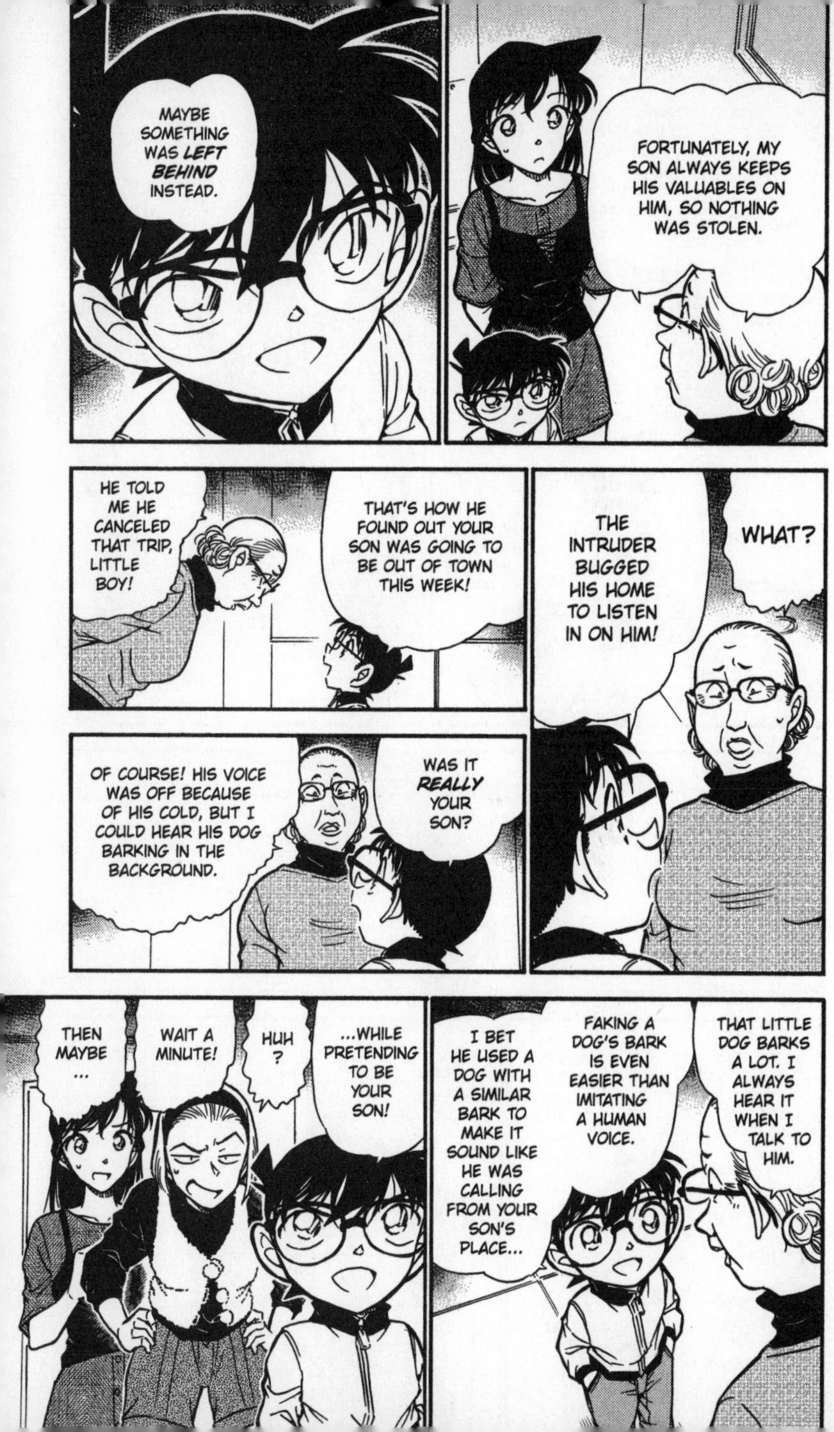

FORTUNATELY, MY SON ALWAYS KEEPS HIS VALUABLES ON HIM, SO NOTHING WAS STOLEN.
MAYBE SOMETHING WAS *LEFT BEHIND* INSTEAD.
WHAT?
THE INTRUDER BUGGED HIS HOME TO LISTEN IN ON HIM!
THAT'S HOW HE FOUND OUT YOUR SON WAS GOING TO BE OUT OF TOWN THIS WEEK!
HE TOLD ME HE CANCELED THAT TRIP, LITTLE BOY!
WAS IT *REALLY* YOUR SON?
OF COURSE! HIS VOICE WAS OFF BECAUSE OF HIS COLD, BUT I COULD HEAR HIS DOG BARKING IN THE BACKGROUND.
THAT LITTLE DOG BARKS A LOT. I ALWAYS HEAR IT WHEN I TALK TO HIM.
FAKING A DOG'S BARK IS EVEN EASIER THAN IMITATING A HUMAN VOICE.
I BET HE USED A DOG WITH A SIMILAR BARK TO MAKE IT SOUND LIKE HE WAS CALLING FROM YOUR SON'S PLACE...
...WHILE PRETENDING TO BE YOUR SON!
HUH?
WAIT A MINUTE!
THEN MAYBE...

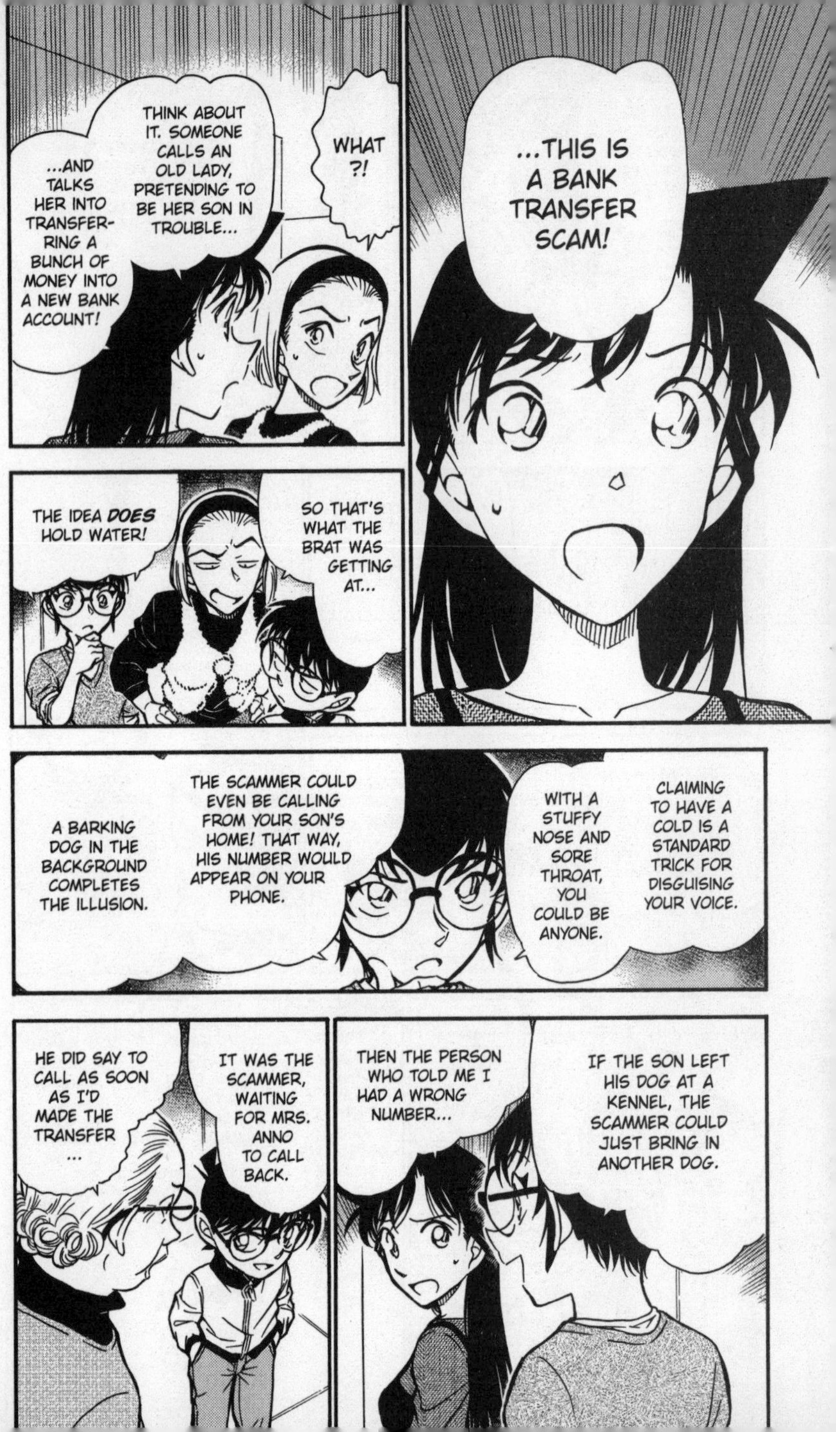
...THIS IS A BANK TRANSFER SCAM!
WHAT?!
THINK ABOUT IT. SOMEONE CALLS AN OLD LADY, PRETENDING TO BE HER SON IN TROUBLE...
...AND TALKS HER INTO TRANSFERRING A BUNCH OF MONEY INTO A NEW BANK ACCOUNT!
SO THAT'S WHAT THE BRAT WAS GETTING AT...
THE IDEA *DOES* HOLD WATER!
CLAIMING TO HAVE A COLD IS A STANDARD TRICK FOR DISGUISING YOUR VOICE.
WITH A STUFFY NOSE AND SORE THROAT, YOU COULD BE ANYONE.
THE SCAMMER COULD EVEN BE CALLING FROM YOUR SON'S HOME! THAT WAY, HIS NUMBER WOULD APPEAR ON YOUR PHONE.
A BARKING DOG IN THE BACKGROUND COMPLETES THE ILLUSION.
IF THE SON LEFT HIS DOG AT A KENNEL, THE SCAMMER COULD JUST BRING IN ANOTHER DOG.
THEN THE PERSON WHO TOLD ME I HAD A WRONG NUMBER...
IT WAS THE SCAMMER, WAITING FOR MRS. ANNO TO CALL BACK.
HE DID SAY TO CALL AS SOON AS I'D MADE THE TRANSFER...

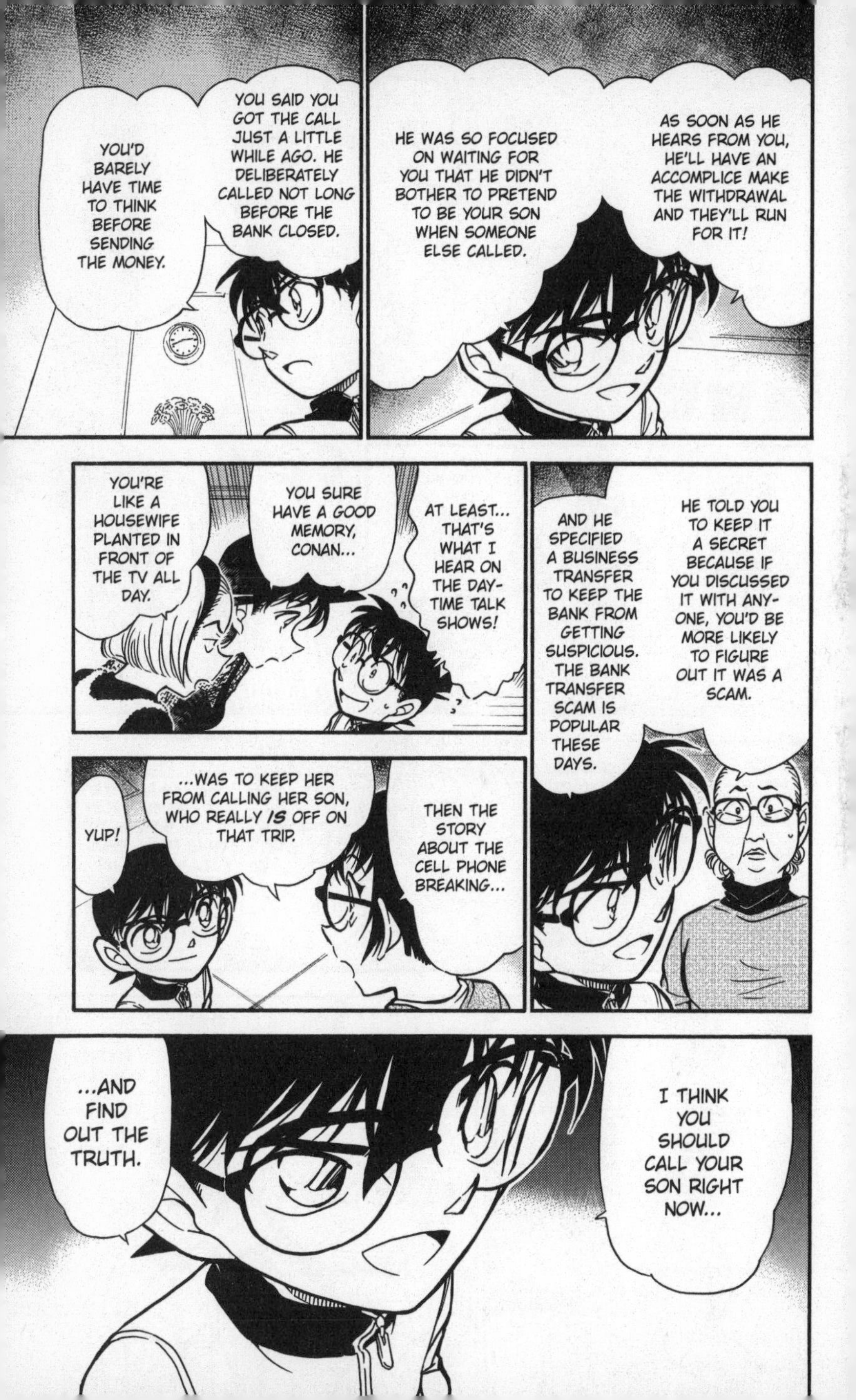
AS SOON AS HE HEARS FROM YOU, HE'LL HAVE AN ACCOMPLICE MAKE THE WITHDRAWAL AND THEY'LL RUN FOR IT!
HE WAS SO FOCUSED ON WAITING FOR YOU THAT HE DIDN'T BOTHER TO PRETEND TO BE YOUR SON WHEN SOMEONE ELSE CALLED.
YOU SAID YOU GOT THE CALL JUST A LITTLE WHILE AGO. HE DELIBERATELY CALLED NOT LONG BEFORE THE BANK CLOSED.
YOU'D BARELY HAVE TIME TO THINK BEFORE SENDING THE MONEY.
HE TOLD YOU TO KEEP IT A SECRET BECAUSE IF YOU DISCUSSED IT WITH ANY-ONE, YOU'D BE MORE LIKELY TO FIGURE OUT IT WAS A SCAM.
AND HE SPECIFIED A BUSINESS TRANSFER TO KEEP THE BANK FROM GETTING SUSPICIOUS. THE BANK TRANSFER SCAM IS POPULAR THESE DAYS.
AT LEAST... THAT'S WHAT I HEAR ON THE DAY-TIME TALK SHOWS!
YOU SURE HAVE A GOOD MEMORY, CONAN...
YOU'RE LIKE A HOUSEWIFE PLANTED IN FRONT OF THE TV ALL DAY.
THEN THE STORY ABOUT THE CELL PHONE BREAKING...
...WAS TO KEEP HER FROM CALLING HER SON, WHO REALLY *IS* OFF ON THAT TRIP.
YUP!
I THINK YOU SHOULD CALL YOUR SON RIGHT NOW...
...AND FIND OUT THE TRUTH.

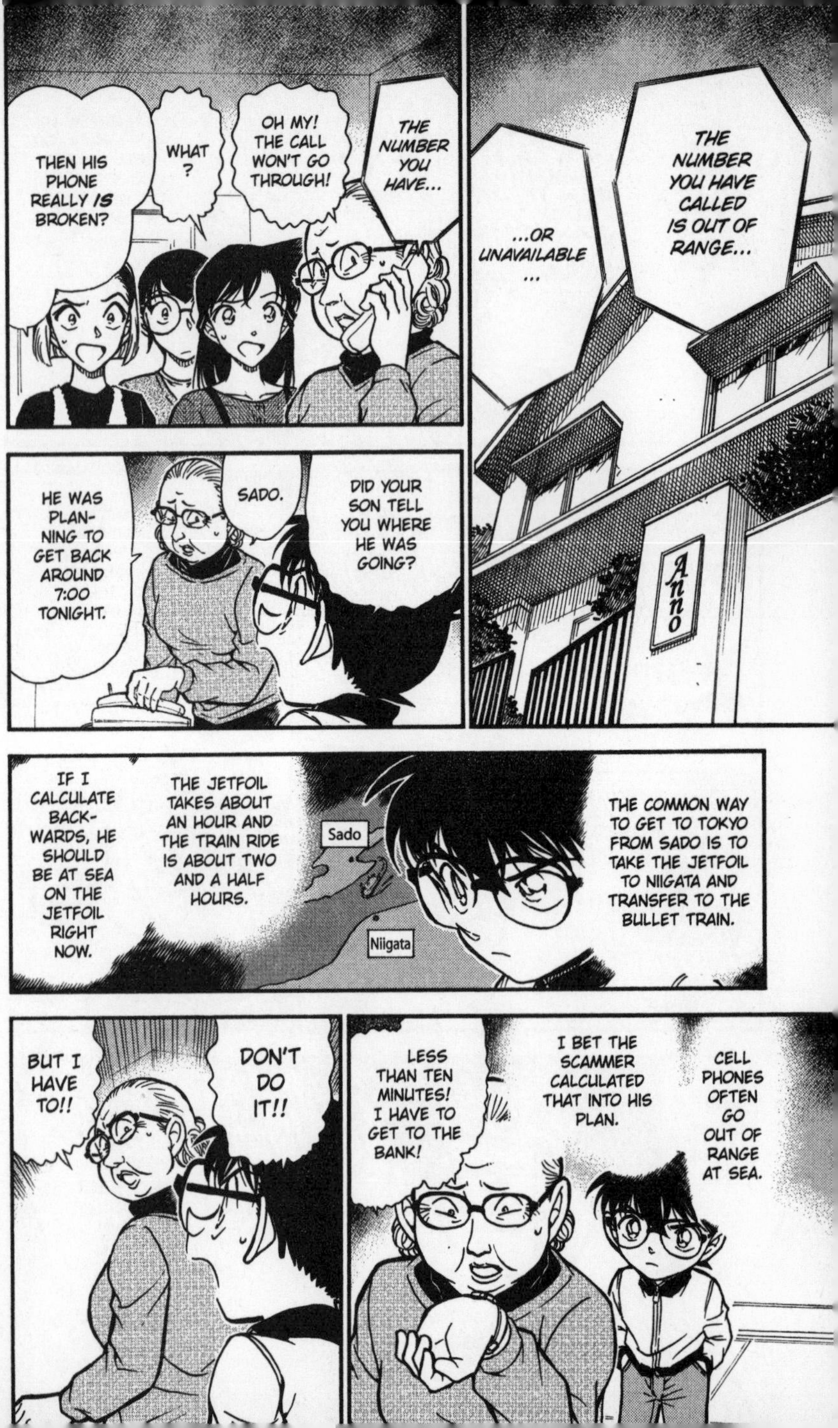
THE NUMBER YOU HAVE CALLED IS OUT OF RANGE...
...OR UNAVAILABLE ...
Anno
THE NUMBER YOU HAVE...
OH MY! THE CALL WON'T GO THROUGH!
WHAT?
THEN HIS PHONE REALLY IS BROKEN?
DID YOUR SON TELL YOU WHERE HE WAS GOING?
SADO.
HE WAS PLAN-NING TO GET BACK AROUND 7:00 TONIGHT.
THE COMMON WAY TO GET TO TOKYO FROM SADO IS TO TAKE THE JETFOIL TO NIIGATA AND TRANSFER TO THE BULLET TRAIN.
Sado
Niigata
THE JETFOIL TAKES ABOUT AN HOUR AND THE TRAIN RIDE IS ABOUT TWO AND A HALF HOURS.
IF I CALCULATE BACK-WARDS, HE SHOULD BE AT SEA ON THE JETFOIL RIGHT NOW.
CELL PHONES OFTEN GO OUT OF RANGE AT SEA.
I BET THE SCAMMER CALCULATED THAT INTO HIS PLAN.
LESS THAN TEN MINUTES! I HAVE TO GET TO THE BANK!
DON'T DO IT!!
BUT I HAVE TO!!

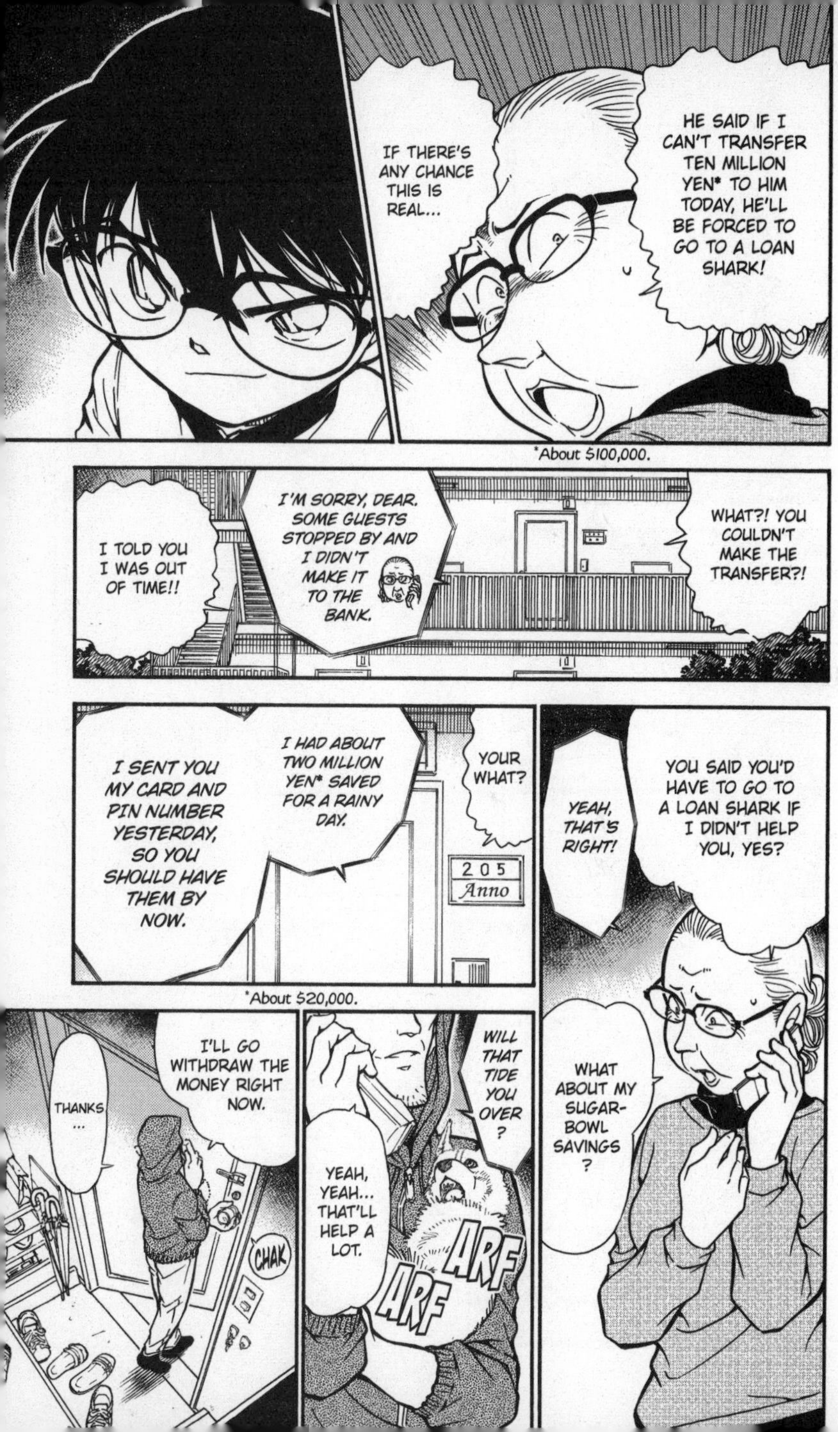
HE SAID IF I CAN'T TRANSFER TEN MILLION YEN* TO HIM TODAY, HE'LL BE FORCED TO GO TO A LOAN SHARK!
IF THERE'S ANY CHANCE THIS IS REAL...
*About $100,000.
WHAT?! YOU COULDN'T MAKE THE TRANSFER?!
I'M SORRY, DEAR. SOME GUESTS STOPPED BY AND I DIDN'T MAKE IT TO THE BANK.
I TOLD YOU I WAS OUT OF TIME!!
YOU SAID YOU'D HAVE TO GO TO A LOAN SHARK IF I DIDN'T HELP YOU, YES?
YEAH, THAT'S RIGHT!
WHAT ABOUT MY SUGAR-BOWL SAVINGS?
YOUR WHAT?
I HAD ABOUT TWO MILLION YEN* SAVED FOR A RAINY DAY.
I SENT YOU MY CARD AND PIN NUMBER YESTERDAY, SO YOU SHOULD HAVE THEM BY NOW.
205
Anno
*About $20,000.
WILL THAT TIDE YOU OVER?
YEAH, YEAH... THAT'LL HELP A LOT.
ARF
ARF
I'LL GO WITHDRAW THE MONEY RIGHT NOW.
THANKS...
CHAK

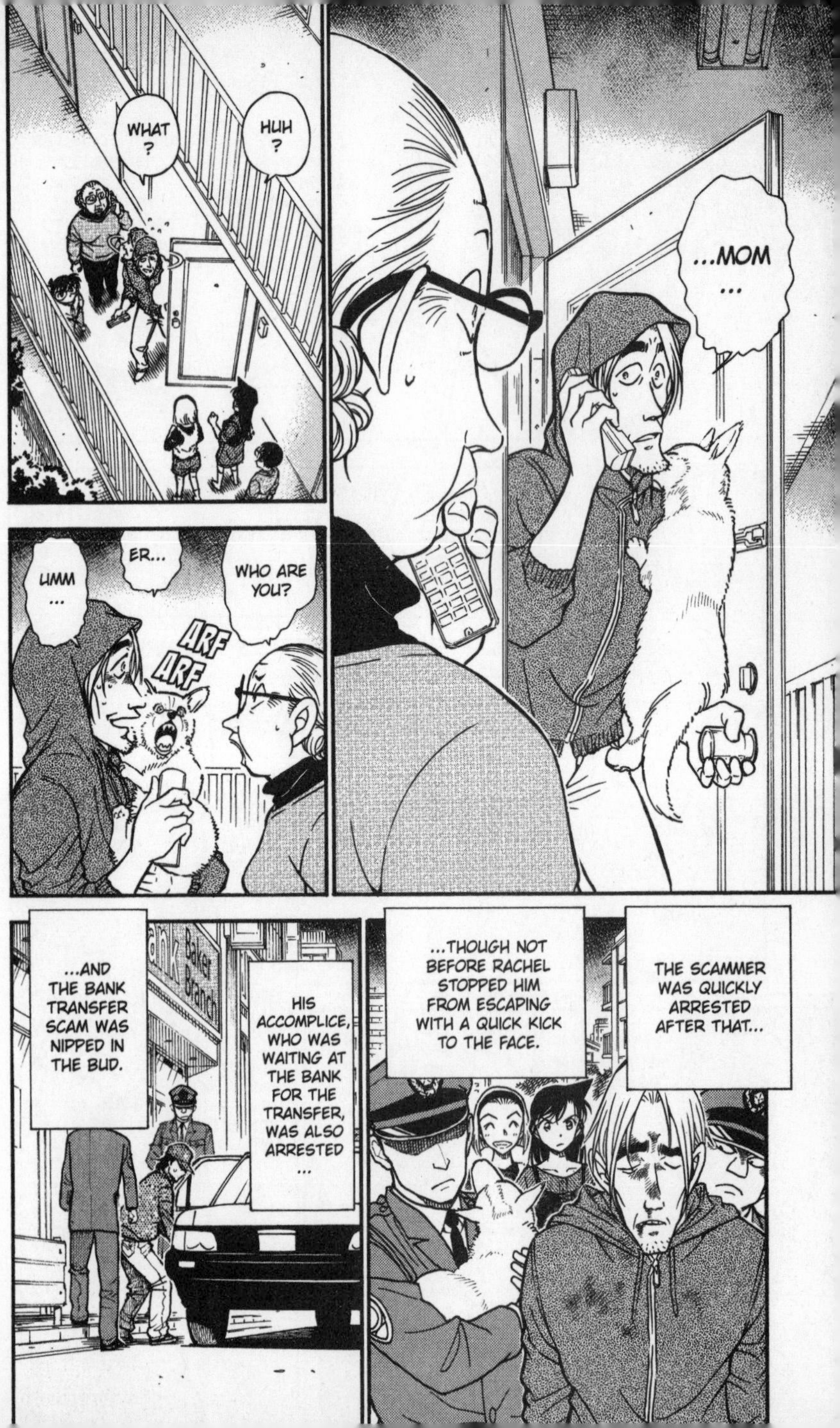
...MOM ...
HUH ?
WHAT ?
WHO ARE YOU?
ER...
UMM ...
ARF ARF
THE SCAMMER WAS QUICKLY ARRESTED AFTER THAT...
...THOUGH NOT BEFORE RACHEL STOPPED HIM FROM ESCAPING WITH A QUICK KICK TO THE FACE.
HIS ACCOMPLICE, WHO WAS WAITING AT THE BANK FOR THE TRANSFER, WAS ALSO ARRESTED ...
Baker Branch
...AND THE BANK TRANSFER SCAM WAS NIPPED IN THE BUD.

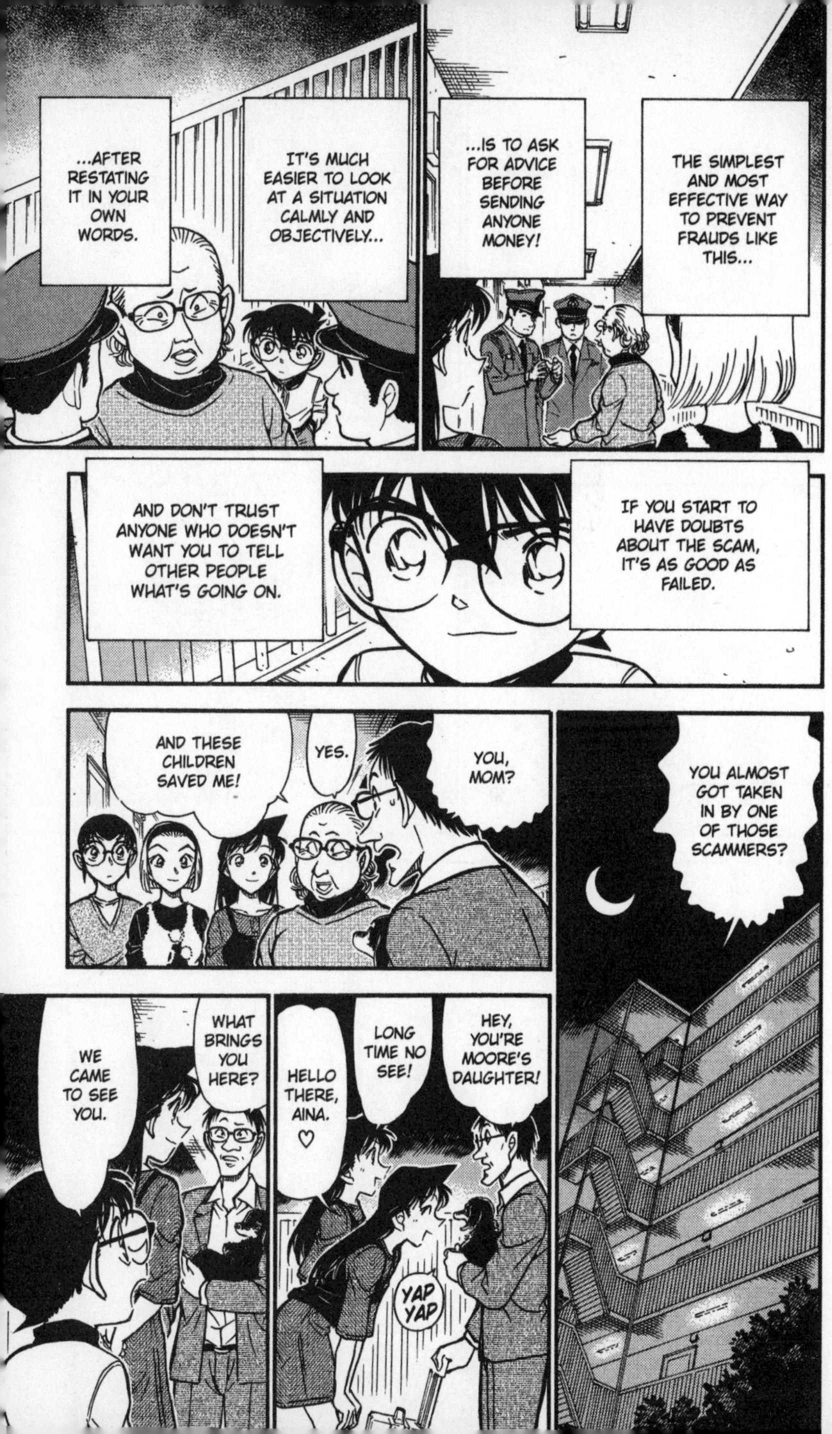
THE SIMPLEST AND MOST EFFECTIVE WAY TO PREVENT FRAUDS LIKE THIS...
...IS TO ASK FOR ADVICE BEFORE SENDING ANYONE MONEY!
IT'S MUCH EASIER TO LOOK AT A SITUATION CALMLY AND OBJECTIVELY...
...AFTER RESTATING IT IN YOUR OWN WORDS.
IF YOU START TO HAVE DOUBTS ABOUT THE SCAM, IT'S AS GOOD AS FAILED.
AND DON'T TRUST ANYONE WHO DOESN'T WANT YOU TO TELL OTHER PEOPLE WHAT'S GOING ON.
YOU ALMOST GOT TAKEN IN BY ONE OF THOSE SCAMMERS?
YOU, MOM?
YES.
AND THESE CHILDREN SAVED ME!
HEY, YOU'RE MOORE'S DAUGHTER!
LONG TIME NO SEE!
HELLO THERE, AINA. ♡
YAP YAP
WHAT BRINGS YOU HERE?
WE CAME TO SEE YOU.

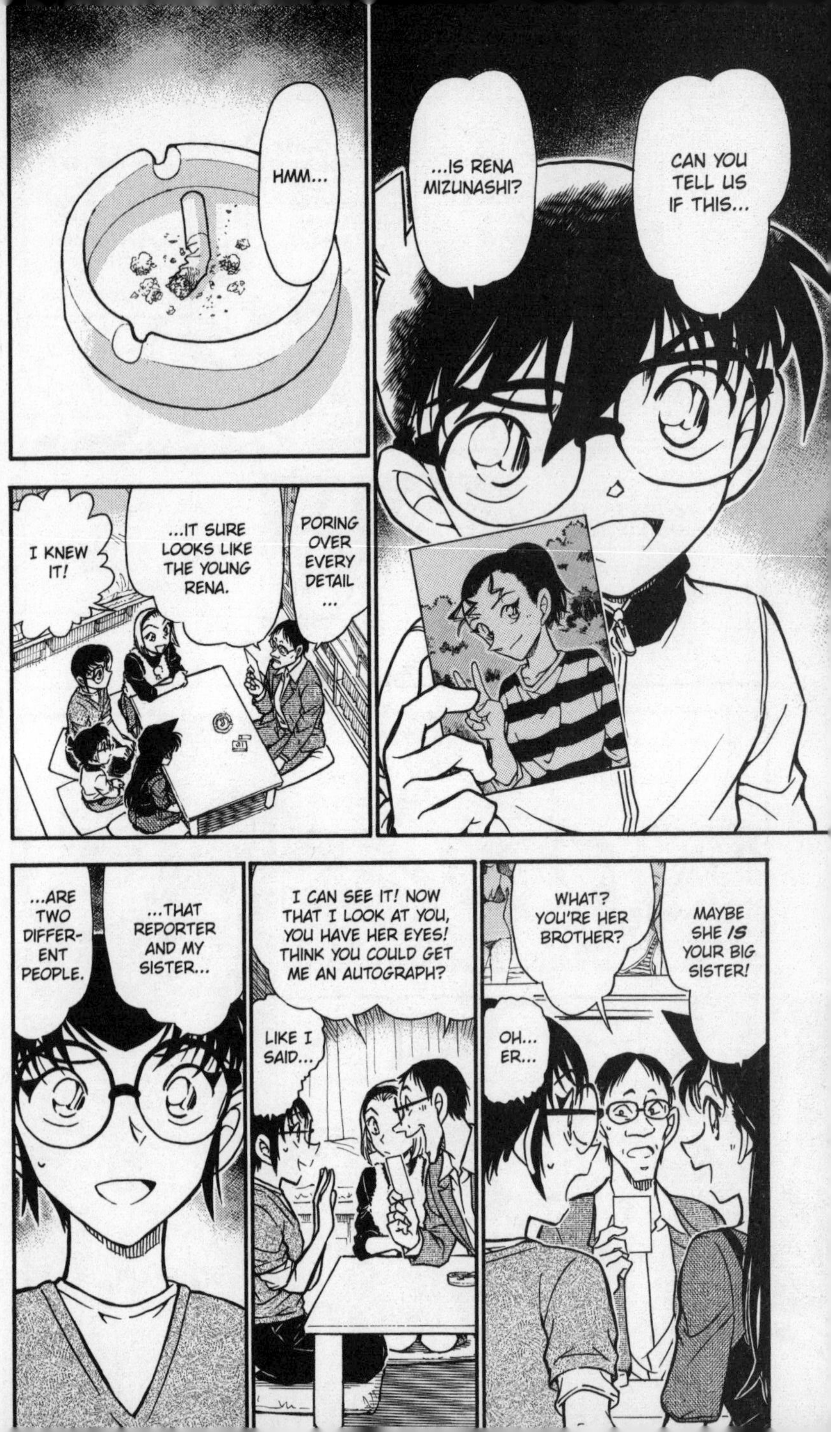
CAN YOU TELL US IF THIS...
...IS RENA MIZUNASHI?
HMM...
PORING OVER EVERY DETAIL...
...IT SURE LOOKS LIKE THE YOUNG RENA.
I KNEW IT!
MAYBE SHE *IS* YOUR BIG SISTER!
WHAT? YOU'RE HER BROTHER?
OH... ER...
I CAN SEE IT! NOW THAT I LOOK AT YOU, YOU HAVE HER EYES! THINK YOU COULD GET ME AN AUTOGRAPH?
LIKE I SAID...
...THAT REPORTER AND MY SISTER...
...ARE TWO DIFFER-ENT PEOPLE.

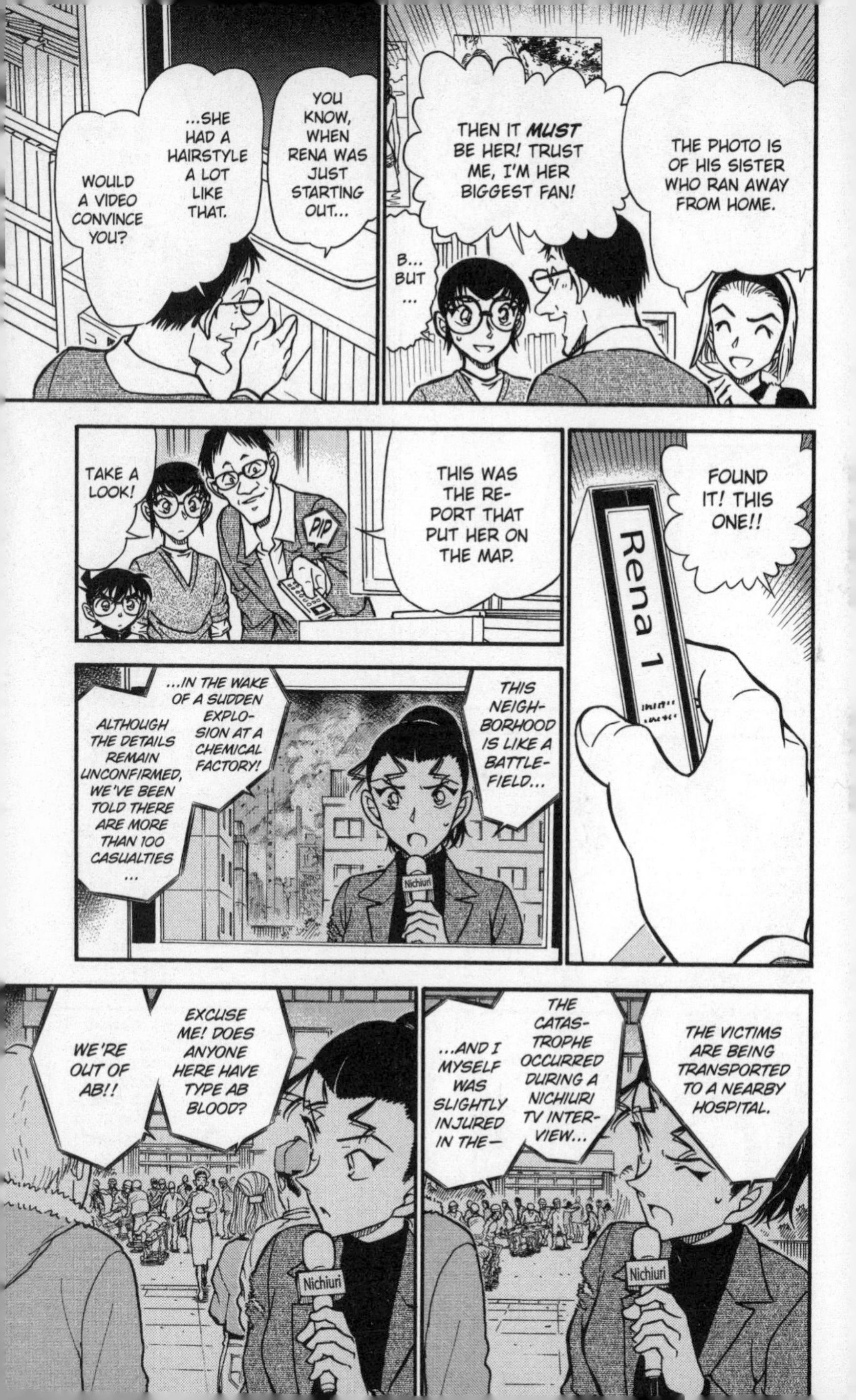
THE PHOTO IS OF HIS SISTER WHO RAN AWAY FROM HOME.
THEN IT MUST BE HER! TRUST ME, I'M HER BIGGEST FAN!
B... BUT ...
YOU KNOW, WHEN RENA WAS JUST STARTING OUT...
...SHE HAD A HAIRSTYLE A LOT LIKE THAT.
WOULD A VIDEO CONVINCE YOU?
FOUND IT! THIS ONE!!
Rena 1
THIS WAS THE REPORT THAT PUT HER ON THE MAP.
TAKE A LOOK!
PIP
THIS NEIGHBORHOOD IS LIKE A BATTLEFIELD...
...IN THE WAKE OF A SUDDEN EXPLOSION AT A CHEMICAL FACTORY!
ALTHOUGH THE DETAILS REMAIN UNCONFIRMED, WE'VE BEEN TOLD THERE ARE MORE THAN 100 CASUALTIES ...
Nichiuri
THE VICTIMS ARE BEING TRANSPORTED TO A NEARBY HOSPITAL.
THE CATASTROPHE OCCURRED DURING A NICHIURI TV INTERVIEW...
...AND I MYSELF WAS SLIGHTLY INJURED IN THE—
Nichiuri
EXCUSE ME! DOES ANYONE HERE HAVE TYPE AB BLOOD?
WE'RE OUT OF AB!!
Nichiuri

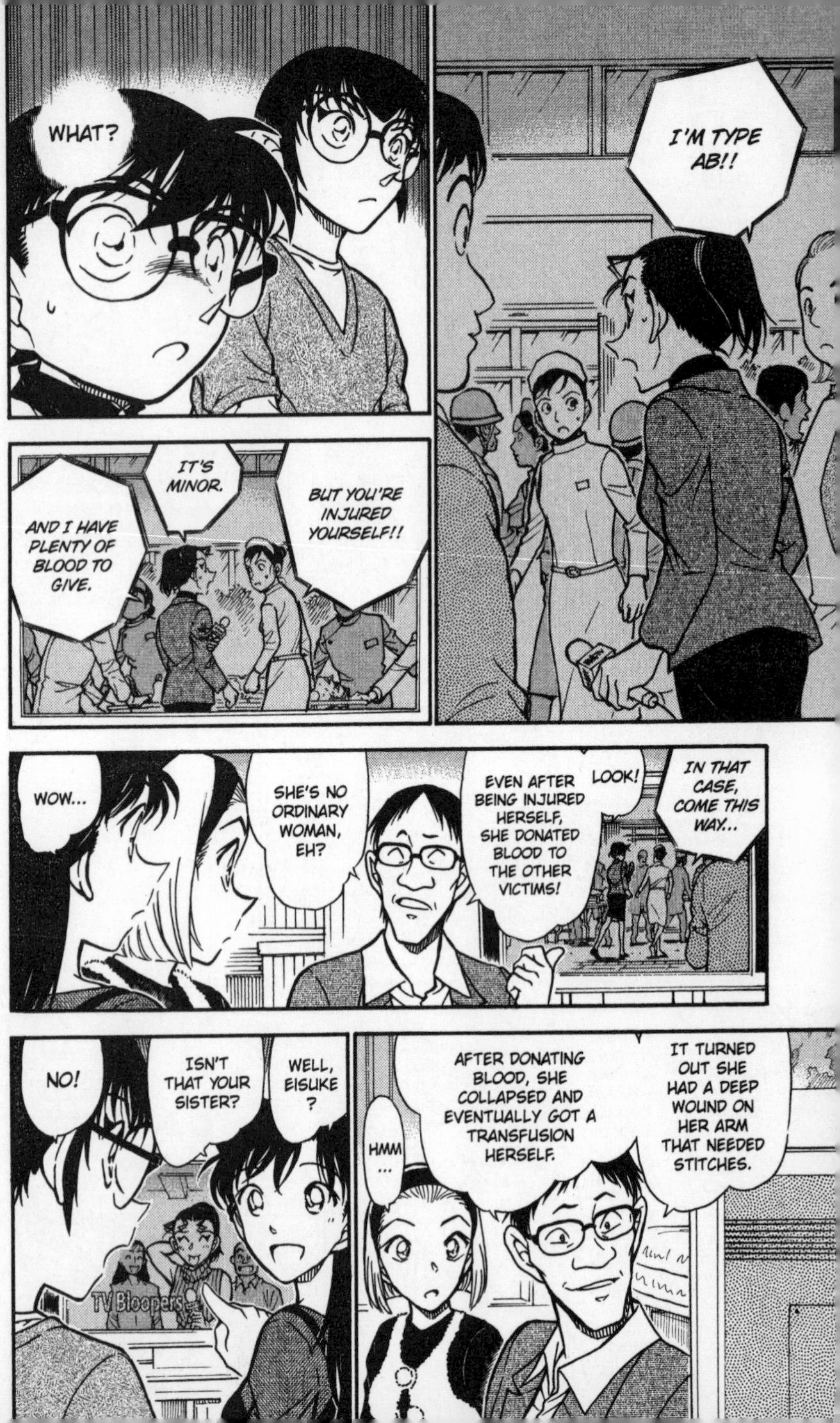
I'M TYPE AB!!
WHAT?
BUT YOU'RE INJURED YOURSELF!!
IT'S MINOR.
AND I HAVE PLENTY OF BLOOD TO GIVE.
IN THAT CASE, COME THIS WAY...
LOOK!
EVEN AFTER BEING INJURED HERSELF, SHE DONATED BLOOD TO THE OTHER VICTIMS!
SHE'S NO ORDINARY WOMAN, EH?
WOW...
IT TURNED OUT SHE HAD A DEEP WOUND ON HER ARM THAT NEEDED STITCHES.
AFTER DONATING BLOOD, SHE COLLAPSED AND EVENTUALLY GOT A TRANSFUSION HERSELF.
HMM...
WELL, EISUKE?
ISN'T THAT YOUR SISTER?
NO!
TV Bloopers

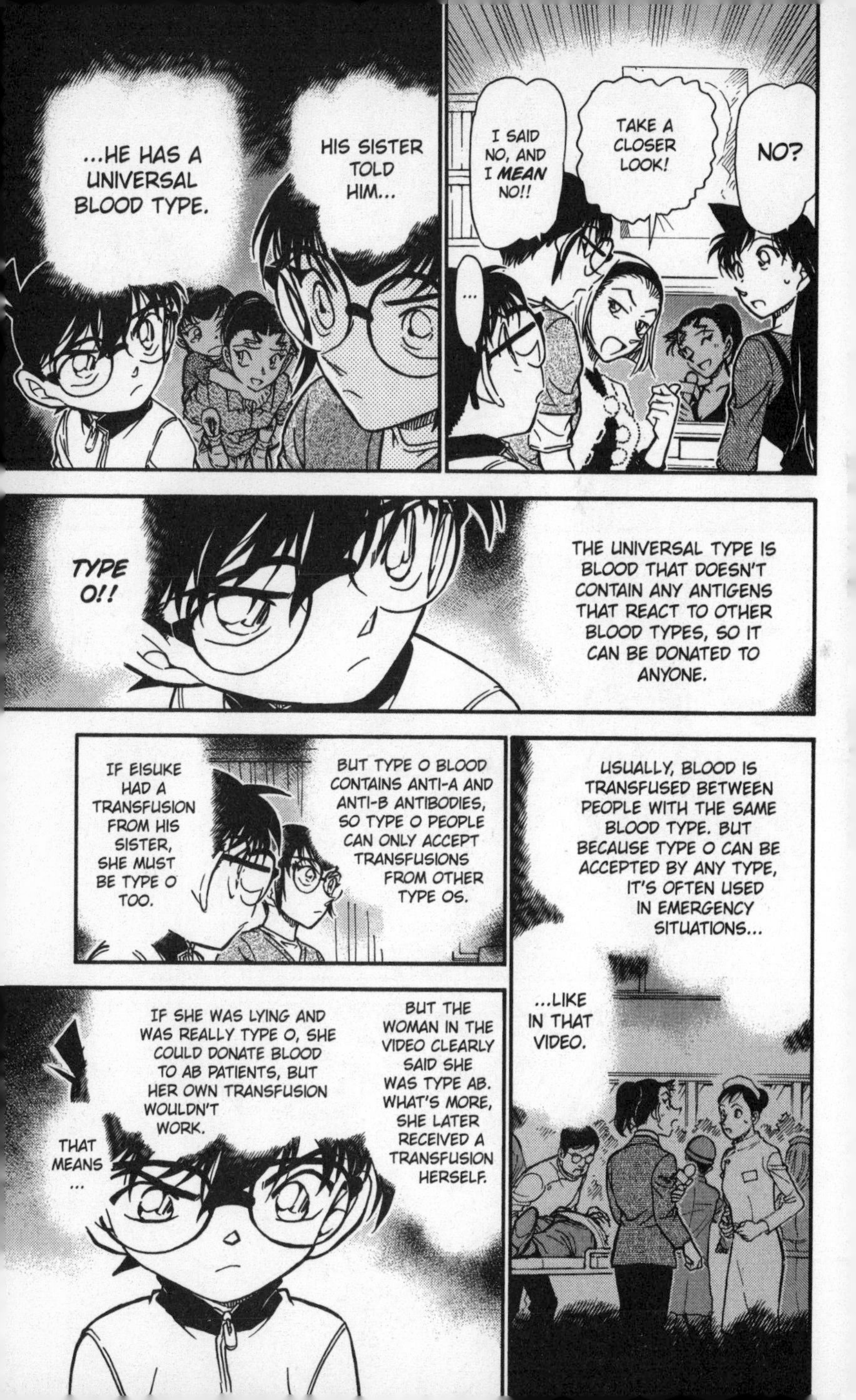

NO?
TAKE A CLOSER LOOK!
I SAID NO, AND I *MEAN* NO!!
...
HIS SISTER TOLD HIM...
...HE HAS A UNIVERSAL BLOOD TYPE.
THE UNIVERSAL TYPE IS BLOOD THAT DOESN'T CONTAIN ANY ANTIGENS THAT REACT TO OTHER BLOOD TYPES, SO IT CAN BE DONATED TO ANYONE.
TYPE O!!
USUALLY, BLOOD IS TRANSFUSED BETWEEN PEOPLE WITH THE SAME BLOOD TYPE. BUT BECAUSE TYPE O CAN BE ACCEPTED BY ANY TYPE, IT'S OFTEN USED IN EMERGENCY SITUATIONS...
...LIKE IN THAT VIDEO.
BUT TYPE O BLOOD CONTAINS ANTI-A AND ANTI-B ANTIBODIES, SO TYPE O PEOPLE CAN ONLY ACCEPT TRANSFUSIONS FROM OTHER TYPE OS.
IF EISUKE HAD A TRANSFUSION FROM HIS SISTER, SHE MUST BE TYPE O TOO.
BUT THE WOMAN IN THE VIDEO CLEARLY SAID SHE WAS TYPE AB. WHAT'S MORE, SHE LATER RECEIVED A TRANSFUSION HERSELF.
IF SHE WAS LYING AND WAS REALLY TYPE O, SHE COULD DONATE BLOOD TO AB PATIENTS, BUT HER OWN TRANSFUSION WOULDN'T WORK.
THAT MEANS ...

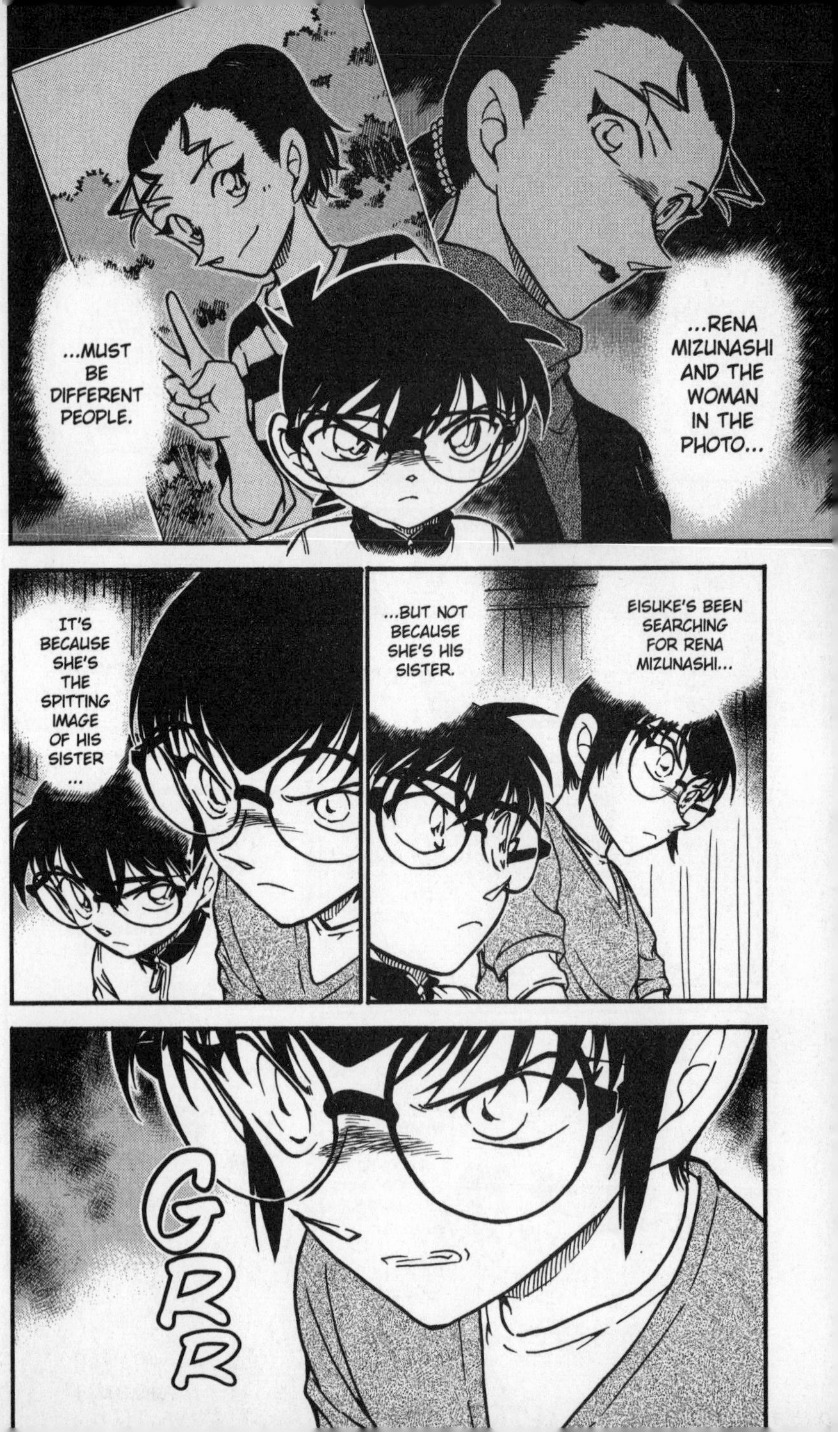
...RENA MIZUNASHI AND THE WOMAN IN THE PHOTO...
...MUST BE DIFFERENT PEOPLE.
EISUKE'S BEEN SEARCHING FOR RENA MIZUNASHI...
...BUT NOT BECAUSE SHE'S HIS SISTER.
IT'S BECAUSE SHE'S THE SPITTING IMAGE OF HIS SISTER ...
GRR

Hello, Aoyama here.

I use the stairs to get to my studio from my apartment two floors below, but lately I notice that I stagger every now and then (yikes). I look in the mirror, thinking "Maybe I'm tired," and notice stubble and gray hair! Am I...old?! Oh no...oh nooo...my deduction is that I just lack exercise. (You call that a deduction?!)

Gosho Aoyama's Mystery Library

56

SASHICHI

If there were a beauty pageant for male detectives, this guy would definitely be representing Japan! Sashichi, master of rounding up criminals, is a police detective who lives at Kanda's Otamaga Pond. He's a pale, handsome man whose looks are almost too perfect to be real, giving him the nickname "Sashichi the Doll." But beneath his delicate appearance, he's a tireless cop who uses his brilliant deduction skills to solve mysteries in the city of Edo. He's assisted by officers Money-Pouch Tatsu and Long-Faced Mameroku—and, last but not least, his loving wife Okume, a beautiful, jealous, sharp-witted former courtesan.

The Sashichi the Doll series is considered one of Japan's three great period mystery dramas. It was written by Seishi Yokomizo, who also created the famous detective Kosuke Kindaichi. Between the Sashichi and Kindaichi series, Yokomizo wrote over 250 novels. If he has so many ideas in his head, I wish he'd share some of them with me (heh).

I recommend *Ghost Yamabushi*.